T0345035

Caribbean Pleasure Industry

WORLDS OF DESIRE
THE CHICAGO SERIES ON SEXUALITY, GENDER, AND CULTURE
A Series Edited by Gilbert Herdt

ALSO IN THE SERIES:

Caribbean Pleasure Industry

Tourism, Sexuality, and AIDS in the Dominican Republic

MARK PADILLA

The University of Chicago Press   *Chicago & London*

MARK PADILLA is assistant professor in the Department of Health Behavior and Health Education in the School of Public Health at the University of Michigan.

The University of Chicago Press, Chicago 60637
The University of Chicago Press, Ltd., London
© 2007 by Mark Padilla
All rights reserved. Published 2007
Printed in the United States of America

16 15 14 13 12 11 10 09 08 07   1 2 3 4 5

ISBN-13: 978-0-226-64435-6 (cloth)
ISBN-13: 978-0-226-64436-3 (paper)
ISBN-10: 0-226-64435-9 (cloth)
ISBN-10: 0-226-64436-7 (paper)

Padilla, Mark, 1969–
  Caribbean pleasure industry : tourism, sexuality, and AIDS in the Dominican Republic / Mark Padilla.
      p.   cm.
  Includes bibliographical references and index.
  ISBN-13: 978-0-226-64435-6 (cloth : alk. paper)
  ISBN-13: 978-0-226-64436-3 (pbk. : alk. paper)
  ISBN-10: 0-226-64435-9 (cloth : alk. paper)
  ISBN-10: 0-226-64436-7 (pbk. : alk. paper)
  1. Sex tourism—Dominican Republic. 2. AIDS (Disease)—Dominican Republic.
3. Gender identity—Dominican Republic. I. Title. II. Title: Tourism, sexuality, and AIDS in the Dominican Republic.
HQ162.5 .A5P33 2007
306.76'62097293—dc22

                                                    2006039087

♾ The paper used in this publication meets the minimum requirements of the American National Standard for Information Sciences—Permanence of Paper for Printed Library Materials, ANSI Z39.48-1992.

Contents

Illustrations

Tables

Figures

Preface

In the year 1516, the first shipment of sugar was sent from the Spanish colony of Santo Domingo, the present-day capital of the Dominican Republic, to Europe, beginning what would become the key export industry in the Caribbean for nearly five centuries, as well as linking the region inexorably to the rise of capitalism in the West. As Sidney Mintz has described in his classic anthropological history *Sweetness and Power* (1985), the Caribbean sugar industry spurred the development of an international division of labor that has persisted throughout the region's history, albeit in forms that are continually adapting to changing political-economic circumstances. Tracing the connections between the black slaves, whose exploited labor fueled the mass production of sugar, and the European working classes who eventually came to be its primary consumers, Mintz argues that "[Caribbean] slave and [European] proletarian together powered the imperial economic system that kept the one supplied with manacles and the other with sugar and rum; but neither had more than minimal influence over it" (1985, 184).[1] The owners of Caribbean sugar companies, as well as the governments that nurtured, protected, and profited from such enterprises, thus fostered a system of capitalist labor exploitation both in the "core" and the "periphery"—a global system driven by the production and consumption of sweetness.

Watching Joselito, a twenty-one-year-old "*sanky panky,*" as he hustled foreigners along a stretch of white-sand beach in the tourist town of Boca Chica, Dominican Republic, I couldn't help but wonder at the paradoxical ways that the echoes of Caribbean history seemed simultaneously distant and overwhelmingly pervasive in this place.[2] It was 1999, during my first months of fieldwork with men who are referred to locally as *"bugarrones"* and *"sanky pankies"*—terms with somewhat complex social definitions described in detail in this book, but which generally refer to men who exchange sex with tourists for money. My head was still swimming with the scholarly discussions of Caribbean society and political economy that I had recently surveyed in preparation for my trip.[3] But here, as foreigners scrambled to claim a well-positioned lounge chair or shrieked in delight as they raced past the dock on banana boats, there was no sign of the sugar plantations that dominate most discussions of Caribbean political economy. The young Dominican men who strolled amidst the sunburnt bodies of European and North American tourists were not carrying the machetes for harvesting sugar cane that many of their fathers had brandished at the nearby *batey*—a sugar plantation that, like a growing number of Dominican *bateyes,* now lies barren. Instead, many of these men carried seafood, souvenirs, "authentic" Dominican artwork, or refreshments, hoping to negotiate high prices (preferably in U.S. dollars) with the sunbathing tourists, most of whom were unfamiliar with the local market and are therefore considered *dinero facil* (easy money). Some young men carried nothing at all, but the way they strategically displayed themselves and flirtatiously greeted the tourists made it quite clear—at least to those foreign men and women who knew how to decode the messages—that the commodity they were offering was their own bodies. Joselito preferred a less subtle approach, casually fondling himself while loudly announcing, "You're on vacation! Enjoy yourself!"

This book is an anthropological analysis of men like Joselito who make a marginal living through informal labor in what is described here as the *pleasure industry*—the diverse informal sector of the Dominican economy devoted to providing a myriad of pleasure-related services to the more than two million foreign guests that visit the country annually. It is the new brand of sweetness that forms the backbone of a rapidly changing economy throughout the Caribbean, one that no longer depends upon the export of the cane sugar for which so many black bodies were forcibly relocated and savagely exploited during the centuries of European colonization. This new commodity is a diffuse but fundamentally pleasurable *experience* that forms a crucial part of the tourist package, and has become a basic feature of the demand for travel to places like the Dominican Republic. As experiences, the commodities that are bought and sold in the pleasure industry are neither stable nor driven by the demands of nameless, faceless consumers in distant and unknowable lands. Rather, they are forged of intimate, close-range, ever-changing desires, and their satisfaction is central to the livelihoods of a growing number of Caribbean men and women who make a living in the informal tourism economy. The growing literature on tourism demonstrates that such touristic experiences possess particular qualities connected to the nature of work and leisure in the contemporary world.[4] They are continually in flux, fickle, escapist, and—as this book demonstrates—inextricably connected to the use and value of sexuality in the contemporary globalized world.

The following pages are filled with the voices of men who work in the Dominican pleasure industry by providing a myriad of services to tourists, and who, either regularly or intermittently, exchange sex for money with foreign gay men. Based on three years of ethnographic research in two cities in the Dominican Republic, the book examines the ways that structural changes in the political economy of the Caribbean—particularly the growth in dependence on tourism and the prominent place of sexual-economic exchanges within the pleasure industry—reverberate in the lives of these men, the vast majority of whom do not identify themselves as gay, and who struggle to maintain a respectable masculine status in their relationships with their wives, girlfriends, extended families, and communities. As bisexually behaving men, these are not the figures who are most visible in cross-cultural studies of non-normative genders and sexualities; indeed, the men described here would likely resist the term *non-normative,* as much of their time is spent in demonstrating—perhaps to themselves as much as to those around them—that they are *hombres normales* (normal men). Yet, as this ethnography endeavors to show, turning the analytical lens upon these men and their experiences has much potentially to tell us about globalization, commodification, gender, sexuality, political economy, and HIV/AIDS.

As a broad project that seeks to link large-scale changes in Dominican political economy to the highly personal subjectivities, identities, and situational vulnerabilities faced by individuals in a specific cultural setting, the analysis developed here further strives to advance the field of medical anthropology, particularly within the growing theoretical and philosophical perspective that has come to be called "critical medical anthropology" (CMA).[5] From the perspective of CMA, health and disease are viewed as embedded within local and global structures of power and inequality, and the interrogation and explication of the linkages between these structures and specific health outcomes are central to the analytic project. The global pandemic of HIV/AIDS has undoubtedly spurred the urgency and relevance of CMA—if not its widespread adoption by international health or governmental bodies—because the devastating magnitude and disproportionate expression of HIV/AIDS among the world's poorest people demands that medical anthropologists engage the fundamental question of how to understand the mechanisms by which social and structural inequalities at a global scale are translated into observable epidemiological disparities in HIV infection rates and AIDS-related morbidity and mortality.[6] As a growing body of evidence demonstrates that the global distribution of HIV infection follows the predictable gradients of poverty and social inequality (Farmer 1992; Farmer, Connors, and Simmons 1996; Link et al. 1998; Link and Phelan 1995; Parker 2001; Parker, Easton, and Klein 2000; Singer 1997), social scientists, public health practitioners, and global health initiatives face the significant challenge of developing new ways of understanding the intricacies of the ways a wide range of social differences—such as race, class, gender, sexuality, and citizenship—combine to influence the risk for HIV infection among specific individuals and groups. While the complexity of the challenge is vast, this book is written with the belief that a broad research approach combining the strengths of a range of disciplines—including anthropology, public health, epidemiology, gender and sexuality studies, history, and the emerging field of globalization studies—can help to trace the linkages between global inequalities and the intimacies of HIV infection. As Jonathan Mann, the distinguished public health practitioner and HIV/AIDS advocate, wrote before his untimely death, "it is clear that multidisciplinary approaches uniting epidemiology with other social sciences may be the most important next phase of development in the science of AIDS research" (Mann 1991, 12).

Ironically, despite the growing number of political-economic approaches to AIDS in the social science literature in the developing world,[7] relatively few analyses have sought to describe how large-scale structural processes are linked to the specific ways that gender and sexuality are constructed and enacted in specific sociocultural settings. Farmer and colleagues, in their foundational book *Women, Poverty, and AIDS* (1996), attribute the paucity of such approaches to the fact that cross-cultural expressions of gender and sexuality are still misunderstood in international public health, and this is worsened by the tendency to rely on rapid assessments that preclude in-depth anthropological research. A growing number of anthropological studies are beginning to respond to this gap, however, offering detailed ethnographic analyses of the ways that women, and particularly poor women, are made vulnerable to HIV by patriarchal gender norms and their intersections with material inequalities.[8] Yet there remains a silence in the literature on how men who are structurally disadvantaged in the global political-economy—as *gendered* beings who are situated within multiple social hierarchies related to race, class, masculinity, and sexuality—are implicated in the patterns of "structural violence" that shape the HIV/AIDS epidemic.[9] Just as men are not simply the reproducers of patriarchy but are also incorporated within its logics, men in places like the Dominican Republic are not always the benefactors of political, economic, or masculine privilege. To truly understand the complex linkages between global inequalities and local cultural systems of gender and sexuality—which is a fundamental goal of a *critical epidemiology* of AIDS—medical anthropology must focus its ethnographic lens not only on the ways that women are marginally positioned in relation to patriarchy, but also on the ways that socially disadvantaged or marginalized men are positioned within hierarchies of gender, sexuality, and power.[10]

This book draws on ethnographic fieldwork among men involved in sexual-economic exchanges with tourists in order to develop a critical epidemiology of the Dominican AIDS epidemic as told from the perspective of the expanding pleasure industry. Perhaps as a symptom of the self-conscious attempt to maintain a broad analytic focus on political-economic processes as well as the local cultural meanings of gender and sexuality, a certain degree of complicity is required on the part of the reader in tracing these linkages through a wide array of social phenomena—from the development of the tourism economy and its relationship to Dominican sexuality; to the globalization of homoerotic identities and the organization of the transnational gay tourism market; to the consequences of male sex tourism for men's familial and conjugal relations; to the economic and affective relations between Dominican men and their foreign gay clients. From the perspective of a political economy of sexuality and AIDS, these are not divergences or tangents; they are the entailments of an ethnographically informed epidemiology, and are fundamental to uncovering the complex and ever changing connections between sweetness, power, and AIDS.

Acknowledgments

This book would not have been possible without the investment and the commitment of numerous friends, mentors, and institutions. I would first like to recognize the support of my Ph.D. dissertation committee members at Emory University's anthropology department: Peter Brown (chair), Carla Freeman, Donald Donham, and Claire Sterk (BSHE department, Rollins School of Public Health), who have encouraged me and facilitated my intellectual and professional development in many different ways. The Center for Health, Culture, and Society (Emory) provided me the opportunity to receive my master's in Public Health in 1997–98, which subsequently permitted the incorporation of quantitative methods into my fieldwork as well as my consulting work in HIV/AIDS and reproductive health organizations in Santo Domingo. I would like to thank Peter Brown in particular for encouraging me to pursue this cross-training, and for his involvement in supporting my application for the fellowship. Carla Freeman has also been an immense source of support for me over the years at Emory, and deserves special thanks for renewing my commitment to the work on several occasions when my own attachment to it foundered. Three dear friends and fellow graduate students at Emory—Michael Hill, Keith McNeal, and Donna Murdock—have been especially important to my intellectual and personal development. Thank you for being there all along the way.

During fieldwork in Santo Domingo, I relied upon the support and practical assistance of numerous people. Tito and Ann Coleman were amazing friends and exceptional mentors in our joint work at AcciónSIDA and PRIME II, respectively. At a particularly crucial point in the research process, Tito assisted in finding additional supporting funds for certain noncovered expenses through the local USAID mission. Tony De Moya at the Instituto de Sexualidad Humana (UASD), Bayardo Gómez (CEPROSH), and Deanna Kerrigan (Johns Hopkins School of Public Health) all provided conceptual and practical support at various stages, as well as their friendship. Deanna also worked with me and my research associates on securing funds for research expenses through the Fogarty AIDS International Training and Research (AITRP) program. Many thanks to Tony De Moya, Rafael García, and Dean Diomedes Robles from the Universidad Autónoma, as well as Ineke Cunningham of the University of Puerto Rico, Rio Piedras, all of whom provided important logistical support in forming a local ethical review committee for the purposes of approving the Fogarty AITRP grant. Thanks to my friends and coworkers River Finlay and Laura Murray for their patience and interest in talking with me about my research over many *Cuba libres.*

My friends and colleagues at Amigos Siempre Amigos (ASA), the nongovernmental organization with which I was affiliated throughout fieldwork, provided immeasurable assistance—as friends, as trusted leaders of the gay community, as research assistants, and as my patient "interpreters" of the meanings of Dominican homoeroticism. In particular, I would like to thank my friends and coinvestigators Leonardo Sánchez (Executive Director of ASA) and Martha Arredondo (physician, counselor, and educator at ASA), both of whom participated in every phase of the study and proved themselves, on numerous occasions, natural ethnographers. While I am solely responsible for the final product, their influence and insights reverberate throughout my work. My research assistants for the survey—Rafael Ferreira and Milka Uribe—also deserve special recognition for their dedication to quality data collection despite our shoestring budget. Thanks also to Laura Vanegas in Bogotá, Colombia, for her excellent transcriptions of the in-depth interviews and her remarkable attention to detail. Finally, four sex workers who must remain anonymous provided excellent assistance in identifying and recruiting potential study participants. Your help and belief in the project were essential.

Three foundations deserve acknowledgment for their generous support in covering my living and research expenses. Fulbright IIE provided living expenses for my first year of fieldwork. The Wenner-Gren Foundation for Anthropological Research and the National Science Foundation Doctoral Dissertation Program funded living and research equipment costs, respectively.

In the process of final write-up as a faculty member at the Department of Sociomedical Sciences, Mailman School of Public Health, Columbia

University, I have benefited greatly from so many inspirational and generous colleagues. I would like to especially thank Richard Parker, who as chair of the department and my mentor has greatly supported me in many ways in moving this book forward, and whose own work has reverberated in my own. Dr. Parker's prior ethnographic work in Brazil and elsewhere has provided the intellectual foundation that has enabled much of the ethnographic project I undertake here. My friend and colleague Jennifer Hirsch provided lucid and insightful commentary on the dissertation in preparation for its adaptation into book form, and has taught me much about applied anthropology in public health. Diane di Mauro and Carlos Decena have also given me their very generous and useful feedback, which has undoubtedly improved the work. Robert Sember and Miguel Muñoz-Laboy have been valued colleagues and friends in SMS and have been sources of inspiration on many, many occasions, perhaps without even realizing it. Vincent Guilamo-Ramos, Associate Professor in Columbia's School of Social Work, has also been a wonderful collaborator, role model, and friend, and a great supporter of my work in the Dominican Republic. I would also like to thank the Center for Gender, Sexuality, and Health in the SMS department, for providing an additional space in which to develop my thoughts in dialogue with other colleagues at Columbia.

Thank you also to the faculty at the Center for AIDS Prevention Studies (CAPS) at the University of California, San Francisco, where I have been enjoying a diverse and stimulating intellectual community through the Collaborative HIV/AIDS Research in Minority Communities program, headed by Barbara Marin and, more recently, Peggy Dolcini. In particular, I would like to thank Héctor Carrillo, who has been an incredible mentor and friend at CAPS, and an invaluable sounding board in helping me to carry these lines of inquiry forward through public health research in the United States and abroad. Thanks to Rafael Díaz for his passionate work among Latino gay men, which in many ways opened the doors for a next generation of scholarly work on the topic.

To the men whose voices fill these pages: I cannot name you here directly, but I deeply thank you for letting down your guard long enough to allow me to glimpse inside. I hope I have done you justice. To my family, Jaime, Sandy, and Bekah: Thank you for your incredible support during the long road to the Ph.D. I couldn't have done it without you. And finally, to my partner, Armando Matiz, who aside from his role as coinvestigator on this project, has accompanied me on so many journeys: You're my hero. This book is dedicated to you.

Introduction

Perhaps it is the image of Joselito on the beach in Boca Chica, marketing a fantasy to foreign tourists, that is most iconic of this book. It embodies the intersections of power, tourism, and sexuality that this ethnography of Dominican male sex work and the AIDS epidemic endeavors to understand. Yet while the following chapters offer detailed descriptions of the unfolding of sexual-economic exchanges between gay male tourists and Dominican sex workers, the ethnographic lens is one that continually strives to transcend a microlevel description of these exchanges by situating them within the larger context of Dominican society and history. Thus, if this image of Joselito is a metaphor for many of the social phenomena examined here, it is useful only as a point of departure, the epicenter from which radiate the social and cultural processes we seek to understand.

As a first step in the project of tracing these reverberations, this chapter introduces the *bugarrones* and *sanky pankies* whose experiences are described in further detail in subsequent chapters, and outlines the relationships between these sexual identities and the growth of the pleasure industry. The collaborative relationships that facilitated this research and the method of inquiry are also described. At the end of this introduction, we will turn to a brief discussion of what is described as the *political economy of sexuality*, the conceptual approach that informs the larger analysis that this book seeks to advance. First, it is necessary to turn briefly to history, in order to situate the subsequent ethnographic discussion in both time and place.

An Initial Glimpse at History

If I could change the past, I'd change it.

JORGE (21) Dominican male sex worker

By way of introduction, it is essential that we frame our considerations within a larger historical context, a project that brings into relief the shifts in the uses of Caribbean sexuality within the changing political economy of the region. Indeed, at the time of this writing, historically informed discussions of sex work are particularly crucial, given contemporary global debates about whether sex work is a legitimate income-generating activity or an inherently exploitative form of "sexual slavery" (Butcher 2003). While this book is not an analysis of human rights discourses or international policies on "sex trafficking," a political-economic analysis of sexuality and sexual-economic exchange cannot stand outside of these debates. For now, the important point is that, at the present time, facile parallels between colonialism and the structure of contemporary sex tourism economies in the Caribbean not only are potentially dangerous to sex workers themselves— since comparisons to slavery are often used as justifications for the policing, surveillance, and abuse of sex workers who, as described in later chapters in reference to Dominican *bugarrones* and *sanky pankies,* are already subject to systematic human rights violations—but these one-dimensional comparisons also have analytical limitations because they foreclose on a deeper and more nuanced historical analysis. Easy and wholesale historical parallels sidestep important questions about the specific ways that contemporary Caribbean sexualities *simultaneously* express certain colonial institutions while also reflecting more recent postcolonial formations. Therefore, the important question to ask is not *whether* Caribbean sex work is related to the uses of sexuality during colonialism—since this is the unavoidable historical reality of the Caribbean—but rather how the historical context of colonialism converges with more recent transformations in *neo*colonial political economy to shape the social organization of Caribbean sex work as it presently unfolds on the ground.[1]

The historical lens used in this book situates contemporary sex work and sex tourism within global structures that have long depended upon the use and value of Caribbean sexuality for projects of economic and political domination by outsiders. Importantly, these structures are not stable; indeed, as described more extensively in chapter 2, they have changed dramatically since the rise of tourism and the wane of the colonial model of dependence on cash crops and raw materials. For the present discussion, it is enough to emphasize that in order to develop a political economy of sex work in the present-day Dominican Republic, it is essential to consider the deep historical parallels between colonial structures and the shape of contemporary sexuality, as well as the influences of more recent formations, such as the growth of the global tourism industry, on expressions of sexuality and sexual-economic exchange.

There are several reasons why we might understand certain forms of contemporary Caribbean sex work as expressions, at least in part, of the centuries of European colonialism and economic exploitation in the region. A number of scholars have described how the sexuality of Caribbean men and women functioned during slavery as a basic resource within the colonial global economy, not only as a commodity that could be bought and sold, but also as the (re)productive capacity that guaranteed a coercible labor force.[2] In his discussion of gender and slavery in Barbados, for example, Beckles (1989) argues that black female prostitutes functioned as a crucial source of revenue for white elites, since "unlike other female slaves, [the prostitute] could generate three income flows: from labor, prostitution and reproduction" (quoted in Kempadoo 1999a, 7). In this sense, sexual labor had direct benefits for the economic interests of the metropolitan powers in Europe, since it permitted the maintenance of a productive system that was driven, in part, by the fertility of the slaves, ensuring in turn the profitability and sustainability of the colonial enterprise.

Thus, while the specific manifestations of sex work described in this book are quite distinct in their expressions from historical descriptions of prostitution during the colonial era, there are certain parallels that may be drawn. Just as the sexual labor of Caribbean slaves was key to the functioning of colonial economies in Europe, sex work in the contemporary Caribbean cannot be understood without reference to the transnational travel and tourism industries—and the governments that nurture and profit from them—which link "consumers" of sexual services in the industrialized world with "producers" of these services in the developing world. Just as the juncture of sexuality, prostitution, and production in colonialism tended to foster racialized, exoticized representations of Caribbean sexuality (Beckles 1989; Findlay 1997), the contemporary marketing of tropical destinations—as well as the motives behind sex tourists' travel to these places—underlines the historical persistence of a particular racialized model of Caribbean sexuality in the modern world system.[3] And just as sex work during colonialism permitted a certain degree of economic independence to some black slaves (Kempadoo 1999a), Caribbean men and women are increasingly using their informal participation in the sex tourism industry as a means to make ends meet in the context of shrinking options for formal wage work in traditional economic sectors. Each of these colonial reverberations is explored in the following chapters.

Yet, at the same time that this book seeks to situate Dominican sex work within these deeper sociohistorical trends, it also describes more recent manifestations of prostitution that have become increasingly pervasive in the Caribbean since the mid-twentieth century, and which cannot be said to have direct parallels to colonial modalities of sexual-economic exchange.[4] These emerging forms of instrumental sex have been made possible by large-scale shifts in the global political economy—for example, the expansion of commercial air travel and the explosion of multinational investment in tourism infrastructure in many developing countries (Crick 1989)—that have enabled vast numbers of middle-class tourists from wealthier nations to travel to the Caribbean on short "getaway vacations." In this sense, Caribbean sex work is closely related to larger changes in forms of capital accumulation, population movement, and information technology that have been described by some theorists as fundamental features of the contemporary "globalized" world (Altman 2001; Appadurai 1996; García Canclini 1995; Harvey 1990). Indeed, the modalities of sex tourism described in this book would not be possible without the development of new methods for commodifying sexuality on a global scale, incorporating technologies such as the Internet, virtual sex tourism networks, and electronic commerce. These historically recent features of the late-modern global economy have permitted more flexible approaches to the production of sexual services, a more rapid response to consumer demand, and a much more segmented, specialized marketing strategy (Truong 1990; see also Crick 1989, MacCannell 1973, and Poon 1989). It is worth mentioning in this context that these processes of market specialization—what we might conceive of as expressions of the growing flexibility and adaptability of late capitalism itself (Harvey 1990)—have also enabled the emergence of tourist services that are specifically oriented toward the gay or lesbian traveler, trends which will be further examined in subsequent chapters as they relate to the commodification of Dominican sexuality (Puar 2002a; Ryan and Hall 2001).

Given the dramatic growth of vacationers who regularly travel to tourism-dependent nations, in conjunction with the particular racialized constructions of Caribbean sexuality that have circulated globally since the colonial era, it is perhaps not surprising that the Caribbean is often constructed by tourists as a utopian space in which to escape restrictive moral-sexual codes at home, as well as to enjoy the greater sexual "freedom" presumably permitted in "primitive" Caribbean societies (Enloe 2000;

Kempadoo 1999b; Kincaid 1988; O'Connell Davidson 1998).⁵ Often, the Caribbean is imagined as a primal, premodern space where "anything goes," a conclusion that may appear to be objectively confirmed, from the perspective of the tourist, by the very pervasiveness and visibility of certain expressions of prostitution in heavily touristed areas. In conducting my ethnographic research in the tourist town of Boca Chica—one of the two research sites where data were collected for this book—I engaged in many awkward conversations with tourists who insisted I explain why Dominicans are "naturally" predisposed to prostitution, reflecting the belief among tourists that sex workers are somehow born, not made. "They are everywhere," one tourist commented. The presumption of a "natural" sex worker, or at least a culture that seemingly facilitates sexual-economic exchange, not only neglects the influence of the tourist him- or herself on local expressions of sexuality—artificially extricating the tourist from the social relations in which he or she is inevitably embedded—but also obscures the ways that sex tourism is structured by both local and global relations of power. As Kempadoo's (1999a) discussion of Caribbean sex tourism argues, attention to the large-scale structures through which sex tourism is enacted permits a critical analysis of the position of Caribbean sexuality within the contemporary world system:

The Caribbean serves as a playground for the richer areas of the world to explore their fantasies of the exotic and to indulge in some rest and relaxation, and the racialized-sexualized bodies and energies of Caribbean women and men are primary resources that local governments and the global tourism industry exploit and commodify to cater to, among other things, tourist desires and needs. In this respect, sex work serves as both a producer and reproducer of capital. Sexual labor and energies are inserted into the production process to fabricate the tourism package, from which profit is accumulated by the state and the tourism industry. Simultaneously, sex work is an extension of physical "care" work that enables the tourist to recuperate his or her energies. . . . Sex work in the region stands as an integral part of the local and global economy, as productive and also reproductive labor, and as a platform upon which the First World (re)creates its identity and power. (1999a, 26–27)

Viewed in this light, there is another way that Caribbean sex work occupies a position in the global economy that bears certain resemblances to its role under colonialism: whereas the sexuality of slaves fueled a system of coerced labor aimed at the provision of cheap sugar calories to the working masses in Europe (Mintz 1985), Caribbean men and women today are increasingly occupied with providing vacationing foreigners an erotic escape from the drudgeries of work in the industrialized world. Thus, despite the dramatic structural changes that have occurred in recent decades—most prominently the wane of traditional agricultural economies and the rise of "King Tourism"—Caribbean people once again find themselves subsumed within a global economy in which their sexual labor functions as a cheap resource that is intimately related to patterns of work and consumption in the "developed" metropolises of North America and Europe.[6] The more things change, it would seem, the more they stay the same.

Yet if the sexual-economic exchanges that occur between Caribbean people and foreign tourists are always already embedded within large-scale historical and structural inequalities, the present research demonstrates that the various configurations of gender, sexuality, and identity expressed in such exchanges are not simply reducible to material conditions. Indeed, the emerging anthropological and critical studies literature on tourism and sexuality has demonstrated that "local" cultural meanings and practices of sexuality are not stable, that what were once "traditional" notions of sexuality are continually shifting as they accommodate and adapt globally circulating ideas of what it means to be a sexual subject or to engage in specific sexual practices (Altman 2001; Cantú 2002; Carrillo 1999, 2002; Puar 2002a). In this sense, sex tourism in the Dominican Republic could never be equivalent to sex tourism in, say, Thailand, since the history of sexuality in each of these settings, and the ways that this history intersects with the development of tourist demand, are markedly different.[7] This culturally and historically contingent quality of global sex tourism as it unfolds in local cultural contexts—and, by extension, its theoretical irreducibility to economic or structural relations—is perhaps particularly evident in the context of the exchanges that occur between gay male sex tourists and the Dominican men who provide them with sexual services, the focus of this book. This is because same-sex exchanges in the context of international tourism highlight so vividly the ways that homoeroticism is variably constructed and socially perceived in different locales, involving the intersection of highly disparate cultural and normative systems for interpreting same-sex desire and practice. Thus, while historical circumstances, such as the Dominican state's escalating economic dependence on international tourism revenues since the 1970s, are often key in structuring same-sex exchanges insofar as they constrain the options available to individuals and increase the demand for homoerotic services, the meanings of same-sex exchanges and their consequences for social relations cannot be fully understood without reference to the specific sociocultural environments in which they unfold.

Despite the fact that a number of Caribbean scholars have discussed the juncture of race and sexual labor in structuring relationships between white male plantation owners and black female slaves, little is known about homosexual exchanges between white male elites and black men during colonialism.[8] While this creates particular analytic problems for the development of a historically informed ethnography of same-sex exchanges in the region, it challenges us to examine how Caribbean homoeroticism operates in the present day and the ways its manifestations are linked to larger structural and historical processes. Unfortunately, an ethnographic analysis of the position of homoeroticism within the Caribbean pleasure industry has been obscured by the fact that most prior studies of male sex work in the region, summarized in chapter 4, have focused almost exclusively on exchanges between Caribbean men and female tourists. The fact that heterosexual exchanges do not challenge normative models of gender and sexuality in the same way or with the same intensity that same-sex exchanges do—and may in fact be a source of symbolic status for some men (see, for example, Press 1978)—has led to the problematic conclusion that sexual-economic exchanges with tourists do not present serious psychosocial challenges to male sex workers, neither do they appear to seriously disrupt their familial or spousal relationships. As argued in the following chapters, in the context of the Dominican Republic, such an interpretation does not reflect the lived experience of the men described here. The sexual exchanges in which these men engage unfold within a much more fluid pattern of behavioral and situational bisexuality than the narrowly heterosexual pattern described in most prior studies, despite the fact that their encounters with male tourists are less readily visible in public space, are often negotiated in clandestine social environments, and are veiled by highly elaborate discretionary practices. Indeed, the fact that same-sex interactions are extensively "covered" in Dominican society may contribute to a persistent underestimation of the frequency of such exchanges in prior research among Caribbean male sex workers, since such "stigma management" presents particular interpretive challenges for social scientific research.[9] This book seeks to understand these cultural silences and their connections to larger structural processes by placing same-sex exchanges within the pleasure industry at the forefront of the analysis. This project is not only essential for conceptualizing the historical position of homoeroticism in today's globalized world, but also provides essential ethnographic context for the analysis of the HIV/AIDS epidemic and its relationship to Dominican tourism dependence that is developed in chapter 6. With this historical context in mind, then, I turn to a discussion of the collaborative relationships with Dominican colleagues that made this study possible.

Team Research and Public Health Affiliations

It is difficult to convey the extent to which this research has benefited from professional exchange and collaboration with local colleagues and public health professionals, some of whom were directly involved in data collection and offered valuable insights into the preliminary interpretation of findings. The most important relationships in this regard were with several members of the local nongovernmental organization Amigos Siempre Amigos (ASA), who became official coinvestigators and contributed immeasurably to the overall quality of the research. ASA is a not-for-profit organization based in Santo Domingo, with institutional roots in the late 1980s, and has received considerable funding from the United States Agency for International Development (USAID) and other international donor agencies to provide HIV-related services to gay-identified men in the Dominican Republic. Based largely on recruitment and outreach to create a nucleus of volunteers to carry out its peer education activities, ASA is the country's only legally incorporated organization run by and for gays. While it also provides certain direct services (principally counseling, support groups, conversation groups, and clinical HIV/STI services) and has served on occasion as a safe space for gay political organizing, its mandate as an HIV-oriented service organization and the restrictions imposed by its funding sources have limited its involvement in purely activist causes (see chapter 6).

Through their outreach work—including special events such as educational shows and theater productions in gay social spaces—the staff members at ASA have become well-known and trusted leaders of the gay community, particularly among the younger, gay-identified men who frequent Santo Domingo's gay bars and discos. The trust ASA members have gained among certain segments of men who have sex with men (MSM)—particularly those who self-identify as gay—made their acceptance of me as an affiliated researcher a clear benefit in my initial contacts with sex workers in Santo Domingo. Many of my first friendships with sex workers were the result of introductions by my colleagues at ASA, and the permission by owners of gay businesses to conduct on-site interviews and focus groups was made possible by their previous collaboration with, and respect for, this organization. Therefore, even if ASA's involvement had been limited to its assistance with social networking, it would have been a significant ally during fieldwork.

In fact, ASA's involvement with my research was much more extensive, including the formation of joint research objectives, the training of personnel for various methods of data collection, the joint administration of research funds, and weekly meetings to discuss ethnographic observations and the ongoing research process. This level of collaboration was made possible by two additional supporting grants (see Methodology, below), which offset most of the logistical, transportation, and personnel expenses required to conduct team research. As a result of conversations between ASA and USAID personnel, facilitated by my dual role as a consultant in the area of HIV/AIDS in the Dominican Republic, financial support was provided to promote: (1) research oriented toward ASA's institutional development and (2) a formative study of a poorly understood subpopulation of MSM who were not being specifically addressed by HIV prevention programs. From the perspective of these donors, the intention of the project was to invest in the capacity and empowerment of existing NGO personnel to formally investigate underserved populations and to incorporate research findings into programs. Chapter 6 discusses some of the directions that this research suggests for HIV/AIDS programs in the Dominican Republic, as well as the ways that it has subsequently reoriented interventions among MSM at ASA.

While my research associates had significant training and experience in the application of behavioral and public health surveys—valuable skills during the survey phase of the research—they had little exposure to ethnographic methods or anthropological analysis. Their desire to participate in certain aspects of the ethnographic process therefore required some training, which was incorporated into the research plan. I trained three ASA members—all with significant professional experience in public health, counseling, and group facilitation—in the basics of participant observation and ethnographic note taking, and they subsequently conducted their own ethnographic observations in male sex-work areas, sharing them with me during regular meetings for this purpose. Our meeting discussions were audiotaped and transcribed to serve as an additional source of ethnographic data, and to triangulate our interpretations of events that we had each witnessed independently.[10]

While each of these coinvestigators made their ethnographic observations and wrote their field notes individually, we organized forty group outings during the first phase of the research to identify, describe, and map the primary sites in Santo Domingo and Boca Chica where male sex workers and clients meet, negotiate, and engage in sexual encounters. These outings produced the information necessary to identify the male sex-work sites discussed in chapter 1 in the section on "Spatial locations and sexual geographies." This approach was particularly useful at the beginning of the research for two primary reasons. First, the existing research on male sex work had not fully described specific sexual geographies in these areas, and the range and extent of urban sites within which male sex work occurred was therefore unknown by our team.[11] Second, since most of the male sex work in Santo Domingo is conducted at night—often in higher-crime areas surrounding discos, strip clubs, and late-night bars—group outings were generally safer until relationships were established with specific sex workers, *maipiolos* (roughly, "pimps"), and the owners of sex work businesses.[12] After this initial phase, my continued ethnographic observations in male sex-work sites, as well as my relationships with individual sex workers and business owners, were largely independent of my colleagues at ASA. Nevertheless, their observations and interactions with sex workers continued to complement my own in ways that contributed greatly to the depth of the research. I, of course, am solely to blame for any deficiencies in analysis or interpretation in this book.

The only tangible liability related to my research association with ASA was the fact that upon first meeting me, some sex workers, as well as gay-identified men, identified my research associates and me primarily as AIDS outreach workers or public health employees. This conceptual association with AIDS prevention, I believe, occasionally skewed self-reports of HIV risk behavior and condom use, since sex workers were often motivated to idealize their behavior in response to sexual questions, or otherwise tended to understand our work as primarily oriented toward the sole objective of HIV prevention (see chapter 6). Nevertheless, this association, while never entirely disappearing, diminished as I began to establish more intimate relationships and friendships with *bugarrones* and *sanky pankies,* and particularly after the first year of fieldwork. As argued in chapter 6, the degree to which sex workers idealize their risk behavior was elucidated by the use of a combined research methodology incorporating both ethnographic-qualitative and quantitative techniques. This combined approach permitted both a methodological check on the interpretation of patterns and a glimpse into the often ambiguous and contradictory dimensions of sex workers' psycho-emotional lives. These and other methodological concerns therefore require further elaboration.

Method of Inquiry

This project involved three years of multisited ethnographic fieldwork between January of 1999 and December of 2001, during which time I lived in two socioeconomically distinct barrios in Santo Domingo, the capital city of the Dominican Republic. My first residence was in Ensanche Luperón, a lower-class, primarily residential neighborhood in the northeastern part of the city, which was geographically convenient to the office of Amigos Siempre Amigos, a fact that facilitated my research collaboration with this organization.[13] While I originally proposed to carry out an ethnographic study of masculinity, HIV/AIDS, and sexuality among a broader cross-section of men (including men who have sex with men) in a single barrio in Santo Domingo, my first months in Ensanche Luperón convinced me to reorient my approach to focus more specifically on male sex work and gay sex tourism. There were a number of reasons for this shift in focus.

First, as suggested in the previous section, one of my primary goals was to develop research objectives along with a local HIV/AIDS organization and to carry out a joint project that would be relevant to their interests and needs. My ongoing conversations with ASA at the beginning of fieldwork, as well as further study and observation of their intervention activities in early 1999, made it clear that the population of male sex workers described here was almost entirely neglected by the exclusively gay-oriented intervention approach then employed by ASA. My observations of ASA's outreach activities at Santo Domingo's gay bars and discos suggested that while the organization's innovative theatrical performances about HIV/AIDS prevention and condom use—as well as their appeal to a gay identity politics— had earned ASA's staff and volunteers a significant amount of respect among gay-identified men, the *bugarrones* and sex workers who are often present in these social spaces were almost entirely neglected by these interventions.[14] Conversations with ASA's administrative and educational staff confirmed that sex workers—and particularly those who do not identify themselves as gay—tend to conceptualize their sexuality very differently than do gay-identified men. For example, while the latter are generally more effeminate in their gender performance and stereotypically (although certainly not universally) participate in *pasivo* (passive, or receptive) sex with their male partners, many *bugarrones* attempt to assimilate to normative constructions of masculinity, are often married, typically request payment for sex, and almost universally claim to participate exclusively in *activo* (active, or insertive) anal sex with their male partners. These men frequent many of the spaces where gay-identified men congregate, and often develop close friendships and long-term relationships with gays. Yet, as described in detail in chapter 3, the boundaries established by cultural constructions of gender and sexuality create palpable divisions between gays and *bugarrones,* making social relations between these groups occasionally ambivalent and contentious.

My growing realization that *bugarrones* were not being reached by HIV prevention interventions conducted by ASA—the only organization in the country conducting public health activities specifically oriented toward MSM was further heightened by my direct professional involvement in HIV/AIDS programs in the Dominican Republic. Beginning in 1999, through contacts made at a conference on HIV prevention approaches among Dominican MSM, I began consulting as a project evaluator for AcciónSIDA, a contract organization funded by USAID between 1998 and 2002.[15] At that time, AcciónSIDA funded and supervised approximately fifteen subprojects in the country, one of them ASA's, to conduct HIV prevention and deliver clinical and social services to various populations. This experience allowed me to engage in more detailed discussions with public health officials both at USAID and at local nongovernmental organizations about approaches to HIV/AIDS intervention and gaps in HIV-related programs. In combination with my preliminary observations among Dominican MSM though my collaboration with ASA, these conversations led to the decision by administrators at AcciónSIDA and the USAID mission to fund some of the expenses related to my ethnographic research among male sex workers, and also stipulated my continued collaboration with ASA and our ability to obtain matching funds from the Fogarty AITRP program.[16] This additional support not only solidified my decision to focus the ethnography on this specific subpopulation of MSM, but also permitted the expansion of the project to include the nearby tourist town of Boca Chica and the different, though closely related, identity of the *sanky panky,* which is discussed further in the following section. It also gave my research associates at ASA a much-deserved, though quite modest, salary for their continued participation in the project.[17]

An additional rationale for the decision to focus the research on male sex work also composes one of the primary themes of this ethnography: the pervasive connections between gay sex tourism and forms of male sex work in the Dominican Republic. The presence of tourists in gay social spaces in Santo Domingo is impossible to ignore, and it was not uncommon for tourists to outnumber locals at some locations during the high tourist season. The fact that gay foreigners are the preferred male clients of most *bugarrones* and *sanky pankies* further drew my analytical attention to the implications of this fact for the globalization of sexual identity, the political economy of sex tourism, and the epidemiology of HIV/AIDS—all of which are central themes of the following chapters. The fact that most studies of male sex work in the Caribbean have focused on local men's relationships with female tourists further solidified my interest in conducting a study focused on the sexual exchanges and long-term transnational relationships developed between local men and gay foreigners. As a result of this focus, the ethnographic analysis in the following pages does not centrally engage with the exchanges that occur between male sex workers and female tourists—exchanges that are considerably more frequent among *sanky pankies* than *bugarrones* (see the following section)—in favor of a more detailed discussion of those between men. As elaborated most clearly in chapters 4 and 5, such a perspective offers a corrective to various interpretive tendencies in existing ethnographic analyses of heterosexual sex tourism in the Caribbean, which have tended to neglect the stigma, shame, and elaborate covering techniques that are so central to sex workers' lives, their construction of identity, and their behavioral risk for HIV/AIDS.

In addition to the ethnographic techniques of informal interviewing and participant observation in sex-work sites that were employed throughout the research period, the length of the fieldwork and the involvement of several research assistants permitted the incorporation of various formal methods, including focus groups, surveys, and in-depth interviews.[18] I incorporated these methods into a phased research plan involving three stages. First, we identified, described, and mapped the primary areas and social spaces in which male sex work occurs in both Santo Domingo and Boca Chica. As mentioned above, this process involved forty team trips to sex work areas in both research areas, during which we used informal interviewing and snowballing from existing contacts in order to identify and observe additional sex work sites. This exploratory phase also included three focus groups with male sex workers in Santo Domingo to examine issues related to self-identification practices, to catalogue local terms and definitions for types of male sex workers, and to check the maps of sex work sites against sex workers' lived experience.[19] The focus groups, which we conducted in a gay bar in Santo Domingo, also assisted in constructing an appropriate survey instrument for application in the second phase, improving the appropriateness of language and the structure of standardized questions.

In the second phase, we conducted quantitative surveys with a total of 200 sex workers in both research sites (of which 199 were usable upon analysis), following a brief validation phase with twenty sex workers in Santo Domingo. I developed the survey instrument through several meetings with ASA team members, during which my initial survey design was discussed and questions were adjusted, removed, or added according to ASA's interests and experience. We sampled survey participants by convenience at a wide variety of sex-work sites, and we used key informants to solicit initial contact interviews with potential participants.[20] As discussed further in chapter 6, that the survey methodology employed purposive, rather than random, sampling has interpretive consequences insofar as it limits gener alizability to a larger population, at least within the epistemological frame-work of statistics. However, the combination of surveys with ethnographic methods broadens the analytical framework for interpretation, and sug-gests that many of the trends demonstrated by the survey data are likely to apply to a broader cross-section of lower-class Dominican men, due to the pervasive influence of the social and political-economic structures that shape sexual-economic exchanges. The following chapters seek to demon-strate this through a comparison of ethnographic and quantitative data.[21]

In the third stage of the research, we conducted audiotaped semistruc-tured interviews with ninety-eight sex workers, exploring issues such as: childhood experiences and traumas; current and past relations with parents and siblings; stigma-management techniques; initiation into sex work; relationships with girlfriends, spouses, and children; stories of worst and best clients; beliefs and fears about HIV/AIDS and condoms; and future as-pirations. Because three coinvestigators besides me were conducting inter-views, I developed a semistructured interview guide to improve consistency in the areas covered, but encouraged the additional interviewers to pursue relevant, important, or unusual lines of inquiry whenever possible. In the case of participants with long-term experience in sex work, or for those who were exceptionally frank or eloquent, interviewers occasionally arranged multiple interviews to explore particular topics more deeply.

Finally, ethnographic techniques—most importantly participant obser-vation, informal interviewing, and ethnographic note-taking—were used throughout the research period. This involved many hours of socializing with male sex workers and clients in various contexts, at first largely in sex work areas—such as bars, discos, parks, restaurants, and streets—and later in more private settings, including some sex workers' homes.[22] The ethno-graphic data continually informed the emerging results from the more for-mal methodologies, allowing for triangulation and verification of data as well as the contextualization of particular findings. This was especially im-portant in the case of the surveys, since straight frequencies of responses can often be misleading when interpreted without reference to sociocul-tural or political-economic context, an epistemological point to which we will return in chapter 6.

Definitions of the Research Population

Throughout this book, the terms *male sex worker, bugarrón,* and *sanky panky* are used somewhat interchangeably. Nevertheless, the referents for these terms are not entirely equivalent, and indeed, these identities are quite complex in their actual social usage and meanings. Even the etic term *male sex worker*—the apparently more objective analytical category often used in public health contexts—should not be understood to refer to a social or linguistic identity that is necessarily relevant or meaningful to the men whose voices fill the following pages. While Dominican employees in HIV/AIDS organizations commonly use the Spanish term *trabajador sexual*—a hispanicization of the English *sex worker* that reflects the globalization of AIDS discourse and the influence of international donor organizations—this is not a term that is salient to all of the men with whom I interacted in the field. While 62 percent of the survey participants answered "yes" to the question, "Do you consider yourself a sex worker" (*¿Te consideras trabajador sexual?*), ethnographic observation clearly demonstrates that this term is very rarely used in actual social discourse, except in unusual cases in which men had experienced a significant amount of exposure to HIV/AIDS organizations, particularly ASA. For example, Ricardo, an experienced *maipiolo* who is discussed at various points in the book, routinely identified himself as a professional *trabajador sexual*, and when I met him he had recently launched what he described as the first locally run "agency" (*agencia*) to provide sexual services to foreign gay men (see chapters 4 and 5). During an interview, he claimed to have developed an *agencia* where he brokered the services of twenty-five "sex workers" to international gay clients.[23] It is not coincidental that Ricardo had had significant contact with outreach workers from ASA, and had even collaborated as a volunteer for this organization on occasion—experiences that had exposed him to the discourses of public health and the technical terms used in such circles to refer to men such as himself. Nevertheless, outside of a formal interview conversation or among men with little or no connection to the institutional cultures of public health, *sex worker* was rarely a term that men ascribed to themselves or to others.

Because *sex worker* is not necessarily a highly salient cultural category or a common term of self-identification, it is used here for analytical purposes, and it was also employed during fieldwork to define the parameters for the selection of participants in the application of the more formal research methods.[24] Nevertheless, even on an analytical level, the term occasionally creates conceptual slippage, for several different reasons. First, while for the purpose of the research *male sex worker* was operationalized as "a man who exchanges sex for money or other benefits," the boundaries of this broad category become blurred in cases in which the "benefits" received are nonmonetary—such as gifts or access to elite hotels and restaurants—or when the instrumental aspects of the exchange are less explicit (or perhaps unconsciously repressed).[25] The latter dynamic, the subject of chapter 5, is common in cases in which romance is a central feature of the relationship, since in such cases sexual-economic exchanges are more indirect and implicit, and monetary exchanges that can be described as simple payments for sex become less common. Despite this analytical fuzziness, it was necessary to include men whose exchanges had been limited to payments in kind, since it is often precisely these exchanges that reveal the diverse ways that sexual-economic encounters with tourists influence local men's immediate material surroundings, as well as the structure of the household economy (see chapter 4).

Another liability of an unreflexive use of the term *male sex worker* is that it may mask the internal variations potentially included in that category. This is implied by a comment made by one of my colleagues at ASA during our initial discussion of the definition of the research population: "So, are we saying that *travestis* are female sex workers?" In fact, our criteria for inclusion in the research had always entailed a somewhat implicit gender distinction between cross-dressing male sex workers—referred to as *travestis* in the Dominican Republic, as well as elsewhere in Latin America (see, for example, Kulick 1998)—and the stereotypical *bugarrones/sanky pankies*, whose gender performance is highly masculine, if not "hypermasculine."[26] As elaborated in chapter 3, this gender dichotomy also reflects a cultural model of active and passive anal sex between men, described in various anthropological studies in the region, in which gender performance and sexual role in anal intercourse are conceptually collapsed and mutually reinforcing (Lancaster 1992; Murray 1995c; Parker 1991, 1999). Thus, within the system of sex and gender in the Dominican Republic, *travestis* and *bugarrones* were quite distinct social and sexual creatures. As an illustration of this, it is likely that *travestis* define themselves as gay much more often than either *bugarrones* or *sanky pankies,* as suggested by the fact that only 3 percent of survey participants in this study identified themselves as gay or homosexual (see fig. 1), and the fact that the *travestis* with whom I interacted socially in the field often considered themselves gay or aligned themselves with the gay community. As argued in the conclusion to this book, this pattern of self-identification—which can be partly explained as the consequence of the fact that it is a particularly non-gay expression of homoeroticism that is sought by most gay sex tourists—has enormous consequences for how we understand the globalization of same-sex desire and practice in the context of tourism dependence.[27]

It is precisely this cultural organization of homoeroticism and sexual identity that would have made it problematic to include cross-dressing sex workers in this research, despite the fact that such research would greatly complement the analysis.[28] This is because of the logistical and method-

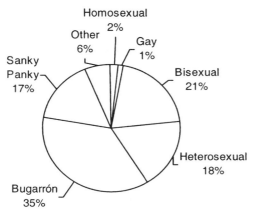

Figure 1. Sexual self-identifications among survey participants

ological constraints of a research project of this scope as well as the decision to focus on the populations least likely to be reached by ASA's gay-oriented interventions.[29] However, it is important to emphasize that, by the very nature of the flexible boundaries of gender constructs, it was not always clear which potential subjects fit our implicit gender criterion. This is illustrated by an incident that occurred during the application of the survey, when one of my research assistants, somewhat perplexed, interrupted my interview to inquire whether he should include or exclude a self-identified *bugarrón* who had painted fingernails. I later learned that this particular *bugarrón* was also a member of a group of *metálicos,* an emerging identity of young men who, as described in chapter 3, project a globalizing heavy-metal aesthetic, often have many tattoos, and frequently paint their fingernails black.[30] This incident demonstrates that while the gender presentation of the participants in this study typically fit the hypermasculine ideal as described in this and later chapters, variations in the performance of gender inevitably blurred the boundaries of selection criteria on some occasions.

While it was tempting at times to restrict the study population to self-identified *bugarrones* and *sanky pankies,* this decision, too, had analytical disadvantages. One disadvantage is suggested by another look at figure 1, which shows that more than half of the men who acknowledged exchanging sex for money or benefits with gay men did not identify as either *bugarrones* or *sanky pankies.* In fact, the idea of using *bugarrón* and *sanky panky* as strict selection criteria entirely neglects the fluid and shifting nature of these identities in actual practice. First, *bugarrón* and *sanky panky* do not connote the rather fixed and publicly acknowledged status claimed, for example, by some gay-identified men in the United States. As described in subsequent chapters, many of these men employ various information management techniques to avoid being publicly "*quemado*" (burned), in the words of one key informant, as a *bugarrón*. Thus, a *bugarrón* sexual identity can be posited only insofar as it is understood as a model of sexual personhood that is highly flexible and dependent upon the pragmatic social context. While a man may refer to himself as a *bugarrón* while in homoerotic social spaces or sex work sites, he is unlikely to do so in the presence of his wife, a potential girlfriend, or male peers who do not frequent these somewhat marginalized spaces. Because of the shifting and pragmatic nature of these categories, their use as a selection criterion for the purpose of surveys or interviews would artificially impose a stable sexual identity that does not reflect social reality. It would also unnecessarily exclude from analysis a wide range of men who share many of the features of self-identified *bugarrones* and *sankies,* but who, for whatever reason, did not choose to refer to themselves as such in the context of an interview.

Another illustration of the fluidity of these categories is evident in the ways that sex workers use them in their speech. The first time I encountered Oscar, a *bugarrón* from Santo Domingo, while conducting participant observation in the town of Boca Chica, he informed me that he had decided to come to the beach for the day in order to "*sanky-panquiar*" (to *sanky panky*). Similarly, the verb form of *bugarrón,* or "*bugarroniar,*" was a very common response among sex workers to questions about what they do for a living. This conversion of the noun *sanky panky* to the verb *sanky-panquiar,* or of the noun *bugarrón* to the verb *bugarroniar,* linguistically constructs these identities as parts that can be played or performed, not fixed dimensions of one's personhood.[31] In many ways, this skill at playing with sexual identities is at the heart of how sex workers sell themselves to clients, as well as the masculine ability to use ambiguity and contradiction to one's advantage. The latter talent—highly developed in the men with whom I interacted in the field—is prototypically represented in the Dominican gender imagery of the *tíguere,* discussed in chapter 4.

Another important definitional distinction between *sanky panky* and *bugarrón* is suggested by the fact that Oscar felt he had to go to the beach in order to "*sanky-panquiar.*" As described in prior studies (De Moya and García 1998; De Moya et al. 1992), the *sanky panky* identity—based on a linguistic dominicanization of the English phrase *hanky panky*—emerged in the seventies and eighties in response to the growing presence of young, well-built Dominican men who made a modest living by hustling foreign men and

TABLE 1: Residence of survey participants by self-identified sexual identity

	Homo-sexual	Gay	Bisexual	Hetero-sexual	Bugarrón	Sanky panky	Other	**Totals**
Santo Dom.	3	1	29	17	63	7	5	**125**
Boca Chica	1	0	8	18	7	25	7	**66**
Other Res.	0	1	4	0	2	1	0	**8**
Totals	**4**	**2**	**41**	**35**	**72**	**33**	**12**	**199**

women in heavily touristed beach areas. The term therefore connotes both a particular masculine style—including, for example, the *trencitas* (small dreadlocks) often mentioned by sex workers as a signature feature of the classic *sanky panky*—and a specific location, that is, the beach. The conceptual linkage between the beach and the *sanky panky* may be, in fact, a reflection of what clients often eroticize about these men, who are viewed as "natural" products of an idyllic tropical climate and whose bodies are sculpted by continual exposure to the sea and the Caribbean sun.[32] Because of this connection between geography and the prototypical *sanky panky*, the ascription of a *sanky panky* identity is conditioned to a significant degree by one's physical location. In the surveys, this linkage was evident in the fact that 76% of the self-identified *sanky pankies* were residents of the beach town of Boca Chica, despite the smaller number of surveys conducted with sex workers in this research site (see table 1).

Bugarrón, on the other hand, has a different social history and entails a slightly different masculine style, although it should be emphasized once again that the boundaries between *bugarrón* and *sanky panky* are fluid and permeable. The word *bugarrón,* which De Moya and García (1998) argue takes its root from the French *bougre,*[33] has a deeper history in the Dominican Republic and, consequently, does not have the same connection to the development of the tourism industry as *sanky panky*. Rather, *bugarrón* was a preexisting identity that was subsequently incorporated into, and commodified by, gay sex tourism in the Caribbean. As an ideal type, *bugarrón* refers to a man who engages in "*activo*" (insertive) anal sex with other men, but who in other domains of life may not be noticeably different from "*hombres normales*" (normal men).[34] A man may refer to himself as a *bugarrón* in certain contexts but not in others, and I have heard the term used both pejoratively—as in "*ese maldito bugarrón*" (that damn *bugarrón*)—and affectionately—as in "*mi bugarroncito*" (my little *bugarrón*). The emotional valence it connotes therefore depends on the context in which it is used, and it may be understood quite differently in the respectable environment of the home than it is on the street or in homoerotic social spaces. As mentioned above, it also takes various grammatical forms, such as *bugarroniar* (roughly, "to bugger") and *bugarronería* (*bugarrón*-like behavior, or "*bugarrón*-ness").

As with *sanky panky, bugarrón* also implies that one requests something of value—whether economic or symbolic—in exchange for sex. As discussed in chapter 3, *bugarrones* are the idealized sexual partners of gay men and, especially, *travestis,* but these relationships invert normative gender models in that it is the symbolically feminized ("passive") partner who is responsible for providing economically for his *bugarrón.* As an illustration, *travestis* frequently commented to me during fieldwork that, in the context of an economic crisis, they were tired of "maintaining" (*manteniendo*) their *bugarrón,* that they wanted to be "maintained" (*mantenida*) by someone themselves.[35] In this sense, Dominican *bugarrones* have cultural analogs in other Latin American contexts, such as the Mexican *mayate* and the Brazilian *michê,* both of which connote a similar configuration of masculinity, sexual positionality, and economic exchange.[36] While, according to De Moya and García (1996, 1998), these exchange relationships may have been less formalized in the traditional Dominican sex/gender system[37]—involving even small gifts of food or alcohol in exchange for sex—the growth in demand for sexual services by gay tourists has tended to further commodify these relationships, leading to greater professionalization and escalating prices. Indeed, studies from the 1980s demonstrate that Dominican gays often complained during the heyday of gay sex tourism in the 1980s that wealthy foreigners were driving the prices for *bugarrones* too high, thereby spoiling them for local gays (De Moya and García 1998). I often heard parallel complaints among local gay men, who felt that it was often prohibitive to have sex with the *bugarrones,* since these men were now "damaged" (*dañados*) by the relatively exorbitant (at least by local standards) payments they were accustomed to receiving from tourists. It is therefore likely that the term *bugarrón* has gradually become associated with more professional or formalized modes of sex work as it has become integrated into the global sex economy, although the term itself has a much deeper sociolinguistic history.[38]

There is a final distinction between *bugarrón* and *sanky panky* that requires further elaboration, as it relates to a number of the following chapters. In both popular understandings and in the few academic accounts available, *bugarrones* are stereotypically associated with same-sex sexual activity, whereas the prototypical partners of *sanky pankies* are foreign women. This study suggests, however, that this difference is more of degree than of kind,

TABLE 2: Sex of clients over previous month, by self-defined sexual identity (N = 172)*

	Homo-sexual	Gay	Bisexual	Hetero-sexual	Bugarrón	Sanky panky	Other	Totals
Women only	0	0	4	21	1	9	4	39
Men only	3	2	18	7	39	4	2	75
Both sexes	1	0	12	5	21	18	1	58
Totals	4	2	34	33	61	31	7	172

*The denominator of table 2 includes only those sex workers who had engaged in sex with a client during the previous month, or 172.

since most *bugarrones* and *sankies* routinely engaged in sexual-economic exchanges with both men and women. As shown in table 2, while those men who identified themselves as *sanky pankies* in the survey did report a higher proportion of female clients than did *bugarrones* during the month preceding the survey, less than a third of them had engaged in sex exclusively with women during this time. The primary difference between self-identified *bugarrones* and *sanky pankies,* in terms of the sex of their clients, is that the relative proportion of *bugarrones* who cater exclusively to male clients is significantly higher than among *sanky pankies* (thirty-nine versus four).

This pattern is consistent with comments by *sanky pankies* during interviews that suggest that while their ideal clients are women, it is often difficult to find female tourists who are willing to *soltar la plata* (let go of money), and women generally require a greater investment of time and energy to negotiate a successful exchange than do men.[39] Thus, even among those *sanky pankies* who preferred female clients, male clients were often viewed as a more consistent source of income, especially when willing female clients were not available or one's economic situation was particularly dire. On the other hand, a high proportion of self-identified *bugarrones* reported never having a female client, while not a single man who identified himself as a *sanky panky* reported having had only male clients during his sex work career. However, these distinctions should be viewed as relative differences along a spectrum of bisexual behavior, and in the survey they did not correspond to differences on a number of related variables. For example, there were no differences between *sanky pankies* and *bugarrones* in preference for male or female sex partners—with a majority of men in both groups indicating they preferred women—nor was there a difference in preferred sexual behaviors with male and female partners. Neither group was more likely to indicate they were capable of falling in love with a man or having a man as a partner, and rates of agreement with various definitions of "homosexual" were similar in both groups (see table A.1 in the appendix).[40]

Taken together, these trends suggest that the identities *bugarrón* and *sanky panky* are intimately related in actual social practice, and their distinctions are best viewed as relative differences rather than as conceptually divergent ideal types. Indeed, because of the greater historical depth of the *bugarrón* category, it seems likely that this construction of Dominican homoeroticism predisposed the emergence of a *sanky panky* identity—catering to both men and women—as tourism began to escalate in the country at the same time that traditional employment options for men were shrinking (see chapter 2). Viewed from this perspective, *sanky panky* is at least partially a historical derivation of a sex/gender system that includes the *bugarrón*, and which is traditionally more permissive of *activo* homosexual behavior among men as well as a notion of sexual-economic exchange in which the insertive partner typically receives some form of payment for his sexual services. In this sense, Dominican models of homoeroticism potentiated the emergence of the *sanky panky*, but the specific cultural expression of the latter identity could not take shape without the structural changes that occurred in the seventies and eighties with the rapid expansion of the tourism industry. Such an interpretation is a plausible explanation for the close conceptual relationship between these identities, as well as the ways that their boundaries are blurred and highly permeable in actual social and linguistic practice.

Because of these dynamics, the analysis in the following chapters frames both of these terms as conceptually linked identity constructions that are shaped by similar political-economic processes. Further, because the overall sexual pattern typical of both *sanky pankies* and *bugarrones* is one of a *fluid behavioral bisexuality* that links same-sex behaviors on the street with heterosexual and marital domains—a connection that is central to the analysis of HIV/AIDS risk in chapter 6—the analysis in the following chapters often represents these identities as more similar than they are different. My focus on the relationships between these identities and gay sex tourism also tends to foreground their similarities rather than their differences, especially because of the ways that these identities are similarly positioned in relation to the fantasized constructions of Dominican masculinity often expressed by gay sex tourists. Finally, it should be reiterated that because of the complexities of identity ascription, not all of the men whom I occasionally refer to as *bugarrones* and *sanky pankies* in the following pages necessarily define themselves as such, or may do so only situationally or contextually. My usage of these terms should therefore be understood as references to prototypical, historically positioned cultural models of masculinity, sexuality, and sexual exchange, rather than as terms of self-reference necessarily employed by specific informants.

∗

The Political Economy of Sexuality

The analytic lens employed here is one that traces large-scale shifts in the global political economy to the lived experiences and practices of sexuality, while continually listening to the voices of the men themselves, their subjective understandings of sexual exchanges with tourists, and their struggles to maintain respect and dignity in a difficult world. The discussion in the following pages therefore hinges on a dualistic theoretical framework in which macro-level political-economic transformations in Caribbean societies interact with the various cultural, historical, and psychosocial meanings of sexuality for the actors themselves.

There is much at stake in the development of such an analytic approach, one that I term *the political economy of sexuality*.[41] First, while theories of globalization have done much to describe in broad terms the macrostructural trends that characterize the contemporary globalized world—including such phenomena as flexible accumulation, acceleration of migration, and the growth of travel and information technologies (Altman 2001; Appadurai 1996; García Canclini 1995; Harvey 1990)—they have less often sought to explicate the linkages between these phenomena and the subjective experiences and local meanings in specific cultural settings. This is perhaps related to the lamentable tendency to see globalization as a process leading inexorably to the homogenization of culture, which contributes to a theoretical flatness in the conceptualization of global processes and a lack of attention to their local texture and variability. Partly in response to this absence of detailed attention to the locality of global processes, some anthropologists have emerged in recent years with important studies of local "queer sexualities" in numerous developing countries, such as Mexico (Carrillo 2002; Prieur 1998), Nicaragua (Lancaster 1992), Brazil (Kulick 1998; Parker 1999), the Philippines (Manalansan 2003), and India (Reddy 2004).[42] These studies have provided a wealth of local "rich descriptions" about sexualities within their cultural contexts as a means of investigating empirically—rather than assuming theoretically—how global processes are expressed in particular places. Yet while these studies have correctly refocused attention to issues such as the hybridity and innovation that characterizes sexuality at the intersection of the local and the global, we are still far from

a holistic understanding of the complex linkages between macrolevel structural changes—such as the growth of the tourism industry in the Caribbean—and changing constructions of sexuality in specific regions of the developing world. As argued in chapter 6, tracing these connections is of more
than theoretical concern, since our ability to understand the intersections
between structural inequalities and local expressions of gender and sexuality directly affects our ability to intervene in human catastrophes that disproportionately affect sexually marginalized populations, such as the global
AIDS pandemic. Until we are able to trace these multilevel reverberations
and reveal their logic, our ability to advocate for human rights and develop
appropriate health interventions will be compromised.

The absence of conceptual tools to make these linkages is particularly
acute in what has been dubbed "queer tourism" (Puar 2002a). While queer
consumers of tourism services—often located in wealthier nations—are
forming a powerful new market niche in many global tourism markets
(Ryan and Hall 2001), we know very little about the impact of these trends
on local populations. As Jasbir Puar has suggested in her introduction to a
recent special issue of the journal *GLQ*, the absence of research on the local
effects of queer tourism may partly result from ambivalence among researchers about acknowledging any relationship between queer travel and
neocolonialism (Puar 2002a).[43] From Puar's perspective, because the world-
wide growth of queer tourism has served on some occasions as a rationale
for championing the emergence of what might be called the "global queer
consumer"—a symbolic being who makes global claims to public visibility
and exerts his or her power by participating in queer touristic consumption—there is an ethical imperative among researchers to describe the dramatic inequalities that enable queer tourism and the consumption of queer
sexual experiences abroad. Following Puar, as well as similar intersectional
approaches advocated by Nagel (2003), my analysis here seeks to highlight
the local and global inequalities that are expressed and maintained through
the exchanges that occur between male sex workers and foreign gay men
in the Dominican Republic. By focusing attention primarily on the sex workers themselves and the ways that their sexual encounters with foreign gay
men influence their personal lives and relationships, I seek to shift the focus
of analysis from the global queer consumer to the local men who make a
modest living by catering to gay foreigners. This shift is critical in developing the political-economic analysis of sexuality that is a key objective of
this book, since it highlights the marginal voices that are rarely articulated
in existing studies of queer tourism. In this case, these voices are of young,
underemployed Dominican men who have decided—in the context of

quite extreme constraints on male employment and the country's growing dependence on the tourism industry—to engage in sexual-economic exchanges with foreign tourists as a means to make ends meet.[44]

An analytical benefit of this attention to marginal voices is that it brings into relief the dramatically contrasting social consequences of engagement in sexual-economic exchanges for the tourist and the sex worker. While gay tourists may feel liberated by the presumably greater sexual freedom and availability of "real men" in places such as the Dominican Republic (see chapter 5), the stigma of homoeroticism in the Dominican sex/gender system requires sex workers to employ elaborate techniques for covering their activities in their intimate familial and spousal relationships (see chapter 4). Similarly, while gay sex tourists are rarely the victims of law enforcement abuses, the sex workers whom they hire are commonly detained by police and forced to pay *multas* (fines) to avoid incarceration. The structure of global gay tourism therefore sets up an *international economy of stigma* that functions parallel to the sex tourism economy, redistributing the negative social consequences of homoeroticism from the North to the South. Thus, while sex tourism may function for some gay men as a means to escape social controls on non-normative sexuality in their home countries, those who are left to manage the consequences of this temporary sexual escapism are the disadvantaged men—disproportionately poor men of color—who do not have access to similar possibilities for global mobility.[45] As illustrated by the narratives of sex workers in chapter 4, this international economy of stigma has myriad effects on the ways that Dominican men who exchange sex for money with gay tourists manage information with and relate to their families, friends, and neighbors in both social and sexual spheres. As argued in chapter 6, it also has much to do with the kinds of sexual risk communication that occurs (or does not occur) in men's relationships with their spouses and female partners.

The latter point emphasizes another benefit of the political economy of sexuality as applied in this research: it offers a corrective to prior studies of homoeroticism in Latin America and elsewhere by highlighting the ways that same-sex exchanges are intimately connected—vis-à-vis the organization of the household economy and marital gender roles—to heterosexual relations and the asymmetrical gender norms that structure them. Following some recent ethnographic work that has begun to break down and critique the presumed divide between heterosexuality and homosexuality in Latin America (Carrillo 2002; Prieur 1998), this book argues that the political-economic, historical, and cultural processes that have fostered homoerotic encounters between gay sex tourists and Dominican men are simultaneously transforming the structure of opposite-sex relations and family life, as well as drawing upon heteronormative gender constructs for the maintenance of same-sex exchanges in the tourism sector. Far from existing in isolation, same-sex and opposite-sex interactions are inextricably interwoven in the sex/gender system that structures the social transactions that occur in the Dominican pleasure industry. Thus, even as male sex workers are disadvantaged in the international economy of stigma that structures their relationships with foreign gay men, they participate in the maintenance of patriarchal gender dynamics that systematically subordinate their female partners. Indeed, as described in chapter 4, heteronormative gender models *enable*, in part, the particular shape of the gay sex tourism market in the Dominican Republic and the practices and identities at play within it. It is therefore analytically essential to situate the social processes described here within a multilevel theoretical framework that permits analysis of the ways that political-economic inequalities related to gender and sexuality are part of multiple and interlocking systems, at times at odds with one another and at times synergistic. A political economy of sexuality must interrogate the entire web of meanings and practices within this sex/gender system and analyze their linkages to larger structural inequalities. In so doing, it resists the ghettoization of ethnographic analyses into either "homosexual" (presumably *exclusively* homosexual) or "heterosexual" (presumably *exclusively* heterosexual) types, particularly in settings where such bipolar categories of sexuality clearly do not apply, as demonstrated by a growing amount of ethnographic literature on behavioral bisexuality in Latin America and elsewhere.[46] Within this broad framework, this book examines the intersections and disjunctures of multiple models of gender and sexuality as they are expressed in the various social and sexual transactions, both same-sex and opposite-sex, in which *bugarrones* and *sanky pankies* engage. In so doing, it offers a new way of understanding the complex web of meanings that link political-economic processes with inequalities of sex and gender at various levels in the social system.

Ultimately, I take the position that the effect of gay tourism on the Dominican sex-gender system must be analyzed in relation to the HIV/AIDS epidemic, since patterns in sexual risk behavior and HIV transmission illustrate so dramatically the ways that local and global sexual inequalities can drive the epidemic while being systematically neglected in public health programs. At the same time, HIV risk among male sex workers and their partners has been largely obscured by the trend in epidemiological discourse to describe the contemporary Caribbean AIDS epidemic (as well as its specifically Dominican expression) as primarily "heterosexual"—a designation that is questioned in chapter 6 through an interdisciplinary dialogue between epidemiological and ethnographic evidence. Indeed, a critical review of the evidence suggests that patterns of HIV transmission in the Dominican Republic cannot be understood without reference to the ways that same-sex encounters in the region have been increasingly commodified by the growth of the pleasure industry, at the same time that development strategies have redirected men's labor from traditional wage work to the informal tourism economy. Such a theoretical framework not only demonstrates that the AIDS epidemic follows the contours of global processes—a quintessential example of what some medical anthropologists have described as the *structural determinants of health and disease*[47]—but also challenges epidemiological depictions of Caribbean AIDS that have often failed to capture the complex linkages between gay sex tourism, tourism dependence, and patterns of HIV risk behavior among "men who have sex with men." Chapter 6 therefore analyzes the Dominican AIDS epidemic from a critical epistemological perspective that interrogates how political-economic and social processes are inscribed on the body while being systematically veiled by the assumptions implicit in theoretical and methodological approaches to the epidemiology of HIV in global public health.

1

Global Sexual Spaces
and Their Hierarchies

The Caribbean region, in the words of Michel-Rolph Trouillot, is "all contact." Here, "there is no way to satisfy anthropology's obsession for 'pure' cultures" (Trouillot 1992, 22). So-called native voices and indigenous constructions are often difficult or impossible to identify in Caribbean societies, where "Pentecostalism is as 'indigenous' as Rastafarianism, where some 'Bush Negroes' were Christians long before Texans became 'American,' where some 'East Indians' find peace in 'African' rituals of Shango" (1992, 24). This pervasive pluralism and mixture have, perhaps, given Caribbean social scientists a privileged ethnographic position from which to engage more recently popularized scholarly discussions of transnationalism and globalization (Basch, Glick Schiller, and Szanton Blanc 1994). The daily manifestations of contact, diffusion, borrowing, blending, and movement are simply too obvious to ignore, and were at the forefront of scholarly analyses of the region long before such ideas were *en vogue*.

What has received less scholarly attention in the Caribbean is the degree to which these globalizing processes are restructuring notions of gender, sexuality, identity, and community for queer men and women.[1] Throughout the region, social networks and gay communities are increasingly forged in a transnational, urban space, bringing together diverse identities, nationalities, languages, symbols, and practices. At the same time, however, these global sexual spaces are cross-cut by social and structural inequalities that constrain the types of social interactions—indeed the types of persons— that are permissible in such spaces. This chapter describes the basic contours of gay social and sexual spaces in the two research sites of Santo Domingo and Boca Chica, with particular emphasis on the ways that the intersections between these spaces and the tourism economy generate social hierarchies that are discernible ethnographically. In the context of the Dominican pleasure industry, a consideration of the position of *bugarrones* and *sanky pankies* illustrates the complex contestations between the processes of globalization that increasingly characterize gay social spaces and the local, particularly Dominican expressions of sexuality and inequality that are implicated in these processes. As we will see through the ethnographic case study of the attempted ban on *bugarrones* at the gay/tourist bar Tropicalia, the politics regarding the inclusion and exclusion of male sex workers from gay businesses in Santo Domingo expose the various ways that the very social shape of Dominican gay space is embedded in social hierarchies at both local and global levels. The chapter ends with a brief description of Boca Chica and Santo Domingo and the specific venues in which participant observation was conducted.

The *Bugarrón* Ban at Tropicalia

In Santo Domingo, global processes are palpable in the gay community's orientation toward all that comes from *fuera* (outside), which unqualified simply means the world beyond the country's borders. In part, this global posture of Santo Domingo's gay community is a reflection of the patterns of population movement, migration, and cultural interchange that are so tangible in all of Dominican society.[2] Yet the types of cultural symbols and knowledge that are brought back home by gay Dominicans who travel or live abroad are distinct in that they are a reflection of their appropriation of global notions of gender and sexuality, often borrowing from styles in Euro-American gay culture that are proudly worn as badges of transnational gay experience. Clothing fashions modeled on urban American gay culture, while much more subdued than in the United States and limited to wealthier gays, are nevertheless discernible in the occasional Dominican in gay uniform, complete with white muscle-T and black signature boots, or sporting imported rainbow-colored jewelry. In the course of my fieldwork, I unwittingly participated in a "suitcase trade" in gay paraphernalia, since the young gay-identified men with whom I worked at ASA often requested gay commercial products from the "outside," which I imported in large quantities in my luggage following trips to the United States. In Santo Domingo's gay bars, the walls are adorned with such borrowed gay icons as Marilyn Monroe and Rock Hudson, and pulse to the rhythm of an eclectic mix of Dominican merengue, Cuban salsa, and Madonna's latest hits. Even as these cultural elements are infused with local tradition and symbolism, then, they provide a constant background reference to a particular off-the-island construction of global gay identity that is being actively interpreted and strategically appropriated by local gays.

As Freeman describes in her analysis of the "foreign shopping missions" of female off-shore informatics workers in Barbados, "'professional' fashion for the informatics worker becomes the 'vent' through which women are able to express themselves creatively and distinctively and a realm of practice through which they also come to feel themselves, and in a certain sense to be, distinct" (2000, 252). In an analogous way, Dominican gay men's consumption of the artistic styles and fashions of Euro-American gay culture—whether through international travel, global media, or suitcase trade—allows a degree of symbolic capital to certain local gay figures who function as cultural brokers or translators in the importation and appropriation of global gay culture. These charismatic figures are cultural innovators in the sense that they are the purported experts on what it means to be gay and Dominican, and creatively combine elements of received knowledge from abroad with local understandings of same-sex desire. The *dragas* or *travestis* (drag queens) that perform in gay bars—particularly those with international travel experience—often function as key cultural brokers, incorporating elements of Euro-American gay style and language into their performances, and forming close-knit social networks through which gay knowledge and international lore are transmitted.[3]

Nevertheless, it would be incorrect to depict Santo Domingo as a burgeoning center of international gay culture, if for no other reason than that these global gay cultural signifiers are accessible to a very small proportion of Dominican men "*de ambiente*" (of the environment) who participate in homoerotic spaces and practices.[4] Many Dominicans can scarcely afford to pay the cover charge for Santo Domingo's gay bars, let alone travel abroad or incorporate gay fashions into their wardrobe. The majority of homoerotic experience in Santo Domingo, then, takes place in the context of a highly depressed economy in which access to many of the signifiers of global gay culture is highly constrained by class and race. As described below in relation to the attempted ban on *bugarrones* in one of Santo Domingo's gay bars, I have witnessed doormen and managers of gay bars and discos in Santo Domingo refuse entry to certain individuals who they feel may "cause problems" or project an inappropriate "image." These decisions are not random; they consistently follow rules of social hierarchy. But as we will see, they also respond to complicated tensions related to the cultural politics of contemporary gay identity and the dependence of many gay business owners on the tourist dollar.

The frequent social and sexual interactions that occur in the Dominican Republic between locals (both queer and straight) and foreigners are emblematic of the Dominican Republic's escalating economic dependence on the tourism industry (which is described in historical detail in the following chapter). While there are no formal statistics on the extent of gay tourism to the Dominican Republic, foreign tourists are prominent fixtures in many gay social spaces.[5] Indeed, in many ways gay life in Santo Domingo rises and falls with fluctuations in the pleasure industry. Owners of gay businesses, despairing the lower profits during the hot summer months of *la temporada baja* (the low tourist season), wait impatiently for the first signs of winter in the United States and Europe that inevitably precede a surge in foreign clients with dollars in hand. A travel agency specifically oriented toward gay tourists to the Dominican Republic is currently operating out of New York, providing personalized vacation packages and travel advice to gay travelers. And there are now several active Internet sites for gay tourists to the country that provide information on local gay businesses and opportunities to arrange social or sexual encounters with Dominicans.[6]

Based on numerous informal conversations with gay tourists in Santo Domingo, primarily from the United States but also from other Latin American and European countries, it is evident that a significant proportion of foreign gay tourists come to the Dominican Republic in order to interact socially and sexually with local men, and often are quite informed about the active sex tourism industry when they arrive.[7] Gay tour groups, numerous Web sites, gay guide books, and local gay hotels and businesses serve to orient them, and—as described further below—local *bugarrones* also work as "tour guides" and interpreters for some gay visitors (either independently or in conjunction with sexual services). At least one local gay business in Santo Domingo, which I call Charlie's, resembles an all-male brothel and caters almost entirely to a foreign clientele of primarily middle-aged clients from the United States (see chapter 5). In nearly all gay bars and discos, foreign sex tourists can be regularly seen, often accompanied by the *bugarrones* who frequent most gay businesses or nearby public areas where they meet potential clients.[8] Gay tourists generally fit into two broad categories: one-time vacationers and regular, repeat travelers. Regular travelers, including Dominican gays residing abroad, often develop social relationships with local gays and establishment owners, facilitating the transmission of privileged gay knowledge and the shaping of Dominican gay culture. An important population in this regard are the queer "Dominican-yorks" who come to Santo Domingo on family holidays or vacations, composing a hybrid queer diaspora that maintains both intimate links and tensions between the Caribbean and New York.[9]

Within this transnational gay space, social interactions are frequently laden with covert or overt contention about the meanings of same-sex desire, as differences in class, race, and identity intersect with both local and global notions of gayness. One of the most contentious issues in Santo Domingo involves the place of the *bugarrón*—or stereotypically *activo,* masculine, heterosexually identified man who often exchanges sex for money—in Dominican gay culture. *Bugarrones* are an undeniable and conspicuous feature of gay life in Santo Domingo, both because of their historical importance as a local expression of homoeroticism and as the men who now accompany many of the gay-identified men in queer social spaces. Nevertheless, their "unsophisticated" dress, hypermasculine demeanor, open flirtation with or *machista* attitude toward women, and frequent self-presentation as *hombres normales* (normal men) all contrast rather sharply with the growing gay identity politics and self-expression of Dominican gay-identified men.[10] Often from lower-class backgrounds, *bugarrones* are regarded by some self-identified gays as *tapa'o*—a Dominicanization of *tapado* (literally, "covered"), which is roughly analogous to "closeted" in gay English—and in Santo Domingo's gay bars one can sometimes hear spontaneous commentaries by gays about *bugarrones* that range from expressions of disgust to pity. Embedded in such commentaries are relatively new assumptions about the construction of gay personhood that echoes many elements of the "coming out" discourse of Euro-American gay culture. But this discourse is distinct in that it simultaneously challenges local, traditional notions of gender and sexuality that, in many ways, are embodied in the figure of the *bugarrón.*

Many of these tensions were evident in the controversial, and ultimately failed, ban on *bugarrones* at Tropicalia, a recently opened gay bar in Santo Domingo. In an attempt to project a more respectable image and upscale social environment, the owners of the elaborately decorated bar-disco announced, through informal social networks, that *bugarrones* would not be allowed to enter the new establishment. The policy was doomed to fail from the beginning. First, it seemed entirely incongruous with the erotic integration—and in many ways, the economic interdependence—of *bugarrones* and gay-identified men. Local *bugarrón*-gay or *bugarrón-travesti* relationships frequently entail an economic arrangement in which the gay/*travesti mantiene a su bugarrón* (supports his *bugarrón*), an inversion of the stereotypical gender division of labor in heterosexual relationships. Further, despite the occasional tensions between them, *bugarrones* still represent the erotic ideal for a significant proportion of gay-identified men, reflecting what Murray (1995c) has described as the sexual system of "homosexual exogamy" in Latin American homoeroticism.[11] Thus, in their attempts to "clean up" the bar, the owners of Tropicalia were planning to purge a primary source of gay men's attraction to the business: *bugarrones*. As many local gay men commented to me, "So, if they keep *bugarrones* out, why would we go there?"

Second, the would-be ban was strangely inconsistent as regards the gay tourists upon which the business depends. Since gay tourists are commonly accompanied by *bugarrones* throughout their vacation, often relying on them as guides and cultural/linguistic translators (see chap. 5), it is not feasible to exclude *bugarrones* without excluding tourists. And the latter is unthinkable, considering the potential loss of profits it would represent.

Given these facts, what is most remarkable about the policy—which was implemented only during the first few days after Tropicalia's opening, and then only haphazardly—is that it was considered at all. Yet despite its practical and economic unfeasibility, it expressed the owners' desire to create a different kind of global gay space—a space they felt would be undermined by the heterosexual identification and presumed "self-deception" of *bugarrones*. Indeed, when my research associate spoke with one of Tropicalia's owners about my ethnographic interviews with *bugarrones,* he said tersely: "I hope you're going to prove what we already know: they're all closet cases [*son unos tapa'os*]." This implies the existence of a deeper, more authentic sexual identity that is being actively repressed by the *bugarrón,* who fails to recognize his own fundamental sexuality and publicly mark himself in terms of his presumed same-sex erotic preference. Such discourses of authenticity are prominent features of North American constructions of gay identity (Levine 1979).

Tropicalia's failed ban on *bugarrones* is useful analytically in that it highlights the contentious and paradoxical nature of the globalization of *gay* in the Dominican Republic, and the ways that sexual spaces are framed within structural inequalities. While Dominican gay life is highly transnational and infused with myriad opportunities for spontaneous social contact with globalizing notions of *gay* that extend far beyond the country's borders, it is also cross-cut by entrenched class differences that limit access almost exclusively to urban elites. The ideologies of gay identity appropriated by certain middle-class and elite gays, while not entirely eclipsing traditional models of sexuality, are nevertheless strategically employed by some to further marginalize those whose "unsophisticated" (read, "unmodern") self-definitions are considered signs of backwardness and sexual repression.[12] These are clearly class-related discourses, but importantly they are also influenced by globalizing notions of what constitutes an appropriate expression of gay identity, and who should be permitted to inhabit its spaces.

Finally, the case of Tropicalia's ban is useful in that it demonstrates how the structures of gay tourism—so prominent in Santo Domingo's homo-erotic environments—place particular constraints on the construction of social and sexual space, since tourist dollars, in a very real sense, are invested in particular expressions of Dominican homoeroticism. As described in chapter 5, gay tourists who purchase sex in the Dominican Republic most often seek an erotic experience with a man who is decidedly non-gay, and *bugarrones* have come to occupy a particularly Dominican expression of this fantasy that is marketable within the global gay tourism economy. An important consequence of this is that the global market for *bugarrones* structures, to a certain extent, the organization of gay cultural and communal space, although it is certainly not deterministic of it. Whereas in the absence of tourist dollars men such as the *bugarrones* described in this book might be systematically marginalized from gay businesses seeking to project a more "sophisticated" global gay image, the connection between *bugarrones* and the flow of gay tourist dollars creates a structural barrier to their absolute exclusion. Gay areas in Santo Domingo are therefore fraught with competing tensions and interests emanating from both local and global levels, and these tensions generate many of the distinct social characteristics of queer spaces.

We will return to many of these issues in chapter 3, which presents an ethnographic case study of contemporary Dominican gay cultural politics that illustrates the contestations that occur in the negotiation of local and global constructions of gay identity, and the ways these continuously display the ripples of structural inequalities. The remainder of this chapter is dedicated to a more extensive description of the social spaces inhabited by *bugarrones* and *sanky pankies,* and the ways the tourism economy influences the movements of sex workers and the geography of homoerotic environments.

The Hierarchies of Tourist Spaces

I remember my disillusionment early in fieldwork when, during a conversation with Antonio, a *bugarrón* with whom I had spent many late nights *tomando trago* (drinking), the subject turned to the larger purpose of my research project.[13] Following a lengthy conversation about his recent symptoms suggesting a sexually transmitted infection, Antonio suddenly flashed me a smile and, with typical directness, offered, "I know why you're doing this study." After a dramatic pause, he observed: "You want to protect the tourists from getting AIDS." While, as a general fieldwork principle I consciously tried to legitimate the opinions of the men whom I was "studying," I found myself sufficiently taken aback in this case that I said nothing at all in response. Antonio didn't seem to notice. He had dropped the comment as easily as he always did, and had already fired a quick "*no' vemo*'" (see you later) and rejoined his group of friends outside a nearby disco before I had fully registered its meaning.

This episode often reverberates in my mind as I attempt to make analytical sense of my fieldwork amidst the ethical and epistemological dilemmas I inevitably faced in conducting ethnographic research on sex work and sex tourism. Antonio's conceptualization of my research agenda as principally HIV-related is perhaps not surprising, given my collaborative research relationship with an AIDS-related nongovernmental organization and my "day job" in HIV prevention with USAID-sponsored projects. What was disturbing to me was the way that his summary of my research emphasized its potential benefits for tourists, whose health I was presumably seeking to preserve by investigating the secret habits of men like Antonio and his friends. Why would he assume, I later wondered, that anything to be gained from my research must necessarily benefit the tourists, perhaps even at his own expense? And why would he assume that I, after nearly a year of socializing and *tomando trago* with him, would prioritize the interests of strangers from foreign lands over his own?

The answers to these questions call attention to the stark inequalities that are characteristic of tourism dependence and neocolonial influence in the Dominican Republic, as well as my own privileged position as a middle-class North American man of mixed white-Hispanic descent. It was more than simple luck, of course, that during three years of fieldwork I was never arrested during a police raid, arbitrarily incarcerated on dubious charges, or forced to pay hefty bribes to the authorities—all common experiences for Dominican sex workers. Dominican *bugarrones* and *sanky pankies* are often persecuted by the police, who take advantage of sex workers' stigmatized status and their association with morally deviant sexual behavior in order to extort money from them. My privileged status as a foreigner who could pass as a tourist allowed me to avoid these dangers, despite my presence throughout fieldwork in spaces in which sex workers are commonly detained or arrested. My "special treatment" in this regard is, of course, more than simple luck; it is the direct result of my privileged position as a person habitually ascribed the status of tourist simply by virtue of my foreignness.[14]

Throughout my fieldwork, I also enjoyed relatively easy access to tourist areas that are off-limits to many locals, particularly those, like sex workers, who are always already under suspicion of being delinquents. Tourist zones are crisscrossed with socio-spatial boundaries that restrict the movements of locals, ranging from the subtle marking of prime beach territory with color-coded umbrellas and "tourist-only" lounge chairs, to the not-so-subtle construction of virtual fortresses around many of the tourist resort complexes. These boundaries may be imperceptible to a light-skinned foreign tourist, for whom freedom of movement is generally taken for granted, but they are as tangible to locals as a sign I once saw posted along a lonely stretch of beach in the heavily touristed town of Puerto Plata: "Dear local residents: Please respect our foreign guests and use the public beach down the road."[15]

Hotel access is a prime example of a context in which I benefited from my ascribed status as a tourist while the men I was "studying" were often at risk of suspicion, expulsion, or arrest. While *bugarrones* and *sanky pankies* spend a considerable amount of time in and around hotels and resorts—making them important spaces for my ethnographic observations—these areas can also be dangerous because of surveillance by hotel staff, security personnel, or the Tourist Police (Policía Turística). This is because sex workers are often automatically suspected of involvement in nefarious activities, such as petty theft and drug use, and are therefore subject to heightened scrutiny. Most of the men with whom I regularly interacted had been detained by hotel personnel while attempting to make contact with a potential client or have sex in a tourist's room, many of them on several different occasions.[16] This bias by hotel staff is illustrated by the fact that hotel managers in Boca Chica universally refused to allow me to conduct interviews with *bugarrones* and *sanky pankies* on the premises, despite the fact that I and my research associates offered to pay full price for our rooms and could legitimate ourselves with supporting documents from public health organizations. Importantly, this prejudice may be more acute for male sex workers than for their female counterparts; one hotel administrator, apparently lamenting the loss of our business, reassured us that "if it were the *muchachas* [female sex workers], well, that would be another thing."[17] Because of these dangers, most *bugarrones* and *sanky pankies* catering to male clients preferred certain gay-oriented or gay-friendly hotels and, especially, *cabañas* (short-term, anonymous drive-in motels), and sex workers commonly share knowledge with one another and with clients about safe and discreet locales for consummating a deal.

While my Dominican research associates and I were often concerned about our vulnerability to police raids during fieldwork—and even devised a research I.D. card to legitimate ourselves in the case of police interrogation—the reality is that I, as a foreigner who was regularly ascribed the status of tourist, was much less likely to be harassed by authorities than either my informants or my (darker-skinned) research colleagues.[18] This protected status is demonstrated by the selective nature of police raids on gay establishments: bars are virtually emptied of Dominicans, leaving only a few bewildered tourists behind. It is not uncommon for police to arrest all young Dominican men fitting the profile of a sex worker, often using the pretext of a *cédula* (national identity card) check, and in a matter of minutes whisk off the "suspects" in police vehicles. Sex workers are incarcerated until they pay a specified "fee," or *multa,* often amounting to a *bugarrón*'s income for a typical week. It is difficult to find a *bugarrón* in Santo Domingo who hasn't been incarcerated in this way, and some estimate that they lose nearly half of their income through such police extortion.

During police raids, the privileged status of the tourist butts up against the selectively applied policies of law enforcement, revealing the fundamental ambivalence of the Dominican authorities as regards gay sex tourism. Gay tourists are largely immune to these abuses, but the local men with whom they associate, if arbitrarily suspected of prostitution, are vulnerable to arrest, extortion, and public humiliation.[19] The juxtaposition of these opposing qualities—of foreign privilege and local vulnerability—can produce surprising and unpredictable interactions. I remember one night on a darkened street in Santo Domingo's Zona Colonial when I suddenly found myself surrounded by *bugarrones* seeking protection from a police officer who, on threat of arrest, was demanding money from sex workers who were leaving a nearby gay bar.[20] Realizing that my ability to pass as a tourist afforded me a potentially protective social status, the *bugarrones* hoped to benefit from the officer's reluctance to make a scene in front of me. The strategy apparently worked, as the officer stopped his approach, and our motley group moved quickly out of sight.

In the context of the persecution and policing experienced by *bugarrones* and *sanky pankies* in various spaces in which they live and work, as well as the hierarchical structure of tourist areas, *bugarrones* and *sanky pankies* employ various strategies to navigate through these environments. One of the most important is their use of the "*cuento,*" a verbal skill that enables them, as sex workers explain it, to *sacar provecho* (take advantage) or *sacarle la plata* (get money out of him). It is to this phenomenon that we now turn our attention.

The Art of the *Cuento* as a Weapon of the Weak

Early in my fieldwork, the structure of the *cuento*—a discursive practice used by sex workers to create an attractive image to the tourist, usually for material gain—manifested itself in a variety of ways in my interactions with *bugarrones* and *sanky pankies,* largely as a result of my unwitting social status as a "tourist-of-sorts."[21] While, as described in the previous section, my tourist identity afforded me certain privileges and protections that were not available to *bugarrones* and *sanky pankies,* it also created a constant background reference to my foreignness that often sabotaged my attempts to separate myself, as an anthropologist and a long-term local resident, from the stereotype of the tourist. During the first year of my fieldwork, most of the sex workers with whom I regularly interacted continued to engage me as they would a tourist, albeit without the linguistic barriers typical of such relationships.[22] Indeed, my field notes from this period are strewn with tormented vignettes of conversations with *bugarrones* that appeared to me at the time—to quote one particularly impassioned journal entry from late 1999—"the same damn rehearsed lines they always tell the tourists." The performative metaphor I employed in this passage is actually quite appropriate for conceptualizing the ways that *bugarrones* typically interact with gay tourists, particularly those whom they ascertain to be potential clients.[23] What I did not fully recognize at the time was that my tourist identity had given me a glimpse of the discourses that frame sex workers' interactions with gay tourists and the strategies they use to *sacarles plata* (get money out of them).

As discussed further in chapter 5, sex workers and sex tourists are engaged in a mutual project of image construction in which both parties attempt to preserve the sense of participating in an "authentic" exchange. For sex workers, this entails the art of the *cuento* (story), a narrative, not necessarily based on fact, that serves to explicate a rationale for one's involvement in sex work, construct oneself as a unique exception to the world of prostitution, or present a tragic drama as a prelude to a request for financial assistance. As an example of the latter, one sex worker explained that, when all else fails, "*matas a una abuela*" (you kill off a grandmother). This refers to the invention of a tragic tale, stereotypically involving a death in the family, which justifies one's dire condition and current state of economic desperation. Another, and more dramatic, example of this use of the *cuento* was provided by Gregorio, a twenty-one-year-old *bugarrón* in Santo Domingo, who explained in an interview how the passing of Hurricane Georges in September 1998 was his "best period," since he was able to convince all of his regular clients to send him sympathy payments totaling 46,000 pesos (nearly U.S.$3,000) to help him rebuild his house. "But my house was fine," he joked heartily, "since it's made of brick!" The important ethnographic point is not that these men are "inventing" extreme economic hardship—since such hardship is not unknown to most sex workers—but rather that the art of the *cuento* is in its distortion and embellishment of hardship for the purpose of garnering empathy on the part of the client—empathy that may have monetary benefits.[24]

Sex workers' discourse about delinquency when marketing themselves to tourists provides an example of another use of the *cuento*. Since *bugarrones* and *sanky pankies* often make initial contacts with potential clients by offering their services as *guías* (tour guides), they commonly warn newly arrived tourists of the many dangers of traveling alone and the recent increases in robberies and violent crimes against foreigners. A sex worker may personalize this *cuento* by offering some first-person examples of crimes he has witnessed or to which he has fallen victim himself. "The streets are full of *tígueres* ["tigers," delinquents]," he might comment casually.[25] "You shouldn't walk around alone, especially as a foreigner." While these observations may or may not have a basis in fact, the important point is that the discourse of local delinquency is strategically deployed by sex workers to convince tourists of the value of their services as *guías*, translators, or would-be bodyguards. To the degree that a *guía*/sex worker is convincing in this regard, he may succeed in establishing a relationship that lasts throughout the tourist's vacation and perhaps beyond—generally a more lucrative arrangement than a brief one-night stand. Thus, a successful *cuento* about delinquency is one that convinces the listener of the need to hire a *guía*, and of the unique moral and physical qualifications of the speaker in this regard.[26] Because of these dynamics, the ways that Dominican male sex workers and gay male tourists interact with each other restrict the boundaries of acceptable discourse, since the successful negotiation of an exchange relies upon the mutual creation of a marketable fantasy. A marketable fantasy in the context of sex tourism is one that facilitates or enables the exchange of sex for money by successfully identifying and guaranteeing the fulfillment of the tourist's sexual pleasure. Because a marketable fantasy is an inherently amorphous phenomenon, successful sex workers are quite remarkably flexible and creative in constructing an "authentic" performance for tourist consumption. The *cuento* is therefore one of the primary means by which sex workers express their creative agency in the course of sex work. Because of the dynamics of the *cuento*, sex workers' relationships with clients are so overdetermined by economic interests, performance, and codes of social engagement that genuine dialogue is often greatly inhibited, and this is only exacerbated by the fact that tourists' Spanish language skills are typically remedial at best.

For these reasons, it was problematic for me to be perceived as a tourist by sex workers, since this status tended to elicit tourist-oriented speech, to limit acceptable topics of conversation, and to muddle the analytical distinction between ethnographic "facts" and "fiction."[27] Early in my fieldwork most of my interactions with sex workers appeared to me as a well-rehearsed "party line," and I had endless hours of conversations with *bugarrones* and *sanky pankies* that began to appear scripted, superficial, and inauthentic. Regarding the delinquency narrative described above, for example, almost no sex workers confided in me during my first year of fieldwork about their involvement in petty theft against clients, a common practice about which later interviews yielded considerable information. Indeed, their responses to my questions about theft revealed a logical inconsistency between sex workers' depiction of their peers and their depiction of themselves. While most would acknowledge that other sex workers steal regularly from their clients, almost none would admit to firsthand involvement in theft; on the contrary, they emphasized how such deception went against their moral beliefs and could result, after all, in substantial economic losses if the victim were to spread the word about the crime to other sex tourists, business owners, or the police.[28] Not coincidentally, these are the same rhetorical devices that they used with sex tourists to convince them that they were safe to take back to their hotel for the night.

In trying to get beyond the *cuentos* and minimize my tourist identity, I had missed the larger analytic point that now seems clear: *cuentos* are woven into the fabric of interactions between sex workers and clients, and function for sex workers as something akin to what Scott (1985) has described as "weapons of the weak"—the everyday, small acts of resistance that are framed within larger structures of inequality and systematic abuse. While Scott frames his analysis within the context of modern industrial enterprises and their exploitation of labor, we might see the use of *cuentos* by Dominican sex workers as an analogous phenomenon in the context of late capitalist formations and, in particular, the structure of the pleasure industry. Indeed, the strategic use of verbal talents is a skill that Dominican men are particularly adept at using—a reflection of the masculine value of *tigueraje* that is discussed later in this book—and *bugarrones* and *sanky pankies* regularly employ this skill to make a living in an environment in which they suffer numerous systematic abuses and restrictions on their mobility.[29] This is a particularly useful framework for examining *cuentos*, since it avoids the interpretation of sex workers' strategies as simply deception at the expense of others, and permits a more holistic understanding of the ways that these behaviors operate as points of resistance within larger systems of power and inequality. We will return to these points at various junctures in the following chapters, as they have analogous expressions in the strategies sex workers use in maintaining their relationships with wives and girlfriends, the topic of chapter 4, and the ways that information is managed with long-term regular clients, or "Western Union daddies," discussed in chapter 5.

Spatial Locations and Sexual Geographies

Because *bugarrones* and *sanky pankies* often face significant amounts of stigma and are regularly subject to abuse by authorities, no specific place names are used in this book, except when they refer to wide geographical regions or barrios. All names of specific businesses have been changed, and certain aspects of their ethnographic descriptions have been altered when necessary to disguise their precise locations. Nevertheless, it is important to describe in broad strokes some of the basic features of the two research sites of Santo Domingo and Boca Chica, as well as specific characteristics of the sex work locations where participant observation was conducted.

In many ways, a comparison of Santo Domingo and Boca Chica presents a problem of unit of analysis. While Santo Domingo, the capital and largest urban center in the country, is a burgeoning Latin American metropolis of over two million people, Boca Chica—located about thirty kilometers to the east—is a small beach town adjacent to a diminishing sugar cane industry that has become a primary *polo turístico* (tourist pole) on the country's southern coast.[30] These contexts are therefore somewhat distinct in the ways they structure male sex work, as well as the identities that circulate within exchanges between tourists and local men. As a large and highly diverse urban center, Santo Domingo has developed specialized commercial environments that appeal to a gay-identified market—both foreign and domestic—and much of the sex work between local men and tourists therefore circulates around specifically gay-oriented businesses. This process has been fostered by the increasing organization of gay sex tourism, which encourages the development of gay-oriented businesses that meet the cultural standards of foreign gays as well as satisfy the erotic demands of gay tourists who are interested in sexual encounters with locals. These gay sites can also function as hubs for the transnational communications necessary to consummate sex tourism encounters. For example, Simon, the owner of a gay bar discussed at the beginning of chapter 5, which caters primarily to sex tourists, regularly received international calls from gay men all over the world seeking to arrange encounters with specific sex workers prior to their trip. This was facilitated by the fact that Simon's bar was discussed by gay sex tourists on various Internet chat sites and Web pages, and was also incorporated into the itineraries of specialized gay tours that brought business to Simon.

Similar gay businesses are not present in Boca Chica, although there are particular networking sites where same-sex encounters are more common.[31] This smaller environment is primarily populated by a highly diverse and continually changing population of European and North American tourists, the employees of the various resorts and tourist businesses that serve them, and the local residents, many of whom make a modest living working in the informal-sector pleasure industry.[32] The lack of specifically gay-oriented businesses creates a social environment in which sexual exchanges between men must be first negotiated discreetly or indirectly, since "producers" and "consumers" may not be immediately recognizable. This explains why many sex workers in Boca Chica made their initial contacts with gay clients while offering their services as *chulos* (pimps) for female sex workers or as *guías* (tour guides). Since potential gay clients often could not be immediately identified within public (implicitly heterosexual) social space—including beaches and resort areas, for example—exchanges between men often involved rather nuanced negotiations to determine the nature of the services desired and the willingness of the sex worker to provide them. The fact that specifically gay-oriented businesses were not present in Boca Chica may also explain why the gay sex tourists with whom I spoke there frequently made initial contacts with Dominican sex workers in gay businesses in Santo Domingo, and later made trips to beach resort areas, such as Boca Chica, along with one or more sex workers/tour guides.[33] It bears mentioning that when sex workers refer to meeting clients "on the beach," they typically include the many tourist-oriented businesses adjacent to the beach and lining the main street of Boca Chica's resort area. Figure 2 shows a typical view of those businesses, which include a mix of bars, discos, *colmados* (small corner stores), souvenir shops, restaurants, tourism companies, and Internet cafes.

However, despite the greater number of specifically gay-oriented businesses in Santo Domingo—presently including four gay bars and discos in the sector of the Zona Colonial alone—it would be inappropriate to assume that all contacts between sex workers and gay tourists occur in openly gay social spaces. Indeed, as shown in table 3, both in Santo Domingo and Boca Chica, a significant proportion of sex workers had made contacts with clients in public and semipublic areas, such as streets, restaurants, shopping centers, and parks. Clearly, though, the primary distinction between Boca Chica and Santo Domingo—in terms of the sites in which male clients are typically met—is represented by the fact that many more sex workers meet clients in bars and *discotecas* (discotheques) in Santo Domingo than they do in Boca Chica, where contacts are typically made on the beach. This pattern is not surprising, giving the foregoing discussion, since the presence of gay bars and discos in Santo Domingo makes it more likely that exchanges with gay clients will occur in such environments. Similarly, the fact that Santo

Figure 2. Tourist-oriented businesses along a Boca Chica street

TABLE 3: Locations of initial contacts with clients, by research site*

	n (%)	
	Santo Domingo	Boca Chica
Bars/discos	101 (84.9)	20 (50.0)*
Hotels	24 (20.2)	8 (20.0)
Beaches	31 (26.1)	38 (95.0)*
Parks/plazas	34 (28.6)	10 (25.0)
Restaurants	25 (21.0)	14 (35.0)
Shopping/commercial centers	17 (14.3)	9 (22.5)
Theaters	11 (9.2)	4 (10.0)

* Indicates differences between sites are highly statistically significant at the $p < .001$ level. Calculations are based on those participants who reported having had sex with male clients (N = 166).

Domingo's tourism industry is not constructed around the beach, but rather around historical cultural sites in the Zona Colonial, explains the much higher frequency of contacts established on the beach in Boca Chica.

In both research sites, then, contacts made in public or semipublic areas required an initial "decoding" of the social cues exchanged in interactions with gay tourists, a process that was described by a number of sex workers during the interviews, as illustrated by Cesar's detailed description of how he negotiated an exchange with his most recent client:

It was an American. He gave me a hundred dollars, and gave me an expensive watch, it was really cool [*chévere*]. At first he pretended to want to meet women with me, and then I said to him—I was the translator because I speak a little English—I asked him if he liked any of [the women], and he told me he liked one, and that he would give her a hundred dollars to go with him. So, I told her and she didn't want to until the next day, she said. So, I told him a bunch of things, and then I started to notice that he was a *maricón* [roughly, "gay man"]. Then he grabbed me and told me, "I like men," and I told him "tell me what you want." And he said "I want you to go with me tonight.". . . So, we left for about four hours, and later I spent the night with him, he gave me a hundred dollars, and later fifty more and a watch.

Here, the decoding of the client's sexual interests was facilitated by Cesar's ability to serve as a *guía* (guide), a role (described further in chapter 2) that often encourages involvement in sexual-economic exchanges among men employed in the pleasure industry. While many of these informally employed *guías* offer to connect male tourists to female sex workers—for

Figure 3. Negotiating a deal outside a gay bar, Santo Domingo

example, by approaching foreign men at night to offer them "*chicas bonitas*" (beautiful girls)—many of them have inevitably made contacts through such work with gay tourists, some of whom become their clients. While walking through Boca Chica with my Dominican research team, we were once approached by a *guía/chulo* offering us "*chicas*." In a moment of experimentation, my male colleague whispered "*chicos*" (boys). The young man suddenly changed his sales pitch, and offered to find us some boys, or to service us himself. Because the social geography of Santo Domingo included gay-oriented businesses, such decoding of sexual desires was often unnecessary, particularly among those sex workers who specifically targeted the gay spaces surrounding gay bars and discos, where it was often presumed that the *bugarrones* who stood outside were potentially for hire. Many of the sex workers who participated in this study were recruited from street areas in Santo Domingo located nearby gay bars and discos, such as the street scene shown in figure 3.

Finally, it is important to note that same-sex exchanges in both research sites overlap with female sex work in a variety of ways, demonstrating the fluid and diverse nature of the pleasure industry in tourist areas. In Boca Chica, for example, spaces that are explicitly oriented toward heterosexual sex tourism, characteristically involving foreign men and local women, are surrounded by more discreet homoerotic transactions between men. Outside one of the popular discos—where fabulously dressed Dominican female sex workers work as "waitresses" while hustling foreign men—*sanky pankies* may be cautiously negotiating a transaction with a group of gay tourists. Similarly, while the well-built Dominican men working at the beach sports shops or as members of "*equipos de animación*" (entertainment staff) at adjacent hotels may flirt openly with female tourists lounging on the beach, many of these same men engage regularly in more discreet exchanges with gay foreigners.

The ways that these transactions are veiled by social taboos and men's elaborate information management techniques are central themes of this book and are considered more extensively in subsequent chapters. First, however, we turn to a different question: How are the same-sex exchanges that occur in the Dominican pleasure industry connected to large-scale shifts in the country's development approach, particularly the exponential growth of the so-called smokeless industry of tourism?

2

"Me La Busco": Looking for Life in the Dominican Pleasure Industry

The cost of living is going up again
The peso which is dropping can't even be seen
And you can't eat beans any more
Or a pound of rice or a measure of coffee
No one cares what you think
Could it be because we don't speak English?
Ah, that's the truth
Do you understand?
Do you? Do you?

El costo de la vida sube otra vez
El peso que baja ya ni se ve
Y las habichuelas no se pueden comer
Ni una libra de arroz ni una cuarta de café
A nadie le importa qué piensa usted
Será porque aquí no hablamos inglés
Ah, ah, es verdad
Do you understand?
Do you? Do you?

JUAN LUIS GUERRA, internationally renowned Dominican *merenguero*, "El costo de la vida" (translation by Fuller 1999)

Dominican Dependency and Tourism Development

One of the central arguments of this book is that contemporary processes of globalization, urbanization, and tourism development in the Dominican

Republic are reconfiguring the ways that men interact materially, socially, and sexually with other men, as well as the ways they interact with girl-friends, spouses, friends, neighbors, and family. While the work of anthro-pologists such as Trouillot (1992) and Mintz (1996) has demonstrated that the Caribbean has in fact been "globalized" for centuries, the argument put forth here is that recent large-scale structural changes in the region have led to contemporary forms of globalization that, in turn, engender a range of new local behaviors and practices. Among the practices that are being trans-formed are the ways that sexual relationships—and sexual-economic ex-changes in particular—are formed, understood, and enacted. Thus, while the particular manifestation of tourist-oriented male sex work that is the subject of this ethnography reflects certain aspects of local norms of gender and sexuality, it is simultaneously an expression of recent political-economic shifts on a global scale that are restructuring the Dominican Republic as a reservoir of a new kind of sexual labor.

In conducting fieldwork with Dominican male sex workers, one of the most striking realizations was the fact that these men were so similar to their non-sex-working peers, a reflection of the fact that they shared many basic characteristics with other men employed in the informal-sector tour-ism economy who did not engage in sex work. When viewed from a political-economic standpoint, the reasons for this become clear, since sexual-economic exchanges in the tourism sector are functionally inseparable from a wide range of tourist-oriented services that young men provide in the pleasure industry. Recent economic trends in the country demon-strate the rapid growth of informal-sector work among lower-class men, and many of these men are filling employment niches that include occa-sional, episodic, or career participation in the pleasure industry—arguably the fastest-growing sector of the Dominican informal economy devoted to the provision of pleasure and recreation to visiting foreign guests.[1] One consequence of these macrolevel processes, increasingly salient since the U.S. invasion of the country in 1965, is that a growing number of young, lower-class men are engaging in sex-for-money exchanges with tourists. A look at the recent history of the Dominican Republic provides some context for understanding why this is so.

Since at least the early 1980s, the Dominican informal sector has em-ployed more men than any other sector of the economy, and the country represents one of the rare cases in which men are approximately as likely as women to be employed in the informal sector (Safa 1995, 107).[2] Indeed, this pattern of the increasing informalization of men's labor—which has been demonstrated in globally comparative studies to be particularly pronounced in the Latin American region (Chen, Vanek, and Carr 2004; Fernández-Kelly 2004)—has provided part of the rationale for recent suggestions in Caribbean scholarship and popular culture that "Caribbean men are in crisis" (Lewis 2004).[3] Caribbeanist scholar Linden Lewis has described two components to this purported "crisis" in Caribbean masculinity. One crisis is economic, and the other is social:

The economic crisis is the result of global restructuring of capitalism which has the effect of reducing and displacing significant segments of the labour force and engendering fear and insecurity among workers. The social crisis is related to the problems experienced in civil society, itself the product, at least in part, of the economic restructuring. Here unemployment coupled with bleak prospects of future work, dwindling chances of realizing the goal of home ownership, for example, and a growing recognition of one's powerlessness to control one's own social reproduction, among other things, have tended to dislocate familiar gender roles for men, leaving them groping for ways to negotiate this new territory. (2004, 251–52)

Lewis's analysis of the purported crisis in masculinity is useful in that while it critiques the inherent gender bias behind the discursive construction of a "crisis in Caribbean masculinity," at the same time it acknowledges the deep structural changes that are occurring in the region, which have unknown consequences for men's gendered identities and practices. How are Caribbean men coping with the loss of traditional formal-sector labor, the "liberalization" of the economy, and recent shifts in the gendered division of labor? The Caribbean scholarship on gender and sexuality is only beginning to address such questions among men, although it benefits in this regard from several important feminist-informed anthropological studies of women's responses to these transformations (Bolles 1996; Freeman 2000; Safa 1986, 1995). In this section, I use Dominican men's increasing involvement in the pleasure industry as a lens for understanding how political-economic forces in the contemporary Caribbean impinge on men who work in the informal tourism economy, and how some men are responding to historically recent shifts toward neoliberalism.

As is typical in the Caribbean more generally, Dominican men have experienced steady proportionate increases in informal- and service-sector employment, gradually catching up to women. The reasons for this are complex and are rooted in several intersecting trends that have escalated over the past three decades: the rapid expansion of the tourism sector, the privatization of major state-owned industries, a greatly reduced emphasis on agricultural exports (most importantly sugar), and the proliferation of free trade zones employing mostly women (Betances 1995; Bray 1984, 1987; Safa

1995; Wiarda and Kryzanek 1992). These macroeconomic trends have been spurred by thirty years of political hegemony by former President Joaquín Balaguer, a holdover from Rafael Trujillo's dictatorial regime, whose policies favored opening the Dominican economy to foreign investment, principally in the areas of tourism and free trade zones (Betances 1995).[4] Indeed, as Barry, Wood, and Preusch (1984) have pointed out, Balaguer's rise to power in 1966, with backing by the United States, was concurrent with the country's transition to a tourism-based economy, and was followed by a regime that was heavily subsidized and guided by the United States, the United Nations, the World Bank, and the Organization of American States in its effort to create an investment climate favorable to tourism.[5] This linkage of development strategies with foreign tourism interests reflects a trend that is palpable throughout the Caribbean. Kamala Kempadoo describes this trend as follows: "Promoted by the United Nations as a strategy to participate in the global economy since the 1960s, tourism was adopted by Caribbean governments at different times as a way to diversify their economies, to overcome economic crises that threatened to cripple the small nation-states, and to acquire foreign exchange" (Kempadoo 1999a, 20).

During the decades of Balaguer's virtual monopoly of political power under an officially democratic state, economic reforms were consistently implemented to attract multinational corporations and tourism developers (Betances 1995, 113–33). In 1971, Balaguer passed Law 153, which provided tax breaks and exemptions for private individuals and conglomerates interested in investing in large-scale tourism enterprises, as well as allowing for the state's arbitrary expropriation of beach-front property for the purpose of tourist development (Freitag 1996, 231).[6] The Dominicanist scholar Emilio Betances describes the consequences of these policies as follows:

During the many years that the Dominican economy relied on the export of sugar, coffee, cacao, and tobacco, the state levied export taxes on these products, thus collecting revenues from the export sectors. By definition, free-trade zones were tax-exempt. As such they did not make contributions to state revenues or to the national economy other than through wages and local expenditures. Tourism generated revenues but was also largely tax-exempt. The transformation from an export-led economy to a service economy with manufacturing increasingly located in free-trade zones eroded the ordinary revenues of the state. This transformation diminished the role of the state in the economy and weakened its ability to meet the needs of an impoverished population. (1995, 130)

Given that in 1990 the Dominican population's standard of living fell to its level of 1980, one can only conclude, as Betances does, that "Balaguer's structural adjustment programs and economic reforms cannot be considered positive from either an economic or a political standpoint" (ibid., 132).[7]

Thus, in recent years the Dominican economy has made a historic shift from a colonial economic model based primarily on agricultural exports to a service-sector economy that depends on the influx of foreign exchange through tourism and free-trade zones, and on the ability to sell cheap local labor that is affordable to multinational investors. Tourism is now the principal industry of the Dominican economy (ASONAHORES 1995), and since 1982 it is been the country's main source of foreign exchange (Freitag 1996). In 1994, according to Cabezas, "close to 150,000 persons were [formally] employed in the tourism sector, making it the largest source of employment in the Dominican Republic" (Cabezas 1998, 96). Nevertheless, estimates of the number of Dominicans formally employed by tourist-oriented businesses overlook entirely the extent to which local Dominicans depend on informal-sector labor within the pleasure industry. More significant for the current discussion, figures of tourism-sector employment do not account for the thousands of individuals involved—either full-time or intermittently—in sexual-economic exchanges with tourists.

These structural changes have had ripple effects that can be discerned throughout Dominican society, as the local economy and culture have become inserted into the global tourism industry. Nostalgic Dominicans sometimes talk about a time not long ago when the "virgin" areas of Caribbean coastline were not inundated with five-star, all-inclusive hotels and resorts. Major tourist enclaves such as those in Puerto Plata, Samaná, La Romana, Boca Chica, Juan Dolio, Barahona, and Bávaro are now attracting over 2 million tourists per year to one of the largest hotel infrastructures in the Caribbean.[8] Public service announcements remind Dominicans to proudly display their "*sonrisa Dominicana*" (Dominican smile) to their foreign guests, and previously quiet fishing towns, such as Las Terrenas, are quickly being transformed into transnational spaces complete with Internet cafes, European cuisine, and New York-style *discotecas*. Between bouts of sunbathing, red-faced tourists browse through the numerous souvenir shops and food stands, or hire a tour guide/interpreter for a trip to Santo Domingo's historic Zona Colonial, before stumbling back onto the cruise liner or into the numerous walled-in resort complexes.

These changes are equally palpable in the large urban centers of the country, but their specific manifestations are somewhat distinct. In a country in which total population size nearly doubled from 4 million in 1970 to 7 million in 1990, more people now live in urban areas than rural (Wiarda and Kryzanek 1992, 9). Faced with lowering agricultural prices, the closure or privatization of state-owned sugar mills, and diminished possibilities of subsistence agriculture, rural populations are pouring into urban areas. The capital of Santo Domingo is presently home to more than 2 million people, most of whom live in the numerous lower-class *barrios marginales* that surround the city's commercial center. Multinational industry is pervasive in large cities like Santo Domingo, Santiago, and San Pedro de Macorís, as are the foreign assembly plants in the numerous free-trade zones.

A growing wealthy expatriate class of businessmen and developers, as well as the supervisory and administrative staff of the myriad international donor agencies, are among the occupants of the dozens of new high-rise apartment complexes that now pierce the ocean view below Santo Domingo's wealthier neighborhoods, such as Piantini, Bella Vista, and Mirador Norte. The city has an increasingly cosmopolitan feel, and wealthy Dominicans and their foreign cohorts can now sip *Cuba libres* in one of several recently developed commercial zones with pricey bars, restaurants, and discos. The government—especially under the administration of President Leonel Fernández—has invested considerable money in "modernizing" the underdeveloped infrastructure of Dominican cities. The new tunnels and *elevados* (elevated highways) of Santo Domingo and Santiago provide a respite from the unending traffic jams, but they cost the Dominican Republic millions, and the constant delays in construction due to lack of equipment and resources have left many city-dwellers wondering if the end is worth the means.

Essentially, these expenditures are a continuation of the country's strategy of international image construction that aspires to attract foreign investment and tourist dollars by providing the necessary infrastructure and economic incentives to ensure globally competitive profits. Such efforts at "modernization" primarily benefit the urban middle class, and they reduce potential investments in education and training that might prepare more Dominicans for higher-level positions in the rapidly globalizing economy. But improved education is antithetical to a service-sector economy in which the low cost of unskilled labor is considered a fundamental asset of the state.[9] Indeed, according to Grasmuck and Pessar (1991, 38), since the 1970s the Dominican Republic has "witnessed an educational mismatch between employment supply and demand," such that students' investment in training and education has resulted in only meager improvements in overall employability and salary. This trend began with the Dominican "Austerity law" in 1966, which froze wages for a decade (ibid., 45). Similar policies have been instituted subsequently, most notably the austerity regulations implemented by the International Monetary Fund in 1983 under former President Jorge Blanco, which led to spontaneous food riots in 1984 and increasing government abuses against a disenchanted laboring class (Black 1986, 138–46).

One of the effects of these and other policies has been to discourage the development of an educated middle class, since returns on educational investments do not offset the rising cost of imported foodstuffs and plummeting wages. Beginning in the 1970s, the proportion of Dominicans receiving higher education increased rapidly in response to a growing demand for skilled labor.[10] Nevertheless, these increases in education could not be absorbed by an economy that increasingly relied on low-skilled labor in the service and export-manufacturing sectors. Grasmuck and Pessar have described how these factors have led to an epidemic of "brain drain," as better-educated Dominican migrants have sought more lucrative employment possibilities in the United States and elsewhere (1991, 44–50).[11]

Ironically, at the same time more Dominicans are being systematically excluded from skilled positions, the country's unskilled laborers are sometimes blamed for stagnating economic growth. The treasurer of the Asociación de Comerciantes de Boca Chica (Boca Chica Business Association) recently announced that the town is losing millions of dollars of potential tourism revenue because local Dominicans are incapable of "attending politely to the visitor and presenting themselves with sophistication and education" (López 2001). Such patterns of blame are illustrative of the systematic devaluation of Dominican labor that has caused a dramatic drop in the basic wage for formal-sector employment, and a rapid transfer of laborers from the formal to the informal sector. Importantly, this trend has been as dramatic for lower-class Dominican men as it has been for women. The closure and privatization of numerous sugar mills, which employ primarily male *braceros* (sugar cane cutters), as well as the simultaneous expansion of free trade zones employing primarily women, have resulted in a growing proportion of men who cannot be absorbed by the formal sector. As immigration restrictions have tightened, migration has also become less viable as a "steam valve" for male unemployment.

The pleasure industry has flourished under these conditions. Fostered by a development strategy that emphasizes the virtually unrestricted influx of foreign exchange and investment in the tourism sector, businesses— both large and small—are increasingly marketing to the middle classes and the wealthy, both foreign and domestic. Given the weakening of local industry and agriculture, a significant and growing proportion of these enterprises are oriented toward recreation and leisure activities. In this way, the economy capitalizes on two of its only remaining resources: the country's tropical climate and its ability to entertain. In short, the Dominican Republic has come to depend—somewhat ambivalently—on the profits from pleasure-seeking behavior, broadly defined.

The great majority of the country's poor are left out of the pleasure industry as major consumers but are crucial as the cheap source of labor that drives it. Some work for wages as waiters/waitresses, chefs, maids, bartenders, disc jockeys, entertainment staff, and security in the bars, restaurants, and hotels in urban areas, or in the many coastal resort complexes. Others discover that they can tap into micromarkets in the diverse informal sector that epitomizes the pleasure industry, from souvenir sales and guided tours to lounge-chair rentals and massage. In coastal towns where there is a significant tourist presence, local informal entrepreneurs swarm along the beaches and boardwalks to sell their products to the "gringos," and may even outnumber foreign visitors during the low tourist season.[12] In part, the popularity of informal work in the tourism sector results from the fact that, as Mullings (1999, 69) argues, "the tourism industry is often seen as a very lucrative route for informal service providers because transactions are often made in foreign currencies and prices are negotiated." The fact that prices are not fixed enables local vendors, artisans, and small-scale entrepreneurs to adjust the prices of their products—and, indeed, the products themselves—to accommodate changes in tourist demand. When tourist demand is high, as in the case of sex tourism, locals have the potential to make more money than would be possible as an unskilled wage laborer in the formal sector.

The loss of viable formal-sector opportunities and the growth of the pleasure industry in the Dominican Republic parallel political-economic changes throughout the Caribbean. Anderson and Witter's (1994) conclusions regarding the consequences of tourism development in Jamaica apply equally to many of the region's tourist-dependent island states; most of the formal-sector employment opportunities that are generated by the Jamaican tourism industry are low-skilled and do not stimulate other types of employment. These patterns fly in the face of earlier promises of Caribbean economies rapidly flourishing in response to tourism development. The much-lauded development approach that posited tourism as the powerhouse of a new Caribbean economy—the "untapped resource" that would enable the accumulation of foreign exchange and the proliferation of jobs—must now confront the harsh realities of dependence on foreign investment.[13] What is often referred to as "leakage" from the local economy—meaning the loss of income due to the industry's tendency to import the products it consumes, hire foreign personnel for its skilled positions, and promote all-inclusive packages whose profits remain in the developed world—has resulted in a very small proportion of tourism revenues actually entering the local economy or creating new jobs (Crick 1989). In conjunction with the fact that most of the multinational tourism enterprises are attracted by generous tax incentives, countries such as the Dominican Republic—having bought wholesale into the tourism-as-development scheme—are now faced with a crisis of lost revenue due to leakage. Indeed, it is estimated that only 15 percent of the revenues from the Dominican tourist industry ever pass through the Central Bank (Freitag 1996, 227).

A number of Caribbeanist scholars have shown that individual responses to these contemporary structural conditions are highly influenced by gender (Bolles 1996; Freeman 1998; Ho 1999; Safa 1995). Due to rising rates of male unemployment and underemployment, women are taking on greater financial responsibility both within and beyond the household. Deere et al. (1990), paraphrased by Kempadoo (1999a, 19), note that during the 1980s four main strategies had been devised by Caribbean women to cope with economic adversity: "they had entered the labor force in large numbers; they increasingly engaged in a wide variety of activities in the informal sector; households diversified their survival strategies; and women joined and even predominated in international migration." All of these processes have had the effect of making Caribbean women more vulnerable to economic crisis and more likely to engage in informal income-generating endeavors—including utilitarian sexual exchanges—as a means of "making do."[14] In contrast, relatively little research has been conducted on the effects of increasing informal-sector participation, including sex work, among Caribbean men. This gap in the literature is perhaps even more striking in the Dominican Republic, given that at least as many men as women are now employed informally.

As is increasingly the case in the contemporary global economy, the expansion of the Dominican informal sector does not reflect a simple transfer of laborers from the formal to the informal sector; in fact, growing numbers of men and women are participating in both sectors simultaneously. In the pleasure industry, the boundary between formal and informal sectors is extremely fluid, with many people engaging in both types of income-generating activities simultaneously, sequentially, or cyclically. Indeed, the nature of the Dominican tourism sector tends to facilitate the strategic diversification of work as a counterbalance to economic uncertainty. The aftermath of Hurricane Georges in 1998 and the post–September eleventh plunge in international travel are just two recent examples of the country's potentially devastating vulnerability to fluctuations in the global tourism economy.[15] Even under the best circumstances, regular fluctuations in tourism are guaranteed by the inherent seasonality of the industry. Low tourism season—the lament of many poor vendors, artisans, taxi drivers, and hotel employees—can create periods of extreme deprivation for poor Dominicans or small businesses that are too reliant on tourist dollars.[16]

The ways that Dominicans relate with one another, both sexually and economically, are also changing as a result of these political-economic shifts. For example, a look at the fragmentation of the Dominican family that is occurring under current conditions is illustrative of the ways that structural changes are linked to sex-for-money exchanges. Indeed, the separations and vulnerabilities that characterize many lower-class Dominican families today are different than the "fragmented," "polygamous" family forms described in early anthropological accounts of the region (see, for example, Clarke 1970; Smith 1962, 1971).[17] While those accounts focused on cultural notions of kinship or the seasonal nature of rural agriculture as explanations of "matrifocality" or "male marginality" from the household, the contemporary Dominican lower-class family is more often structured by the economic pulls of urban spaces and tourist enclaves, in combination with growing dependence on informal-sector income. The number of men leaving formal-sector work in the agricultural industries increased thirty-two times between 1998 and 2000, due to the numerous closures of the state-owned (CEA) sugar cane plantations (Secretaria de Estado de Trabajo 1998, 2000). This dramatic shift in the agricultural base has led many rural families to search out better options in an urban environment. Many of these families are no longer dispersed because of agricultural cycles, but rather because of the boom-and-bust cycles of informal-sector opportunities such as the pleasure industry, which provide sporadic economic opportunities in particular (mostly coastal) regions.

Dominican sugar cane communities, or *bateyes*—consistently showing the lowest levels of health and development in the country (Martinez 1995; Tejada 2001)—epitomize the forces that are dispersing many families. In areas like San Pedro de Macorís, the closure or privatization of state-owned *ingenios* (sugar mills) has left *batey* communities in geographically isolated areas with no industry and few, if any, jobs. Rates of unemployment in these *bateyes* are extraordinarily high. As a result, many *batey* residents have moved out of the community to seek out better options, but others—having invested brick-by-brick in humble homes—have decided to remain in the *batey*. Due to the extreme economic constraints in *batey* communities and the diminishing possibilities for work, residents must frequently leave the *batey* to make money, perhaps working in a nearby tourist enclave or—

with some luck—in a free trade zone. Depending on the geographical iso-
lation of a given *batey*, income-generating activities can result in long ab-
sences by spouses, adult children, or other members of the extended family.
Indeed, the accelerating dispersal of *batey* residents—many of whom are
Haitian or Haitian-Dominican—has begun to rekindle the omnipresent
Dominican prejudice against Haitians, as ongoing debates rage in the Do-
minican media and the public sphere about the inundation of "unsightly"
Haitian beggars on the streets of Santo Domingo.[18]

In many ways, these migratory patterns are not so different from those
of rural-urban migrants throughout much of Latin America and the Caribbean, but the crucial point is that these movements also reflect neoliberal transformations in the Dominican economy that are directly related to
increasing tourism dependence. As the formal-sector economy shrinks and
options for informal income generation in the pleasure industry multiply,
the frequency of sex work inevitably increases. Nevertheless, as demonstrated throughout this book, these processes should not be understood in
purely functional economic terms, since the structural constraints on individual decision making are not deterministic of the specific manifestations
of sex work or the ways they are conceptualized by the actors themselves.

Looking for Life

As the structural processes described above continue to escalate, a growing
number of Dominicans are taking advantage of their ability to provide a
wide variety of products and services to visiting foreigners. This market
diversification is perhaps more likely in an economy based on the profits
of pleasure-seeking behavior, since the types of goods and services that are
marketable in a pleasure-based economy are highly varied and fluid. The
male sex workers with whom this research was conducted illustrate one of
the ways that some young Dominican men are filling this diverse market
niche, partly as a means to cope with rising male unemployment and economic crisis.

Ranging from highly opportunistic casual encounters to international
prostitution networks, Dominican sex work—not legally prohibited between consenting adults over eighteen years old—has become one of the
fastest growing sectors of the informal economy.[19] Of course, the precise
value of the cash and gifts that changes hands in sex-for-money exchanges
is impossible to determine, but this is perhaps insignificant in comparison
to the profound effects of sex work on Dominican society and culture more
generally. Large cities like Santo Domingo now have complex networks and

urban spaces where various kinds of sex-for-money exchanges occur. Female sex work is more conspicuous than male sex work, and is a pervasive and visible feature of Dominican life, particularly in urban and tourism areas. Estimates of the number of female sex workers in the Dominican Republic range from 50,000 to 250,000 (AIDSCAP 1993; Gallardo Rivas 1995; MODEMU 1997; CESDEM 1997; International Organization for Migration [IOM] 1996), remarkable in a country in which total population size is only 8 million.

Analysts of Dominican female sex work have emphasized the centrality of the country's sex trade in international prostitution networks both within and beyond the Caribbean, an observation that spurred one of the first regional studies of sexual trafficking (Kempadoo 1999b; see also Imbert Brugal 1991). By 1996, estimates were 50,000 for domestic Dominican sex workers, and another 50,000 were estimated to be working in prostitution abroad (IOM 1996). Kempadoo describes the results of studies of Dominican female sex-work networks as follows:

Research in the Caribbean identified multiple trafficking routes within the region and internationally for purposes of prostitution and domestic work, establishing that the most common forms of trafficking involved situations of indentureship. Women were contracted as workers, prostitutes, dancers, or domestics through an agent in their home country and assisted with travel to another country or region, ending up in a situation where they would have to pay off large debts for travel expenses and travel documents. (1999a, 15)

Presently, Dominican female sex work is undergoing a process of political organization and institutionalization, with a number of nongovernmental organizations working directly or indirectly with sex workers.[20] The female sex-work industry is expanding in urban barrios and is rapidly diversifying into new modalities, such as the *car wash* and the *liquor store* (Kerrigan et al. 2001).[21] Due in part to the compact and eclectic nature of Santo Domingo's barrios, nodal points of female sex work are often located within or easily accessible to residential areas, increasing the visibility of sex work in daily life, if not always its wholehearted acceptance. When I asked one of my Dominican colleagues, a public health educator who became involved in HIV prevention with female sex workers early in the epidemic, why she had chosen to work with this population, she commented simply, "In the barrio where I live, there are sex workers everywhere, so I just considered it working with my community."[22]

Dominicans living or working in tourist enclaves such as Boca Chica are continually confronted with female sex work, arguably the largest informal-sector niche in the tourist economy. Large, all-inclusive resorts and hotels—growing in number and geographical extent as the Dominican government continues to offer incentives to foreign developers—are always convenient to the pervasive *discotecas,* hotels, *cabañas,* and bars catering to sex work.[23] Transactions between female sex workers and male clients are readily visible in these areas, as scantily-dressed *camareras/meseras* (waitresses) negotiate with potential clients, *novios* (boyfriends), *chulos* (roughly, "pimps"), or *maridos* (husbands).[24] Fantasies of marrying a foreigner and moving abroad are common among female sex workers working with a tourist clientele (Brennan 2004), fueled by a relatively small but significant number of mythic success stories. Indeed, small enclaves of Dominican female sex workers have been described in various European and Caribbean countries, usually associated with a client demand for a *mulatta* skin tone (Brussa 1989; Koenig 1989; Martis 1999).[25]

Some broad features of female sex work are described here because they are important in understanding the context of male sex work in the Dominican Republic. Male and female participation in sex work have distinct features and social consequences, but they are also inextricably linked through the informal social networks of the pleasure economy. Some of the male sex workers interviewed for this study were also *chulos* for female sex workers, and many had paid women to have sex with them. In one prior study of seventy-six *palomos* (adolescent male sex workers) and *bugarrones* in Santo Domingo, for example, Ruiz and Vásquez (1993) reported that 43 percent of study participants had engaged in intercourse with female sex workers, and one-fourth of them indicated they were *chulos* for these women. In general, these men accept money for sex when the opportunity presents itself—and under specific conditions that are both culturally and individually circumscribed—but they also engage regularly in a diverse set of parallel activities in the pleasure industry that bring them into regular contact with female sex workers.

The term *buscársela* is commonly used in the Dominican Republic to describe an unspecified set of informal income-generating strategies that people use to make a living. The conjugated form *me la busco*—literally, "I look for it"—is one of the most common replies that one hears from male sex workers when asked about what they do for a living (*¿A qué te dedicas?*). While the referent of the direct object pronoun *la* in "*me la busco*" often remains intentionally ambiguous in actual discourse, it is likely that it refers to the feminine of "life," or *vida,* yielding the semantic approximation, "I look for life." Yet perhaps the ambiguity of the term reflects its most important function in actual discourse, since the phrase "*me la busco*" immediately indexes a fundamental uncertainty about how to make ends meet in a difficult world. Importantly, while the term is used very commonly among both male and female sex workers—giving it particular context-bound meanings in this community—it is also used outside of sex-work circles. Dominicans use the phrase to describe a highly diverse set of survival strategies, including borrowing, sharing, and myriad informal income-generating endeavors.

The concept of *buscársela* in the Dominican Republic is similar in overall structure to what some scholars (Mullings 1999; Senior 1991) have described as the "coping strategy" of "making do" in Jamaica. Senior (1991) has defined the Jamaican notion of "making do" as: "a social phenomenon which is widely accepted: that is, it is a fundamental role of poor women to make do with what they have or better still, 'make something from nothing' in order to maintain their families. At its simplest level 'making do' involves 'cutting and carving' or 'cutting and contriving,' i.e., being resourceful in using whatever is available to maximize its utility to oneself and family" (1991, 130–31). Paraphrasing this literature, Kempadoo (1999a, 19–20) notes that "Senior emphasized that Caribbean women's survival strategies were based on multiple 'sources of livelihood.' Sex, she argued, was just one of the many resources that women relied upon to 'make do,' concluding that 'to feed their children, women will exploit any option, including their bodies'" (1991, 134).[26]

Similarly, many lower-class Dominican men are combining various activities in the informal sector in order to make ends meet, a pattern that is particularly evident in the pleasure industry. The diverse strategies that *bugarrones* and *sanky pankies* use in "looking for life" are illustrated by the fact that, in addition to their sex work, they participate in a wide variety of jobs primarily based on informal negotiations and commissions rather than steady waged labor. Indeed, the ad hoc and shifting nature of the economic activities in which sex workers—and indeed most individuals employed in the pleasure industry—engage can make it difficult to determine in a specific case whether sex work or a "supplemental job" is the primary income-generating activity. Among the participants in this study, economic activity ranged from highly professionalized sex workers who relied principally on sexual-economic exchanges, to individuals who supported themselves primarily through other activities and had engaged in sex work only on an intermittent or situational basis.

Figure 4 summarizes the survey data on the various jobs that sex workers used, in addition to sex-for-money exchanges, as a means of making do. Of the sex workers surveyed, 124 (62 percent) engaged in at least one additional income-generating activity.[27] In constructing figure 4, open-ended responses were organized post hoc into higher-level conceptual categories

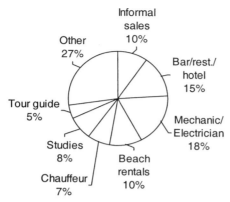

Figure 4. Income-generating activities in addition to sex work

generally corresponding to domains or clusters of economic activities that, taken individually, are extraordinarily diverse.[28] This diversification of informal-sector activities is adaptive in the context of an uncertain economy and shrinking opportunities for formal wage labor.

Yet the economic activities summarized in Figure 4 provide only part of the picture, since such static figures cannot fully capture the highly dynamic and situational strategies for money-making that characterize the informal tourism economy. In fact, an individual's income is conditioned by his willingness to engage in a broad range of economic activities, as well as his ability to establish and maintain strong social networks through which future income-generating opportunities might arise. Proficiency and respectability in various types of exchanges can therefore be highly profitable, since much of the pleasure economy is mediated by inside contacts. Well-connected and charismatic individuals can more effectively tap into the enormous flow of foreign exchange in the informal sector if they are able to situate themselves as middlemen in diverse transactions. Men use a variety of strategies to make themselves "indispensable" for these transactions, such as befriending and "protecting" tourists; securing rights to broker certain transactions; working as *taxistas* (taxi drivers) and *motoconchistas* (motor cycle drivers); and becoming proficient translators. Those who are successful middlemen can charge commissions or fees for negotiating transactions, including illicit activities such as drug sales and underground pornography productions.

One of the most visible examples of the ways that many Dominican men are inserting themselves as middlemen in the pleasure industry—particularly pervasive in heavily touristed areas—is the phenomenon of the "*guía*" (guide) or "*guía turística*" (tour guide). Most of the specialized *guías* are men—although women engage in similar kinds of informal networking—and in tourist areas like Boca Chica, male *guías* overlap with the sex work identities *bugarrón* and *sanky panky*. Working as a *guía* does not necessarily mean that one is situated within a formal tour agency, and indeed most of this work is highly opportunistic, independent, and unregulated. The term *guía* is therefore used here as a cultural category and an informal-sector niche, not as an official designation.[29]

As discussed further in chapter 4, the informal title of *guía* has additional advantages for young men who engage regularly or intermittently in sexual-economic exchanges with tourists: it offers a "cover" for engagement in stigmatized behavior, since it provides a logical justification for frequent interactions with tourists and extended absences from home. In this sense, a *guía* identity is analogous—in terms of its social functions—to the *camarera/mesera* (waitress) identity adopted by many female sex workers to distance themselves from the stigma of their engagement in prostitution.[30] Indeed, for female sex workers, the protective symbolic status of being a *camarera* is one of the most important benefits that the job provides, since the material compensation generated through sex work often far outweighs that provided by waitressing.

In the Dominican pleasure industry, the primary responsibility of the *guía* is to facilitate pleasure. A *guía* can work within the sex industry or not, and not all sex workers are *guías,* but these domains tend to overlap because of the nature of demand in the informal pleasure economy. *Guías* benefit materially from their ability to facilitate the fulfillment of desire, and they employ various strategies to ensure their success. One of the most important of these strategies is to gain enough *confianza* (trust) with their clients to either personally provide or to broker all their requests. When the request is sexual in nature, the *guía* has various potential courses of action: he can break off the interaction; he can refer the client to someone willing and able to provide the service; or—the most lucrative option—he can provide the service himself.

Dominican male sex work, then, is situated within an informal economy in which the ability to successfully manage diverse social networks is highly adaptive. The income-generating activities of male sex workers are not, therefore, strictly limited to direct sex acts but include a variety of (often illicit) goods and services that can be accessed "by referral." The successful transactions that these go-betweens broker in the informal pleasure economy often entail a commission, the size of which depends on the service provided. Men who are talented at managing a significant proportion of such transactions within the sex industry may therefore become successful *chulos* or *maipiolos,* exercising a degree of power over their social peers.

✶

Gender, Space, and the *"Puta"* vs. the *"Maricón"*

Male and female sex workers are inextricably linked in the diverse transactions that occur in the pleasure industry, despite the fact that studies tend to view them in isolation. Often they are linked as lovers, casual partners, or spouses; sometimes they are linked professionally as coworkers in bars, restaurants, or hotels; and they are certainly linked epidemiologically through the transmission of HIV and other sexually transmitted infections. Yet the ways that the activities of male and female sex workers in the pleasure industry are spatially circumscribed, and the ways they are incorporated into commercial and governmental institutions, are highly differentiated by gender.

In general, negotiations between female sex workers and their clients occur within various sex-work establishments in which they are working in some formal capacity, such as waitresses or dancers. Despite the visibility of street sex workers in certain parts of urban centers, non-establishment-based sex work represents a minority of the female sex industry. The relative formality of female sex workers' position within sex establishments—while apparently attenuating in Santo Domingo's evolving sex industry—is evidenced by the fact that rules are often institutionalized regarding the payment of a portion of the women's earnings from sex work to the establishment owner.[31] Some female sex workers also receive certain employment benefits from their work as waitresses in sex-work establishments, such as their annual *bonos* (end-of-year double wage) (Kerrigan, personal communication). Kerrigan et al. (2001) report that many sex workers and the owners of sex establishments describe their work environment as "familial" and mutually supportive, despite occasional dissention and conflict. Finally, the development and growing recognition of grass-roots advocacy organizations afford female sex workers certain avenues of recourse if they are mistreated or exploited in their work, however limited these avenues may be.

In contrast, the male sex workers described here have few formal ties to the businesses in which they often meet *clientes,*[32] and the ties that occasionally exist with management are generally informal, tenuous, and contested. Indeed, social relations between male sex workers and business owners are at best ambivalent, and sex workers are often prohibited—either individually or as a group—from entering certain businesses. Usually these bans are temporary, resulting from a specific incident of petty theft, aggressiveness with a client, or problems with the police. In some cases, however, entry bans are the result of simple prejudice on the part of the owners, administrators, or *porteros* (doormen). As described in interviews with sex workers, for example, some of the more upscale bars and *discotecas* in Santo Domingo are known to refuse entry to male sex workers who are "inappropriately dressed," referencing their lower-class status.[33]

Partly as a result of their more tenuous relationship with specific sex work establishments, male sex workers are highly mobile, often moving between various bars, *discotecas,* restaurants, and other businesses where they are simultaneously "clients" (of the business) and sex workers looking for potential clients.[34] In Santo Domingo, many sex workers follow nightly routes that begin at an establishment with an earlier closing time and move progressively to the late-night bars and discos. In no businesses—other than hotels—are there on-site beds or rooms where clients and male sex workers can have sex, as is typical of the brothels in female sex work. In addition, a significant proportion of male sex workers' contacts with clients are made in streets, parks, plazas, restaurants, beaches, bathrooms, and other public places, rather than in specialized sex-work establishments.

Perhaps the most important contrast with female sex work, however, is the fact that male sex workers have virtually no institutional representation, and had been incorporated only marginally and sporadically into social service programs when the present research was undertaken.[35] There are no self-advocacy or support organizations for male sex workers, and there has been no sustained effort to expand relevant services to include them.[36] There are a number of reasons for this, as discussed in more detail in chapter 6, but it is ethnographically significant that the relationships between sex workers and various institutions—both commercial and social-service-related— are much more tenuous than those typifying female sex workers. As a result, social and health-related services currently have no infrastructural basis upon which to reach—much less to understand the cultural nuances of— men who engage in sexual-economic exchanges in the pleasure industry.

In many ways, these contrasts between male and female sex work—while always relative rather than absolute—reflect differences in the gender positionality of men and women more generally, as well as the divergent contours of social stigma for male and female sex workers.[37] Some of the earliest anthropological depictions of gender relations in the Hispanic Caribbean discussed the normative bifurcation of lower-class space into the domain of female respectability in the "home" (*casa*), on the one hand, and the male domain of reputation and the "street" (*calle*), on the other (Manners 1956; Mintz 1956; Scheele 1956; Wilson 1969). Yet while ongoing debates about the utility of this conceptual division have contributed important correctives and nuances (see chapter 4), there has been little discussion of the specific ways that the figure of the "*puta*" (prostitute, or more semantically accurate, "slut") functions to establish normative boundaries that constrain women's activities to the home. Indeed, a woman's presence in certain areas at night, or her employment in certain questionable businesses, can provoke gossip among her family, friends, and neighbors that she is a *puta*.[38]

Female sex workers, for obvious reasons, bear the brunt of this prejudice,[39] but the normative power of the *puta*—as the symbolically denigrated pole of what has been called the "madonna-whore complex" in Judeo-Christian gender imagery (Whitehead 1997; see also Bastide 1968)—extends well beyond the community of sex workers, continually redefining the boundary between appropriate and inappropriate feminine behavior. By negative example, the *puta* in the Dominican Republic functions as a threat to all women who would deviate from certain notions of appropriate female sexuality, loading the term with negative affect and stigma. Female sex workers use various techniques to mitigate the stigma of their "spoiled identity" (Goffman 1963), including the common conceptualization of their occupation as waitressing rather than as sex work and, more recently, the political reconfiguration of female sex work through the empowerment activities of advocacy organizations. The most important point is that the ways that female sex workers behave and conceptualize themselves are refractions of a larger sex/gender system, since sex workers continuously navigate the margins of the morally acceptable.

In an analogous way, male sex work refracts important features of male gender identity and sexuality, but the field of social stigma is distinct. For the male sex workers examined here, it is not the frequent engagement in sexual-economic exchanges or their participation in activities associated with street life that threatens their social reputation. Rather, it is the type of sexual behavior in which they participate that makes them vulnerable to social prejudice and censure. Of critical importance to understanding the lived experience of *bugarrones* and *sanky pankies* is that a significant proportion of their sex-for-money exchanges are with men—despite frequent assumptions to the contrary—and they only rarely identify themselves as *gay* or *homosexual*. In fact, roughly speaking, the stigmatized figure of the *loca* or *maricón* in Dominican male sex work is, in some important ways, analogous to the *puta* in female sex work: the *maricón* represents the ever present danger of a social death as a man. Male sex workers use a number of techniques to avoid the attribution of a *maricón* identity, a more stigmatized status by far than their participation in sex-for-money exchanges per se. As illustrated by the sex worker narratives analyzed in chapter 4, these self-making practices—relying fundamentally on deception, discretion, and covering—tend to foster shame and ambivalence in sex workers' emotional lives. At the same time, however, these strategies are consistent in important respects with the gender expectations of certain lower-class men, symbolized by the masculine image of the philandering, street-carousing "*tíguere*" (roughly, "tiger"; see chap. 4). The logic of Dominican gender ideology therefore fosters a social permissiveness toward men's street activities and provides them certain options for stigma management that are not available to women. Conversely, the position of female sex workers within the gender structure seems to have afforded them certain opportunities for the creation of self-advocacy organizations, as well as the establishment of more stable—if occasionally conflictual—networks with business owners. Indeed, the relatively high degree to which female sex workers are integrated into sex-work establishments is one of the primary reasons that a recent (and highly successful) HIV/AIDS intervention with this population has taken a "structural" approach that incorporates business owners to support prevention measures (Kerrigan et al. 2003). No analogous structure exists for male sex workers, a point that is elaborated further in chapter 6.

Recent changes in communication are also influencing the ways that sexual-economic exchanges are organized, as well as the ways that stigma is managed by male and female sex workers. The ever widening Dominican sex-work networks now take advantage of twenty-first-century communications technologies to broker contacts between sex workers and clients. Some Dominican sex workers—both male and female—can be found on various Internet sites dedicated to sex tourism or pornography.[40] Throughout my fieldwork, I was struck by the extent to which male sex workers rely on their cell phones to plan airport pick-ups and resort weekends with their visiting foreign clients, or arrange an evening with a regular. And a few "agencies" and Internet groups are now specializing in the organization of packaged tours to the Dominican Republic that involve, implicitly or explicitly, intimate exchanges with the "natives."

The irony of these expanding communication networks is that these very networks systematically inhibit other types of communication. The increasingly urban and tourist-oriented focus of Dominican male sex work has spurred a "delocalization" of sex-for-money exchange that fosters anonymity and discretion.[41] These are many sex workers' psycho-emotional allies as they struggle to maintain the boundaries that separate their sex-work lives from their intimate familial relationships and spousal partnerships. The high-tech, modernized systems that are transforming the structure of sexual exchanges, then, are also facilitating a protective, anonymous space in which growing numbers of Dominican men can experiment in sex work (or other non-normative expressions of eroticism) beyond the watchful eyes of their neighbors, friends, and families.

Indeed, in addition to the perception that tourists are "rich" (*ricos*), many *bugarrones* and *sankies* explain their overwhelming preference for foreign clients by noting the protective anonymity that they provide. They feel that tourists are safer—in terms of their potential social consequences—because they are not integrated into local social networks, often do not speak Spanish, and are generally on a short trip. Therefore, sex workers believe that emphasizing exchanges with tourists provides a buffer against the ever present danger of being socially "burned" (*quemado*) by an unwitting or purposeful breach of the boundary that so tenuously separates their two lives.[42]

In sum, the ways that Dominican sex work is organized, both institutionally and socially, are strongly influenced by gender norms that specify different spatial boundaries and codify different social consequences for deviation from gender expectations. Female sex workers, vis-à-vis their mobility and visibility in "male" public space, defy conservative notions of women's appropriate place—a gender transgression that is symbolically denigrated through the patriarchal image of the *puta*. In contrast, the street activities and late-night carousing typical of male sex workers do not transgress normative models of masculinity, and indeed such behavior is largely expected of men, if not always embraced by their wives and girlfriends. For male sex workers, then, the potential threat to masculinity is embodied in the *maricón*, since the social consequences of same-sex activity—while less severe when one is exclusively the "active" sexual partner (see chap. 3)—are defined by hetero-normative gender models that relegate *maricones* to the bottom of the masculine hierarchy. The challenge for *bugarrones* and *sankies*, then, is to use the public mobility granted them by their gender privilege to cover their potentially stigmatizing sexual activities with men, a strategy that is largely untenable for female sex workers, who are always, already *putas*. These gender distinctions, in turn, place different constraints on the development of institutions and self-advocacy organizations for male and female sex workers, a point elaborated further in chapter 6 as it relates to HIV/AIDS.

✶

From the Campo to the Resort: Migration, Mobility, and Sex Tourism

The political-economic transformations discussed at the beginning of this chapter have led to some complex changes in population mobility and migration in the Dominican Republic over the last three decades. While increases in rural-urban migration began early in the twentieth century in response to growing dependence on imported Haitian labor on Dominican sugar plantations,[43] the economic forces that have influenced both domestic and international migration dramatically changed in response to the Balaguerista economic reforms implemented since the late sixties. As free trade zones and tourist enclaves have become primary employment draws for those who have been squeezed out of the shrinking rural economy, the country's cities have seen dramatic population increases due to internal migration. By 1970, half of Santo Domingo's population was comprised of internal migrants (Georges 1990, 34), and other research suggests that this proportion is significantly higher in the poorest barrios of the capital city.[44]

Most rural-urban migrants are women, according to a somewhat outdated 1978 survey (Ramírez 1984, cited in Georges 1990, 101), although more recently Rogers (1995) reports that the female-headed households in her sample were disproportionately urban, a finding consistent with a higher proportion of women migrating to the cities. Georges attributes this gender bias in rural-urban migration to the fact that most agricultural jobs in rural areas are available only to men, which, as the rural economy has shrunk, has tended to push women more forcefully toward urban areas, where there is greater demand for their labor in factories, free trade zones, service industries, and domestic service (1990, 99–105). Nevertheless, it is important to note that the research supporting a bias toward women among rural-urban migrants may be out-of-date, given the escalation of agricultural closures in the late 1990s, which have reduced the demand for male labor in rural areas and led to the accelerating mobility of Dominican men. This new economic environment will require further study to determine the influence of agricultural closures on contemporary migration patterns.

As several anthropological studies of Caribbean sex work have demonstrated (Farmer 1992; Kane 1993; Kempadoo 1999b; Kreniske 1997), one of the by-products of the increasing mobility of the rural poor is that young migrants are often left without supportive family members nearby, or available family members are already too overburdened by the rising cost of living expenses and plummeting wages. These circumstances make it more likely that young people—left without a safety net in an increasingly anonymous urban space—will choose (or be forced) to engage in sex-for-money exchanges. Frequently, scholars have pointed to the association of female sex work and risk for HIV/AIDS with poor women's employment as domestic servants—itself a by-product of what Georges terms the "commodification of the domestic economy."[45] Many of these dynamics are eloquently examined in Farmer's (1992) ethnographic study of the relationships between North American imperialism, rural decay, population displacement, and the AIDS epidemic in Haiti.

This trend toward rural-urban migration is evident in the results from surveys conducted with male sex workers for the research reported here. Of the sex workers surveyed, 191 were residing in either Santo Domingo or Boca Chica at the time of the interview. Nevertheless, 98 of these (51 percent) were originally from other, mostly rural, parts of the country. The internal migrations of the Santo Domingo and Boca Chica residents who originated elsewhere are shown in figure 5. Forty percent of the sex workers who were residing in Santo Domingo at the time of the interview originated from other parts of the country, whereas 73 percent of Boca Chica residents originated elsewhere. As discussed in more detail in chapter 4, this pattern of familial dispersal is a theme in sex workers' life histories. Often spurred by parental neglect, alcoholism, and extreme economic constraints in the natal home, a significant proportion of sex workers had migrated to Santo Domingo or Boca Chica, sometimes staying temporarily or permanently with extended family members who had migrated previously. This pattern of internal "chain-migration" reflects a more general tendency among Dominicans to develop extended family networks that connect rural and urban areas. What is, perhaps, unique about sex workers' migration stories is that the migration experience often occurs at a very young age and is frequently the result of traumatic experiences of abuse or neglect. Some sex workers tell stories of moving from the *campo* (countryside) alone, becoming "*niños de la calle*" (street kids), and finding intermittent informal-sector jobs as *limpiabotas* (shoe shiners) or *chiriperos* (street vendors). Those who begin sex work as children do so out of economic desperation, either at the suggestion of more experienced peers or due to an unsolicited offer from a potential client. The growth of the pleasure industry has only intensified these trends, as young migrants are increasingly likely to confront the opportunity to engage in relatively lucrative sexual exchanges with foreigners.

It is also important to consider these processes in the context of larger patterns of Dominican international migration, given the unusually high proportion of Dominicans who reside or travel abroad. Population movement from the Dominican Republic to the United States increased dramatically following the assassination of Trujillo, since the dictator had employed a somewhat paranoiac isolationism in his attempts to prevent political dissidence abroad (Crassweller 1966). These policies were reversed in the mid-sixties, as the American occupying forces were pressured to use a strategy of openness to Dominican immigration as a "vent" for local political unrest (Grasmuck and Pessar 1991, 12). Estimates of the number of

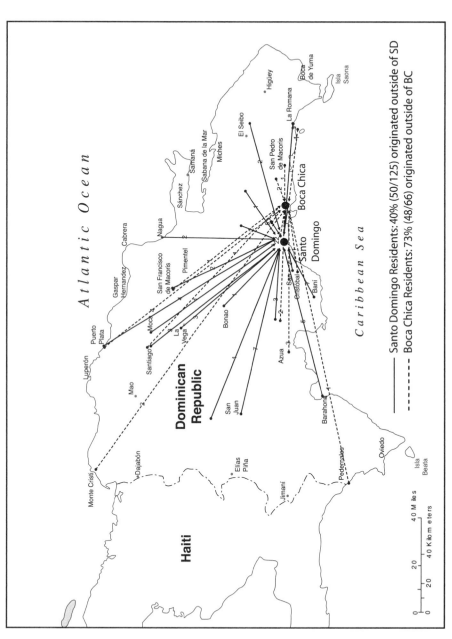

Figure 5. Internal migratory pathways of Dominican male sex workers (N = 98)

Dominican immigrants currently in the United States vary widely, with some as high as a million (Georges 1990, 43).[46] More conservative estimates are closer to a half million, or equivalent to 6 percent of the population of the Dominican Republic itself (Grasmuck and Pessar 1991, 20–22).[47] However, travel and tourism to the United States and other countries are much more common than immigration statistics imply. Since the 1960s, the number of Dominican nonimmigrants traveling to the United States officially as "tourists" has increased much more rapidly than has the number of immigrants, and by the mid-1970s, over 150,000 nonimmigrants were being legally admitted from the Dominican Republic each year (Grasmuck and Pessar 1991, 38–40; Howard 2001, 98). Tourism and family visits to the United States are now a fact of life for many middle-class Dominicans, and among Santo Domingo residents it is very common to have at least one extended family member who resides abroad.[48]

A significant and growing proportion of Dominican immigration is illegal, and especially for women, much of it—perhaps particularly that oriented toward Spain (Gallardo Rivas 1995)—involves domestic work and/or sex work. The frequent news reports of Dominicans captured or drowned in failed attempts to *cruzar* (cross over) the Mona Passage to Puerto Rico in *yolas* (small fishing/trolling boats) attest to the growing number of lower-class Dominicans who have settled in the United States illegally. Díaz (1987), cited by Georges (1990, 40), estimates that 60,000 Dominicans may have been living in Puerto Rico by 1987, a figure that is consistent with the commonality of migration stories to this destination among the participants in this study.[49] In this study, most of the male sex workers interviewed who had been to Puerto Rico had crossed the Mona Passage illegally, and many of these had returned to the Dominican Republic due to capture and deportation.

Return migration is also quite common, and was estimated at 12.3 percent in one household survey conducted in 1993 (Howard 2001, 99–100). Grasmuck and Pessar (1991, 14) interpret these patterns as the consequence of a strong "ideology of return" among Dominicans abroad that emphasizes the investment of earnings in the construction of houses in wealthier neighborhoods "back home" in the hopes of someday returning. In the context of this growth in circular migration to and from the United States, as well as high rates of deportation of illegal migrants apprehended abroad, the figure of the *Dominican-york*—a Dominican with extended periods of residency in New York—has come to occupy an important position in the transnational imaginary of those who remain on the island. Ironically, while residency in the United States is a status marker for Dominicans, the growing number of *Dominican-yorks* who are deported from the United States for criminal activities is the target of a considerable amount of scapegoating by local residents. Many Dominicans believe that the recent growth in violent crime and delinquency on the island is directly related to criminal repatriations from the United States, the vast majority of which are men.

There is a common belief among Dominicans that many *Dominican-yorks*—particularly those who are repatriated for criminal activities abroad—are "damaged" (*dañados*) by their experience of urban life in the United States. When they return to the island, they bring bad habits (*malas costumbres*), engage in illicit activities, and form mafias that are developing connections to international drug cartels. One analyst argues that such attitudes are the product of a conservative backlash by the island's nonimmigrant elite who have sought to distinguish themselves from the young "*nuevos ricos*" (new rich) returning from New York (Howard 2001, 102–8). Viewed from this perspective, the stereotypes of criminality that often circulate about *Dominican-yorks* are at least partially the consequence of power struggles in which traditional markers of class status—based primarily on family name and land ownership—are being challenged by the society's increasing engagement with a transnational Dominican identity that straddles the "core" and the "periphery." The following excerpt from an article in the Miami newspaper *El Nuevo Herald* illustrates many aspects of this ideological construction of the *Dominican-york:*

> Nearly 3,000 Dominicans incarcerated in the United States, the majority for drug trafficking and assault, will be deported this year to their country of origin, upon completing their sentence with a "graduate degree" in delinquency. . . . They are the "tígueres" (the tough ones, in colloquial Dominican language) that are adding to the growing "tigueraje" of the barrios of Santo Domingo, where poverty pushes thousands of youth into drug addiction, prostitution, and delinquency. . . . In the Dominican capital armed incidents at night have risen, but the "Dominican-yorks," the ex-residents of New York who return to the Caribbean with the habits and the environment of the New York "ghettos," are not the only guilty ones . . .
> (Contreras 1999, translation by author)

This author's description of the parallels between the masculine identity of the *tíguere* and the growing presence of the *Dominican-york* exemplifies some of the ways that Dominican masculinity is changing as the island is integrated into an increasingly transnational world. For young Dominican men, the contemporary field of gender performance is quite different from that of their fathers, now accommodating a range of "imported" attitudes, styles, identification practices, and income-generating activities. Among the *tígueres* of Santo Domingo's barrios today, the influence of New York hip-hop clothing fashions—with their accompanying brand-name fetishism—is palpable, and advertisements continually bombard the country's youth with images of smiling sports heroes touting the very products whose off-shore assembly exploits cheap Dominican labor in the country's numerous free trade zones.

Thus, while Dominican male sex work is perhaps particularly emblematic of the growth of a distinctly globalized *tigueraje,* it also reflects changes in the social construction of masculinity that resonate for many—if not most—young lower-class men. I remember the pride with which one sex worker displayed his new Air Jordans to me during an interview and, detecting my interest, proceeded to model his entire ensemble, skillfully accessorized with the numerous gifts of clothing and jewelry he had received from various foreign clients. Through the imported fashions of Tommy Hilfiger and Nike, he displayed many of the icons of contemporary *tigueraje* that are now so intimately related to a particular commodity fetishism that resembles certain aspects of Afro-Hispanic enclaves in the urban United States. In a foundational study of Puerto Rican crack dealers in Spanish Harlem, anthropologist Philippe Bourgois (1995) described how the subcultural style of "fly clothes" provides cultural capital to male dealers within the illegal underground economy but also alienates them from formal-sector employment, as they are criticized for dressing like "hoodlums" (157–62). In a similar way, the emphasis on particular kinds of conspicuous consumption among Dominican *bugarrones* and *sankies* is symptomatic of the symbolic status of certain appropriated fashions within their lower-class peer group, even as it positions them squarely within the larger cultural stereotype of the delinquent, troublemaking *tíguere.*

Some of the sex workers with whom I interacted during fieldwork acquired these tastes through their own experiences of international travel, but given the extent to which locals are exposed to global fashions and consumer trends through the influx of foreign products, images, and people, actual border crossing is not a necessary precursor to one's internalization or appropriation of global styles. Nevertheless, nearly one-third (30 percent) of the sex workers surveyed had traveled internationally, most commonly to the continental United States or Puerto Rico, but also to a number of developing countries in Latin America and the Caribbean (see table 4).

An additional thirty percent of those who had traveled abroad indicated that they had participated in sex work while they were abroad, with the United States and Puerto Rico accounting for exactly half of the reported instances.[50] Nearly ninety percent of the sex workers who had conducted sex work abroad affirmed that they had "lived with a client" during this time,

TABLE 4: Sex workers' international travel destinations (N = 60)*

Destination/country	Frequency	% of sex workers mentioning
Aruba	3	5.0%
Canada	2	3.3%
Colombia	2	3.3%
Cuba	1	1.7%
Curaçao	4	6.7%
France	1	1.7%
Germany	1	1.7%
Haiti	7	11.7%
Holland	3	5.0%
Honduras	1	1.7%
Italy	6	10.0%
Mexico	4	6.7%
Panama	5	8.3%
Puerto Rico	28	46.7%
Saint Thomas	1	1.7%
Spain	2	3.3%
Switzerland	1	1.7%
Turks and Caicos islands	1	1.7%
United States (continent)	13	21.7%
Venezuela	4	6.7%

* Table includes all destinations even when participants indicated they had traveled to more than one country. Therefore, while the data derive from 60 sex workers, the frequency column represents a total of 90 cases of international travel.

and in most cases (62 percent), these clients were contacted abroad, that is, *after* traveling rather than before. It therefore appears that while for some sex workers international travel may be instigated by relationships with specific clients—clients who probably resemble the "Western Union daddies" described in chapter 5—such relationships do not appear to be necessary precursors to the decision to travel abroad.

There was a positive statistical correlation between years of education and international travel experience ($p < .05$), but this correlation was not consistent across all levels of education. Less ambiguously, participants who indicated they had received "technical training" or had a "profession" were significantly more likely to report travel abroad ($p < .01$ and $p < .05$, respectively).[51] Further, those whose households owned a motorcycle, car, or truck ($p < .05$), or whose families paid for cable television at home ($p < .05$), were also significantly more likely to have traveled abroad. These findings suggest some tentative parallels with conclusions by Grasmuck and Pessar

(1991) and Bray (1984), who suggest that Dominican migration is more often undertaken by those of higher education and training, reflecting in part
a frustration with the limitations of the shrinking local market for skilled
labor. In any case, among *bugarrones* and *sankies,* international travel—at
least among those who have subsequently returned to the island and could
therefore be interviewed—does not appear to be predominant in the lowest educational and socioeconomic levels. In part, this may be the product
of intensifying immigration restrictions, particularly to the United States,
which often require proof of significant domestic assets prior to issuing
even a single-entry tourist visa. Therefore, these patterns may be less a reflection of individual decision making than of the growing legal constraints
on international migration, leading many of the most desperate migrants
to fend for themselves in the tumultuous seas of the Mona Passage.

The Pleasure Industry as Viewed from Above

From a structural perspective—one that focuses not only on the specific cultural expressions of sex work but also on the large-scale political-economic
processes that condition it—the *bugarrones* and *sanky pankies* described
here can be seen to share many of the characteristics common to a growing
number of young, poor Dominican men employed in the country's informal
tourism economy. As national development strategies have shifted toward
a policy that has prioritized the tourism sector while phasing out many traditional sources of male employment, relatively lucrative opportunities for
informal income generation have proliferated in response to the new demand for a wide range of products and services by tourists. The need for low-
cost service providers to staff the tourist-oriented businesses, as well as the
many opportunities provided by an informally negotiated dollar economy,
increase the likelihood that local men will migrate to tourist enclaves, in
closer proximity to tourists. In conjunction with the deepening economic
crisis, these conditions make it more likely that sexual-economic exchanges
will occur. Later in this book we will examine how the structure of the pleasure industry facilitates same-sex exchanges through analyses of the narratives of initiation into sex work provided by *bugarrones* and *sanky pankies.*

   While all of these large-scale processes have implications for same-sex
exchanges between gay tourists and Dominican men, they are often veiled
by the social taboos and discretionary practices that so often surround homoeroticism.[52] As elaborated in the following chapters, same-sex exchanges
in the Dominican Republic, while certainly grounded in culturally situated
notions of masculinity and male sexuality, have also been shaped by macro-

level changes that have encouraged sex tourism, commodified certain elements of Dominican male sexuality, and restructured the local sexual economy. The linkage between homoeroticism and political-economic processes demonstrates that sexual exchanges between men are embedded in relations of power that extend far beyond the shores of the Dominican Republic, and highlights the material foundations that underpin local negotiations of sexual identity and practice. It is with this attention to structure, therefore, that we turn to a deeper discussion of the interplay between the contemporary Dominican political economy and the complex politics of "*orgullo gay Dominicano*" (Dominican gay pride)—a discussion that illustrates the ways that tourism and sex work have shaped the evolution of Dominican gay politics.

3

"Orgullo Gay Dominicano": Shifting Cultural Politics of Sexual Identity in Santo Domingo

Same-sex relations and gay life can in many ways be a prism through which global processes become visible.

RICHARD PARKER

As suggested in the introduction, the political economy of sexuality requires us to view the globalization of sexuality in light of the large-scale inequalities that frame and condition the structures through which globalizing processes unfold. In this sense, it is analytically essential to view the transnational expansion of a range of contemporary gay cultural symbols—whether these be forms of dress, movement politics, or discourses of sexual identity—as much more than the simple diffusion of meanings of homoeroticism from the "West" to the "non-West." Indeed, in the context of Caribbean history and political economy, it is highly problematic to frame these questions in such mutually exclusive terms, given the numerous and profound dimensions of contact and creolization with external powers that have characterized Caribbean history for centuries (Knight 1990; Williams 1984). Indeed, as Mintz's work has shown most effectively, the Caribbean might be regarded as the symbolic cradle of Western industrialization, to the degree that its extracted riches powered the development of European and American industrial capitalism (Mintz 1985). Now as then, Caribbean sexuality is intertwined in the fabric of the global economy, as patterns of labor, migration, and travel shape the ways that individuals and groups relate to one another, the degree and kind of economic constraints they confront, and the strategies they employ in "looking for life." Given the neoliberal development policies in the Caribbean described in the previous chapter, an underpaid, unskilled Caribbean tourism worker provides not only a necessary *human* resource for multinational tourism conglomerates, but also a potential *erotic* resource for the informal sex economy among tourists. The men who participated in this research are therefore constrained by the exploitative system in which they participate at the same time that they exercise sexual agency in their use of the informal tourism economy to gain some degree of economic and social advantage. Their practices of sexuality are both limited and enabled by the structures of the pleasure industry.

This tension between the structural affordances of the Dominican tourism sector and the sexual agency of local actors is the theoretical lens for this chapter. Here, I examine how the underlying structures of the pleasure industry influence how local LGBTQ sexual identities and the meanings of homoeroticism are understood and enacted in the Dominican Republic.[1] As argued throughout this book, international gay tourism in the Dominican Republic commodifies—that is, produces a global demand for the "production" of—certain expressions of masculinity and male sexuality. These compose what I have referred to as a "marketable fantasy," a socially constructed desire that drives touristic sexual practices and consumption patterns, as well as providing an opening for local entrepreneurs to, in the terminology of sex workers, *sacarles plata a los turistas* (get money out of the tourists). Vis-à-vis this marketable fantasy, tourist dollars are "invested" in particular performances of gender and sexuality, and this fact has a range of consequences for the social organization of local sexual communities, as well as sexual practices more generally. Chapter 1 mentioned one way in which the global gay tourism market structures Dominican gay life: the ebb and flow of the tourism sector creates a seasonality to local rhythms in gay spaces, and these rhythms have very real material consequences for both gay-oriented businesses and a broad range of informal-sector service providers who target the gay market, including—but not limited to—*bugarrones* and *sanky pankies*.[2] In this chapter, we examine more closely two different effects of the tourism industry on local queer populations: the influence of neoliberal policies and tourism dependence on the nascent Dominican LGBTQ movement; and the influence of the growing sex tourism market on the construction of gender and sexuality among *bugarrones* and *sanky pankies* employed in the informal tourism economy.

Examining a key ethnographic case—the first gay pride march in the Dominican Republic, occurring in 1999—the first half of this chapter illustrates how the structure of the pleasure industry shaped the particular local tensions and ad hoc affiliations that ultimately led to a historical moment of LGBTQ resistance. The theoretical approach is one that looks through the ethnographic evidence to uncover the structural factors related to the tourism economy that shaped the generation of social tensions and the ultimate expression of sexual resistance enacted by a small, diverse group of marginalized gay-identified men. Their great courage notwithstanding, I argue that the appropriation of global gay cultural symbols and modes of protest in this particular case ironically effaced a critical stance on the larger structural inequalities and dependencies that were implicated in the patterns of anti-gay abuse by police in Santo Domingo.

In the second half of the chapter, I turn again to the Dominican sex-work identities *bugarrón* and *sanky panky*, and consider what consequences the tourism economy may have for the cultural persistence of these "*activo*" (sexually active, or penetrative) homoerotic figures. Here, I critically engage the existing ethnographic literature in Latin America on the globalization of gay identity, which often entails an implicit assumption that the traditional *activo* is an "endangered species"—an artifact of local sexual systems that will ultimately be displaced by globalizing notions of sexual identity. By reframing this discussion in structural terms, I avoid analyzing Dominican *activo* identities as reflections of a presumably "older" or more "traditional" sex/gender system—an approach that tends to essentialize Dominican sexuality and to decontextualize it from the larger global connections in which it is embedded. Instead, I ask two very different questions: How are these identities *already* integrated into global patterns of sexual consumption through the tourism industry, and what kinds of consequences does this integration have for the psychosocial experiences of men who profess these identities?

Orgullo Gay Dominicano

On March 23, 1999, a historic event occurred in one of the most historic sites in old Santo Domingo. Here, in front of the first Spanish colonial cathedral in the New World, flanked by foreign tourists, strolling young couples, playful children, and scattered groups of domino players, fifteen gay men adorned themselves with rainbow flags and marched the full length of El Conde, the popular pedestrian mall and the most active commercial area of the Zona Colonial. The march was not visually spectacular, and it lasted only about twenty minutes, the minimum time required for a group of this size to make its way from the cathedral through the crowded length of El Conde. But it was history nonetheless, and it represents a willingness to publicly confront societal homophobia that is unprecedented in this conservative Catholic country.

The event, which I attended and documented through photographs at the request of the participants, was my first key ethnographic moment in fieldwork, and in many ways is a refraction of many of the primary concerns of this book. One of the most fascinating features of this first Dominican "*orgullo gay*" (gay pride) event—as it was later described by the participants—is the way that it embodied both the local concerns of the nascent gay community in Santo Domingo and the appropriated symbols and modes of public expression that are broadly representative of global gay discourse. Indeed, as described below, the international model of the gay pride parade had a paradoxical dual effect on the country's first conscious public engagement with Dominican homophobia: it potentiated an unprecedented mode of public expression by the gay community at the same time that it effaced many of the local tensions and abusive state practices that were motivationally salient for the gay men who took to the streets. Thus, while international gay cultural symbols and practices provided a widely recognizable means by which to critique societal prejudices, they also eclipsed the local voices and discursive practices that could have expressed opposition to the various structures and inequities that operate on the ground to marginalize gay Dominicans. As we shall see, the state's dependence on tourism, as well as the desire to project a respectable public image to tourists in highly touristed areas of Santo Domingo, was centrally involved in the conflicts with police that led to the first gay pride event, even though these connections were ultimately erased by the use of generic global gay signifiers that did not address themselves to these larger structural factors.

The place of the Dominican Republic in the international political economy, particularly its growing dependence on the tourism industry, is key to understanding the history of tensions that led, in part, to the first discussions among gays of organizing a public "*protesta*." In early 1999, gay men in Santo Domingo were increasingly preoccupied by sharp increases in incidents of police abuse in the Plaza España, a heavily touristed area of the Zona Colonial known in the gay community as El Drake.[3] Located at the original Spanish colonial port on the mouth of the Rio Ozama, El Drake faces Diego Colón's majestic colonial home, and former President Balaguer's ironic monument, El Faro a Colón (Columbus lighthouse), is clearly visible at night on the eastern horizon from this vantage point.

By the late 1990s, the administrators of neighboring businesses near El Drake had become concerned about the presumably negative effect on tourism of openly gay men gathering in and around the plaza and had encouraged the police, allegedly with bribes, to arrest gays found "loitering" in the area.[4] While some gays lamented that a part of their community had virtually provoked a police response by engaging in sex acts in the pseudo-public areas surrounding the plaza, others pointed to the arbitrary profiling of gay men, based largely on "inappropriate" gender expression, and to emerging stories of sexual abuses perpetrated by law enforcement personnel during incarceration.[5]

The contentious nature of the social/sexual space surrounding El Drake must be framed within the context of local business owners' concerns about projecting an appropriate and attractive image for tourist consumption, thereby encouraging the growing numbers of foreign visitors to pay the exorbitant prices for gourmet dishes and the privilege to feast in the midst of the Western hemisphere's oldest colonial ruins. Now lined with upscale, tourist-oriented restaurants offering fine international cuisine, El Drake is therefore a key site in Santo Domingo where a well-known gay place—in the sense of a physical location imbued with cultural meaning for gay men— has spatially overlapped with the expanding tourism interests of local business owners and the state. It is also a metaphorical space in the sense that it is a microcosm of large-scale changes in the country that increasingly necessitate a concern, at the levels of both policy and social interaction, with "appropriate" local representations of Dominican-ness and the ways they affect tourists' consumptive choices.

As a number of scholars have described, sexuality is a highly contested domain in tourism representations of local places and peoples, as it is paradoxically a cultural resource that can enhance the global marketability of specific destinations as well as a potential source of societal shame and scapegoating (Bishop and Robinson 1998; Hobson and Dietrich 1994; Kempadoo 1999b; Lim 1998; Truong 1990). Barbara Mullings (1999) makes reference to this contradictory nature of sexuality in her discussion of female prostitution and the state in Jamaica: "The disdain that is expressed for sex workers by many in the tourism industry is all the more contradictory when the industry as a whole routinely utilizes hedonistic imagery of 'sun, sand and sex' that relies heavily on racialized constructions of women as 'exotic' and 'wild' to market the island as a tourism destination" (1999, 65). Similarly, the potential benefits to be gained by police and the Dominican state vis-à-vis their complicity in male prostitution and gay sex tourism is exemplified by the *multas* (fees) regularly extorted from sex workers, which are frequently paid for by gay tourists.[6] Such benefit for the authorities, juxtaposed with the stigma and shame associated with these activities, places the authorities in an ambivalent structural position that can lead to an unpredictable and inconsistent posture toward male sex workers and clients.

An analogous, though not entirely equivalent, ambivalence characterizes attitudes toward gay men in the Dominican Republic more generally—regardless of their participation in sex work—and is sufficient to rationalize abusive policies when gays are believed to engage in "obvious" or "inappropriate" public behavior. In the Dominican Republic, such effeminate behaviors are often described using terms such as *loca* (effeminate) or *muy obvio* (very obvious).[7] Paralleling ethnographic descriptions of homosexuality in other parts of Latin America and the Caribbean, there are particular times and places in which homoeroticism and cross-gender behavior are more or less tolerated in the Dominican Republic.[8] While open effeminacy and even transvestism may be a source of relatively benign amusement among neighbors in one of Santo Domingo's lower-class *barrios marginales* or in the rural *pueblos,* there are particular spaces in which such behavior is considered a more serious breach of normative models of gender and sexuality. Such breaches are more likely in social spaces that are symbolically coded as sanctified icons of nationalism and cultural heritage. The Zona Colonial in Santo Domingo is just such an area for Dominicans, inspiring much patriotism and national pride in both political rhetoric and public discourse. It also stands as the most vivid symbol of what has been described as a kind of Dominican "hispanophilia"—an exaggerated identification with all things of peninsular Spanish origin, and a simultaneous denial (and repression) of the African cultural influences on contemporary Dominican society and culture (Cambeira 1997; Crassweller 1966; Murphy 1991; Wiarda and Kryzanek 1992; Winn 1992).[9] Encapsulating a string of "firsts"—the first Catholic cathedral, the first colonial fort, the first Spanish outpost—the Zona Colonial makes continual symbolic reference to the colonization of the New World and the "privileged" place of Santo Domingo as its divine port of entry.

While such representations express a kind of colonial nostalgia that effaces the human devastation of the conquest and the realities of its legacy in the modern Caribbean, they also serve what some scholars would describe as *neo*colonial functions in that they have become central in the marketing strategy of the country as a historic tourist destination (Cohen 1972; Enloe 2000; Fanon 1963; Graburn 1983). The union of the Dominican Republic's colonial heritage with tourism marketing strategies reached its pinnacle during the early 1990s, as former President Balaguer's generous incentives to multinational tourism conglomerates coincided with the five-hundredth anniversary of the Spanish conquest—the latter being perhaps the most symbolic moment of Balaguer's political career. Culminating in the inauguration of the mammoth Columbus Lighthouse and the ritual interment of Christopher Columbus's remains in its inner tomb by Pope John Paul II, the long-awaited *Quintocentenario* celebrations were a spectacular manifestation of the colonial nostalgia Balaguer expresses so eloquently in his *Guía Emocional de la ciudad romántica* (Emotional guide to the romantic city) (1978). Yet, in addition to the tragic-ironic colonial nostalgia that marked the event, politicians and investors were also "banking on the [re]'discovery' of the country in 1992 as a bonanza that will generate hundreds of millions of dollars in foreign currency" (Wiarda and Kryzanek 1992, 90). As Krohn-Hansen explains of the inauguration of the Columbus lighthouse: "Columbus was not only a Dominican ancestor. He was also an incarnation and a source of modern values, the patron saint of Pan-Americanism and a tourist attraction and potential source of income" (Krohn-Hansen 2001, 172).[10]

Thus, the Zona Colonial has become a key site in Santo Domingo where the resurrection and preservation of Spanish colonial heritage is a characteristic feature of the physical and social landscape, as selected features of "authentic" Dominican cultural identity, or *Dominicanidad,* are offered up for tourist consumption (MacCannell 1973). From the perspective of locals and the Dominican state, then, there is much at stake in the politics of representation in the Zona Colonial, and huge investments in the reconstruction of colonial ruins, maintenance of tourist infrastructure, and a visible police presence are signs of an increasing preoccupation with projecting an appropriate image for visitors to "America's first city." Analogous to state policies in other Caribbean tourist settings (Kempadoo 1999b), Dominican beautification campaigns have occasionally marginalized particular groups of locals who are seen as an eyesore or as a potential moral insult to the foreigners strolling down the gangplanks of the cruise liners or streaming from the many tour buses that line the Plaza Colón (Ferguson 1992, 2). For example, Dominican television news channels broadcast numerous reports in the fall of 2001 on the presumably negative effect of homeless Haitian beggars on the streets of Santo Domingo. Anti-Haitian commentaries frequently centered on the potential damage of a visible Haitian presence to the "image" of the city, implicitly or explicitly citing the detrimental effect on tourism.

While the state's marginalization of locals for the sake of the moral comfort of wealthy foreigners seems a quintessential example of Fanon's depiction of national elites as neocolonial "managers of Western enterprise" (1963), the case of the persecution of gays in the Zona Colonial demonstrates that such beautification programs are as much about local politics of gender and sexuality as they are motivated by concern for the presumed moral stance of tourists. In fact, the colonial zone has the highest density of gay bars and establishments in all of Santo Domingo, conveniently located within walking distance of the many tourist-oriented hotels and *pensiones* (small guest-houses). Within an area of approximately two square miles, there are four specifically gay-oriented bars—two of which double as primary network-ing sites for gay sex tourists to meet local sex workers—several gay-friendly or tolerant restaurant-cafés, a pornographic cinema frequented by many gays, and innumerable gay cruising and socializing areas. Thus, if local au-thorities and tourist-oriented businesses were solely concerned about the effect on profits of a visible gay presence, the high number of gay tourists implies that such concerns are unfounded. Indeed, as Truong (1990) argues regarding heterosexual sex tourism in Southeast Asia, the Dominican tour-ism sector benefits from the dollars spent by both tourists and locals at gay establishments in the Zona Colonial.[11] But in the case of gay sex tourism, the attitudes of law enforcement and local businesses are not based purely on rational economic analysis.

In fact, homosexuality and gay sex tourism have been depicted in local discourse as one of the most troubling social consequences of the coun-try's increasing dependence on tourism. One exemplary newspaper exposé, entitled "Lack of Legislation Inhibits Detainment of Increases in Homo-sexual Prostitution," was published in 1984, when state incentives for tour-ism development were just beginning to produce visible changes in the social landscape of the Zona Colonial (Cepeda 1984). After several intro-ductory caveats about the "dark dimensions" of the "taboo" topic at hand, the article continues:

But as part of the accelerated disintegration that Dominican society is undergo-ing, we are confronted by a growing phenomenon: homosexuality in its phase of male prostitution. Go to any area of the Zona Colonial and you will find scenes that don't permit uncertainty and explain why one North American tour com-pany has promoted the Dominican Republic as a "paradise for homosexuals." And this advertisement isn't the fault of that company, which, imbued with an excess of liberalism as is possible in the United States, has simply conducted pro-motion based on the observed realities of our country. (Cepeda 1984, 13; transla-tion by author)

Ending on a note that ominously recalls the heavy-handed state policies of former dictator Rafael Trujillo, whose homophobia culminated in the establishment of homosexual concentration camps in the early 1950s (De Moya and García 1996, 125), the author laments the lack of police will-ingness to employ more coercive tactics in order to curb the "moral degen-eration of the country" (Cepeda 1984, 13).[12]

Such reactions may have been more visceral in the initial years of gay sex tourism in the early 1980s, exacerbated by the sudden visibility of foreign "*vicios*" (vices) and the high demand for Caribbean male sex workers in the pre-AIDS era (De Moya and García 1998; Farmer 1992). While public discourse may have given way in recent years to a more sedate resignation toward the country's "degeneration"—as tourism has become so totalizing that its social consequences are increasingly regarded as a simple fact of life—an assumption of police permissiveness toward local gays would be seriously misguided. One recent example of the authorities' continued antigay policies is the high-profile campaign by the chief of the national police, Pedro de Jesús Candelier, to purge all homosexuals from his ranks. Based on an erroneous reinterpretation of police code 210 on "diverse infractions," a spokesman for Candelier boldly announced in February 2001 that "the chief of police gave instructions to carry out the investigation and proceed to putting them [homosexuals] in formation to publicly humiliate them as an example to the rest" (Cabrera 2001; see also González 2001, González and Pérez 2001, and Staff 2001). A more recent example is provided in incensed proclamations by the Dominican cardinal Nicolás de Jesús López Rodríguez, who announced that the Dominican and foreign homosexuals who had invaded the colonial zone of Santo Domingo were "social scum" (*lacras sociales*) who should be forcibly removed by the police. As reported in the local newspaper *Listín Diario,* the cardinal made his provocative proclamations after giving mass at the first cathedral of the New World—which is surrounded by many active areas for sex work and homoeroticism—where he commented to reporters that "we cannot permit that this place, the historical center of Santo Domingo, be converted into a patrimony of foreign and Dominican degenerates" (Medrano 2006).

Thus, it is clear that homosexually behaving Dominican men continue to be the target of institutionalized discrimination and abuse. However, the roots of this abuse at this particular time and place, and the ways that it was enacted in the Zona Colonial, is another question entirely, and it is here that the connections to tourism come into focus. A crucial fact about the events leading up to the first Dominican *orgullo gay* event is that the *discourse* among gays about police abuses in the Zona Colonial often emphasized local business owners' desire to clean up the area for tourists, as well as the coercive union of business owners and the police. Some local gays told me stories of individual homophobic owners who were involved in the recruitment of their neighbors, effectively forming an economic front by which to manipulate the authorities. This gave owners considerable power to control the social space within the plaza, and their financial leverage was further buttressed by existing policies of beautification and the traditional antigay stance of the police.

While the truth of these allegations against owners is impossible to con-
firm, they are key in understanding the perception among gays of the structures that contributed to their vulnerability in El Drake, and which, by early
1999, some were plotting to publicly resist. In gay men's narratives, the tensions and abuses of gays were therefore embedded within a network of
power relations that calls attention to local class inequities, global tourism
dependence, and the institutionalized homophobia of law enforcement. As
described in the following section, however, many of the elements that
structured gay men's motivations to protest and their awareness of systemic
abuses were ultimately effaced by the way in which global gay symbols and
modes of public expression were adopted. A closer look at the dynamics of
the debates that occurred preceding the protest permits a deeper understanding of the local contestations and strategic alliances that were never
ultimately represented in the country's first "gay pride" march.

Metalicos, Raperos, and *Gays:* War of Position in the Zona Colonial

In February and March of 1999, I witnessed a number of heated conversations among Dominican gay men about the escalating police "attacks" on
gays in El Drake, whether they should be met with some form of organized
resistance, or whether gay men should comport themselves differently in
this public (presumably heterosexual) space. One aspect of these conversations was most intriguing to me: I heard two local identities—the *metálicos*
and the *raperos*—described for the first time.

Significantly, along with the gays, the police had also targeted other
gender-transgressive groups that gathered in the area of El Drake, most importantly the *raperos* (or *Joes*) and the *metálicos.* The *raperos,* whose baggy
pants and "B-boy" persona are modeled on North American hip-hop styles,
and the *metálicos,* whose body piercings, tattoos, and black clothing signify
identification with the heavy metal crowd, are historically recent social identities among Dominican youth, many of whom gather regularly in the Zona
Colonial. Both groups are closely associated with North American music
styles and are regarded locally—at least among more conservative, and usually older, Dominicans—to be one of the many negative consequences of the
growing number of *Dominican-yorks,* who import the latest and strangest
fashions from the urban United States.

Like gay men, *metálicos* and *raperos* experience social censure in Santo
Domingo because of their transgression of highly conservative gender norms
for dress and public demeanor, as well as stereotypes of their involvement
in criminal activities such as petty theft and drug use. In the weeks preceding the march, the gays, *raperos,* and *metálicos*—groups which had only

rarely interacted previously—began to create a utilitarian alliance, culminating in an invitation by a group of *metálicos* to participate in a joint protest to voice opposition to police repression in the Zona Colonial. A meeting was arranged involving key members of each group, which some gay leaders attended.[13] The date was set for the protest, and it was decided the march would originate at the Plaza Colón, in front of the first Catholic cathedral in the New World, and would proceed down the entire length of El Conde, ending at the Parque Independencia. This route would take the protesters through the prime commercial sector of the Zona Colonial, in clear view of tourists and police officers patrolling the area, and had the symbolic benefit of making a public statement amidst the city's most sacred monuments.

The alliance between the gays, *metálicos,* and *raperos* was not only unlikely, but also highly unstable. A number of gay men—some of them self-described activists who would presumably welcome such a protest—decided not to attend, because they considered associating with *metálicos* and *raperos* to be disreputable, politically counterproductive, or lower-class. Rumors spread in the gay community in the days preceding the protest, and there was much discussion about whether to attend, whether the event would occur at all, and how to handle the police in the event of a conflict or mass arrest. There were scattered reports of the impending march—which had not been granted official recognition—on local radio and television, but no widespread coverage occurred.

The precariousness of the alliance was most evident on the day of the protest. As participants began to arrive in front of the cathedral, a small group of *metálicos* formed in one section of the plaza, while the gays gathered on the adjacent section of El Conde, a safe distance away. The *metálicos* were apparently hesitant to claim common cause with the gays, whose effeminacy and increasingly boisterous campiness had begun to draw a significant amount of negative attention from heterosexual onlookers in the vicinity. As the homophobic comments escalated—culminating in a threat by an angry tour guide to knife several of the gay protesters—rumors quickly spread that the *metálicos* had decided to "postpone" their protest until the following Friday, and their contingent quickly vacated the area.

After a few moments of debate among the remaining gay protesters about the most prudent course of action, a small group of gay marchers arrived with a bundle of rainbow-colored gay pride flags, which were quickly distributed to the apparent approval of all.[14] Moments later, the group, now composed entirely of gays and suddenly reconfigured—although certainly through no systematic consensus-taking among the participants—as a gay pride march, began a rapid but conspicuous procession down El Conde.

With the exception of a few jeers and some relatively benign commentary from onlookers, the marchers' progress was not impeded in any way, and the police officers that witnessed the event apparently did not regard the group as meriting any special response on their part. This outcome was likely because the reaction of the public along El Conde was generally one of amusement, rather than outrage or disgust, and the protesters dissipated quickly upon reaching their symbolic destination at the Parque Independencia.[15]

There are two aspects of the first Dominican "gay pride" march that require further comment. First, until the disappearance of the *metálicos* and the arrival of the gay pride flags, the *protesta* had not been configured as a "gay pride" event, nor was there consensus about the messages and symbolism to be employed by the participants. Rather, the inspiration for action was sparked by a series of police abuses in El Drake against which the protesters, through their ad hoc coalition, were reacting. Thus, the discursive framework for narrating the public expression of discontent was, from the beginning, grounded in the realities of a specific set of local power relations, even as these were simultaneously tied to large-scale inequities related to the country's dependence on tourism. Indeed, the uneasy union of the *metálicos, raperos,* and gays is interpretable only within the context of their shared status as local non-normative identities and the parallel prejudices they face in relation to the authorities. The ways that gays talked about their decisions to participate in the event were embedded in the local tensions and perceived differences between gay men, on the one hand, and the *metálicos* and *raperos,* on the other—the same tensions that ultimately led to the collapse of the alliance on the day of the protest. And finally, it should be reiterated that it was the *metálicos,* not the gays, who originally proposed the idea of a public protest, further emphasizing that the event was not originally conceived as a gay pride march, but rather as an ad hoc reaction to abuses of power that were situated within a specific set of local places and practices.

The second aspect of the event that should be highlighted is that the common oppression experienced by the *metálicos, raperos,* and gays was related to their shared marginalization with respect to highly restrictive norms of appropriate gender expression in public space, rather than presumptions about their sexual behavior or orientation. This is further evidenced by the fact that at no point did *bugarrones* express interest in joining the coalition, to protest their discriminatory treatment by the police in El Drake. As described in previous chapters, *bugarrones* are routinely arrested without formal charges and forced to pay *multas* as a condition of release. Nevertheless, it is not their public gender expression, but rather their private engagement in sex-for-money exchanges with other men, that is justification for police abuse and (potential) social censure. Indeed, it is precisely *bugarrones'* reticence to mark themselves publicly that represents one of the key distinctions between *bugarrones* and the members of the *metálico/rapero/*gay alliance. While the public gender expression of *bugarrones* generally falls within the masculine norm, the *metálicos, raperos,* and gays engage in modes of gender performance that are immediately apprehended as inappropriate within the public sphere, particularly in the image-conscious social space of the Zona Colonial.[16]

These intricacies of local identity politics make the ultimate configuration of the protest as a gay pride march somewhat paradoxical. Yet, as the tenuous coalition began to crumble in the face of escalating public hostility, the appropriated meanings of the gay pride flag—undoubtedly familiar to the marchers through global media, gay lore, and international travel—gave the participants a useful model for public expression that potentiated action. Without the momentum provided by the global symbolism of the gay pride parade, it is quite possible that the unprecedented event would have been entirely diffused upon the withdrawal of the *metálicos.* At the same time, the strategic appropriation of the gay pride model tended to undermine the original configuration of the protest as a resistant moment of targeted social action against abusive local practices.

The fact that fifteen gay men marched the length of the New World's oldest colonial city in what was apparently the first public engagement with societal homophobia in the country is remarkable and truly courageous, considering the tradition of intense state repression of such open expressions of social discontent. During the country's thirty-year reign of terror under Trujillo, for example, such public displays of resistance were regularly met with state-sponsored assassinations and "disappearances" (Crassweller 1966), and former president Balaguer's long history of repressive responses to protesters has been well documented (Betances 1995; Bray 1984; Cambeira 1997; Wiarda and Kryzanek 1992; Winn 1992). In the case of the first gay pride march, however, the unreflexive way in which global models of gay social action were appropriated tended to dilute the expression of resistance against the specific local practices that were motivational for the participants. It also entirely effaced a potentially astute social critique of the ways that classism, racism, and tourism dependence were facilitating a coercive collaboration between business owners and the police to purge the Zona Colonial of "undesirables." It therefore left unaddressed the abusive power relations that would continue to make gay men vulnerable to arbitrary police abuse in the area of El Drake.

Finally, the reconfiguration of the protest as a gay pride march tended to convert a critical stance on conservative definitions of gender norms—

which marginalized gays as well as *metálicos* and *raperos*—to a statement about sexual identity or preference.[17] This undermined a critique of the ways that restrictive codes of public expression victimize a range of gender-transgressive groups, thereby placing gays in a structural position similar to other non-normative identities. In sum, the potential symbolic power of the motley coalition between the *metálicos, raperos,* and gays was ultimately eclipsed by the strategic appropriation of global gay discourse.[18]

Sexual Positions, Bodily Frontiers

The above discussion illustrates the ad hoc and somewhat surprising negotiations of global gay signifiers at the juncture of the local and the global. In this section, we turn to a different question related to the globalization of *gay:* For Dominican sex workers, what does it mean to be increasingly exposed to global expressions of same-sex desire, behavior, and identity? How are we to understand the ways that men who exchange sex for money with gay tourists are situated within globalizing discourses of gender and sexuality?

Fortunately, there is now sufficient ethnographic research on male homosexuality in Latin America to provide a useful starting point for this discussion. While few Latin American anthropologists have taken as their central goal to examine the influences of the international gay movement on Latin American homosexuality and its particular cultural expressions (see, however, Parker 1999), scholars have offered implicit or explicit hypotheses about the effects of global gay culture on local sexual identities and practices. One of the most important hypotheses in this regard concerns the effects of the diffusion of global gay identities on the persistence of more traditional, role-based definitions of sexual identity in Latin America, and specifically, the consequences of globalization for the "*activo.*"

The traditional model of Latin American male homosexuality posits that sexual role in anal sex rather than sexual object choice is the primary criterion for the ascription of sexual identity. That is, among Latin American men who have sex with men, the social attribution of sexual identities is more dependent on one's position in anal intercourse and the specific uses of one's sexual organs than it is on the biological sex of one's partners. Specifically, *homosexuales* (or their specific local approximations) are defined as men who take the "*pasivo*" (passive) position in anal sex, and are frequently given labels that incorporate linguistic references to their stereotypical sexual role.[19] Lancaster (1988, 1992), for example, describes the Nicaraguan *cochón,* the local identity term for the passive homosexual, who most likely takes his name from the Spanish *colchón,* or mattress, making metaphorical reference to his participation in receptive anal sex. Similarly, my own research shows that in the Dominican Republic, the identity terms *volteado* (turned over), *doblado* (bent over), and *quetcher* (derived from "catcher") are clear references to the presumed passive position of homosexuals in anal sex.[20]

What is perhaps more controversial is the social position of the active participant in anal sex between men. A number of scholars have observed that the Latin American active/passive model not only demarcates the boundary between what can be roughly translated as *homosexual* and *heterosexual* identities, but also distributes stigma unequally between the two. Indeed, some anthropologists have noted that the active participant in anal sex is not necessarily stigmatized by his engagement in homosexual relations. Lancaster, for example, finds that in Nicaragua "the prevailing discourse distinguishes, not between men who have sex with men and those who do not, but between a stigmatized passivity and an unstigmatized activity" (1997). For Brazil, Parker similarly observes that the "*homen* who enters into a sexual relationship with another male . . . does not necessarily sacrifice his culturally constituted *masculinidade*—at least so long as he performs the culturally perceived active, masculine role during sexual intercourse" (1999, 30–31). Other anthropologists have echoed these findings in diverse Latin American contexts, including Mexico (Alonso and Koreck 1993; Carrier 1995), Cuba (Lumsden 1996), and the Dominican Republic (De Moya and García 1996).[21]

Many of these authors have offered linguistic evidence for the presumed lack of stigma attached to the insertive participant in homosexual anal sex: there are rarely specific identity terms to refer to the *activo*. Adam (1989, 77), for example, observes that in Nicaragua "it is the *pasivos* who are usually equated with *homosexuales* by both *homosexuales* and the larger society, while *activos* are largely indistinguishable from the rest of the male population and generally escape unlabeled," a finding that is echoed by Lancaster (1988, 122). Similarly, Parker (1999, 33–34) shows that the derogatory terms for homosexuals in Brazil, such as *bicha, viado,* and *baitola,* all refer to sexual passivity, suggesting that the receptive participant in anal sex is allotted significantly more lexical elaboration—and social stigma—than his insertive counterpart. And Murray goes so far as to say that in Latin America, the "'active' male in homosexual copulation is an *unmarked male,* not officially regarded (and especially not by himself) as 'homosexual'" (1995b, 11).

More recent work on male homoeroticism in Latin America has begun to describe how these traditional role-based models of homosexuality in the region are transforming as emerging models of masculinity and same-sex desire are increasingly available, perhaps particularly in urban areas.

Héctor Carrillo (2003a), for example, has found that among contemporary urban Mexican men, the image of a decidedly *masculine* man who prefers sex with other men has become more common and is causing shifts in popular thinking about traditional notions of homosexuality. This emerging model of homoeroticism—which enables the enigmatic possibility of a *macho homosexual*—challenges traditional thinking because it does not entail the emphasis on sexual position (since who is penetrated is less important in this framework than the fact of same-sex desire itself), and because it does not conflate male effeminacy with homosexuality (since it envisions no necessary relationship between masculinity and heterosexuality).[22] Carrillo finds that this contemporary notion of Mexican gender and sexuality allows some Mexican men who desire same-sex interaction to understand themselves—and for others to understand them—in new ways that may mitigate some of the stigma associated with the disparaged effeminacy of the stereotypical "*maricón*" (fag). It might also make it more feasible for homosexually behaving men to disclose their sexual preferences and behaviors to friends and family, since the stakes of sexual disclosure may be reduced if one can still make claims to being a "normal masculine man."

Given the intense hybridity in the meanings of homoeroticism that are occurring in the region, how do Dominican *bugarrones* and *sanky pankies* fit into globalizing models of gender and sexuality, particularly as they influence the social transformation of the Latin American *activo*? In answering this question, it is crucial to consider how the contemporary construction of the *activo* in the Dominican Republic is tied to global capitalist markets through the pleasure industry. From this perspective, the key question is not how globalization will impact these identities—since the contemporary meanings of *bugarrón* and *sanky panky* are already so enmeshed in global sexual circuits as to be uninterpretable outside of them—but rather how *existing* structures of globalization, particularly as they are expressed through the tourism industry, are shaping and constraining the ways that these identities are understood and enacted. Framed in these terms, transnational structures can be seen to provide the *parameters for the performance of gender and sexuality,* and as elaborated further in chapter 5, *bugarrón* and *sanky panky* identities become not "local identities," but global commodities, circulating and taking on value within the pleasure industry. In this sense, the masculinity that is performed by Dominican male sex workers is different than the modern masculinity expressed by Carrillo's "macho homosexuals," largely because of the disparate ways that identity is connected to material interests and needs in each case, as well as variations in how sexual practices are connected to a fundamental sense of self.

Regarding the latter point, and unlike Carrillo's informants, the majority of the sex workers with whom I spoke did not seem to feel that being a *bugarrón* or *sanky panky* expressed a basic aspect of their identity or personhood. This is partly due to the fact that, as discussed in the introduction, these identities do not function in practice as stable social statuses—as might be more typical for a gay-identified man, for example—but rather can change from place to place, situation to situation. It was therefore somewhat difficult for some men to interpret questions that framed these identities as fixed personal traits. Indeed, in the in-depth interviews, one of the most complicated questions for sex workers to answer concerned how they defined their sexual identity, since this often required a certain degree of reflection that many of them had not (apparently) experienced before—at least not in the directed and formalized manner of an interview. In some cases, as with twenty-two-year-old Julio, a sex worker in Santo Domingo, the conversation centered on participants' self-perception as "*hombres normales*" (normal men)—men whose unmarked sexuality and masculinity was presumably so normative that it required no specific comment or terminology. An interview excerpt with Julio illustrates this kind of relatively common exchange. When asked what he considered his sexuality to be, Julio responded:

Julio: What do I consider myself?
Interviewer: Yes, how would you describe your sexuality?
Julio: I consider myself a man in sex, always a man. It doesn't matter with whom—women, of course, and men.
I: Do you consider yourself homosexual, bisexual, heterosexual . . . ?
Julio: No, not homosexual. I don't consider myself homosexual.
I: Okay, can you tell me more about how would you describe your sexuality?
Julio: I feel—That's what I mean. I'm not homosexual, not bisexual, not anything. I consider myself a man always in sex. Always the man. Nothing more.

As described further below, the repeated references to his being "always a man," in addition to reflecting a notion of normative masculinity and disavowing homosexuality, are also sexual references to Julio's presumed "manliness" in bed, communicating that he is the "active" partner who only penetrates during sex with men, not the symbolic "woman" (or *maricón*) who is penetrated. Similarly, Josué, a twenty-seven-year-old in Santo Domingo, insisted on avoiding any particular term to describe his sexuality, describing himself as *una persona normal* (a normal person), who "does his things in his own way" and "simply takes advantage of any opportunity that is presented in life."

The tendency by these men to avoid terms of non-normative self-identity is likely related to the fact that, in the words of one self-described *bugarrón,* identities like *bugarrón* and *sanky panky* are "outside of society" (*fuera de la sociedad*); that is, they are identities that are, by their very definition and operation, expressed only in private and socially marginalized contexts, and are generally enveloped in silence in the public sphere. As already mentioned, there is no *bugarrón* advocacy organization or movement, and I sensed no felt need on the part of the sex workers with whom I interacted to develop anything resembling a collective political voice.[23] One consequence of this is that the concern with whether or not to disclose one's "true" sexual orientation to friends and family—which was clearly expressed by Carrillo's masculine homosexuals—is less relevant to these men, because it presumes that there is a deeper or more authentic sexuality that an individual feels compelled to publicly acknowledge or negotiate. As described in more detail in chapter 4, many of these men do feel the need to manage their potentially stigmatizing non-normative *behavior,* but they very rarely express the desire to voluntarily disclose their sexual *identity.* For men like Julio and Josué, this is because they consider themselves to be simply "*hombres normales*" who engage in sex with men for money, rather than men who are repressing a deeper, more authentic, or more personal sexuality.[24]

In general, the men who described themselves as *hombres normales*—as opposed to directly claiming an identity such as *bugarrón, sanky panky,* or *bisexual*—also tended to deny a sexual desire for men or to describe a markedly lower attraction for men than for women. At times, these men seemed to be motivated by an apparent attempt to convince both the interviewer and themselves that they felt no true sexual interest for men. For example, Lorenzo, a twenty-four-year-old in Santo Domingo who reported that his only source of income was "*bugarronería*" (*bugarrón*-like behavior), elaborated as follows when I asked him if he thought he could fall in love with a man:

I know that I am going to quit [sex work] because inside me, still, inside myself, I don't feel like a gay man. I feel like a man. And I'm telling you, I've seen people— like I told you the other night—damn, they deserve for someone to at least think "How good that guy looks!" You know? "How handsome he is! He looks good in this or that." But I haven't felt that attraction yet to be able to say "Damn!" to a guy, "You look good!" You know? I haven't said it inside me. . . . I still haven't gotten to that extreme.

Here, in addition to his denial of feelings of attraction for men, Lorenzo confesses that he has asked himself questions "inside" about whether he is really attracted to men—an "extreme" situation that he hopes to avoid by removing himself from sex work as soon as possible. His implication here that leaving sex work would be better for him emotionally was also a theme in the interviews, since men frequently felt that the nature of their work—involving numerous vices, excesses, and sexual taboos—did not bode well for their emotional health over the long term. Further, Lorenzo's internal questioning about his sexuality demonstrates how involvement in the pleasure industry can lead some of these men to question—and to obsessively test—their sexual attractions in order to reassure themselves that they are, in fact, *hombres normales*.[25] For other men, however, such insecurity was not expressed, with many men insisting that they had absolutely no sexual interest in men, and making statements such as those by eighteen-year-old Cristian: "Never. I could never be attracted to a man. I mean, I do this, but it's not because I like it, but out of necessity [*por la necesidad*]."

In fact, this later comment—emphasizing exclusively economic motives for having sex with men—was echoed by many sex workers, who rationalized their participation in what they considered to be morally questionable behaviors by pointing to their dire economic situation. In other words, these men side-stepped questions about their sexual identities by framing the discussion exclusively in terms of the utilitarian benefits of sex work, which allowed them to disavow emotional or sexual connections to clients. As discussed in chapter 5, this denial of emotional connection is actually a simplification of reality, since affection and even love can develop in the longer-term relationships with clients or tourists whom I call "Western Union daddies," and these situations need to be somehow managed by sex workers.[26] Yet it is also clear that many of these men did not view their exchanges with men as sexual outlets for their identities or fantasies, but rather as ways of making "easy money." While a minority of men reported having had exciting or erotic experiences with men or longer-term male partners (often *travestis* or effeminate gay men), most participants were emphatic in their denial of feeling sexual attraction to men. An unusual exception to this general rule was eighteen-year-old Arturo, who was one of a handful of men in this research who identified himself as "homosexual" in the in-depth interviews, confessing that "to tell you the truth, I like both women and men." Arturo was unusual in that he directly expressed sexual attraction for men, rather than seeking to find ways of justifying or disavowing it, even though he framed this attraction in terms of gay men's sexual talents: "On the one hand I like them because, at least, I like the sensation of men, the sensation when they suck you, then I feel—at least I feel accustomed to it that way, I'm accustomed to it now and I like it better."[27]

This notion of becoming "accustomed" (*acostumbrado*) to sex work and same-sex activity was another common theme. While in general these men did not express attraction for men, they were clear about the fact that sex work provided both economic and symbolic benefits to which they had become accustomed. Lorenzo—who, as quoted above, denied that he had gone to the "extreme" of being sexually attracted to men—elaborated on why he sometimes found his work "pleasurable" (*una diversión*): "I mean 'pleasurable' in the moment that you're enjoying some things, when you're enjoying a good resort, a good hotel, some good food, a good drink. You know? Good clothes, maybe a good game, a good casino. In some cases this happens." These attractions, though not a part of the direct monetary compensation that these men receive for their work, provided an additional rationale for participation in sex work and are part of the reason that some of these men described their work as *dinero fácil* (easy money). For example, after explaining that he had "changed" as a result of his work in the sex tourism industry, Eugenio (18) commented,

I've changed because now I don't have the same mentality. Now what I think is: "I want more tourists so they can give me more money [*cuartos*]." Because many of them give us one hundred or even two hundred dollars! Tourists come from over there [*allá*, meaning abroad], *maricones,* and you want to be with one of them because he buys you everything. You tell him [to buy] this, that, and you get married to him [*te casas con él*]. But it's because he makes you "heavy," he buys you everything [*to' la vaina*], and you're always in jeans—always stylish [*paradísimo*].

Thus, while it was fairly common for sex workers to describe getting "accustomed" to these symbolic and material benefits of sex work, some men also expressed some anxiety over what would become of them—morally, socially, and physically—as a result of their involvement in such "vices." See, for example, the case of Miguel in chapter 4, who expressed regret about the unknown psychological consequences of his many years of involvement in the pleasure industry. At the same time, many men also clearly enjoyed the luxuries and the possibilities for accessing certain kinds of global signifiers through their foreign clients.

In understanding how Dominican male sex workers conceive of their identity, it is critical to emphasize that one of the characteristics most consistently expressed by these men is that they do not participate in passive sexual acts, and particularly receptive anal sex. This was a refrain that reverberated throughout the interviews and functioned—in a manner quite consistent with the traditional active/passive model of Latin American homosexuality—as a way to establish socio-sexual boundaries between sex workers and the *maricones* who are symbolically feminized vis-à-vis their

penetrable bodies. Sexuality for these men was shaped by their deep commitment to being *un hombre normal,* which for them meant being vigilant
in guarding against anything that would threaten the necessary concordance
between their public masculinity and their (exclusively penetrative) sexual
practices. They had to be, in Julio's words, "always the man." Indeed, pre-
serving social status as a normal man is likely much more crucial for *bugarrones* and *sanky pankies* than for men who do not engage in sex work, since
they are continually navigating the frontier between masculine activity and
feminine passivity in the course of their work, always in danger of falling into
the symbolic abyss of *mariconería.* It is because of this danger, for instance,
that *bugarrones* often joke about the liminal figure of the *"bugaloca"*—a
bugarrón who has been seduced by the temptation to engage in passive sex
and who has been symbolically converted to a *"loca"* (queer, fag). The men
in this study often mentioned to me that one or another of their peers was
known to *"dar el culo"* (give their ass) on occasion, which often produced
much hilarity on the part of the storyteller. It is therefore important for these
men to maintain an *"activo"* reputation, since they are under surveillance
by others and are continually in danger of becoming known as a *bugaloca.*

Because of the perceived social dangers of engaging in passive sexual acts,
many men insisted that they had *always* refused to engage in such acts, even
when submitting to them might have led to significant economic gain. When
asked whether he had ever been asked to engage in receptive anal sex, Alfonso,
a twenty-six-year-old in Santo Domingo, told a detailed story of an incident
in which he had protected his masculinity despite a client's persistent attempts to manipulate him financially into adopting a passive sexual role.

Once a foreigner offered me $500 for me to penetrate him, and later he told me—
after I penetrated him—"I'm going to give you $500 more now for me to pene-
trate you," he told me. And he took out the 500 and put them in my hand, and I
said "I don't let myself get fucked in the ass [*no me dejo dar por el culo*].". . . And
the fag [*el pájaro*] said, "Okay, that's fine, no problem. Come by tomorrow." And
I came back the next day like normal, for me to give it to him, and he wanted to
give it to me! He handed me the money again, but I gave the 500 back. But I didn't
let myself be penetrated! I never want to be penetrated. Because I'm going to tell
you the truth: I'm not a *maricón.* I look for life [*me la busco*] out of necessity, but
I don't feel anything back there. Here in front, around my dick [*mi huevo*], yes. It
gets hard as soon as they put a hand on it, right away. But for them to penetrate
me?! No, I don't feel anything back there.

Alfonso's narrative offers insight into the symbolic boundaries that
envelope cultural models of sexuality and the ways that participation in

sexual-economic exchanges can create phenomenological challenges to *bugarrones* and *sanky pankies* as they navigate the precarious terrain of the pleasure industry. The extent of narrative elaboration in sex workers' descriptions of these moments of bodily boundary-maintenance—which nearly always entail an emphatic denial of engagement in passive sexual acts—suggests that these narratives express a considerable amount of anxiety, despite the fact that it is possible that many of these men have never experienced a direct attempt by a client to "turn the tables," as described by Alfonso.[28] I interpret this anxiety as an expression of the shame that is symbolically distributed in the body, since many of these men, drawing on Dominican cultural models that equate sexual passivity with the disparaged *maricón,* have constructed their sense of masculinity around an exclusively penetrative notion of self.[29] It is not arbitrary, after all, that Alfonso feels nothing "back there" but is confident that he can perform "in front" at a moment's notice. Indeed, one scholar of Dominican gender and sexuality has described a Dominican boy's upbringing as involving intense socialization into a "strongly restrictive and prohibitive environment" in which parents—and frequently mothers—are obsessively vigilant about creating in their male children a strong "threshold of resistance to taboo homosexual—phallicist—temptation" (De Moya 2003, 73). This socialization involves the creation of an environment in which passivity in both word and deed are severely stigmatized, and in which masculine domination of others is essentialized or "naturalized" (Yanagisako and Delaney 1995). According to De Moya, the domination-subordination duality that is generated by this sex/gender system manifests itself in Dominican men's neuroses about protecting themselves from symbolic (or actual) penetration by dominant male peers.[30]

This phallic construction of Dominican men's sexuality has been incorporated into the calculus that structures the economic negotiations between sex workers and clients. As implied by Alfonso's narrative, the sexual roles played by *bugarrones* and *sanky pankies* have value on the global market, and these values can be used strategically by both sex workers and clients. This is a point that is further developed in chapter 5. For the moment, it is important simply to highlight that these phenomenological features of the Dominican *activo* are reflected in the ways that sex workers and clients negotiate prices for particular sexual acts. Interestingly, this was quite evident in the survey data as well, since sex workers were asked detailed questions about the prices they would typically charge to engage in particular sex acts. As shown in table 5, the prices reported for passive sexual acts were significantly higher than those for active sexual acts, and passive anal sex

TABLE 5: Prices per sex act reported by male sex workers, by type of sex act (N = 199)

Sex act	% Refusing act for any price	N (men reporting a price)	Minimum (pesos DR*)	Maximum (pesos DR*)	Average (pesos DR*)
Active (insertive) oral sex	14.6	170	100	15,000	1,080
Passive (receptive) oral sex	80.4	39	300	19,200	2,428
Active (insertive) anal sex	17.1	165	200	19,200	1,807
Passive (receptive) anal sex	89.9	22	200	32,000	4,272

* Approximate exchange rate in 2001: U.S .$1 = 17 pesos

was, quite predictably, the behavior provoking the highest reported price. That is, the prices sex workers reported were informed by an implicit logic in which shameful, passive sexual acts were significantly more expensive than those considered "normal" expressions of masculinity. This logic combines the traditional moral economy of the body in which passivity is stigmatized with the contemporary Dominican notion—promulgated by the rapid expansion of the informal tourism economy—that nearly everything has a price on the global market. Thus, while most of the sex workers claimed that there was no price that they could be paid for passive sexual acts (either anal or oral sex), some of them reported that they would violate these taboos for the right price.

What is perhaps most significant about sex workers' responses to these survey questions is that the average prices they gave for passive sexual acts were grossly inflated. Ethnographic observations clearly demonstrate that *bugarrones* and *sanky pankies* typically receive between 500 and 1,000 pesos (approximately U.S.$25–50 in 2001) for a single transaction, and this payment would be considered a great success in most cases. Indeed, under particularly dire circumstances, some sex workers will go with a client for the promise of a meal or a place to stay for the night. Yet the average price reported for engaging in passive anal sex in the survey was 4,672 pesos (U.S.$1,882), ten times the price I typically heard reported by both sex workers and clients in the field. Importantly, the prices of active sexual acts were slightly inflated as well, but not unreasonably so, and showed an average price that generally corresponded to the prices I observed ethnographically over the same time period (1,800 pesos, or approximately U.S.$94). The prices quoted by sex workers in the surveys therefore reflect either a conscious or an unconscious inflation, in which the reported prices were directly proportional to the shame associated with the specific sexual behaviors involved. Predictably, this effect was most pronounced in the case of passive anal sex. My interpretation of these unanticipated results is that the exaggeration of the payment required to engage in passive sexual acts was offered as a kind of (over)compensation for hypothetical participation in these stigmatizing activities, and served to equalize the moral frame by which these men would be presumably judged—both by themselves and by others—for sacrificing their masculinity and taking the passive position.

An epistemological point should be made here, since the combination of quantitative and ethnographic data is what permits a psychosocial interpretation of these survey results. That is, examined within the larger cultural context of Dominican sexual exchanges, the numbers themselves are clearly not expressions of "objective" price structures for sexual-economic exchanges—and should not be taken as such by the reader—but rather are an epiphenomenon of the stigma and shame associated with passive homosexual behaviors, here represented in the gross inflation of the material compensation these behaviors would hypothetically provide. If there were no other source of ethnographic data beyond these self-reported prices, one might reach very erroneous conclusions about the typical payments sex workers receive. The ethnographic reality on the ground, however, is that both bodily frontiers and prices are much more flexible in the practices that occur in the pleasure industry, since moments of economic deprivation often take precedence over men's desires to place limits on the instrumental uses of their bodies. The symbolic cost of defiled masculinity may be perceived as a relatively small sacrifice when one is desperately looking for life.

In the remainder of this chapter, I move from this specific ethnographic discussion of the sexuality and bodily practices of Dominican *bugarrones* and *sanky pankies* to a broader consideration of the Latin American *activo* in the context of the global structural transformations that are shaping gender and sexuality in the region. For this analysis, I draw further from the regional ethnographic literature on Latin American homosexualities, but seek to reframe the discussion to focus attention on the ways the cultural meanings and practices of the *activo* intersect with the structures of the pleasure industry. This discussion anticipates a more extensive elaboration of these issues in chapter 5.

The Dominican *Activo* as an Endangered Species?

In this section, I focus on the hypothesis that the Dominican *activo*—the active participant in anal intercourse in traditional Latin American constructions of homoeroticism—will disappear from the sexual landscape as a result of the presumably homogenizing effects of the globalization of "Western" notions of gay identity. In general, prior ethnographic analyses in Latin America have suggested that there are two potential influences of the globalization of gay identity on the structure of traditional sex/gender systems in the region: (1) the gradual breakdown of the role-based model of sexual identity in favor of one based on sexual object choice (or sexual orientation); and (2) the development of a personal and community politics that is manifested in the public declaration of *gay* identity and same-sex preference. This discussion follows Richard Parker's (1999, 27–51) analysis of stages in the incorporation of same-sex global identities in Brazil, and therefore deserves a more detailed summary of his specific points here.

Parker argues that in the late nineteenth century in Brazil, with the progressive urbanization and industrialization of the country, the active/passive gender system typical of traditional agrarian society began to gradually incorporate new notions of sexuality based on medical/scientific modes of sexual classification. The effect of these medicalized terms was to introduce an alternative scheme of potential identity definitions based primarily on sexual orientation or preference:

In particular, a new medical/scientific model of sexual classification—introduced into Brazilian culture through the writings of medical doctors, psychiatrists, and psychoanalysts, and translated only gradually into the wider discourse of popular culture—seems to have marked a fundamental shift in cultural attention away from a distinction between active and passive roles as the building blocks of gender hierarchy, and toward the importance, along Anglo-European lines, of sexual desire and, in particular, sexual object choice as central to the very definition of the sexual subject. . . . In practical terms, this new emphasis on sexual attraction, on sexual orientation, resulted from the invention of a new set of classificatory categories—notions such as *homosexualidade* (homosexuality), *heterosexualidade* (heterosexuality), and *bisexualidade* (bisexuality)—for mapping out and interpreting the sexual landscape (Parker 1999, 37–38).

As identity terms based on a notion of sexual desire and object choice have become popularized in Brazilian culture, they have offered men and women new ways of understanding their sexuality and resisting the stigma and discrimination of the traditional sex/gender system. Parker's informants provide poignant ethnographic evidence of the salience of these terms as means of affirming one's identity while avoiding the derogatory labels typical of the active/passive model of homosexuality.

The second globalized model of sexual identity discussed by Parker is related to the more recent formation of gay social spaces organized around a particular notion of self-ascribed sexual identity. The global gay liberation movement, especially in its post-AIDS manifestations, has produced a new discourse about the *personhood* and *community* of gay men and women that transcends the more clinical focus on sexual behavior or orientation typical of historically older cultural models. In Europe and North America, the modern gay movement has also developed a massive institutional base, a corporate infrastructure, and a consumer culture through which it disseminates, on a global scale, a particular representation of gay community and identity politics. As Parker emphasizes, however, it remains an open question the degree to which local sex/gender systems in developing contexts have incorporated, altered, or recombined the specific cultural elements of global gay identity. In the case of Brazil, he finds indications of both the appropriation of certain aspects of international gay culture and the persistence of traditional, characteristically Brazilian features of the active/passive model.

For the purposes of analytical discussion, the potential local effects of these two ideal types of global sexual identity models—that based on sexual orientation and that based on *gay* identity—can be conceptually divided into two parallel historical processes. First, traditional Latin American sex/gender systems may be gradually weakened by the introduction of a globalizing model of sexual orientation, and the concomitant effects on sexual practices and local identity constructions may be ethnographically observable. While research on this question is limited, there is tentative evidence from Brazil (Parker 1999), Mexico (Carrier 1995; Carrillo 2002), and California (Magaña and Carrier 1991), for example, that the incorporation of foreign notions of "sexual orientation" have diminished the role rigidity associated with traditional active/passive gender models and, perhaps, altered patterns of sexual behavior as well.[31] Further, it is likely that the gradual incorporation of a notion of homosexuality based primarily on sexual object choice has the effect of broadening the local conceptual frameworks used to identify and label participants in homosexual relations. That is, we might assume that the *activo* would tend to lose his unmarked ("normal") status within a cultural setting in which all same-sex sexual behavior is homosexual-typing. The division of sexuality into *heterosexual* and *homosexual,* then, has a tendency to reorder the traditional landscape of homoeroticism by positing a more generalized definition of same-sex desire that blurs the conceptual boundaries between marked (passive) and unmarked (active) categories. It also redistributes stigma by placing the *activo* in a potentially "discreditable" position in relation to his participation in same-sex activities (Goffman 1963), at the same time it provides him a new, potentially affirming identity label by which to resist social discrimination.

The second possible effect of globalizing models of same-sex desire is the incorporation of a *gay* identity around which a particular construction of personhood, social space, and community can develop. As Parker argues, while the formation of "gay identity" and institutions in Latin America has occurred parallel to the development and popularization of a modern notion of sexual orientation—following, for example, the growing use of these terms in medical and scientific discussions of homoeroticism throughout the twentieth century—the development of "gay" is distinct from earlier notions of "homosexuality." A key index of the appropriation of global gay identity is the degree to which local actors define their sexuality through idioms of self-identification with a community of peers. Thus, whereas the traditional model of Latin American homosexuality is generally more ascriptive and derogatory in its designations of the *pasivo,* and the language of sexual orientation is more descriptive and clinical, the language of *gay* makes reference to the processes of *self*-ascription and community association that are in many ways definitional of global gay discourse (Levine 1979).

A key implication of this book is that the position of the Latin American *activo* in the context of globalization—as represented in the Dominican Republic in the figure of the *bugarrón*—cannot be understood without addressing the ways that the local meanings of homoeroticism are incorporated into the larger political and economic structures of the contemporary world. While many prior analyses have tended to depict the globalization of gay identity as a phenomenon that acts *upon* the *activo*—as if an external force that gradually obliterates "traditional" non-Western categories of homoeroticism—the analytic approach used here is one that examines the ways that the *bugarrón* category is *already* incorporated into global systems of consumption, and then seeks to explicate its linkages to these systems. Taking this perspective involves critically interrogating the assumption that contemporary expressions of the *bugarrón* are truly "traditional" or "authentic." Indeed, there is no reason to assume that the meanings of *bugarrón* today—incorporated as they are into tourism markets and processes of sexual commodification that extend far beyond the country's borders—have direct or unambiguous connections to the "traditional" Dominican sex/gender system, since these meanings are now the products of global discourses and evolving representations of Dominican masculinity, *as well as* local cultural expressions. As described in chapter 1, the meanings of the *bugarrón* and *sanky panky,* and the social ascription of these identities, are now inextricably linked to the international tourism economy, and indeed, the very existence of the *sanky panky* identity is tied to the historical growth of the pleasure industry. What does this mean for the men who participated in this study? How have these men resolved the various tensions between the knowledge about sexuality that they received in the course of their socialization and the rapidly changing world in which they live?

These questions will be further explored in subsequent chapters. In concluding the current discussion, I would simply like to suggest that the globalization of *gay* as it unfolds in the Dominican Republic should not be understood as a process that leads to the inevitable erasure of traditional identities and practices, but as one that incorporates, reworks, and commodifies particular constructions of sexuality vis-à-vis global capitalism. To be clear, this is not synonymous with saying that *bugarrones* and *sanky pankies* exert no agency in the ways that they engage these large-scale structures in their own lives—as discussed in the previous chapter, the art of the *cuento* is one such "weapon of the weak"—but rather emphasizes that the structures themselves are not of their own making. Men like Julio, Alfonso, and Lorenzo are deft and creative in negotiating daily life in the pleasure industry, but they do so from a position of great disadvantage within it. Tourism and sexuality theorist Jasbir Puar has asked, "Who benefits the most and the least from queer tourism? One could say that those who are already enabled and rewarded by capitalist formations can most easily harness the positive effects of increased queer tourism" (Puar 2002b, 127). In chapter 5, I similarly argue that some gay foreigners who visit the Dominican Republic seek to "harness" the effects of queer tourism by using their privileged access to global mobility as a means of obtaining what they perceive as uniquely "Dominican" sexual experiences. The identities of *bugarrón* and *sanky panky* are therefore an essential part of a globally marketable fantasy, composing the metaphorical "edge" of what Joane Nagel calls an "ethnosexual frontier" (2003).[32] As long as these local *activo* identities continue to occupy a central place in this fantasy, and as long as the global inequalities that enable these exchanges persist, it is likely that *bugarrones* and *sanky pankies* will continue to converge on Dominican beaches and historic sites— in search of a buyer.

The two ethnographic forays that compose this chapter—a critical analysis of the first Dominican gay pride parade and the sexual narratives of *bugarrones* and *sanky pankies*—have been used here as a lens onto the ways that the pleasure industry shapes the sexual identities, cultural politics, and bodily experiences of two non-normative male sexualities. While the first gay pride event grew out of tensions between Dominican gays and the local Dominican authorities, police abuses against gays were rationalized (and perhaps financed) by the tourism businesses in the Zona Colonial that would presumably suffer from the distasteful image of homosexuality in this tourist-dependent area. The politics of sexuality was therefore caught up in discourses about the kinds of Dominican-ness that were appropriate for tourist consumption, demonstrating both the power of appeals to tourism as political rhetoric and the ways that it can be wielded to justify social cleansing campaigns. As Cardinal Nicolás de Jesús López Rodríguez's recent proclamations have made clear, Santo Domingo's primary tourism area— the colonial zone—will no longer tolerate open displays of "perversion," forecasting a new era in police abuse and mass arrests against local LGBTQ populations (Medrano 2006). From the perspective of the political economy of sexuality, the important point to highlight here is that state tourism interests were used in this case as ideological leverage to justify the persecution of non-normative genders and sexualities. These interests were an invisible undercurrent to the sexual politics of the first gay pride event, although they were never openly addressed or politically challenged in the ultimate configuration of this moment of "gay pride." It remains to be seen whether future acts of LGBTQ resistance to systematic state abuses will seek to generate a social critique of the structural dependencies that often frame the politics of sexuality in the Dominican Republic.

In the subsequent discussion of sexual identity among Dominican *bugarrones* and *sanky pankies*, I have drawn on the ethnographic literature from Latin America to make two overall suggestions. First, men's participation in the pleasure industry can shape the way they conceptualize and experience their sexualities and bodily frontiers, although it does so ambivalently. This is because while Dominican sexuality has instrumental value in the pleasure industry—allowing men to access and even to become "accustomed to" certain material and symbolic benefits—it also creates internal questions for them as they attempt to maintain a somewhat precarious masculinity and avoid slipping into a demonized "*mariconería.*" This socialized anxiety about passive or feminine genders and sexualities is expressed in these men's hypervigilance about avoiding the passive position in sex—a position that, nevertheless, might be purchased for a sufficiently high price on the global market. The commodification of men's sexual positions itself entails a significant transformation in Dominican models of homoeroticism, because it generates global material "investments" in the uses that *bugarrones* and *sanky pankies* make of their bodies and orifices. Since masculine socialization has established sexual boundaries that are not necessarily congruent with these global investments—at least in some specific cases, such as that described by Alfonso—sex workers must learn to cope with and manage these disjunctures while maintaining a masculine social image both in their own and in others' eyes. This, as with masculinity itself, is always a precarious balance.

The second suggestion I have made in relation to the Dominican *bugarrones* and *sanky pankies* is a theoretical one. Ethnographic studies of homosexuality and globalization have implicitly or explicitly framed the figure of the *activo* as a "traditional" phenomenon that is in tension with, and may ultimately be eclipsed by, currently circulating notions of global gay identity. This framing, however, presumes a lack of integration of *activo* sexualities into global cultural flows and economic interests, a presumption that can in no way be confirmed by the ethnographic evidence presented in this book. Global gay identity and its meanings are transmitted not only by cultural diffusion, but also through the hierarchies and structures that enable queer touristic practices. As further elaborated in subsequent chapters, these structures set the parameters for the sexual interactions that occur in the pleasure industry and have numerous consequences for the ways that local sexualities are understood and enacted.

4

Familial Discretions: Unveiling the Other Side of Sex Work

A similar though not necessarily identical feature seems to be characteristic of Caribbean societies. It is surely not accidental that the very activities most central to the achievement and maintenance of manhood and reputation are those proclaimed illegal by the total society. . . . In fact, in its most general sense a reputation is gained according to the degree to which a man is proficient in undermining, disobeying or circumventing the legal system of society.

PETER WILSON

Within the family the *de ambiente* man wears a transparent mask . . .

PAUL KUTSCHE

Miguel's Story

During an interview, Miguel—a thirty-two-year-old *bugarrón* who has twenty years of experience in the Dominican sex trade—recalled events in his childhood that were anything but idyllic. Born in the eastern pueblo of La Romana, an area that would later be developed into one of the Dominican Republic's most lavish tourist zones, he remembered:

My father was, as they say, an alcoholic. Everything he earned he drank, and he never gave a dime [un chele] to my mother, because everything was—everything he earned he drank. There were problems between them, so I decided to leave the house, and that way they avoided [another] problem. . . . The problem with me when I was little was that I was really mischievous [travieso] and my mother was always beating me, and I always had little problems. And between the beatings that she gave me, and the tormenting, what they did to me is tear me apart, and I got so that I didn't even want to see my house. When I looked at my family it was like looking at the devil, so when I left it was like fleeing. . . . At the end of it all, you have to leave the house and get by alone.

At age nine, Miguel left his family home and became, in his words, "a street kid" (*niño de la calle*): "I was raised in the street. Mainly I was raised with the tourists. I worked with them. Some were gays and I stayed with them, and that's how my life went. I raised myself alone." Two years after leaving home, he relocated from La Romana to Santo Domingo to try his luck in the city.

Well, when I came to Santo Domingo the first time, I began working with a triciclo [tricycle] in the street . . . looking for bottles, looking for cardboard in the street.[1] And I always stopped there in El Conde around a hotel that was called the Hotel Anastasia, and they [the tourists] always waved to me, and they started to give me things, and they said "come," and from there I continued. I went every day, I passed by every day, since then I knew that they gave me—that they gave me a sandwich, they gave me ten dollars, they gave me five pesos. . . . And I got a person, a guy, an American friend, and from the age of twelve I stayed almost—almost four or five years working with him in the hotel. I was the one who—who did it to him, who did it to him. And there I stayed.

Today, Miguel is a well-known *bugarrón* in Santo Domingo with relatively lucrative connections to the international sex trade, a success which he attributes to his sociable personality and his English-language proficiency. "I learned [English] easily," he commented, "because aside from the fact that I don't know how to read or write, I'm very intelligent." These language skills have served him well, since they have allowed him to continue making a living in the sex industry despite competition with younger *bugarrones* who are often in higher demand. Now, as a well-connected *maipiolo*, he has even been able to reduce his direct involvement in sexual exchanges without seriously compromising his income, since his networking services earn him regular *comisiones* (commissions):

Basically, I don't have to be wandering around having sex with lots of people, because I always get something translating, or taking him [a tourist] to Boca Chica, or taking him to such and such a place to buy this or that. And they send for me if they need a person: "Hey! Get me that one." And I go and I look for him. In general, I don't have to have sex [*tener relaciones*], since now I almost don't use sex to, to get money.

Miguel's success with the tourists has allowed him to provide a relatively stable income for his common-law wife, Sonia, and their three children, the eldest of whom is now twelve. The family has a small house in Los Mameyes, a lower-class barrio just across the Rio Ozama from the city's colonial zone. Miguel believes that the higher income one can attain through sex work has allowed him to provide a better life for his children. "I was a kid who suffered a lot on the street," he reflected, "and I know what that is like, and I don't want to throw kids out to suffer on the street because I can't take care of them." Sex work has also provided other benefits for his family, including a more flexible schedule, since "in my free time, I can be at home with my kids, sometimes playing Nintendo, sometimes we go to San Cristóbal to the river, to the beach, lots of things."

Nevertheless, he admits that when he is busy with tourists, he sometimes has "problems" with Sonia, who, while she is aware of his work and has even entertained tourist-clients in her home, is not wholeheartedly supportive of Miguel's occupation:

"You know how women are. They always want to have their husband beside them, so the problems always come because of that, because I have to go out to the street and sometimes I'm out until two, three o'clock in the morning, and those are, most of the time, the problems that we have. We've argued to the point of hitting each other."

Despite these arguments, Miguel feels that his wife has no grounds to criticize him for what he considers legitimate work that provides for his family's needs: "The man always has to be in the street looking for money for the woman's food, and from that she eats. . . . You can't go on what everyone tells you in the street, because you know that I'm in this environment and, if you're my partner and we're living together, you're eating from what I bring here, you have to accept what—what I'm involved in."

Many of these tensions come to the fore when one of Miguel's regular clients, Larry—a North American executive in his early sixties—comes to Santo Domingo on his annual vacations. For the past eleven years, Larry has been traveling to the Dominican Republic to visit Miguel at least once a year, usually staying for two months at a time. Miguel recalls being introduced to Larry through another *bugarrón* who had established him as a regular client. When he was invited to accompany the couple to dinner, Miguel took the opportunity to impress the tourist.

I took him a basket of fruit, and I got him with that, because when I went [to the hotel] I took him that present and he said to my friend, "Of the two or three years we've been seeing each other, you've never given me anything, I'm always giving you things. And look, yesterday I invited this boy to have dinner here, and look what he came here with!". . . And then we went on a trip to La Romana, with my friend driving and us in back, and he started falling in love with me. And that was when he told my friend that he didn't want to have anything to do with him anymore. . . . And later [from New York] he called me at my house, and he told me that he was coming at such and such time and that I should wait for him. And that's when he started sending me money.

Larry now sends Miguel "a monthly payment of 150 dollars, and mainly with that [he] can get by."

During Larry's trips to Santo Domingo, Miguel has to spend significant amounts of time away from home in order to accompany him and serve as his tour guide and translator: "The problem when he's here is that I have to spend one night there [in the hotel] and one night in my house, one night there and one night in my house—because I have to divide myself." While Sonia complains of these absences, Larry is understanding when Miguel needs to spend time at home with his family. In fact, he says, "[Larry] is the one who buys me what I need. If I need a fan, if I need a television, if I need a radio—it's always him that buys everything. He's bought almost everything I have in the house." Nevertheless, Larry is not accepting of Miguel's involvement with other male tourists, warning that "if [anybody] tells me that you're working, I'm not going to Santo Domingo anymore." This is a tangible threat, since Miguel has come to depend on the regular remittances he receives from New York. When asked how he convinces Larry that he is not working with other tourists, Miguel shrugged and remarked, "No, it's not about convincing, because he's in the United States and I'm here; he doesn't know what I'm doing."

Despite his feeling that his career in sex work has provided him "easy money" (*dinero facil*), Miguel is not quick to conclude that it is harmless.

The foreigners come here and do a lot of damage. . . . How can I explain it? It's never really known because it stays with them, but the foreigners sometimes do a lot of damage to the boys. . . . They're the ones who get them used to it [*los acostumbran*], because if I'm a person who's making two hundred or three hundred pesos a day [ten to fifteen dollars], and you come to me and say, "Look, come with me and I'm going to give you four thousand or five thousand pesos" . . . that boy will get used to it. That boy gets used to a life. And what life? Drinking every day, and drugs. And he gets accustomed to it. And that's where the problem comes from: when the boy doesn't have a dime, he has to rob the tourist.

However, he feels that this world of "vicios" (vices) in which he has spent most of his life has helped him to provide for his family, including his parents, whom he has always visited on occasion. Until his father's recent death, he had regularly supported both of his parents—who had been subsequently divorced and remarried—with whatever he could manage, despite the fact that he feels they neglected him as a child. He continued these contributions even though his father's new wife treated him very poorly, often objecting openly to his occasional visits. Miguel feels that his father, though certainly a neglectful parent, suffered from a weakness and inability to control his drinking and his women. Indeed, Miguel seemed to find a certain poetic justice in the manner of his father's passing, which—at least in Miguel's own imagination—was partially related to the old man's agonizing sense of guilt about his lifelong neglect of his child:

"That was something that tormented him a lot, and he started drinking, because he was saying, 'Damn, I wasn't with my son when he was a boy.'. . . And he started drinking, and drinking, and drinking, and then he fell off the bed and had a stroke."

Childhood and the Natal Family

Here we have a proverb: "The mouth of the devil and the heart of God." It means when one fights a lot—fights all the time—but the heart is noble. That's my mother and my father.

VICTOR, *bugarrón*, Santo Domingo

In many ways, Miguel's story is typical of the life stories of many of the *bugarrones* and *sanky pankies* with whom I spoke. In talking about their childhood, these men frequently mentioned parental neglect, mistreatment, or alcoholism, often punctuated by memories of traumatic early ruptures from the natal household leading to a more vulnerable existence on the street. Miguel's sense that his departure from home was "like fleeing" provides a glimpse into the early context of childhood socialization—including regular beatings by his mother, as well as his father's drunkenness and neglect—that contributed, at least partially, to his initiation into the world of the street. Nevertheless, these factors should not be viewed as simplistically "causal" of Miguel's being "raised with the tourists," if for no other reason than that he—and indeed most of the sex workers with whom I spoke—frames his departure from home as his own agentive decision. Phrases such as "so I decided to leave the house" are common in sex workers' narratives, but they are often used to describe the thought process of a child who is far too young to make an informed, rational decision about living on the streets. In general, then, there seem to be relatively strong "push factors" in the natal household leading to the rather extreme "choice" on the part of a young child to fend for himself on the streets, despite the fact that sex workers' narratives often emphasize their own agency in the decision to leave home.

While he does not say so directly, it is possible that Miguel's leaving home at the age of nine was motivated by certain messages from his family—whether implicit or explicit—that he should support himself economically. Indeed, his comment that "at the end of it all, you have to leave the house and get by alone" is similar to comments made by many sex workers concerning their early break with the family. Such comments are suggestive of a belief that male children of lower-class families should be more independent and self-supporting, especially as they approach adulthood. This is particularly true when there are many children in the family, when there is only one parent, or when a boy is considered old enough to cover part or all of his own expenses through formal or informal work. This expectation may explain why a significantly greater number of the sex workers surveyed in this study were among the older siblings in their natal families, suggesting that parents may prioritize younger children over older children who are expected to be significantly more independent. As with Miguel, many of the men with whom I interacted had become street children by an early age, often working as *limpiabotas* (shoe shiners) or *chiriperos* (street vendors)—occupations that tended to expose them to the opportunity, the vulnerability, and the temptation to engage in sex work. Indeed, a study of thirty homeless boys aged fourteen to seventeen who were living on the streets of Santo Domingo concluded that by fifteen, 80 percent of these boys had already had experience exchanging sexual favors for money with adult gay men, most of whom were foreigners (Vásquez, Ruíz, and De Moya 1990).

The theme of parental neglect is clear in sex workers' narratives. Memories of alcoholism—typically on the part of the father—are common and are often associated with habitual abuse. Andrés, a twenty-year-old *bugarrón* in Santo Domingo, described as follows his most vivid childhood memory:

Well, I was a shoe shiner when I was really little. I cleaned shoes. . . . And he [my father] took my money from me, to store it, to buy whatever he wanted. He bought me what he wanted, and he controlled me. Sometimes on the weekends I had to come home early, at seven or eight, and he would get home drunk and start to fight and bother us. Really bad. And in December during the holidays, when everyone goes to bed later, he would get drunk and we would have to go to bed early. We had to listen to all his ranting lying down. I suffered a lot.

In some cases, sex workers connected their own problems with substance abuse to the influence of their fathers. When I asked him what he would change about his relationship with his parents, Ricardo, a thirty-two-year-old self-identified *maipiolo*, responded: "[I would change] the addictions, like the alcohol, the drug addiction, we have. Between my father, alcoholic; my brother, drug addict and alcoholic; and me, drug addict and alcoholic—I would change all that I know were problems and that caused suffering to my family. If I had a magic wand, I'd make time go back to change all that, to reverse the suffering and the addiction."

Many men mentioned divorce, separation, or remarriage as instrumental in negatively affecting the configuration of the childhood home, often leading to an early introduction to the streets. These narratives typically highlight problems with a stepparent, a finding consistent with the relatively high frequency of serial and simultaneous consensual unions among lower-class Dominicans, resulting in children commonly being raised by several caregivers (Brown 1975a).[2] Rafael (18) explained to me why he believed his stepmother, rather than his father, was the one who had actually forced him into a life on the streets:

Maybe I don't blame [my father], or maybe I blame him for being really weak, because a woman controls him, like, manipulates his mind. So this woman made me leave the house! She hates me and he runs here and there to do whatever she says. You understand? So, she wants to see me drown, to see that I never go to the university or study anything, that I'm always poor, and doesn't allow him to help me. I mean, I don't know what she puts in his head, because that's what my family tells me: that it's because of my stepmother that he doesn't help me.

Martín (33) tells a similar story of his reasons for moving, at the age of twelve, from the city of San Pedro de Macorís to Santo Domingo, a journey that he paid for by bartering some of his toys for a "*bola*" (ride) from a truck driver: "I lived with my stepmother, who treated me badly. My father never treated me badly, but I never let him know that my stepmother treated me badly, because . . . he suffers from diabetes [*sufre de azucar*] and I don't want him to [get upset]. . . . So, I moved here with my brother from San Pedro, to the capital, because of a beating that our stepmother had given us."[3]

Despite the trauma that is associated with leaving home, these ruptures are often viewed ambivalently by sex workers. In some cases, "fleeing" the natal home is also associated with independence from an abusive home life and is perceived as a kind of liberation that permits one to engage more freely in certain sexual and economic activities, including prostitution. This is commonly the case when sex work begins while one is still residing with family, since coresidence with parents and siblings lends itself to the unavoidable indiscretions and questions about one's nocturnal activities that can be perceived as oppressive familial restrictions, often culminating in the decision to move away from home. Nevertheless, nearly half (43 percent) of the sex workers surveyed in this study were still living with their father and/or mother, and not surprisingly, those who were still living with their parents at the time of the survey were significantly younger than those who were not ($p < .01$). This figure increases to 52 percent living with family when we include those who resided not with parents but with siblings, aunts, uncles, or other extended-family members—a scenario that is particularly common among rural-urban migrants (see chapter 2). The breakdown of coresident family for survey participants is shown in figure A.1 in the appendix.[4]

The effect of the commonality of coresident family is that young men are subject to greater surveillance, leading many to seek an independent residence at the first opportunity. Martín explained to me how his decision to leave his father's house and rent a small room across the street had given him some relief from his father's constant surveillance.

Martín: I used to arrive late, and [the neighbors] would tell [my father] that I was with so-and-so. . . . Since San Pedro is so little, they started to realize and people commented things. So, he told me he didn't want to see me with so-and-so, because sometimes [a regular client] took me nearby my house, and he would drop me off. . . . And I would go straight to my house and in ten or fifteen minutes it had already reached my father. And that had consequences. Problems. And so I had to move across the street.

MP: And now is the situation better?

Martín: Yes, now I practically don't have to depend on him, I depend on myself. What happens is that when you live with your parents and they put a roof over your head, you have to respect the—the example they want to give you. Now I can live my life the way I want to.

Similarly, Rafael explained how he had avoided problems with his family by distancing himself from them: "I am, as they say, separated from my family right now. At least, I decided to distance myself a little from my family, because they are really on the pulse of everything [*muy sobre el pulso*], and I can't depend on anyone. I'm in this and nobody knows. I mean, they know I'm a little crazy, I get home late, I'm out all night—stuff. But I tell them I'm with my friends." While he had distanced himself from most of his family, Rafael was still living with his older brother when I interviewed him. When I asked if his brother ever inquires about where he gets the money he brings home, he replied: "No, actually, he doesn't know about it."

I mean, I don't show him the money. You understand? Instead, I say: 'I'm doing a job [*una chiripa*], something around here. Here: Take 100 pesos. They gave me 200 pesos. You take half.' I show him the money little by little, you see? And later I tell him, 'I'm going to do another job. Here. You need twenty dollars? Forty dollars?'"

While many sex workers believe that engaging in sex work while living with family is both impractical and stressful, most of them are unable to become sufficiently economically independent to live alone. This reliance on family to meet living costs is demonstrated by survey data on the amount of economic support that sex workers receive for specific household expenses. Participants were read a list of common household expenses and asked to indicate whether they alone paid for these expenses, whether they shared these expenses with another member of the household, whether someone else in the family paid for these expenses, or whether they did not have the indicated expense. Their responses are summarized in figure A.2 (appendix). These figures demonstrate that a significant proportion of sex workers rely on members of their household to cover all or part of their routine expenses—one of the primary reasons that establishing a separate residence is out of reach for most *bugarrones* and *sankies*. Nearly half of those sex workers who paid rent for a house or apartment, for example, received help from other household members for all or part of this expense. Other expenses show a similar pattern.[5]

If we examine Rafael's above statement more closely, we can observe a technique employed by many sex workers to mitigate the familial consequences of their engagement in stigmatized behavior. The methods Rafael uses to "cover" his involvement in the sex industry—for example, inventing an unspecified "*chiripa*" (informal-sector sales job) to which he must urgently attend—are typical of the strategies used by many *bugarrones* and *sanky pankies* in their close kin relationships.[6] Indeed, much informal socializing among sex workers involves telling humorous stories about methods used to evade detection by family members, and friends often collude to create mutually beneficial alibis. During an interview, Humberto (22) recalled the agreement he had made with a friend when he was just beginning to see clients, several years earlier, while still residing with his aunt and uncle:

MP: So your aunt and uncle didn't know anything about this work?
Humberto: No. I told them that I slept at a friend's place.
MP: They didn't have any idea what you were doing?
H: No. I told them, "I slept at a friend's."

MP: And they never said anything to you?

H: Yeah, they said stuff, but my friend covered me [*me tapaba*].

MP: OK. And this friend knew what you were doing?

H: Yeah.

MP: What did he think?

H: Nothing. He didn't say anything to me because I gave him some of what I got so that he would cover me with my aunt.

In fact, it is quite common for sex workers to pay their peers to provide a credible explanation—always prearranged—for their absence from home, in the event of a more extensive inquiry by a suspicious family member. Thus, the need to cover one's involvement in sex work generates an additional demand for "alibi services," creating a niche for those who are *del ambiente* (in the know) to make a small amount of supplemental income by selling credible stories.[7]

As described in chapters 1 and 2, another covering technique employed by sex workers is to present themselves to their family as "*guías,*" since this is a less stigmatizing explanation for extended or frequent absences from home and has the additional benefit of being a reasonable explanation for regular interaction with tourists. Miguel, whose story is summarized at the beginning of this chapter, described how his relationship with his mother had benefited from the cover provided by his self-presentation as a professional tour guide. When I asked him if his mother knew about his involvement in sex work, he replied:

Yes, because I've even taken tourists to her house. I mean, she doesn't know exactly what I do, because one thing doesn't necessarily have to do with the other. Sometimes I go there with tourists who don't have anything to do with that [sex work], and sometimes I go there with tourists who have a lot to do with that. You understand? But you don't ever let your family know, even if they start to realize.

The ambiguity that Miguel describes is common in sex workers' relationships with family, since mutual pretense, rather than direct communication, is often preferred by all parties. The status of a tour guide thus provides just enough cover to avoid open conflict with family, permitting momentary denial to lapse into years of mutual pretense.[8]

Many sex workers believe that such techniques for avoiding detection are necessary because of the potential consequences if the true nature of their occupation were to be exposed to the family. Jaime, a twenty-four-year-old student at the country's largest public university, described how he imagined his mother would react if she were to learn about his involvement in sex work:

If I tell her that I have sex with gays and all that, I know that she isn't going to understand. She'd tell me not to do it, and if she asks me why I do it, I'm going to tell her, "Well, with that I get money," and then she'll tell me to get a job. She's not going to understand that there are no jobs that a person can make good money with because—For example, I study marketing. If I'm going to buy my materials for class and I take another job, I'm not going to have time to do the homework anyway. And she wouldn't understand those things.

Fears about discovery are reinforced by cases in which family members learn the truth about a sex worker's activity, or develop strong suspicions. Edgar (19) narrated as follows his brother's recent discovery of his work, and the conflict that resulted from this realization:

My brother and I had a fight [*un pleito*] near my house, because a client of mine, a homosexual, took me to my house in a Mercedes-Benz. And my brother and some of his friends were watching, like, "Is it a man or a woman?" And I heard them. . . . And then one of them started to say that I was going around with a fag [*maricongo*], fucking around. I grabbed him and threw a couple of rocks at him. Later the police came by my house, but they couldn't send me to jail, because you have to fight with a machete or a knife to go to jail.

Following this discovery, the family changed significantly in their treatment of Edgar:

They were ashamed that people would know that I was a relative of theirs, they were ashamed of me, and that made me feel really bad. So, when I'm at home they bother me, and when I go out they bother me for going out or for not coming back. . . . But they don't worry about giving me money to leave—or to come back.

Concern about neighbors' suspicion and gossip is heightened by the fact that most sex workers live in lower-class barrios in which privacy is at a premium and surveillance is often intense. As with Martín's description of his father's network of neighbors who would inform him within minutes of any questionable behavior by his son, the men I interacted with were nearly always occupied with devising various schemes to evade their neighbors' curiosity. This is because it is frequently neighbors—rather than family members—who first witness potentially discrediting interactions with clients, and later comment about them to family and friends. Cesar (23) explained to me how his family was informed by curious neighbors of his involvement in sex work:

Cesar: Of course, you know how the old people and women are in the barrios. They live to talk about, like, the guy who screws around with fags, that—that this is bad, since they think that fags are something from another world.

MP: Did your family ever see you with anyone?

Cesar: They never saw me, but with the neighbors—how should I say it?—I was always talked about. I was burned [*quemado*] in the barrio as a bugarrón. . . . I was with him [indicates a client across the street], and I always had money, and was always buying clothes and going everywhere with him. So they deduced and did the calculations: "He's a bugarrón [*está bugarroniando*]."

Thus, being socially "burned" in the barrio was often a precursor to problems with family, both because neighbors might inform family members of questionable behavior and because families are frequently preoccupied with maintaining the respectability of the household in relation to their social peers.

Ricardo—a well-known *maipiolo* who founded what he described as the first sex-work "agency" (*agencia*) specializing in brokering contacts between local *bugarrones* and foreign tourists—was unusually direct in his interactions with overly curious neighbors. He described his confrontational technique as follows:

I live in a five-story building . . . so there are always two or three [neighbors] that you categorize as the newspaper *El nacional,* another as the newspaper *Hoy.* [laughing] You know, like reporters, who don't have anything to do. Old ladies who spend their lives observing everything that happens in the barrio—the one who cheats, the one who fucks the fags [*maricones*], how you work, if you rob, sell drugs. So, I take care of those people. So a woman came to ask me questions, and I said to her, "What I have in my house is an office of sex workers. Foreign guys come, we fuck them up the ass [*les damos por el culo*]—excuse the phrase—they pay us. But there are also some women who call, so if you need anything, let me know and I'll take care of you!" She turned her back to me and has never talked to me again! [laughing]

The surprisingly direct style of Ricardo's dealings with neighbors is, in fact, the exception that explains the rule. His unusual brazenness was undoubtedly related to the independence he has gained through his success as a professional *maipiolo,* and in a certain sense his apparent imperviousness to social critique was required if he was to make his private home—where he lived with his wife and infant daughter—the headquarters for his sex-work "agency."

Despite intense social pressures, some informants had managed to achieve some openness about their sex work with certain family members, and a handful had attained a degree of acceptance (or perhaps resignation) from their families regarding their "other life." Most often, sex workers understood this acceptance as the result of their economic contributions to the household, which tended to defuse, in their view, any strong objections from family regarding their work. Indeed, financial contributions to the family were often constructed as a way of mitigating the potential consequences of engaging in stigmatized behavior, as illustrated by Rafael's reply to his brother's overly curious inquiries: "You need twenty dollars? Forty dollars?" This technique minimizes excessive curiosity by implicitly offering financial compensation in exchange for silence and complicity. Orlando (27) made this logic explicit when I asked him if his sister, with whom he was then living, had any suspicions about his sexual exchanges with tourists: "No, because she never sticks her nose in my life, and neither does my brother. I leave without a curfew. If I go out, I come back the next day, and she doesn't ask me anything because I always give her a monthly payment [*una mensualidad*]." Orlando's last phrase makes clear the logic behind his conceptualization of his sister's silence: his provision of economic assistance—as well as his sister's acceptance of it—invalidates any presumed right to moral criticism about his sexual activities. As discussed in the following section, this logic is also evident in the ways that sex workers relate to their wives and girlfriends, and is reinforced by conservative notions of male gender roles in the household.[9]

A few sex workers attributed the relative acceptance of their occupation by their family members to their recognition that sex work with men is a viable, if highly stigmatized, strategy for achieving upward mobility. As discussed further in chapter 5, relationships with male tourists occasionally lead to sustained economic assistance by a client that can have a significant effect on one's ability not only to provide for basic needs, but also to continue education and training that can improve long-term employability and salary. For example, a significant proportion of *bugarrones* pay for either their own or their children's educational expenses with the money they make through sex work. I remember a conversation with Ernesto, a *bugarrón* in his mid-twenties, who described to me how difficult it is for him to pay his university tuition during the low tourist season. "You have to turn a trick to buy a book," he chuckled. "You think we don't have to study when the tourists stay home?"[10]

Another strategy for upward mobility involves the establishment of long-term relationships with upper-class Dominican men, since such relationships can be highly beneficial for men of meager economic means. A number of sex workers described how their relationships with wealthy and powerful Dominican men would eventually assist them in improving their overall socioeconomic condition. These perceptions seem to be borne out by the regular comments I heard from *bugarrones* about their reliance on wealthier local clients as a reservoir of resources upon which they could draw during scarce economic times, as well as a means by which to invest in such things as education and home improvements. While foreign clients also contribute to these expenses—and probably in higher overall proportions—local clients are beneficial because they more often lead to sustained relationships that provide a degree of longevity and economic stability that is not typical of the more transient relationships with tourists. Relationships with local men, while not providing the lucrative income typical of transactions with tourists, provide a kind of safety net for sex workers that mitigates the boom-and-bust cycles associated with any tourist-oriented product or service. Thus, during hard times, *bugarrones* and *sankies* often rely to a greater degree on their more sustained relationships with local men.[11]

Because of my focus in this book on the influences of the tourism industry on Dominican men's lives, and because sex workers express a strong preference for exchanges with foreigners (see chapter 5), I have not developed a fuller analysis of sexual-economic exchanges between local men. Nevertheless, local exchanges do occur, and a small number of participants in this study had a larger proportion of local versus foreign clients. It seems quite possible, based on my conversations with *bugarrones* and *sanky pankies,* that age-graded local exchange relationships are a distinct modality of sex work in Santo Domingo worthy of more systematic study. For the current discussion, the most important point about these local relationships is that at least some sex workers believed that their family's tolerance of their work was related to their recognition of the potential economic benefits of these local relationships. Edgar, for example, described as follows how his family reacted to their discovery of his relationship with a steady local client:

"They made fun of me, but they didn't ask me to stop doing it, because they know that I make contacts through this and I know a lot of people who can help me in the future, a lot of people who have connections, who are homosexuals who have a high position in the government, in politics, and this also helps me."

Such notions are not entirely far-fetched, since the long tradition of clientelism and the patriarchal structure of Dominican institutions make contacts with powerful men quite useful in opening doors to education, employment, and a variety of social and legal services. Powerful local clients may also be more successful at negotiating a release from jail—a highly useful potential benefit in the context of systematic police abuse. Indeed, as discussed in chapter 5, after foreign tourists (58 percent), survey participants indicated that their preferred male clients were wealthy Dominican executives (11 percent), which is partially related to the belief that such relationships can facilitate class mobility.[12] In sum, while one's family may have moral objections to sex work, it may be more difficult for them to dispute the potential benefits of these relationships as a counterbalance to rising male unemployment and a highly unreliable income.

Those family members who knew about and, to some degree, accepted one's involvement in sex work also made relatively frequent references to the dangers of the occupation in terms of potential exposure to HIV and other sexually transmitted infections. Cesar, for example, explained that after his mother's initial shock and a series of difficult conversations about his career choice: "She started to leave me alone, except that she always says, 'Be careful you don't get AIDS.'" Similarly, Martín observed regarding his relationship with his sister, with whom he now openly discusses his work, "She doesn't really give any opinions now. She just tells me to take care of myself, to use a condom, and, in case anything happens, to talk to her about it first." Such comments suggest that family may provide a significant reinforcement of safer sex practices among those sex workers—generally the minority—who are able to be more open with their families about their engagement in sexual-economic exchanges with men. However, the contours of stigma and silence that surround male sex work, and homoeroticism more generally, place significant constraints on men's ability to safely disclose information about their involvement in sex work to their families, a point to which we will return in chapter 6 when we turn to a discussion of HIV/AIDS.

Finally, relationships with siblings were often quite strong in this study, and sex workers were generally more open about their activities with their brothers and sisters than they were with their parents, spouses, or partners. Particularly when informants did not have their own children, they often felt strong economic obligations toward their siblings, nieces, and nephews, and a significant proportion of sex workers who no longer had close relationships with their parents continued to live with or regularly visit their siblings. During semistructured interviews, siblings were also the family members most commonly mentioned in sex workers' replies to a question about the family member to whom they feel the closest.

This sense of closeness is at least partially related to the fact that it is often older brothers who initiate their younger brothers into sex work, resulting in greater trust and openness with them regarding sexual exchanges. Jaime, for example, described his brother's role in socializing him into sex work when he was an adolescent:

Well, I knew that he left home all the time, but I didn't really think anything. But then I saw that I was killing myself working, and he would go, for example, one night to a disco, and he came back with a lot of money. And he bought clothes and jewelry and stuff. And I thought, "But wait a second. How is it that this guy goes dancing at the disco and he comes back with money [*cuarto*], and I'm killing myself all week working and I'm completely broke [*en la olla*]?" And later he asked me if I wanted to go, and I said "let's go," and so I went to see.

Jaime's story demonstrates one of the ways that some adolescents come into initial contact with the possibility of sex work, as they observe their older brothers' successes in displaying the material icons of the middle class, including the prized designer fashions from abroad.[13] His story is also significant in that it demonstrates the ways that siblings can have a protective influence on those sex workers, particularly minors, who are just beginning and who lack the knowledge and experience to successfully navigate the social, physical, and emotional risks of sex work. As Jaime later described to me, his brother eased the otherwise traumatic experience of his transition to sex work—a trauma that is a common theme in sex workers' narratives of initiation—by taking him under his wing and patiently teaching him the best ways to select clients and negotiate exchanges. Thus, while he is partially responsible for Jaime's initiation into sex work, he also limited his younger brother's exposure to the dangers he would have encountered if he had attempted to discover this world on his own. This is a socialization role that is often assumed by older *bugarrones* in their relationships with younger *bugarrones*, but the blood ties between brothers raise the stakes of these relationships and appeal to the older sibling's sense of familial obligation and fraternal caretaking. This generally has a buffering effect on the subjective experience of younger sex workers such as Jaime, who can rely on advice, protection, and an understanding ear if they should require them.[14]

Wives, Girlfriends, and Evasion

Late one night in July 2001, I was drinking with Orlando across the street from Tropicalia, a gay disco on Santo Domingo's *malecón* where sex workers frequently make contacts with clients. Orlando, while only twenty-seven, had considerable experience in the sex trade and was well known and friendly with most of the *bugarrones* in the area—qualities that would serve him well as he approached an age at which his networking skills, rather than his direct sexual exchanges, would be his primary economic resource. He had joked with me on several previous occasions about the "*lío*" (big problem) that had developed as a result of his involvement with two women, as well as his somewhat ineffective attempts to prevent his sister, with whom he was then living, from learning about his sexual exchanges with men. Since we had chatted before, I asked him if I could audiotape our conversation, to which he agreed. During the course of our conversation, we had the following exchange, which I quote here at length because of its vivid illustration of the cover *bugarrones* struggle to preserve amidst the surveillance of their wives, girlfriends, family, and clients:

MP: Do your girlfriends know that you "look for it" [*te la buscas*] with men?
Orlando: No, because maybe if they knew, they wouldn't be with me.
MP: You think they'd react badly?
Orlando: Yeah, because—also if my friends [regular clients] knew that I had others, for example, my friend the doctor, if he knew that I had others, he'd dump me [*me botaría*]. Or if he knew that I have a girlfriend, he'd think the same.
MP: He'd dump you?
Orlando: Yeah, because he says he would.
MP: So, is that difficult for you, to have, like, two lives, because you have your life with your girlfriend, and she doesn't know that you—
Orlando: No.
MP: And the doctor doesn't know anything either.
Orlando: No.
MP: Is that difficult for you?
Orlando: [No response]
MP: Do you feel bad that you have to tell lies sometimes?
Orlando: No.
MP: No?
Orlando: I sometimes have to tell little lies [*mentiritas*].
MP: What kinds of lies?
Orlando: Well, sometimes I even have to tell them [regular clients] that I have an uncle that's been feeling bad, that I have to go for a week to the country, but it's a lie, because it's to be with my girlfriend. And sometimes I tell my girlfriends that I—I have a job, that I'm painting a house really far away and that I won't be back until really late, so I won't be able to go by their house, but it's a lie, since that's when I'm with my friends, right?
MP: But that doesn't bother you, to tell those lies?
Orlando: No.
MP: Is it easy?
Orlando: [Laughing] Yeah, because since the lie was invented, it hasn't betrayed anyone [*desde que se inventó la mentira, ya nadie queda mal*].
MP: [Laughing] Oh! So they don't suspect anything?

Orlando: No.

MP: Are you a good liar?

Orlando: [Long pause] No, because sometimes I make mistakes.

MP: Give me an example of a mistake you've made.

Orlando: Like, the other day I told the doctor that I was going to the country for a week, and the next day, or like two days later, he called my sister's house, and it was me who answered the phone. But it was because I wanted to see my girlfriend, or to divide my time between my girlfriends.

MP: And the doctor? What did he say when you answered?

Orlando: Nothing. He came right over to my sister's house. He said, "Let's go drink some beers," and that's when we started to argue.

MP: Did he get mad? What did he say?

Orlando: [Laughing] Yeah! He was furious!

MP: And you argued?

Orlando: Yeah, of course. We had a bad argument, and he went like four days without calling, and later he called and said that he wanted to talk to me, and I said that I know I shouldn't have lied to him but that I did it because I wanted to hang out and relax at my sister's. He didn't know about my girlfriend.

MP: What did he say? Did he believe that? Did he believe you?

Orlando: I don't know if he believed it. I did it so he would relax [laughing]. I don't know if he believed it.

MP: Sometimes they find out, and sometimes they have suspicions, I imagine.

Orlando: I guess so. Sometimes he even calls my sister's house, and he asks her about me, and sometimes I think that even my sister suspects.

MP: Really?

Orlando: Yeah.

MP: But she never asks you anything?

Orlando: No.

MP: Why do you think she suspects, then?

Orlando: Because guys call me in the morning, in the afternoon, every day. She has a right to suspect something. And there are times when I'm not there and he [the doctor] just shows up at my sister's.

MP: Really? He drives by in his car, or what?

Orlando: No, there's an alley by my house, so he leaves the car around the corner and comes through the alley to my sister's.

MP: How often does he do that?

Orlando: Sometimes—almost every day.

MP: Really? Oh, I can understand why your sister might suspect something.

Orlando: Yeah, she might be suspecting something.

MP: So, when you're at your sister's and he shows up, you go out with him then?

Orlando: Yeah, because he's not obvious [*no se le nota nada*].

MP: And do the neighbors have—do they bother you or gossip in the neighborhood or anything?

Orlando: No.

MP: No?

Orlando: No, because the neighbors have always seen me with lots of women.

MP: OK, so they don't have any idea—

Orlando: No, and I sometimes—like every once in a while I go by to, as they say,
to "kill the bad thoughts" [*matar la mala mente*], or kill the bad tongues of the
neighbors. I go to my sister's house with my girlfriend.

MP: To avoid gossip [*evitar los chismes*].

Orlando: Yeah. Because a few months ago my sister said to me, "Listen, you always used to bring girlfriends here, almost weekly, and now you're—it's been
a long time since you introduced me to a girlfriend," and I said, "I have a girlfriend, but I didn't think you'd want me to bring women here." So later I
showed up with my girlfriend.

Orlando's narrative is, in many respects, an apt example of the complex,
multifaceted techniques that *bugarrones* and *sankies* employ to manage information about their extrarelational sexual activities—including, but not
limited to, their sexual-economic exchanges—with their wives, girlfriends,
boyfriends, and clients. In many cases, these strategies are consciously employed to create the illusion of fidelity or to defuse questions about involvement with men or with sex work. Some are used primarily to justify one's
physical absence, as in Orlando's "little lie" to his girlfriend about a painting job that requires him to work until late at night. Others, such as his taking a girlfriend to his sister's house in order to "kill the bad thoughts" of the
neighbors, are intended to dispel any suspicions about engagement in potentially stigmatizing behavior. In both of these examples, the strategies
employed are "premeditated" in that they involve planning and coordina-
tion in order to create a convincing "scene." This is most dramatically illustrated by cases in which other sex workers or persons "in the know" are paid
to buttress a particular alibi, usually by vouching for one's presence in a
nonincriminating location. These techniques are therefore highly performative, requiring a continuous awareness of potential reactions and a talent for eliciting desired impressions.

These techniques are important for *bugarrones* and *sanky pankies* for two
primary reasons. First, a substantial proportion of them are married, either
legally or—more commonly—consensually (sometimes described collo-
quially as "*casado sin papeles*," married without papers). Figure A.3 (appendix) shows the marital status of the survey participants, of whom nearly

one-fourth (23 percent) were married, either legally or consensually. Nevertheless, these numbers do not account for the commonality of relationships with *novias* (girlfriends), which were perceived as quite distinct from consensual wives. Generally, a woman was considered a *novia* rather than an *esposa* (wife, whether legal or consensual) when the couple was not cohabitating and/or they had no children together. Most of the relatively stable *novia* relationships that did not yet include mutually recognized spousal obligations are therefore not represented in the survey data, or rather, would be categorized as "single." In fact, the vast majority of *bugarrones* and *sanky pankies* are involved with one or more *novias* at any given time, ranging from casual visiting relationships to long-term engagements.

The commonality of relationships with women is linked to the second, and related, reason sex workers require strategies for covering their activities: most of their wives and girlfriends are unaware that they are involved in sex work or that they regularly have sex with men. The vast majority of *bugarrones* and *sankies* do not engage in open conversations about their outside sexual activities with their significant others, and deception and covering are almost always preferred to open discussion or dialogue. Interestingly, when asked if their wives or girlfriends "know about" their involvement in sex work, *bugarrones* and *sankies* often respond in the affirmative. This is apparent in the survey data, in which slightly more than half of the participants (57 percent) answered "yes" to an opinion question about whether most sex workers' wives and girlfriends know about their partners' involvement in sex work with men. Nevertheless, when asked in semistructured interviews if they have "talked about" it specifically with their partners, very few men responded with an unequivocal "yes." In fact, their responses were usually similar in form to the way that Miguel, quoted in the previous section, qualified his earlier assertion that his mother "knows" about his work: "Well, she doesn't know exactly what I do." The reality is that it is quite rare for explicit conversations to occur with spouses and girlfriends about sex work, with a few exceptions, such as when both partners are employed in the sex industry.[15] This is related to the fact that open communication about the details of one's private sex life—perhaps particularly with wives and girlfriends—is not a strong value in Dominican culture, especially when this involves highly stigmatized sexual activity. It is generally taken as a more serious breach of social relations to discuss nonnormative sexual activities than it is to engage in them privately and discreetly.[16] Indeed, when family members learned of one's involvement in sex work, their primary concern was often the social consequences of any potential indiscretion, as illustrated by Orlando's summary of his mother's initial reaction upon discovering the nature of his work: "She just said for me to be careful because the people are talking a lot, that I should do my things discreetly." It is interesting to note in this context that the vast majority of gay-identified men with whom I regularly interacted had not explicitly "come out" as such to their families, and often gave responses to my inquiries that paralleled those of sex workers: everybody knows, but we haven't talked about it. Thus, the cultural emphasis on discretion tended to reinforce sex workers' resolve to remain silent about their sexual activities, rather than discuss them explicitly with their families and partners.

However, the constant preoccupation with evasive techniques demonstrates that sex workers not only are engaged in a passive game of mutual pretense with their partners and families, but are actively trying to deflect curiosity through the use of deception and "little lies"—described in Goffman's (1963) formulation as "stigma management techniques." The pervasiveness of these techniques raises the question of what partners and family really know about their activities, and also suggests that the presumption that family "already know" may function more as a justification for not speaking about extrarelational activities than as an accurate depiction of the family's awareness. Ironically, then, the notion that family members are already aware of one's engagement in sex work—whether or not this is actually the case— may function to reinforce sex workers' noncommunicative stance, since there is no reason to discuss that which is presumably shared knowledge.[17] As discussed in the next section, the silences that characterize sex workers' relationships with spouses and partners are also reinforced by the sexual permissiveness afforded to men in the Dominican sex/gender system, and the gendered expectation that most men are "*tígueres*" (roughly, "tigers").

The centrality of these stigma-management techniques for sex workers' psychosocial lives is perhaps best explained by the great lengths at which they spoke with me about them, sometimes resulting in highly emotional conversations about anxieties related to wives and girlfriends. For many sex workers, the ethnographic interview was the first time they had talked extensively about the various lives they were struggling to keep in balance, usually quite precariously, and often causing significant emotional stress about the potentially damaging consequences of their work for their intimate relationships with women. For example, Héctor (27) became visibly anxious when I asked him about how his wife would feel if she knew about his sex work with men. "That's why I want to leave this [sex work] forever," he explained. "Because, you know, I have my woman now, you see? If my woman realizes that I have sex with men, maybe she'll leave me, you under-stand?" Similarly, Edgar, who had hurled rocks at his neighbor for spread-ing rumors about his involvement with *maricones,* described to me his fears about the fallout from this very public conflict: "My girlfriend will dump me, of course, because she's going to think that I don't love her and I don't respect her, and I can infect her with some strange disease. She loves me and she wants to marry me, and I'd like to marry her too, but if she finds out about this she's going to look for something—something better."

Sex workers' fears about the potential problems with their wives and girl-friends caused by their engagement in sex work seem to be borne out by sto-ries of actual conflict in the household. Orlando, whose interview is quoted at length above, had almost daily arguments with his girlfriend about his frequent absences from home and his late-night carousing. By the end of my fieldwork, he had decided that the conflicts had become too much for both of them. "It's because I practically don't dedicate the time I need to dedicate to her," he told me in our last interview:

Orlando: Because a lot of the time, a guy will call me—to give an example—in the morning, and he says he's going to call me at 8 o'clock at night, and I have to be at my sister's waiting for the call. So, I have to call Elizabeth [his girl-friend] to tell her I have to go out, and that it won't be until the next day that we'll see each other.
MP: And is that a problem for you?
Orlando: Of course! That's why we've left each other so many times.

Humberto, who often commented to me, usually in the later hours of the night or early morning, that his wife "must be waiting up" for him, said that the main problem in his relationship was the conflict generated by his late nights on the street. Things had gotten so intense of late that each night he feared that he would return in the early morning to find an empty house.

Fears about the end of relationships with women were often connected to larger concerns about raising a family and having children—highly valued goals for most *bugarrones* and *sankies.* Edgar's concerns about a public sham-ing, for example, were connected to his masculine reputation in the barrio, since he believed that "*chismes*" (gossip) about his alleged "*bugarronería*" could make it difficult for him to marry and raise children in the area.

Edgar: It makes me really ashamed, because any woman . . . if she asks around about me, they [the neighbors] are going to talk badly about me and scare her away . . .

MP: Has that ever happened to you? Has a woman ever found out?

Edgar: Yeah, I'm telling you because it's happened to me, and later they were making fun of me.

MP: What happened?

Edgar: Well, I never knew who said it, but she [a potential girlfriend] was interested in me, and she started to ask people about who I was, who I hang out with, and they told her I'm a bugarrón, that I'm always in Tropicalia, that I'm always taking maricones around to eat in strange places—they told her a bunch of stuff.

MP: "They" were the neighbors?

Edgar: Yeah, and what hurts me [*me duele*] is that I'd like to have a son, and if I have a son, I'm not going to be able to raise him there, because if they tell him that, it's a huge shame [*vergüenza*] for him.

Indeed, the desire to have children was strong among sex workers, and nearly half of the 200 survey participants (47 percent) already had children. This is even more significant when we consider that the average age of participants was only twenty-four. Indeed, having fathered children was often considered more important than doing so within a stable cohabitating relationship or marriage. Francisco, for example, explained that he had recently begun an extramarital relationship because his wife had not yet given him a child. When I asked him if this was his main reason for the affair, he exclaimed, "Of course! I'm twenty-two and I still don't have even one [child]!" The value that these men placed on their fertility—independent, to some extent, of their participation in actual child rearing—is also suggested by the fact that nearly half of those who had fathered children were not living with any of their children at the time of the survey (44 percent). Despite this, 83 percent of fathers indicated that they help to support their children economically, and the cost of raising children was often cited as a primary reason for participation in sex work.[18] The latter is illustrated by Martín's response when I asked him whether his income from sex work covers all his expenses: "No, it doesn't cover all of my expenses, but it helps me to take care of my children . . . which is the most important thing."

Nevertheless, while sex workers frequently expressed the desire to support their children, in a significant number of cases this does not appear to be the only or even the primary motivation behind their participation in sexual-economic exchanges. This is further evidenced by the types of expenditures that *bugarrones* and *sanky pankies* cover with their income from sex work, as shown in figure A.4 (appendix). While "basic needs" for either themselves or their families were cited most frequently, a significant proportion indicated they also spent sex-work income on "entertainment" (e.g., alcohol, drugs, luxury items), "dating," and "travel."[19] The "dating" category was broadly conceived to include expenses ranging from casual dating with "*novias*" to payments for female sex workers. This broad definition was useful for the survey, because it is often difficult to rapidly distinguish between casual dating relationships and paid exchanges, for two primary reasons: (1) both types of relationship often presuppose financial contributions by the male partner, and (2) the regular male clients of female sex workers are commonly conceptualized as "*novios*" (boyfriends) after only three or four dates.[20]

Paralleling observations made in the previous section, contributions to wives and children were often framed within a gender logic that invalidated a woman's right to criticize any objectionable activity. Thus, despite their expressed fears about being discovered or "burned," many sex workers reacted to questions about a hypothetical future indiscretion by emphasizing the supposed immunity to moral criticism that was afforded them by their role as household provider. Cesar made this clear when I asked him what typically happens when he argues with his wife about his late nights.

No, she doesn't argue too much, because I stop the conversation right there if she comes to criticize me. I always—I say, "What you need, when you ask for it, don't I get it for you? When you want some new shoes, or something for me to buy you, don't I buy it without looking back? I mean, I always have money. So, what you need, you know that I get it for you [*me lo busco*], so don't come to talk to me about that!" And I stop the conversation right there, and I leave.

Similarly, while Rafael was expressly fearful about his wife's discovery of his exchanges with men, his assessment of her possible reaction to the truth was somewhat incongruously nonchalant: "She wouldn't do anything . . . Or maybe she'd say, 'Shit, what a pig!' But it's for my money, and I'd tell her, 'Well, you enjoy this also,' and she'd keep quiet. She wouldn't say anything more, you understand?"

Thus, it is significant that despite their anxiety about being exposed by their significant others, many *bugarrones* and *sankies* appealed to their role as household provider in order to rhetorically justify their participation in stigmatizing behavior, and to deflect any real or potential criticism from their wives or girlfriends. Such strategies point to the tenuous nature of their support for their female partners and children, since built into this logic is a veiled threat: if you object to my behavior, I may choose to withdraw my support. It is also quite evident that many sex workers overemphasize their role as provider partly as a means to compensate for their engagement in stigmatizing behavior that is potentially discrediting of their masculine reputation. This is a particularly useful psychosocial strategy, since it counteracts what would otherwise be considered a masculine failing—participation in homosexual exchanges—with presumed success in another masculine role: household provider.

The narratives that sex workers tell of their stigma management techniques demonstrate the ways that their patriarchal gender privilege provides them with particular resources, both symbolic and material, which they use to minimize the social effects of their stigmatizing behavior. That is, *bugarrones* and *sanky pankies* are not prevented from accessing normative masculinity—since they have not chosen to disclose or make public their "spoiled identity"—and therefore can make strategic appeals to masculine privilege in order to justify their behaviors, to "cover" the nature of their exchanges with men, and to place limits on their wives' interrogation of their activities. Hegemonic constructions of Dominican masculinity are embedded in the strategies that these men employ to manage stigma in their daily lives, demonstrating the complex intersections of normative and non-normative gendered practices that pervade their lives. This calls for the development of intersectional cultural theories for understanding how "liminal" genders and sexualities—that is, individuals who fall in between the salient categories that organize a particular sex/gender system—draw on, reproduce, and resist contradictory gendered meanings and expectations.[21]

One such approach emerges out of recent ethnographically informed discussions of "sexual silence" in Latin America and among Latino populations in the United States (Carrillo 2002; Díaz 1998). Sexual silence has been described as a key feature of the strategies that are implemented by sexually marginalized individuals to avoid certain kinds of sexual disclosure in the context of their social identities as presumed "normal men." It is therefore similar to the stigma management techniques described above, but it involves a more complex cultural nuance that has been discussed by Héctor Carrillo in his eloquent book on Mexican sexuality, *The Night Is Young* (Carrillo 2002). Beyond functioning as a way of avoiding sexual communication, the system of sexual silence allows for and even fosters other kinds of veiled communication that are implied or "between the lines." Because sexual silence permits a constant ambiguity and uncertainty, it provides a highly productive system for indirect communication in a cultural context that does not permit (or at least encourage) more frank or serious expressions of sexuality.[22] It also allows for what Carrillo describes as "tacit agreements": "The unspoken message is sent by 'those who know' [that] 'I tolerate you and your behavior so long as we never talk about it.' The message in return is: 'I know you know, and I also know that you don't want me to talk about it'" (2002, 140).

Beyond these tacit agreements, the ambiguity of sexual silence allows for veiled modes of discourse that can be strategically deployed by sexually marginalized individuals in their relationships with a wide range of social peers—from "accomplices" (those who know the real truth and tolerate the behavior), to the "deceived" (those who have no idea about the truth), to the "suspicious" (those who are somewhere in the middle). The ambiguity of sexual silence provides social flexibility, since it permits the necessary communicative "fuzziness" to correct or disavow undesired interpretations if they should occur, while also, in some cases, allowing a great deal of communication about one's "other life" without ever explicitly broaching the topic.

Sexual silence is evident in the relationships between the participants in this study and their female partners, although it expresses itself differently in the Dominican context. First, sexual silence results in different kinds of communication because of the ways that *bugarrones* and *sanky pankies* make claims to normative masculinity as a result of their disavowal of homosexual identity, attraction, and the receptive sexual role. As discussed in the previous chapter, the majority of sex workers denied being physically attracted to men or possessing a homosexual identity, and often sought to demonstrate this by "always being the man," that is, never becoming a penetrable *maricón*. During moments of potential breaches of discretion with their family members and partners, some of these men therefore drew on these notions of Dominican masculinity to avoid further sexual communication or to communicate that they were, in fact, "*hombres normales.*" One useful example is provided by twenty-one-year-old Gerardo, who explained what had happened when his girlfriend heard rumors that he was living with a *maricón*:

One of my friends is a big charlatan, and he started to joke around and stuff [with my girlfriend], "This guy's running around with some guy." And she said, "And who is he?" Because it seemed like she knew him, because he was one from the barrio. And my friend said, "Go over there, he wants to talk to you," and I was telling him to shut up. But she saw the guy, and—on top of everything the guy was a real maricón—and I told her, "No! He's a maricón! I'm not a maricón, I'm a bugarrón!"[23] . . . And she said "What do you mean you're not a maricón, if you live with a man?!" And I said they weren't the same thing. "What do you mean?" And I said, "No, because he's the one who receives, and I'm the one who gives." And she went two or three days really mad, and then I went back and convinced her [I wasn't a maricón], and we went back to her house.

Gerardo's narrative provides a rather dramatic example of how the particular positionality of *bugarrones*—both socially and sexually—produces a uniquely Dominican brand of "sexual silence." On one level, this particular case of relational conflict does not seem to reflect sexual silence at all, since it involved very explicit communication about sexuality and sexual roles. However, here I would like to suggest that arguments such as Gerardo's may contribute to sexual silence in the Dominican Republic, because they dispel concerns about being a "true" *maricón*. By appealing to active/passive models of sexuality that are pervasive in Dominican gender socialization (see chapter 3), some *bugarrones* and *sanky pankies* seek to normalize their stigmatizing behaviors by reinstantiating the symbolic and bodily boundaries between themselves and the *maricón*. Further, in the context of the pleasure industry and the common instrumental uses of sexuality by both men and women, asserting one's identity as a *bugarrón*—as Gerardo did in this case when backed into a corner—also suggests that these behaviors are compensated monetarily, a fact that further justifies them as a means of "looking for life." Thus, while not entirely eliminating the stigma associated with a *bugarrón* identity, traditional notions of masculinity can be strategically drawn upon within a system of sexual silence to allay concerns about sexual deviance or "*mariconería*" and avoid other kinds of sexual communication.

This strategic assertion of a *bugarrón* identity is related to another important reason that sexual silence takes on a particularly Dominican expression among sex workers: *tigueraje*. As described in the following section, *tigueraje* is a specific Dominican expression of masculinity that valorizes (and sometimes disparages) ambiguity, trickery, and opportunism among men. In this sense, *tigueraje* is the great Dominican complement to sexual silence among *bugarrones* and *sanky pankies*, allowing men to maintain a degree of masculine esteem through their opportunistic behaviors, while contributing to the gender inequalities and communicative breakdowns that characterize their spousal relationships. It is to this concept that we now turn our attention.

Global Sex Work, *Tigueraje*, and Stigma Management

On the popular radio programs that continuously emanate from the *colmados* (small corner stores) throughout the Dominican Republic, *bachateros* and *merengueros* often sing of the tragicomic strategies that men employ in their (variously successful) attempts to evade detection during extramarital affairs.[24] Conversely, women are frequently depicted as either entirely deceived by their *maridos/esposos* or as tragically martyred by their husbands' uncontrollable philandering. In one popular merengue by Luis Días, "Me dejaste sola" (You left me alone), the female protagonist laments (translation by Austerlitz 1997, 118):

Te emborrachaste, pagué la cuenta,	You got drunk, I paid the bill,
Y tú, de jumo, no [te] diste cuenta.	In your stupor, you didn't even notice.
Tenía[s] queri[d]as por todas partes.	You had girlfriends all over the place.
No te hice nada y me deshonraste.	I didn't do anything to you, and you
	degraded me.

The cultural models that circulate through popular merengue and bachata are refractions of Dominican gender relations, even as they represent highly stereotyped notions of masculinity and femininity.[25] What is overwhelmingly evident in the lyrics of these songs is a certain antagonism between men and women that is often rooted in infidelity, betrayal, and deceit. Frequently cast in a humorous tone, the gendered discourses that are promulgated by these musical forms reflect a characteristic feature of Dominican gender relations: the idea that men are incorrigible "*mujeriegos*" (womanizers) or "*tígueres*" who are continually deceiving their female partners. The complex notion of *tigueraje* is central to the construction of Dominican masculinity. Many of its primary features—such as its emphasis on sexual conquest and infidelity—are also characteristic of what Peter Wilson (1969, 1973) has referred to as "reputation" among lower-class Caribbean men. It is therefore useful to briefly summarize some key elements of Wilson's influential argument.

Wilson constructed his model of Caribbean gender relations on the bipolar concepts of "reputation" and "respectability," which represent a spectrum of ideological options available to people in constructing their gendered moral selves. Taking anthropological studies of machismo in the Hispanic Caribbean as his point of departure, Wilson proposed that lower-class men and women subscribe to distinct value systems informing their gender identities, household structure, and sexual/reproductive behavior.[26] For men, norms of masculinity require the maintenance of one's reputation through the active demonstration of sexual prowess, virility, aloofness from the household, aggression, and heavy drinking. Women, on the other hand, are functionally excluded from the value system of reputation and subscribe to the European-derived, legally encoded system of respectability. This entails an emphasis on legal marriage, sexual morality, fidelity, fecundity, and confinement to the home. Importantly, Wilson also ties these dichotomous gender norms to class status by noting that one's ability to display the icons of respectability requires access to material resources. For lower-class men who are structurally excluded from the realm of respectability, reputation thus offers an alternative and transgressive gender ideology through which to achieve a degree of social esteem by subverting the (respectable) values of the larger society.[27]

A defensible critique of Wilson's model is that it does not address the ways that men and women of all social classes may strategically borrow from a polyvalent set of gendered meanings, combining or contesting them in practice and discourse. Indeed, Jack Alexander's important work on the Jamaican family argues that many middle-class men are "on two tracks at the same time"; they value the sexual responsibility associated with a "serious covenant" in marriage but simultaneously engage in "illegitimate" relationships with outside women—the latter behavior being associated with the lower class. Thus, "the middle-class male has both a 'responsible' legal family and an 'irresponsible,' illegitimate, 'outside' relationship" (1984, 162). Using a dichotomy that is reminiscent of Wilson's reputation/respectability distinction, Alexander argues that middle-class Jamaican men are positioned midway between two cultural stereotypes—one associated with the lower class and coded as "black," and the other associated with the upper class and coded as "white." Having been forged in the liminal space between lower-class slaves and British landowners, the Jamaican middle class has never been able to successfully separate itself from a lower-class notion of its identity, and it therefore "harbors a belief in its own dishonor" (1984, 173).

The ways that the middle-class men in Alexander's research recruit the meanings associated with a "lower-class" masculine identity are similar in certain respects to the ways that Dominican men of all social classes recruit the notion of *tigueraje*. It is impossible to live in the Dominican Republic without hearing the term *tíguere* on an almost daily basis, and it is not inconsequential that *bugarrones* and *sankies* are considered quintessential *tígueres*, by both themselves and others. Indeed, sex workers often use the term *tíguere* to refer to themselves or their social peers, and—as discussed in chapter 5—they strategically exaggerate certain features of their *tíguere* identity as a means of marketing their sexual services.

Tíguere seems to have its root in the Spanish word for "tiger" (*tigre*) and has been interpreted as a partially resistant response on the part of urban men to the particular configuration of state repression under the Trujillo dictatorship (1930–61) (Krohn-Hansen 1996). The term is central to the construction of masculinity for men of all social classes, and it embodies a set of polyvalent meanings that are associated with a particular gender identity. The *tíguere*, while stereotypically lower-class, is also a certain kind of man that is superficially similar to Wilson's man of reputation. In Santo Domingo, the term *tíguere* is often used to describe a man who regularly engages in a range of street behaviors, including drinking in all-male groups, carousing, womanizing, infidelity, aggression, and various kinds of delinquency. Yet the notion of *tigueraje* encompasses other qualities that are, perhaps, unique to Dominican gender constructions. In daily discourse, *tíguere* frequently indexes a kind of self-serving opportunism, deception, or avarice that is simultaneously disparaged and valorized. Men who take advantage of others for their personal gain are likely to be labeled *tígueres* by their social peers, a designation that can serve as both social critique and admiration. *Tigueraje,* then, is associated in important ways with the ability to "*aprovecharse de otros*" (take advantage of others), whether the context be sexual, economic, or political. This parallels Krohn-Hansen's depiction of the Dominican *tíguere* as a "trickster" precisely because of his ability "to resolve, in an acceptable way, the dilemmas which have to be faced as a consequence of a tough environment" (1996, 121). The skill with which the *tíguere,* as trickster, confronts difficult situations—relying on verbal skills and a chameleon-like ability to convince—brings Krohn-Hansen to describe his essence as fundamentally ambiguous:

The symbol of the *tíguere* (precisely because of its semantic and moral complexity) makes it possible to express what otherwise seems difficult to grasp and classify: paradoxes and ambiguities associated with the exercise of power in relationships. This is so because—according to people themselves—the essence of the image of the *tíguere* seems to be one of ambiguity. Being cunning but not a criminal, the *tíguere* stretches what is socially permissible and orthodox, but without losing moral balance. As the image literally suggests, the man who sees himself, and is seen by others, as a "tiger" is dangerous, tough, flexible and irresistible; even so, this man, this "animal," is not rejected by society—on the contrary, he often arouses others' admiration (1996, 123).

These paradoxes and ambiguities are discernible in the erotic construction of the *tíguere*. Dominican women and gay-identified men, for example, often lament their relationships with *tígueres,* who are believed to embody two somewhat contradictory qualities: they are both the symbol of masculine (erotic) prowess and the frequent perpetrators of myriad abuses and "*engaños*" (betrayals). In informal interviews with Dominican gay men, interviewees often described to me their frustration and dissatisfaction with the *tígueres* with whom they had developed intimate relationships but simultaneously felt a sexual compulsion for this "type" of man. While I did not directly study attitudes toward male partners among heterosexual Dominican women, informal conversations with numerous female friends—including many female sex workers at a local NGO—suggest a similar ambivalence toward the figure of the *tíguere,* who is seen as both a masculine ideal and an all-too-common prelude to unhappiness.[28] The normative construct of *tigueraje,* then, imbues the *tíguere* with both positive and negative masculine attributes, since he is simultaneously the pinnacle of manliness and the cause of considerable suffering by his partners.

The dualistic nature of the *tíguere*'s erotic construction parallels De Moya and García's (1996) description of the sociohistorical development of lower-class Dominican attitudes toward male homoeroticism, which they see as stemming from the juxtaposition of strong colonial proscriptions against homosexuality and an enduring, "transgressive" value placed on male-male sexuality and bonding. This configuration of public performance and private subversion, they argue, leads to a bifurcated notion of Dominican masculinity in which men "displayed a strong public homophobia, although comradeship and enduring friendship between males continued to be perceived as superior to relationships with females, who were frequently seen as 'cunning' and 'treacherous'" (1996, 124). They continue: "From those days on, it seems that inhabitants of the island utilized a paradoxical logic though which the simultaneous denial and assertion of the self became a generalized approach to social life, a magical resolution of Hamlet's dilemma ('to be' or 'not to be'), in which 'to be' and 'not to be' could smoothly coalesce and be confounded with each other" (ibid.).

Given such interpretations, the ways that male sex workers manage their intimate spousal relationships—avoiding conflict and detection through the skillful use of elaborate stories and "little lies"—reflect many of the distinguishing features of masculine *tigueraje*. Indeed, from one perspective, the identity of the *tíguere* would seem to predispose men to succeed at the social exigencies of sex work, since the continual management of information, described in the previous section, necessitates expertise in using ambiguity and paradox as "cover." Conversely, engagement in sex work might be seen to reinforce one's reputation as a *tíguere*, since it epitomizes in many ways the types of masculine behavior expected of the *tíguere*. Thus, it is important to ask how men's increasing activity in the sex tourism economy intersects with existing notions of Dominican masculinity, such as the qualities associated with a *tíguere* identity.

There is some precedent for such questions in the Caribbean, due to the growing literature on sex work from an anthropological or psychosocial analytical framework. Nevertheless, this literature is noticeably incomplete as regards a specific manifestation of Caribbean sex work that is of particular relevance to the research discussed here. The vast majority of anthropological or social scientific research on sex work in the region has either focused on female sex workers (Brennan 2004; Cabezas 1998; Castaneda et al. 1996; Kane 1993; Kempadoo 1999b; Pruitt and LaFont 1995) or analyzed male sex workers principally or solely in their roles as "gigolos" for female sex tourists (Phillips 1999; Press 1978; Pruitt and LaFont 1995). Yet what is precisely so compelling about the case of Dominican *bugarrones* and *sankies* is that while they are in many ways quintessential examples of lower-class masculine *tigueraje,* they engage in regular—albeit usually elaborately hidden— sexual-economic exchanges with other men. This fact has profound consequences for the ways that they understand themselves and relate to others as gendered beings in the world.

A focus on the heterosexual exchanges between male sex workers and female clients has meant that most studies in the Caribbean have tended to deemphasize the conflict between normative models of masculinity and engagement in sexual-economic exchanges. That is, several studies have reported that tourist-oriented male sex work in the Caribbean is not entirely antithetical to normative constructs of masculinity, as sex workers can enhance their masculine reputations through their (hetero)sexual conquests as well as draw upon rather conservative gender repertoires to improve their marketability to tourists. According to Pruitt and LaFont, for example, the Jamaican phenomenon of the "rent-a-dread" or "rent-a-Rasta" demonstrates how male sex workers "frequently draw on traditional models of male dominance to initiate relationships" with foreign women (Pruitt and LaFont 1995). Similarly, Phillips finds that a beach boy in Barbados is "able to demonstrate his 'skills of strength and knowledge' . . . in his role of tour guide and escort," since the female tourist "also allows him to be 'a man' and to adopt a dominant role in the relationship" (Phillips 1999, 197). This interpretation echoes Press's (1978) earlier study of Barbadian beach hustlers, which argues that men's exchanges with female tourists are a form of resistance to the restriction of economic options available to young males, as well as a way to enhance masculine esteem among their peers (see also Momsen 1994 and Kinnaird et al. 1994, 26). Kempadoo summarizes these interpretations as follows:

In settings where young men are economically and racially marginalized, expressions of this type of heterosexuality allow them access to one of the few socially respected power bases available to them. Sex with a female tourist who holds the economic dominant position in the relationship appears not to threaten or disrupt this culturally approved expression of masculinity but rather to enable feelings of personal worth and self-confidence. Although perhaps shunned by "decent" working men and women for their hustling activities, fundamental hegemonic constructions of Caribbean masculinity are not questioned or denied to the male heterosexual sex worker. An exchange of sex for material and financial benefits with a female tourist, instead, reaffirms conceptions of "real" Caribbean manhood, creating a space for . . . the liberation of a masculinity that, within the international context, is subordinated to an economically powerful, white masculinity. (Kempadoo 1999a, 24–5)

In the context of the Dominican sex workers with whom I conducted research, there is some evidence that men may gain access to certain avenues of masculine status through their participation in sex work. This is perhaps best evidenced by the use of global fashions and brand-name fetishism, discussed in chapter 3, to project a particularly globalized masculine identity. Nevertheless, the unqualified notion that their participation in sex work does not pose any serious challenges to their status as men neglects entirely the commonality of discreet sexual exchanges with other men, the shame and homophobia that is often associated with these exchanges, and the ways that such exchanges are meticulously "covered" in intimate and familial relationships. The centrality of these covering techniques to sex workers' subjective experience poses particular challenges to ethnographic interpretation, since that which is most readily observable regarding sex workers' exchanges does not always accurately reflect the reality of their sexual behavior. Mullings (1999, 76), for example, has noted that in Jamaica male sex work with female clients is "perhaps the most visible part of the Jamaican sex trade." Indeed, the "beach boy" phenomenon—with the *sanky panky* as its specifically Dominican cultural analog—seems to be a highly conspicuous expression of male sex tourism throughout the region. However, the high visibility of exchanges between male sex workers and female clients should not lead to a priori assumptions about the relative frequency of such exchanges, since—as described in chapter 5—discreet contacts between Dominican male sex workers and gay male tourists are more common, and represent a larger proportion of sex work income, than contacts with female clients, despite social stereotypes to the contrary.[29] The key difference, therefore, is in the ways that information about each type of exchange must be managed in order to minimize the negative social consequences of any potential breach of discretion. This is not intended to imply that scholarly accounts of male sex work in other Caribbean contexts have necessarily neglected the commonality of hidden homosexual exchanges, but merely to highlight the complexity of ethnographic interpretation given the vested interests sex workers have in covering their stigmatized activities.

The sociologist Erving Goffman has explained as follows the quandary faced by the stigmatized individual in his social relations: "The issue is not that of managing tension generated during social contacts, but rather that of managing information about his failing. To display or not to display; to tell or not to tell; to let on or not to let on; to lie or not to lie; and in each case to whom, how, when, and where" (1963, 42). This description seems an apt summary of the scenario confronted by many of the men discussed in this book, since they are continually evaluating whether, and to what extent, they can divulge information about themselves to others.[30] The stress that this generates for some men is evidenced by the catharsis they often felt during the interview process—occasionally resulting in the interview becoming a kind of therapeutic context—since many men had never before openly discussed the challenges of their continual information management. Thus, our conversations often focused on the shame sex workers felt about their engagement in sexual relations with men, as well as their anxieties about any potential discovery.[31]

Importantly, however, it seems to be sex workers' shame about their same-sex sexual behavior—rather than their evasive or deceptive behavior per se—that causes them the greatest anxiety. That is, intentionally misleading wives and partners does not apparently create a moral dilemma for most sex workers, as illustrated by Orlando's above comment that telling "little lies" is actually quite simple. This is also evidenced by the humor with which sex workers discuss their evasive techniques and collaborate to create mutually beneficial alibis. While it is quite plausible that the humorous tone of these conversations reflects the use of joking as a means to cope with anxiety or shame, it is also the case that these behaviors are consistent with the notion that the quintessential *tíguere* is one whose performative skill allows him to escape any difficult situation. Thus, evasion and covering, in and of themselves, are not necessarily stigmatizing, and indeed are expressions of many of the masculine qualities associated with *tigueraje*.

In addition, it is important to highlight that sex workers' strategies for information management are often supported to a certain degree by their families' emphasis on discretion—rather than direct communication—regarding male sexual "deviance." Whereas female sexuality in the Dominican Republic is relatively more guarded and controlled, male sexuality is not similarly subject to public surveillance. In this regard, Dominican masculinity allows for particular freedoms that mitigate the stigmatizing effects of sex work, recalling Kutsche's (1995, 117) description of the "*de ambiente*" man—a bisexually behaving man who does not self-identify as gay—in Costa Rica:

What any man does with his free time is his own business, so long as he supports his family and so long as he is discreet enough not to become publicly obnoxious. A "proper" man seeking other men is therefore not conspicuous. He is flamboyant, if at all, only during the leisure part of the day, when no one has a right to ask where he is, and only inside the walls of establishments which straights would not want to enter.

Thus, the relative permissiveness toward male sexuality and the gendered expectation of men's philandering assist *bugarrones* and *sankies* in evading detection, since men's sexuality is not as intensely policed as women's.[32] Further, the emphasis on discretion regarding men's sexual transgressions, as distinct from sexual restraint, means that men are unlikely to be confronted by family members unless there is a relatively public breach of social/sexual decorum—such as that described by Edgar when his brother and some friends witnessed him getting out of a client's Mercedes. To prevent such a breach, many sex workers attempt to compartmentalize their lives, separating their familial and spousal relations from the world of their sexual exchanges.

Kutsche's reference to the importance of men's "provider" role as a means by which men can circumvent objections by their wives points to the importance of men's economic contributions to the household as mitigating factors in the management of stigma. Similarly, Chevannes's work on Jamaican masculinity also mentions a rather dramatic case in which a bisexually behaving man beats his wife and tells her that "if she could not be satisfied with the little he could provide she could leave" (2001, 189). Such examples parallel comments made by *bugarrones* and *sanky pankies,* described above, and demonstrate the ways that their household support can be used to place limitations on a woman's right to object to infidelities or involvement in sex work. This technique, of course, embodies an implicit threat: men's economic contributions to the family are conditional and can be withdrawn if a woman complains excessively. Indeed, it is not inconsequential that the precarious nature of men's support for their wives and children—which has been described in widely varying Caribbean contexts— has also been connected to women's initiation into sex work (Farmer 1992; Kempadoo 1999b).[33]

In sum, what is perhaps most interesting about the strategies employed by male sex workers to avoid stigma and familial conflict is that they combine diverse, and somewhat incongruous, elements of masculine gender models to escape social censure. On the one hand, Dominican *tigueraje*— which shares many broad characteristics of Wilson's man of "reputation"— provides an ideological rationalization for men's infidelity, deception, and late-night carousing. On the other hand, men's "respectable" role as household provider can always be drawn upon to counter any potential criticism or indiscretion. The case of Dominican male sex workers thus provides another illustration of Alexander's (1984) argument, since it demonstrates that masculinity is a contested, polyvalent domain from which men can strategically draw, depending on the exigencies of the moment and the social or economic constraints they encounter.

5

"Love," Finance, and Authenticity in Gay Sex Tourism

The most sophisticated thing is to be in the new exotica. To be at the leading edge of modern capitalism is to eat fifteen different cuisines in any one week, not to eat one. It is no longer important to have boiled beef and Yorkshire pudding every Sunday. Who needs that? Because if you are just jetting in from Tokyo, via Harare, you come in loaded, not with "how everything is the same" but how wonderful it is, that everything is different.

STUART HALL

Transnational Space at Charlie's

A few blocks from the bustling pedestrian mall of El Conde is a small, inconspicuous corner bar called Charlie's. Every night of the week, as the sun goes down and Santo Domingo's colonial architecture begins to take on its distinct amber-gold hue, the forty-something, slightly overweight bartender, Héctor, opens the wooden front door facing a narrow side street. The iron security gate remains noticeably closed, allowing passersby a hazy view of the darkened interior through the black metal bars. At this early hour, children are still playing along the adjacent sidewalks of this mostly residential barrio, and the men who gather at the *colmado* across the street prepare for a lazy evening of dominoes, rum, and animated political commentary. After nearly twenty years of operation, Charlie's seems to blend almost imperceptibly into the local rhythm of life, despite the relatively peculiar nature of the activities that occur there. Neighbors have grown accustomed to the taxis that pass by to drop off or pick up their passengers—tourists from one of the gay-friendly hotels or, perhaps, arriving directly from the airport—and often stop by to chat with the *bugarrones* who prop themselves for hours against the weathered concrete wall outside the establishment.

Leonardo, the husky *portero* and well-known *maipiolo,* arrives around 7:30 and takes his usual seat on the stool just inside the iron gate. From here, he maintains a steady watch over the activities on the street, prepared to come to the assistance of clients whose incautious display of dollars or jewelry occasionally attract the attention of muggers, or to warn his fellow *bugarrones* at the first signs of a police patrol. It was Leonardo who came to my rescue one night when a side window of my car was broken and a backpack full of research materials stolen by a young *tíguere* known to torment tourists in the neighborhood.[1] But on a busy night at Charlie's, most of the patrons and sex workers that gather inside the bar do not appear to be concerned with these potential dangers. They are too occupied with *la búsqueda* (the search). Gay tourists, often bleary-eyed from ingesting obscene amounts of rum, and red-faced from a weekend at the beach, size up the young, muscled men who strategically display themselves at the tables along the perimeter. During the high tourist season, or when gay tour groups are in town, the small bar can become so crowded that *bugarrones* who can no longer squeeze through the doorway gather instead along the street outside and attempt to solicit from clients as they stumble into their taxis. Translators and *guías*—such as the famous "El Loco" (the crazy one), an ex-*bugarrón* whose age and diminishing physical condition now preclude direct sexual exchanges—function as middlemen between clients and sex workers, hoping to broker contacts that will bring commissions roughly equivalent to five dollars per contact. Héctor, in his relatively powerful position as bartender, manages to make a living by strategically overcharging the drunken tourists, extracting commissions from sex workers, or flirtatiously soliciting generous tips. And the police officers who regularly pass by on their motorcycles extort payments from *bugarrones* as they leave the bar with a client or attempt to walk home after an unsuccessful evening.

All of this is presided over by Charlie's somewhat unlikely owner, Simon, a gay British ex-pat whose air of sophistication—symbolized by the large picture of the queen of England that graces one wall—seems somewhat out of sync with the bar's otherwise humble surroundings. Simon, enticed years ago by the erotic allure of the Dominican Republic, sold his businesses in Spain and England and began Charlie's as an extension of his private home, which is located adjacent to the bar and easily accessible through a door that reads simply "*Privado*" (private). A slight old man and self-defined alcoholic who continues to sip his imported gin despite advanced cirrhosis of the liver, he seems to take a certain pleasure in quietly watching over his "boys" and joking with the tourists who make their way in and out of his otherwise insular world. Despite the fact that he speaks little Spanish and rarely leaves his home, he continues to advise his tourist clientele—who treat him as a sort of grandfatherly expert on the local men-for-hire—on the best ways to enjoy the *bugarrones*. "One of the most common questions they ask me is 'How big is he?'" Simon told me in an interview. "That's foremost on their mind. It's just the interest in their dick. But, of course, you would expect those kinds of questions in a bar of this type."

Perched on his personal barstool with a cigarette balanced precariously in one hand and a drink in the other, Simon seems to enjoy discussing his past with me amidst the cacophony of merengue mixed with inebriated laughter. "It's not a bad life they're leading," he reflects when I ask him about the *bugarrones'* choice of profession. "I don't know what the average Dominican wage is right now—maybe 2,000 pesos a month [approximately U.S.$117 in the year 2001]—and they can make that with a tourist, you know, in four or five days, maybe less. Maybe all at one go." As we watch a middle-aged, overweight New Yorker select three boys, and the entire entourage squeeze into a taxi outside, I comment to Simon (who is giving them a delicate wave goodbye) about the apparently great variety of tourists that come into his bar/home. "Oh, dear, here we get the kinky ones and the first-timers. We've had several porno directors, who film the boys in one of the hotels around here. And, of course, we get the weird fantasies." With an unexpectedly loud shriek of laughter, Simon proceeds to tell me about the infamous repeat visitor "Mr. Poo-Poo," so named by the local boys because of his notorious fecal fetish. "But he always manages to pay enough to get what he wants," he reflects, in a suddenly hushed tone—as if out of fear that one of his boys might overhear him.[2]

The "Western Union Daddy"

I remember the first time I encountered one of my "informants" in a Western Union office in Santo Domingo. His name was Rogelio, and he worked regularly as a stripper at one of the gay discos near the Parque Olímpico. Rogelio, known for his impressive physique, was one of the *bugarrón* success stories—at least for the moment—and was enjoying the peak of his popularity among the tourists. As I was filling out my paperwork for a balance transfer from the United States, I overheard Rogelio chatting in extremely broken English over one of the international phone lines along the wall. A few moments later, he strolled over and stretched out his hand to me, and by way of greeting, we exchanged the obligatory "*¿como tu 'ta?*" (how are you?). Before I could stop myself, I blurted, "*¿Qué tu haces aquí?*" (What are you doing here?). Perhaps the abruptness of my question, which I later regretted, was motivated by the cognitive dissonance that I, like many sex workers themselves, often felt upon encountering a "knowing other" in the context of public space. In any case, Rogelio seemed nonplussed. "I'm here picking up a little present from a friend," he winked, as he flashed me the wad of bills he held in his hand.

In the course of my fieldwork, I had several such encounters with *bugarrones* in Western Union offices, and even assisted some of them in receiving payments from their "friends" abroad.[3] As described for Miguel in the previous chapter, who receives a steady monthly payment of U.S.$150 from his regular client Larry, these remittances can make the difference between meeting basic expenses and living on the street, particularly for those who have no support from family. Thus, while exchanges with tourists are, in general, transient encounters, they can be highly lucrative when they develop into longer-term relationships that transcend direct sex-for-money exchanges. Indeed, a prior study of seventy-six male sex workers in Santo Domingo found that half of them had foreign clients who sent them remittances from abroad or brought them gifts during their regular visits to the Dominican Republic (Ruiz and Vásquez 1993, 58).[4] Tourists such as Larry, who send regular payments to their Dominican "boys" while abroad, do not appear to be seeking the impersonal, dehumanized sexual object associated with a certain modality of sex tourism.[5] Indeed, in many ways these relationships resemble what Pruitt and LaFont (1995) have described as "romance tourism," a phenomenon that is also given considerable attention by the contributors to the recent volume on Caribbean sex tourism *Sun, Sex, and Gold* (Kempadoo 1999b).[6] Nevertheless, these analyses have focused exclusively on "romantic," long-term exchange relationships between male sex workers and female clients. How are these dynamics the same or different in same-sex interactions?

The men I refer to as "Western Union daddies"—because of the nature of their remittances and their generally older age—resemble certain features of the male clients of female sex workers in the coastal town of Sosúa, Dominican Republic, as described by anthropologist Amalia Cabezas (1999). Cabezas observes that many of the female sex workers with whom she spoke preferred entering into longer relationships with foreign clients who sent them monthly remittances for "buying gifts such as electrical appliances and clothing for [their] children" (ibid., 99), and who often returned to visit. She notes that sometimes these clients provide the women "plane tickets and visas for travel," the latter being the goal of many female sex workers who fantasize about reaching "La Gloria" (ibid.). In their narratives about the best types of clients, many of these women express a clear preference for foreign tourists over locals, as described by Cabezas in her discussion of women who work in tourist-oriented establishments:

The majority of the women interviewed in this category had not worked with a local clientele. Those that had, indicated that they much preferred to work with foreigners, because Dominican men are considered rough with the women, mistreating them and calling them names; they are verbally and sexually abusive, and they are always reluctant to wear condoms. Foremost, women make a lot less money in these establishments [those oriented toward local clients], they cannot control their hours, and the business owners dominate and abuse them. In comparison, foreigners pay them a lot more money, and they have the possibility of migrating or traveling to other countries (ibid., 98)

Cabezas subsequently quotes an informant, Leonor, who recalled that her grandfather had given her the following advice: "Instead of getting pregnant by one of those *tigres* [pimps] from here that only want to beat you and live off of you, that it was better for me to sleep with a gringo [foreigner] so that way I can support my kids" (1999, 109).[7]

This preference for foreign clients is also reflected in prior studies among male sex workers in the Dominican Republic. In a study by Ruiz and Vásquez (1993) of seventy-six lower-class *bugarrones* in Santo Domingo, the average number of male clients per year was thirty-six, of which nearly half (17) were foreign tourists. Tourists were described as "better" clients because of the higher price that they were generally willing to pay for sex, a finding that is consistent with De Moya et al.'s (1992) study among *sanky pankies* in the tourist town of Sosúa. Similarly, in a KABP (Knowledge, Attitudes, Beliefs, and Practices) study of 188 Dominican bisexual men, Ramah et al. (1992) found a high rate of participation in sex work among lower-class men, for whom foreign tourists or higher-class men were their preferred clients.

In their exchanges with male clients, the *bugarrones* and *sankies* in this study similarly show a strong preference for foreigners, often alluding to the fact that such clients represent *dinero fácil* in the context of an otherwise difficult economic environment. Martín, for example, explained to me as follows the reasons he prefers tourists as clients: "I've gone for about ten or twelve years without work. So, you know, here in the Dominican Republic things are really hard, so since there are some opportunities with some guys

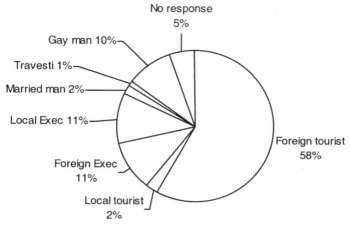

Figure 6. Preferred male clients

who come from abroad, and they offer you money or something to be with them, you grab it, you understand? It's the easiest way to get money. That's what's going on."

The preference for foreign clients is evident in the survey data on preferred clients, as summarized in figure 6, which shows an overwhelming bias toward foreigners.[8]

A preference for foreign clients is also reflected in the nationalities of sex workers' last male clients, of whom 64 percent (107/168) were foreigners.[9] For these 107 sex workers, the breakdown of last-client nationality is shown in figure A.5 in the appendix. Of interest here is the fact that the greatest proportion of tourist-clients originated from the United States (36 percent), followed by Puerto Rico (16 percent) and Italy (14 percent).[10] These percentages are roughly similar to the distributions for sex workers' last regular male tourist-clients. For the purpose of the survey, regular male clients were defined as those with whom participants had engaged in at least three separate encounters, generally considered a marker for a more involved, steady relationship. These regular clients are also those with whom it was more likely for sex workers to develop long-term economic relationships involving remittances from abroad. There were 118 participants who indicated they'd had regular male clients, of whom seventy-two (61 percent) indicated that their last regular client was a foreigner.[11] The breakdown of client nationality for the last regular tourist-client is shown in figure A.6 (appendix).[12]

Survey participants were also asked to estimate the age range of their last regular tourist-client, and the modal age range was between thirty-five and thirty-nine years (19 percent). Interestingly, last tourist-clients were significantly older when they were classified as "regular" clients as opposed to "new" clients ($p < .05$). That is, the modal age distribution is significantly higher for regular tourist-clients than for first-time tourist-clients, a finding that is consistent with ethnographic observations. Tourists I observed on repeat trips to the Dominican Republic for the purpose of visiting one or two specific sex workers were generally older than those who divided their time among numerous men or expressed interest in a greater variety of erotic experiences. This suggests a life-course pattern in which younger clients use sex tourism as a means of erotic exploration with multiple partners, while older clients seek more stable and intimate relationships with specific sex workers.

Similarly, a number of sex workers expressed a preference for older clients. For example, I had the following exchange with Jaime in an interview:

MP: So, who are your favorite clients? I mean, what are they like?

Jaime: Well, what can I tell you? I don't know exactly which ones are my favorites, but what I do know is that older clients [*clientes de mayor edad*] pay more for the young guys.

MP: So, they tend to pay more?

Jaime: Yeah.

MP: But that must be difficult because older clients don't always look so good, like you just told me, so it must be more difficult with them [sexually]. So is it better for you to leave with an older client who pays more or a young client that looks better?

Jaime: I think with the older client, because—how can I explain it? The idea isn't that I like him, but rather the end: getting the money.

Further, to the degree that older clients are more oriented toward regular, intimate relationships, it is likely that they provide a steadier source of income than younger clients. It is also quite possible that older clients, by virtue of their stage of professional career, have more disposable income, enabling them to provide more extensive economic support through remittances and gifts. These findings are consistent with those of Ruiz and Vásquez (1993, 60), who report that 62 percent of the male sex workers they surveyed preferred older clients, many of them because these "viejos" (old men) were believed to have more money.

As suggested in the previous chapter, steady clients, whether foreign or local, often provide a safety net for men who have no steady wage or whose income does not meet their basic needs. Sex workers often explained to me that these longer-term relationships are more reliable than simple one-night

TABLE 6: Types of economic support from last regular tourist-client

Remittance	Basic needs	Child support	Other
1,000 pesos RD / month	Food (4)	Daughter's cradle	Household items
Money when needed	Clothing / shoes (9)	Children's clothes	Cable T.V.
300 dollars / month	Rent for apartment	Baseball fees	Travel
50 dollars / week	Home construction	School tuition (2)	Jewelry
50 dollars / month	Motorcycle (5)		Cellular phone
	Furniture		Misc. gifts

Note: N = 66. When more than one participant mentioned a given type of support, the number of participants is indicated in parentheses. Multiple answers per participant were permitted.

stands, as illustrated by Martín's response when I asked him why he had chosen to focus more attention on his regular clients: "Listen, what happens with the gays and the money is that most of the time it's momentary. You grab a guy, he gives you something, and that's what you made that night, like I told you. But if you have two regular ones, they're more definite than those that you grab for the night, you understand? Because when you need them, they're going to be there to help you."

The importance of regular clients to sex workers' general economic situation is further demonstrated by the types of economic support received from steady foreign clients, as shown in table 6, which summarizes survey responses regarding the types of economic support received by sex workers from their last regular tourist-client. Of the seventy-two sex workers who reported having regular male tourist-clients, sixty-six (92 percent) said these clients had provided them economic support that went beyond direct payments for sex. Further, types of support from steady clients are much more diverse than the simple cash gifts typical of the more direct sex-for-money exchanges with new clients. Table 6 shows that support from regular clients, while frequently including cash, is often oriented toward assisting sex workers with a wide variety of expenses, including such items as household construction materials, automobiles or motorcycles, and educational expenses. It is also noteworthy that sex workers occasionally cite support for their children in their descriptions of regular clients' forms of assistance, a pattern that parallels statements by Dominican female sex workers (Cabezas 1998).[13]

Importantly, the remittances received from regular foreign clients must be understood in the larger context of the dependence on remittances from abroad that characterizes the Dominican economy more generally. Grasmuck and Pessar estimated that in the year 1981, the single city of Santiago, Dominican Republic, received approximately U.S.$13 million in the form of regular remittances from migrant family members abroad (1991, 71). As their work aptly demonstrates, the influx of remittances from abroad functions for many Dominican families as a means to cope with falling real wages and the restriction of local employment options, while enabling them to acquire certain foreign consumer goods that are increasingly symbolic of the "middle class" (ibid.: 71–74). Indeed, in Latin America and the Caribbean, the volume of remittances to the Dominican Republic is surpassed only by Mexico and Brazil, and in 2001 the value of Dominican remittances was three times the value of all its agricultural exports (Multilateral Investment Fund 2001, 6).[14] Viewed in this light, the cash gifts sex workers receive from their regular clients abroad are a microcosm of a global economic flow from the "core" to the "periphery" upon which the local economy has come to depend. It is perhaps not surprising, then, that sex workers value their regular foreign clients, since the commonality of support from migrant family members has undoubtedly taught many of them about the importance of regular remittances from abroad. It is also worth noting that standard estimates of the value of foreign remittances entirely neglect the payments received from sex work clients abroad, which may be quite significant in countries with a significant sex tourism industry.

Given the level of economic support from regular male clients and the relatively greater intimacy that characterizes these relationships, how do sex workers feel toward the men with whom they develop such long-term relationships? This is a complex question, since such exchanges are infused with contradictory interests, motivations, and emotions. As described throughout this book, *bugarrones* and *sanky pankies* often express shame about their sexual exchanges with men, suggesting a fundamental ambivalence about their relationships with men. As discussed in chapter 4, many sex workers mitigate the shame they feel about their same-sex encounters by employing information management techniques that decrease the possibility of discovery by family, friends, and neighbors. This, however, does not necessarily eliminate the anxiety and emotional turmoil many of them feel regarding their own sexual behavior and identity, regardless of whether others are aware of the nature of their activity. These anxieties can intensify when relationships with male clients develop into longer-term arrangements involving a certain degree of intimacy, because clients often expect more "authentic" expressions of affection from their partners, and because sex workers may begin to develop feelings for their long-term clients that conflict with their own self-perceptions and definitions.

The ambivalence sex workers feel toward regular clients manifests itself in a number of ways. In their conversations with me, for example, sex workers frequently avoided the use of terms of emotional attachment in describing their relationships with regular clients. This is related to the common belief that it is gay men, not *"hombres normales"* (normal men), who develop strong emotional feelings for other men. Thus, the denial of an emotional bond with regular clients—and especially a bond that would imply an inappropriate level of attachment to another man—served to preserve their macho self-image and allay any fears about becoming a *maricón*.[15] Nevertheless, their efforts to maintain a safe emotional distance from their regular clients were often complicated by their growing affection for them, and many emphasized how well their "amigos" treated them. The result is that their descriptions of their relationships with regular clients often reveal a tension between expressions of genuine affection and the desire to maintain an appropriate level of emotional distance. For example, I had the following exchange with Cesar in our conversation about his relationship with Jacob, a regular client from the United States:

MP: So, do you think you're in love with him?

Cesar: No!

MP: No? Why not?

Cesar: I haven't fallen in love, but just—when he leaves on trips, I miss him [*me hace falta*], like, hanging out with him, you understand? It's like when you're used to eating a particular dish, and the day that you don't eat it, you feel bad because you didn't eat rice. You understand?

MP: Yeah.

Cesar: That's how it is when he's not here.

MP: You miss him?

Cesar: Yeah. Well—we're always running around on the beach and everything, you know?

MP: Ahum. Okay. You miss that: the experience, the sharing, and everything with him.

Cesar: Yeah.

Here, Cesar is struggling to achieve a balance between an accurate description of his feelings for Jacob and his desire to avoid an admission of strong emotional attachment, resulting in a narrative that reveals contradictions, hesitations, and partial retractions. His metaphorical comparison of his feelings for Jacob with an acquired taste for rice—a bland dish, in any case—seems to be an attempt to downplay his prior assertion that he "misses" him, as well as to counter my somewhat threatening question about his "falling in love." Later, my clarifying question about whether he "misses" Jacob seems to elicit an affirmative answer, yet this is quickly followed by a retraction that focuses not on Cesar's feelings for Jacob, but rather the impersonal experience of "running around on the beach." Taken together, these linguistic strategies reflect his desire to configure his feelings for Jacob as "normal" rather than inappropriately affectionate or romantic.

Sex workers' tendency to distance themselves emotionally from regular clients is also demonstrated by survey responses about affective relations with last regular clients. Several yes/no questions were designed to explore participants' reactions to a series of phrases describing progressively deeper emotional attachments to regular male clients. These questions followed an extensive inquiry into the history of participants' relationships with their last regular tourist-clients that included questions about sexual activities and safer sex practices (see chap. 7). The relevant questions are:

- Do you feel your last regular client treats you well?
- Do you trust your last regular client?
- Do you feel affection for your last regular client?
- Do you love your last regular client?[16]

The proportion of "yes" responses to these questions is shown in figure A.7 (appendix). As expected, sex workers tended to answer affirmatively in lower proportions to questions that implied a greater degree of emotional involvement. From one perspective, this seems to be a logical result, since it is reasonable that fewer relationships would develop to a level that would represent mutual "love." Nevertheless, there is more to these patterns than is immediately apparent.

For example, the comparison of answers to two additional survey questions is telling. When participants were asked a general question about whether a *bugarrón*—that is, any *bugarrón*—could fall in love with another man, responses were overwhelmingly positive, with 79 percent (158/199) agreeing that this was possible. On the other hand, when they were asked a direct personal question about whether they themselves could fall in love with another man, only 35 percent (70/199) acknowledged that this was possible. The difference between these answers represents the degree to which sex workers are motivated to deny their own emotional attachments to other men, as these are considered "abnormal" expressions of eroticism and signs of homosexuality that are threatening to their sense of self.[17]

In our conversations, the ambivalence that sex workers felt regarding their own emotional attachments to regular clients often manifested itself in their rhetorical emphasis on the performative aspects of their "love." That is, they sought to depict their outward affection for their regular clients as an exigency of their occupation and often joked about the "ridiculous" things they have to do to convince their partners of the authenticity of their feelings. "I feel like an idiot sometimes," one *bugarrón* explained about his romantic performances for clients, "but I do it super well." These performances are often necessary because the credibility of their "love" and affection can have a direct bearing on clients' willingness to continue visiting Santo Domingo or to send remittances from abroad. It is useful in this context to recall from chapter 4 the explicit threat by Larry, Miguel's regular client: "If [anybody] tells me that you're working, I'm not going to Santo Domingo anymore." This sets up a financial scenario in which Miguel is forced, if he is to continue receiving the lucrative remittances from New York, to give a convincing show of love, affection, and—in this case—fidelity.

Precisely because of the need to perform romance, a certain proportion of sex workers refuse to enter into longer-term relationships with clients, preferring the more mechanical, instrumental, and impersonal encounters typical of exchanges with new clients. Rafael, for example, explained to me that he avoided steady clients, because they required him to do things that made him feel uncomfortable as a "macho" and therefore were not worth the potential economic benefits:

Rafael: Actually, the ones that come from *allá* [over there, meaning "abroad"], some of them want to have, like, a relationship. But you see, you have to do lots of things for that, and that doesn't happen with me.

MP: Why doesn't it happen?

Rafael: Because I'm not going to make you feel—I don't do whatever you want. You have to satisfy a *maricón* with things that you don't—if you're a *machista*—you wouldn't do, you understand? So, they tell me, like, that I'm cold, but I tell them, "No, man!" because I don't do that. . . . I'm telling you, honestly, sometimes you try to make them fall in love with you and they don't give you anything. It's not worth it, you see? Keep that away from me! Look, shit, I treat you with affection [*cariño*] and nothing. . . . You know, you go with them and you give them a little caress [*caricia*], and later you tell him, "Sweetie, I'm in love" [*estoy enamorado*]. And me, lying down with him hugging me—it looks bad. I don't like that shit.

Thus, individual sex workers must weigh their own willingness to perform romance—which occasionally requires behavior that is decidedly un-macho—against the potential economic benefits of these performances.[18]

Nevertheless, as illustrated by figure A.7, it is important to emphasize that a significant proportion of sex workers acknowledge feeling affection for, or even being "in love" with, one or more of their regular clients. How are we to understand the affective dimensions of these relationships, particularly when they are so fraught with differences of race, class, and nationality? In fact, even in those cases in which affection or love was openly expressed, emotional attachment was very often framed within the context of the material benefits that resulted from these relationships. In sex workers' discourses about favorite clients, for example, one of the primary rationales for feeling genuine "*cariño*" for a client was the provision of extensive economic benefits and gifts. "Best clients" are almost always described as those who are financially generous, as opposed to the contemptible "*tacaños*" (stingy ones) who are constantly devising ways to cheat the "boys." Often, these stereotypes are couched in nationalistic terms. That is, there are those countries from which clients tend to be more generous or more *tacaño*, although I could detect no clear consensus among sex workers on this point.[19] What is clear is that a positive emotional valence toward a client is more consistently associated with generous material benefits than with nearly any other personality trait. And, as described in the following section, this is precisely the source of anxiety for many Western Union daddies, since the fact of their economic contributions never allows them to feel entirely secure about the authenticity of their partners' affection.

"No Romance without Finance": Gay Tourist Narratives of Authenticity

[Tourism] involves for the participants a separation from normal "instrumental" life and the business of making a living, and offers entry into another kind of moral state in which mental, expressive, and cultural needs come to the fore. It is no wonder, then, that tourism is often identified with "re-creation"—the renewal of life, the recharging of run-down elements—so necessary for the maintenance of mental and bodily health which characterize a balanced life style—*mens sane in corpora sana.*[20]

I met Jeffrey, an early-forties paralegal from New York, through an Internet chat group oriented toward gay tourism to the Dominican Republic, where I had posted a message about conducting interviews with sex-work clients during their trips to Santo Domingo. After corresponding, we agreed to meet during his next trip to Santo Domingo, and we conducted our first interview at a gay hotel near the Zona Colonial in May 2000. This interview was the beginning of a regular correspondence relationship over the next two years in which Jeffrey kept me informed of his "adventures" in the Dominican Republic and his developing relationship with Fernando, a regular *bugarrón* at Charlie's bar. I also interacted regularly with Fernando throughout my fieldwork, both in the presence of Jeffrey and during the latter's long absences in New York, and Fernando participated in various formal stages of this research. In addition, Fernando and Jeffrey solicited my translation services for their long-distance phone calls between Santo Domingo and New York, since the occasionally complex negotiations of their transnational relationship often required a linguistic precision that exceeded their language abilities. The longitudinal quality of the ethnographic material with Jeffrey and Fernando is useful in illustrating many of the dimensions of authenticity that are central to sexual-economic exchanges. It also permits a glimpse into the complex emotional attachments and economic arrangements that develop as relationships based on "sex tourism" are gradually reconfigured as those based on "romance"—a transformation that is always fraught with questions of authenticity.

During our initial interview, Jeffrey described his relationship to the *bugarrones* as one based primarily on anonymous sexual exploration, although he had already established a regular relationship with two sex workers, one of whom was Fernando. Nevertheless, as he later wrote to me from New York, his initial infatuation was not with Fernando, but with Leonardo, the husky doorman from Charlie's:

I remember telling you something along the lines of I have no problem separating my emotions from the whole scene and not emotionally falling for these boys. Well, I've been having a little bit of problem with that since returning to NYC this time. I certainly wouldn't call it Love (if it is—I will REMAIN in denial). But I have a strong infatuation with Leonardo. Now I've been through enough in life to know that infatuations don't last. But still, all in all, I'm feeling these things for him. And I don't particularly like it. All of his kindness and sincerity put aside, the bottom line is that he is a PROSTITUTE. But feeling this infatuation with him leaves me open and vulnerable. For instance, I told him that I would wire him $50 on my payday. Now, Mark, honestly, I live paycheck to paycheck and really can't afford to be sending these boys money. Unlike a lot of these queens who go there all the time, I have to save money for my little jaunts to Santo Domingo. And then I think that if I send Leonardo $50, then I should send Fernando the same—to keep from hurting Fernando's feelings. It's crazy. But I know I'll do it anyway.

This initial correspondence represents the beginning of Jeffrey's ongoing internal debate about the fundamental nature of his relationships with Dominican *bugarrones,* a debate that centered principally on the meanings of his financial contributions and the underlying motivations for his "boys" to continue their relationships with him. These questions intensified as his trips to Santo Domingo became more frequent, trips which he described to me in an interview as a kind of "obsession." The latter is epitomized by the compulsive nature of his remittances, which is a theme of his letters, and is represented in the above correspondence by the final line, "But I know I'll do it anyway." Such linguistic constructions demonstrate the degree to which Jeffrey perceives his remittances as something beyond his voluntary control, and much of his correspondence revolves around his attempts to understand the psychological roots of his own obsessive financial relationships with Dominican men. Indeed, he confided in one letter that he often found his correspondence with me somewhat cathartic, in contrast to his conversations with fellow sex tourists who display similar compulsive tendencies:

You know this corresponding with you has really helped me to sort out my feelings. I tried to get into a similar dialogue on the phone with one of my fellow "traveling sisters" in Atlanta, but Miss Thing is already carrying around so much emotional baggage of her own, that she really couldn't offer me any constructive feedback. She's been to Santo Domingo 15 times in the last 10 months! But Miss Thing is loaded and can afford it like that. God only knows if I had that kind of money, I'd be doing the same! She said she has 3 of these boys constantly calling her for Western Union gifts.[21]

In later correspondence, Jeffrey began to reflect more directly on the psychological motives behind his own financial contributions, as well as on the authenticity of the affection that Fernando and Leonardo expressed to him. He narrated as follows the final day of one of his trips to Santo Domingo:

You see, I was running out of money on my last day (as I always do), and I knew I wasn't going to have anymore to give them, and I certainly wanted some more Pinga before I left![22] They have both told me that unlike their other clients, I can give them what I want. Matter of fact, Fernando never asks for anything. And the only thing Leonardo will say is "I have to go to see my family now and I need to take them 500 pesos," or something similar. They tell me that I am their friend, not just a tourist. It is very touching. Whether it is an orchestrated and rehearsed scene or not (but I don't think it is), it is very touching to me. But after I had said to them at the beach that I would wire them money next week, somehow I felt in control and in charge of the whole situation again. Nothing changed about them after I mentioned money. They were their same festive selves as before. Would they have continued to stay with me the last night if there had been no money offered? I would like to think so, and I think that may have been the case—but I don't know for sure. At any rate, they never allow me to go from point A to point B in Santo Domingo without one of them escorting me. And that's very touching.

Here, Jeffrey displays more introspection in his understanding of his own financial contributions, making explicit reference to his feeling "in control" after making his financial offer to Fernando and Leonardo. Nevertheless, he is unable to entirely dispel the suspicion that his boys' affection is actually "an orchestrated and rehearsed scene," despite the fact that he ultimately finds their "act" convincing and "touching." In this narrative, Jeffrey makes one of his first references to what he later calls the "what-if question"— referring to the hypothetical consequences if he were to discontinue his financial support—a question that seems to cause him considerable emotional turmoil. In one message, for example, he writes, "If I REALLY wanted to know the answer, I'd stop with the $$." As far as I am aware, however, Jeffrey has never actually carried out this test, preferring to continue sending remittances and coping with the constant questions about the authenticity of his partners' affection. This is preferable to the pain of verifying what he has suspected all along, as illustrated by his closing remark in one message: "Is it really 'No Romance without Finance?'"

In several of Jeffrey's letters, there are scattered references to the distinctions between Dominican *bugarrones* and hustlers in New York, a pattern in gay sex tourists' narratives and a primary motive for their attraction to the country. Jeffrey, for example, described to me the "jaded" attitude of the "strung-out," drug-addicted hustlers in New York, and the fact that Dominican *bugarrones* are "clean" and "predictable" in comparison.[23] Such tourist narratives often incorporate references to cultural differences that are eroticized, including, for example, the ways Dominican men move their bodies when dancing the merengue, or the machismo expressed in their gestures. Many gay sex tourists also eroticize the fact that Dominican sex workers do not generally consider themselves to be gay, allowing the tourist to realize a fantasy that is not "thinkable" within the sex/gender logic of the United States and Europe: to have sex with a truly "straight" man.[24] Finally, the poor economic condition of the Dominican Republic—and of sex workers in particular—is a common feature of these tourist narratives, and often functions as a justification for continued remittances as well as a way to mitigate ambivalence about the combination of "romance" and "finance."

Many of these narrative features are evident in a notable passage in one of Jeffrey's messages from June 2000:

In March, Leonardo took me to meet his family and have dinner with them (his sister, nieces, nephews and mother—I saw no girlfriend or wife). And I saw the conditions they live in. Granted it was very clean considering the circumstances. But they had no running water, electricity was haphazardly strung up everywhere and cement floors. Which is something I love about the Dominican people who have never been here. They haven't been exposed to the blatant materialism we have here, and they appear to have a tranquility about them. They seem to love their culture, their language, the food, their music, etc. But when I saw the way they lived I knew that even a few dollars would go a long way to help them. And it seems that almost all the money that Leonardo gets goes back to them. And I'm sure Fernando's family is the same way. And Leonardo and Fernando are not alcoholics or drug addicts who are going to blow every dime you give them on getting fucked up. They put the money to good use—whether it's for their family or for something for them to wear or eat.

Here, Jeffrey is explicit about the fundamental differences between North Americans and Dominicans, particularly those who have not been "exposed" to the negative (modern) influences of the developed world—an ironic contrast given the commonality of transnational migration and exchange that characterizes Dominicans of all social classes.[25] The idea that his remittances were "put . . . to good use" seems to be one of the primary ways that he was able to reach a tentative resolution to the "what-if" dilemma of his financial contributions. This is because his focus on the conditions of poverty and deprivation allowed him to psychologically reconfigure his payments as a kind of humanitarian assistance, rather than (or, perhaps, in addition to) compensation for sex, affection, or companionship. Thus, while providing a way to configure himself as an empathetic benefactor rather than a sex tourist, his focus on his boys' poverty permitted him to alleviate the ambivalence he felt about sending remittances to Leonardo and Fernando. In this context, it is also important to note that sex workers are well aware of the potential economic benefits of performing poverty for their regular clients, and often expressed this as a strategy for gaining empathy that could lead to more generous payments from tourists.

By March 2001, more than a year after his first remittances to Fernando and Leonardo, Jeffrey reported that he had begun to suspect Leonardo's motives, particularly because he seemed to be trying to cheat Fernando out of his portion of the payments. "I'm wondering if Leonardo wasn't going to one Western Union to pick up his money with his I.D.," he wrote in one letter, "and then going to another Western Union and getting Fernando's money." The conflict that ensued between Leonardo and Fernando typifies the tension that often develops between competing sex workers when a regular client proves to be particularly generous. Subsequent correspondence with Jeffrey revealed that Leonardo and Fernando were no longer in communication, and each had a different—and conflicting—story about the other's motives in relation to Jeffrey.[26] At the same time, Jeffrey began to express greater affection for Fernando, and his subsequent trips to Santo Domingo focused almost exclusively on this relationship.

Some of the correspondence from this period is noteworthy in that it demonstrates the ways that sex tourism can become a fundamental feature of one's psychological coping style—a kind of "drug," as Jeffrey once described it to me—leaving one feeling empty and depressed between vacations. Jeffrey often spoke to me about his desire to live in the Dominican Republic, but his linguistic limitations and "paycheck-to-paycheck" existence in New York made this untenable. In one message, he clearly expresses his emotional state upon his return to New York following a trip to Santo Domingo:

I am still in a FUNK. I'm feel like as if I'm walking around like a programmed robot. Get up, get dressed, take the f-ing 7 train to the City, work all day and half the night, go home, go to sleep and do it all over again. And all this just so I can go back to the DR again. I have absolutely no interest in anything going on in this City. My dearest friend is not speaking to me now because he says all I have is the DR on my mind. He's right, you know. I am so f-ing DEPRESSED! I feel so NEEDY!!!

Passages such as this, echoed in various messages from Jeffrey, illustrate a dimension of sex tourism that is rarely addressed in scholarly discussions: the ways that it can be used, perhaps largely unconsciously, as a means to deal with emotional problems "back home." While for obvious reasons I cannot (nor do I wish to) assess Jeffrey's emotional health, it is nevertheless clear that his behavior—including a highly obsessive relationship with Dominican *bugarrones*, a compulsive overtime work schedule in order to pay for the next trip to Santo Domingo, and a generally depressed attitude toward life in New York—suggests that his participation in sex tourism be understood within the larger framework of his emotional life. As a forty-something, somewhat overweight gay man living a marginally middle-class life in New York, the Dominican Republic has provided him the opportunity to see himself as desirable by men whom he views as fundamentally different from the hustlers (and perhaps all men) in New York. *Bugarrones* are real men; they are true machos who are not "jaded" by the "materialism" of the modern world; they are happy in spite of their circumstances; and they are pleased to accept whatever he is willing to send them to "help out." Indeed, in Jeffrey's conceptualization, Santo Domingo is everything that New York is not, suggesting a kind of splitting or bifurcation of his emotional/ geographical universe into the modern turmoil of New York and the idyllic fantasyland of the *bugarrones*. Being able to control the affection of others through economic resources—something that would be impossible for him among the more expensive hustlers in New York—allows him to gain a degree of control over what may otherwise be a more difficult erotic terrain at home. Thus, Santo Domingo provides him a temporary escape not only from the unsatisfying grind of work, but also, in a certain way, from a sense of himself that he finds in some way unfulfilling. As a Western Union daddy, he is able to see himself in a different light, as someone worthy of the attention of men, as an empathetic benefactor—as anything but ordinary.

At the time of this writing, Jeffrey and Fernando continue their visiting relationship, which has developed into one they both characterize as "love." Jeffrey has continued to send regular remittances and provides Fernando with relatively expensive gifts, most recently a car. They have spoken of the possibility of Fernando moving to New York, although this is a step that they are still negotiating, partly because of Jeffrey's insistence that Fernando become literate before moving abroad.[27] Despite the progression of their relationship, however, Jeffrey continues to express doubt about the authenticity of Fernando's affection. His last update on the status of their relationship ends with his typical combination of hopeful romanticism, nagging suspicion, and gay camp: "It has been confirmed and verified that Fernando no longer goes to the *bugarrón* spots anymore. I know this is most likely because I give him a monthly allowance, but it's still a lifestyle change for him. . . . Maybe I'm a fool, but right now I'm just a fool in love."

Othering and the Exotic

Santo Domingo has been the target of homoerotic projection by outsiders since at least as early as 1540, when Spanish *fray* Bartolomé de Las Casas condemned the indigenous male residents of the first New World colony for the "abominable" practice of sodomy (Trexler 1995, 2).[28] Nevertheless, scholars have had surprisingly little to say about the discourse and practice of homoeroticism as it relates to the global structures of power that have framed Caribbean history. There is now a significant body of literature on sexual-economic exchanges between male colonists and black female slaves that demonstrates the many ways that women's sexual labor has been exploited throughout Caribbean history to increase economic productivity, to provide an erotic outlet for powerful (white) men, and to open certain avenues for women's resistance (Abraham-van der Mark 1993; Beckles 1989; Castañeda 1995; Findlay 1997; Henriques 1965; Kempadoo 1999a; Kerr 1995; Moitt 1996). In the postcolonial era, a number of scholars have similarly framed female sex work within a global political economy that has systematically disadvantaged Caribbean women, resulting in an international commerce in black women's bodies and the racialized sexual fantasies of foreigners (Bolles 1992; Brennan 1998; Cabezas 1998a, b; del Olmo 1979; Fusco

1998; Kane 1993; Karch and Dann 1981; Kempadoo 1999a; O'Connell David-son 1996; Schwartz 1999). Caribbean men's sexual-economic exchanges with foreigners, however, have received much less attention, and where they have been examined it is almost exclusively in the context of their exchanges with female tourists (Phillips 1999; Press 1978; Pruitt and LaFont 1995). It is likely that these trends are related to the relatively more clandestine nature of same-sex exchanges, as well as an underestimation (or denial) on the part of researchers regarding the extent of covert homosexual behavior among so-called normal, heterosexual men.[29]

As a consequence, relatively little is known about the nature of sexual-economic exchanges between gay sex tourists and male sex workers in the Caribbean. Specifically, how are the economic and affective relationships between gay tourists and local men the same or different from those described in studies of heterosexual sex tourism in the region? To what extent are negotiations of power, control, and racial "othering" operative in gay sex tourism, and what specific forms do they take? And how are we to understand male sex workers' responses to these processes, the effect on their self-understanding, and the larger influence of their participation in same-sex exchanges on their social relations?

The present research can only begin to address these questions. What is clear is that, in the Dominican context, gay sex tourism displays certain parallels to heterosexual sex tourism as described by other researchers, while also showing clear points of departure. For example, both gay male and heterosexual female clients' motivations for participation in sex tourism must be understood within the context of a symbolic construction of masculinity and of Caribbean men's bodies that incorporates racialized fantasies of sexual difference. As suggested by Beverley Mullings (1999) in her discussion of Jamaican sex tourism, erotic constructions of Caribbean masculinity appear to be distinct from those characterizing other regions, as demonstrated by the greater involvement of men in sex tourism enterprises.[30] As described in chapter 2, this is also related to the greater demand for men's sexual services in the Caribbean, in addition to the increasingly limited employment options available to them and their growing incorporation into the region's informal sector tourist economies. Tourist demand for Caribbean men's sexual services, whether heterosexual or gay, is often structured by fantasies of the presumably "animalistic" nature of black male sexuality,[31] which Phillips aptly describes as follows in her discussion of Barbadian beach boys: "The Barbadian male embodies the primitive, aggressive nature of the black man, having an animal-like quality, which is constructed as opposite to the white man, the gentleman. This is the type of man who 'would fuck you in the sand and wouldn't think anything the matter with it'" (1999, 193). The racial projections of male sex-work clients thus eroticize their submission to an uncontrollable black male sexuality that belies, to some extent, the control that tourist-clients gain through their economic contributions. The fantasy of being ravaged by a sexually dominant black man appears to be one of the primary distinctions between gay clients of male sex workers and heterosexual clients of female sex workers, since the latter often express a nostalgia for a traditional gender order that has been lost in the context of Western feminism, in which women are compliant and submissive to all male demands (O'Connell Davidson and Sanchez Taylor 1999).[32] On the contrary, gay tourists to the Dominican Republic most often seek exchanges with men whom they perceive as (hyper)masculine "machos," an aesthetic that conforms quite closely to the stereotypical *tíguere* described in chapter 4.[33]

Gay tourists' desire to be sexually dominated is perhaps best illustrated by the fact that they almost universally seek to engage in receptive anal sex with Dominican sex workers, and only very rarely do they express the desire to be the penetrative partner or to engage in a variety of sexual roles. Indeed, Internet chat sites for gay travelers to Santo Domingo, where experiences are shared among sex tourists, frequently warn potential visitors not to expect sexual "versatility" among the local men, since the "boys" are known to be almost exclusively "one-way." This assessment is also consistent with what sex workers themselves say about their sexual activities, although their incessant concern to represent themselves as "*hombres normales*" most likely motivates a certain proportion of them to deny their occasional participation in receptive anal sex.[34] Nevertheless, in the in-depth interviews our team conducted with sex workers, one of the most common responses to questions about their sexual behavior with clients was to immediately clarify—just in case there were any ambiguity on the topic—that they were "*hombres de verdad*" (real men) or "*hombres normales*" (normal men). This pattern is illustrated by the following exchange between my colleague and Josué, a *bugarrón* in Santo Domingo:

LS: Normally, what is it you do with your clients sexually?
Josué: [laughs] That I can't tell you!
LS: Okay, but do you normally give in to the requests that they make of you?
Josué: No, no, no. I'm going to do my work with them, but I've always told them: "I'm a man." They've never penetrated me. Never. And I haven't sucked anyone's penis either. And I've been in this a long time. And I've always felt myself a superman [*superhombre*].

What is perhaps most revealing of Josué's response is its emphatic nature, which is tied to the desire to emphasize his "normal" sexuality—vis-à-vis his impenetrability—as well as to make a statement about his gender performance or masculinity. We will return to this point at the end of this chapter. For the moment, the important point is that sex workers' presumable participation in exclusively penetrative sex does not seem to be a cause for concern among the gay sex tourists with whom I have spoken, since their fantasies most commonly involve being sexually dominated (read, "fucked") by a Dominican "stud."

The racial othering inherent in these fantasies is further elaborated in beliefs about the large penis size of Dominican men. It is worth recalling the comment by Simon, the owner of Charlie's bar, that one of the most common questions he is asked by gay tourists is, "How big is he?" demonstrating the high tourist demand for the largest phallus available. Kobena Mercer (1993), in his analysis of the racial imagery in the work of the late gay photographer Robert Mapplethorpe, notes that one of the key features of exoticization in such works is the tendency to reduce the black male subject to an enormous penis, which serves as the dehumanized centerpiece of a projective, racialized fantasy.[35] Similarly, the obsession of many gay sex tourists with hiring the man with the largest penis demonstrates their desire to fulfill a preconceived fantasy in which the animalistic sexuality of Dominican men is iconically represented in a "monstrous" phallus. Importantly, sex workers are well aware of the importance of penis size for many gay clients, and often claim to know precisely the relative size of their peers.[36] It is also fairly common for those *bugarrones* who are particularly well endowed to display their penis for potential clients, by either strategically accentuating it through their clothing or lowering their pants to permit a full visual inspection (see fig. 7).[37]

As shown by several researchers, the conceptual linkage between race and the erotic in tourist fantasies is often embedded in the imagery and language employed by marketing campaigns targeting foreign vacationers (Canan and Hennessey 1989; Selwyn 1993; Urry 1991). Caribbean women's sexuality in particular is commonly used in subtle and not-so-subtle advertising campaigns to foster demand for tourism in the region—a quintessential example of what hooks (1992, 25–26) has described as "the commodification of the Other." Within this framework, in Mullings (1999, 74) words, "the 'gendered' and 'raced' body has become a signifier for certain forms of post-Fordist consumption," resulting in tourism marketing approaches that, almost by necessity, appeal to the racial-sexual fantasies of foreigners. A reflection of the "flexible" economic strategies that increasingly typify local responses to tourism dependence (Crick 1989), the imagery and

Figure 7. A *bugarrón* displays himself for inspection by tourists at one of Santo Domingo's gay bars

language employed by Caribbean governments and tourism developers frequently exoticize Caribbean bodies and traffic in racial stereotypes. Somewhat ironically, the economic benefits afforded to the state vis-à-vis its implicit marketing of erotic services—referred to by Kempadoo and Ghuma (1999, 301) as "state pimpage"—contrasts rather markedly with the intermittent attempts by local authorities to arrest sex workers caught "harassing" the tourists. This contradictory posture of the state in relation to its own construction of itself is, in part, a reflection of a larger societal ambivalence about the global exigencies of tourism development, which lead marketers to depict "authentic" local people and practices through stereotyped, naturalized, and exoticized representations.[38]

In contrast to the heterosexual imagery in tourism marketing, however, homoerotic representations and their "readings" by gay tourists must be understood in relation to the non-normative status of same-sex desire. In the vast majority of cases, homoeroticism is not directly represented in tourism marketing that is intended for general dissemination.[39] How, then, do gay tourists develop particular exoticized beliefs about local men's sexuality, such as those expressed by Jeffrey?

At least part of the answer lies in the growth of gay institutions and publications devoted to the gay and lesbian traveler, and more recently the enormous influence of the Internet on the organization of sex tourism to the Caribbean. Essentially, the Internet has streamlined flexible marketing approaches and permitted advertising to "special interest" populations on a global scale and through largely anonymous channels. In the Dominican Republic (and undoubtedly elsewhere), these characteristics of the Internet have proven instrumental in the development of a delocalized sex trade through which sexual-economic exchanges—and the fantasies that fuel them—can be forged "virtually." There are now several Internet sites devoted specifically to gay tourism to the Dominican Republic, where information is published about local gay businesses, cruising areas, and sex work, and through which clients can share stories and images of their sexual adventures with Dominicans.[40] At least two gay tour companies based in New York specialize in organizing gay tourist packages to Santo Domingo, and both reach their clientele principally through Internet Web sites. And several of the more professionalized sex workers with whom I interacted had personal Web pages, where they published erotic pictures of themselves, elaborated on their physical or personal qualities, or posted their contact information for the convenience of potential clients.[41]

As Appadurai describes, the "mediascapes" that typify the flow of information in the contemporary world facilitate a subjective experience in which delocalized subjects are barraged by "a complicated and interconnected repertoire of print, celluloid, electronic screens, and billboards" such that "the realistic and the fictional landscapes they see are blurred" (1996, 35). The more people recombine imagery and text from distant locations within new contexts, "the more likely they are to construct imagined worlds that are chimerical, aesthetic, even fantastic objects, particularly if assessed by the criteria of some other perspective, some other imagined world" (ibid.). Appadurai argues that one of the effects of global mediascapes is that "scripts," or conceptual models, "can be formed of imagined lives, their own as well as those of others living in other places." It is in the process of forming scripts out of decontextualized cultural artifacts that othering practices are particularly discernible: "These scripts can and do get disaggregated into complex sets of metaphors by which people live (Lakoff and Johnson 1980) as they help to constitute narratives of the Other and protonarratives of possible lives, fantasies that could become prolegomena to the desire for acquisition and movement" (1990, 35–36).

Within this theoretical framework, the scripts that circulate in what we might call "homoerotic mediascapes" are constitutive of the fantasies of the Other that, in part, drive the demand for gay sex tourism. In other words, "the desire for acquisition and movement" typical of sex tourism is a partial consequence of the types of scripts of Caribbean sexuality that circulate "back home," and the ways these canalize imagined erotic worlds. In this way, as Urry (1991, 1995, 2002) has argued, the imagery used in tourism marketing can be understood to have a much larger effect on the construction of global racial-sexual fantasies than would be implied by the relatively intermittent, short-term travel by a privileged few.

Importantly, many of the images of Dominican men that are published abroad for gay male consumption are of sex workers who were paid by foreigners to be photographed or filmed. A number of the sex workers with whom I interacted, particularly the more professionalized ones such as the regulars at Charlie's bar, had participated in pornographic video productions, which were commonly filmed in a gay hotel in Santo Domingo. An American porn video director with whom I interacted on several occasions travels regularly to the Dominican Republic to film gay porn movies, which are marketed in adult video stores abroad and over the Internet.[42] Often, the plots of these movies are interspersed with images of "natural" Caribbean scenes—an unspoiled tropical swimming hole, a virgin white-sand beach, or an idyllic rural home in the *campo*—and these representational techniques tend to reinforce the "naturalization" of Dominican homoeroticism that characterizes these texts (Yanagisako and Delaney 1995). Here, same-sex behavior is depicted as a manifestation of a natural Dominican masculinity that is less constrained by (hetero)sexual morality and more permissive of homoeroticism. In the minds of the gay men who decode these scripts abroad, this depiction of Dominican masculinity provides a useful catalyst for the formation of "imagined worlds" that are fundamentally different from "ours"—an exoticized fantasy of cultural/sexual difference. As described above, these patterns are evident in the expressions of erotic othering in Jeffrey's narrative of the fundamental differences between Dominicans and New Yorkers: Dominican men lead simple, uncomplicated lives; they are isolated from the negative consequences of the modern world; and they are naturally more masculine and sensual than North Americans. Thus, the scripts of Dominican masculinity that commonly circulate in foreign gay media, and particularly in gay pornography, are reflections of gay men's fantasies of the Other as well as constitutive of those fantasies, providing the raw material for the imagination of "possible lives" in, for example, a distant tropical paradise populated by "real men."

The mutually reinforcing nature of the relationship between erotic representations and the othering fantasies of gay men is useful in conceptualizing the processes by which sex tourism can become a fundamental feature of some men's identity and practice—a part of their "*habitus,*" in Bourdieu's (1977) terminology. As Western Union daddies, men like Jeffrey—vis-à-vis their experiences of travel, cultural and racial difference, and the consumption of sexual services—are able to envision themselves and their erotic lives in a new light. Thus, as suggested by Kempadoo (1999a, 26), "Caribbean masculinity and femininity alike . . . become the tableaux upon which a reshaping and retooling of Western identity occurs." Nevertheless, this "Western identity" is never entirely stable, for at least two reasons. First, the erotic power of the Other depends on a particular construction of essentialized difference that, in turn, necessitates a certain degree of distance. A consequence of this is evident in a comment that Jeffrey made repeatedly when we discussed the possibility of his moving permanently to the Dominican Republic: "But if I lived there, it just wouldn't be the same." According to Mullings (1999, 72–73), the inverse relationship between familiarity and eroticism that characterizes sex tourism is one of the reasons that the "traditional" destinations for international prostitution, such as Southeast Asia, are now showing signs of market "saturation," as tourists are seeking unspoiled, "virgin" areas for sexual exploration. For clients seeking "romantic" encounters abroad, then, sex tourism requires a compromise between distance and intimacy, permitting a degree of emotional involvement while keeping the erotic charge of otherness intact.[43] As illustrated by Jeffrey's story, however, the drawback of this division of one's erotic universe is that it sometimes leads to a kind of fissioning of identity, an aching nostalgia, and a sense of personal alienation upon return "home." As one's identity and fantasy world become rooted in an exotic faraway place, it becomes increasingly difficult to find oneself trapped in the mundane grind of "modern" urban life.

A second reason this so-called Western identity, as constructed through the Other, is unstable is that it depends on socioeconomic differences whose very existence undermines the authenticity of a partner's fantasized "love." As more intimate relationships develop, the dramatic economic inequalities that frame global sex work never permit the sex tourist absolute security about the degree to which his affection is genuinely reciprocated, despite the various strategies that both parties employ to obfuscate the instrumental aspects of the relationship. As O'Connell Davidson and Sanchez Taylor (1999, 40) argue, in global sex tourism the commercial nature of the sex worker/client exchange essentially strips all mutuality from sexual relations and "provides a conveniently ready-dehumanized sexual object for the client." Yet in the context of "romance tourism"—or the longer-term, more intimate relationships typical of Western Union daddies—this tendency toward dehumanization must be in some way resolved, insofar as it is understood to be antithetical to true intimacy and emotional mutuality. Thus, while sex tourism opens certain avenues by which Westerners can rework their identities vis-à-vis the Other, it can also create dilemmas for them as they struggle to imagine themselves as worthy beings amidst the inequalities that can never be entirely erased from consciousness.

6

AIDS, the "Bisexual Bridge," and the Political Economy of Risk in the Dominican Republic

> Models of disease emergence need to be dynamic, systemic, and critical, uncovering connections and patterns that are often obscured by conventional epidemiology and examining the role of social forces and inequalities.
>
> PAUL FARMER

Having guided the ethnographic analysis through a broad range of social spaces in which Dominican male sex workers live and work, and having analyzed the intricate ways that local and global norms of gender and sexuality intersect through the pleasure industry, I can now turn to a more urgent issue: the HIV/AIDS epidemic and its relationship to the global structures in which the Dominican Republic—and the men whose voices have filled these pages—are embedded. This chapter expands on the ethnographic material presented in previous chapters by reframing these various phenomena—the historical development of the pleasure industry, the globalization of homoerotic identities, the context of familial and conjugal relations, and the instrumental relationships with foreign gay clients—within the theoretical perspective of *critical medical anthropology* (CMA). This project allows us to develop what Paul Farmer has called a "critical epidemiology" of Dominican AIDS—the examination of the political, economic, and social forces underlying disease patterns, and using this structural framework to inform epidemiological interpretation. This conceptual approach has two primary benefits. First, it enables us to trace the relationships between global inequalities and epidemiological patterns, a fundamental goal of CMA, and thereby allows us to reveal the connections—so often obscured by traditional epidemiology—between "structural violence" and HIV/AIDS.[1] Second, it requires that epidemiological interpretations themselves be understood as embedded within global structures and inequalities—a perspective that demands us to be critical of epidemiological "truth," to avoid the tendency to simply accept scientific discourses as statements about an "objective" reality. The latter approach is essential for the epistemological analysis of the "bisexual bridge" metaphor that is developed in this chapter, which provides a critical rereading of epidemiological models of sexual orientation in international public health discourses on the Caribbean AIDS epidemic.

Further, this chapter seeks to advance CMA as applied to the global HIV/AIDS pandemic by combining it with what has been described in this book as a *political economy of sexuality.* It is only through a true political economy of sexuality—one which considers global structural processes as well as individual subjectivities and the local cultural meanings of sexuality—that we are able to discern the ways that large-scale structures are internalized, enacted, and experienced. Indeed, the neglect of this macromicro linkage has been a conceptual weakness of prior analyses of HIV/AIDS from the perspective of CMA, precisely because the meanings of gender and sexuality within the local cultural system are easily obscured by the broad analytic lens required for the analysis of global structural processes. The discussion in this chapter therefore seeks to follow these macro-micro connections in both directions—from the global structures of dependency that position the Caribbean region as a reservoir for a new kind of sexual labor, to the specific identities, behaviors, and practices of *bugarrones* and *sanky pankies* in the Dominican Republic—in order to develop a critical epidemiological interpretation of Dominican AIDS as told from the perspective of the Caribbean pleasure industry. This requires us to continue the dialectical approach that has been used throughout this book, alternating between the analysis of broad political-economic processes and their particular ethnographic reverberations.

AIDS in the Caribbean: Context and Interpretation

Much has been made recently of the growth of the AIDS epidemic in the Caribbean, the world region currently showing the highest prevalence rates of HIV infection outside of sub-Saharan Africa (UNAIDS 2002, 36). The urgent need to address the spread of HIV in the region has been the primary rationale for prioritizing the Caribbean, along with Africa, in the recent commitment of U.S.$15 billion by the United States government to finance global AIDS prevention and service programs in the coming years.[2] It is estimated that 40,000 people died of AIDS in the Caribbean in the year 2001 alone, and approximately 2.4 percent of the adult population is currently HIV-infected (Gonzales 2003). Nearly a half million people in the region are estimated to be infected (UNAIDS 2002, 35). The highly mobile nature of Caribbean populations has contributed to high prevalences of HIV among immigrant enclaves in areas such as New York, where half of HIV-infected immigrants are of Caribbean origin (Camara 2001). As is typical globally, the Caribbean AIDS epidemic primarily affects persons who are at the peak of their productive potential, with more than a third of total AIDS cases occurring among persons between the ages of twenty-five and thirty-four (ibid.). The epidemic has therefore had devastating economic effects ranging from the microlevel of the household economy to the macrolevel of regional development projects, in addition to the immeasurable human costs in terms of suffering and loss.

That Africa and the Caribbean share a disproportionate amount of the global burden of AIDS may tend to mask the divergent geographical, historical, and political-economic conditions that have shaped the epidemiology of HIV transmission in these world areas. Indeed, as Paul Farmer's foundational ethnographic work on the AIDS epidemic in Haiti has vividly demonstrated (1992), racist and nationalist stereotyping at the beginning of the epidemic often led to wild theories about the purported epidemiological linkages between Africa and the Caribbean—theories that seemed to explain the "simultaneous" emergence and rapid spread of HIV in these distant areas but entirely neglected the different ways that these regions are incorporated into the contemporary world system.[3] One important contrast between the structural conditions of the African and Caribbean epidemics concerns the relationships between HIV transmission and the timing and focus of capitalist development. Whereas the AIDS epidemic in Africa has often been driven by the relatively recent emergence of large-scale capitalist enterprises dependent on isolated enclaves of migrant male laborers (Caldwell, Caldwell, and Quiggin 1989; Jochelson, Mothibeli, and Leger 1991; Larson 1989; Moodie 1988; Obbo 1993; Standing 1992)—structural changes that have led to long separations by spouses and the development of nodal points of prostitution—the Caribbean epidemic is related to recent shifts in global capitalist dependencies that are themselves centuries old (Mintz 1985, 1996; Trouillot 1992). Many of the structural conditions that have contributed to the escalation of the AIDS epidemic in the Caribbean are therefore not historically new, as they represent a continuation of patterns of intense intra- and interregional population mobility, large-scale capitalist labor exploitation, and sexual-economic exchanges between powerful foreigners and subjugated locals that have characterized both the colonial and postcolonial periods (Kempadoo 1999a).

What has proven to be an ill-fated change in Caribbean political economy, at least insofar as it made the region even more vulnerable to the AIDS epidemic in the early 1980s, began in the 1960s with the transition to a development approach that diminished dependence on traditional exports and increasingly prioritized the so-called smokeless industry of tourism (Momsen 1994; Pattullo 1996). While the Caribbean has long been vulnerable to epidemics because of its historically unfortunate position as a crossroads for international travel, commerce, and exploitative modes of resource extraction (McNeill 1976), the dramatic escalation of travel to the region as a result of the post-Fordist development of the tourism and airline industries—spurred by global representations of the Caribbean as an idyllic escape from the drudgery of work in the developed West—has undoubtedly increased the risk of exposure to imported diseases among Caribbean people. Susceptibility to sexually transmitted infections is further exacerbated by the marketability of sexual services to tourists, combined with the growing desperation of an increasingly urban, underemployed, landless lower class.

Given these conditions, it is not surprising that the region's AIDS epidemic has been closely linked with the tourism industry since the first cases appeared in the early 1980s. As poignantly demonstrated by Farmer's (1992) life-history accounts of the first victims of AIDS among the residents of the rural Haitian village of Do Kay, for example, sexual contact with tourists or with those employed in the tourism industry were strong markers of HIV risk during the first years of the epidemic. Indeed, a recent regional report on trends in HIV infection by the director of the Caribbean Epidemiology Centre (CAREC) in Trinidad argues that those countries that are the most economically dependent on tourism—the Bahamas, Barbados, Bermuda, the Dominican Republic, the Turks and Caicos, Jamaica, St. Maarten, and Tobago—are precisely those showing the highest prevalence and incidence rates of HIV at the present time (Camara 2001).[4] Such epidemiological patterns suggest not only that tourism was a primary means by which HIV was initially introduced into Caribbean societies, but that it continues to function as an important source of new infections, exerting an ongoing influence on the scope and impact of AIDS in specific locales.

Given this, it is ironic that almost no HIV prevention programs in the region have attempted to directly target the tourism industry—either its employees or its clients—in an effort to reduce the impact of AIDS.[5] This omission is likely the result of the perception among public health officials and policymakers that the exigencies of tourism marketing prohibit open discussion of HIV, since both the recognition of an "AIDS problem" and the suggestion that people should behave "safely" contradict the escapism, exoticism, and consequence-free environment that compose at least part of the tourism package offered to foreigners (see chapter 5). Afraid of fostering negative associations within a highly competitive and fickle global tourism industry, Caribbean governments have often preferred to avoid the presumably detrimental consequences of explicit HIV prevention campaigns aimed at the tourism sector, and indeed, denial about the existence or extent of the local AIDS epidemic has been an all-too-common response among Caribbean governments.[6]

The epidemiological linkages between the Caribbean AIDS epidemic and the tourism industry can be fully understood only by considering the historical emergence and expansion of gay sex tourism to the region in the seventies and eighties. Indeed, Camara argues that in Haiti, Jamaica, and Trinidad and Tobago, the first AIDS cases detected were among men who had sex with North American gay tourists (2001).[7] Similarly, Pape and Johnson (1988) note that during the initial years of the AIDS epidemic in Jamaica, the Dominican Republic, and Trinidad, "sexual contact with American homosexuals rather than promiscuity per se appeared to be associated with increased risk of infection" (quoted in Farmer 1999, 118). Farmer has described this scenario in Haiti, arguing that the pre-AIDS growth in gay tourism to Haiti was related to representations in North American gay publications that promised that "handsome men with 'a great ability to satisfy'" abound in Haiti—for a small price (1992, 147). He connects the rise in gay sex tourism to the epidemiological pattern of the country's first AIDS cases, concluding that "sufficient data now exist to support the assertion that economically driven male prostitution, catering to a North American clientele, played a major role in the introduction of HIV to Haiti" (1992, 145). Farmer also reviews epidemiological evidence of a similar pattern in other Caribbean nations, demonstrating that during the early 1980s, the "major risk factor for HIV seropositivity was homosexual contact with a partner from a foreign country, primarily the United States" (Farmer 1999, 119). As described in the following section, studies in the Dominican Republic demonstrate that this country epitomizes the pattern described by Farmer and suggest not only that initial AIDS cases were primarily among men involved in sex work with gay foreigners, but that the continuing connections between male sex tourism and HIV transmission are dangerously under-recognized by dominant public health interpretations of the country's AIDS epidemic.

Despite this initial pattern of HIV infection primarily among men categorized as "homo/bisexual"—a category that may obscure more than it reveals (see below)—contemporary interpretations of the Caribbean AIDS epidemic describe it as one that is predominantly "heterosexual." This conclusion is often supported by the epidemiological evidence of a continually shrinking male-to-female sex ratio of HIV infection, demonstrating that at the present time, on average, one woman for every two men is HIV-infected (Camara 2001). Surveillance data on cases of HIV/AIDS estimate that somewhere between 76 and 80 percent of infections are currently due to "heterosexual" transmission, with "homo/bisexual" transmission accounting for around 12 percent of cases (PAHO/WHO 2002, 12–13). Importantly, the relatively low proportion of HIV infections that are attributed to same-sex activities in the Caribbean contrasts rather sharply with some other countries in Latin America, most notably Mexico and Brazil, where the homo/bisexual category accounts for 56 percent and 35 percent of all AIDS cases, respectively (ibid., 9–11). Thus, despite the fact that the initial cases of AIDS were among homosexually behaving men, most contemporary analyses depict an epidemiological transition in the Caribbean from a primarily "homosexual" pattern to a primarily "heterosexual" one, or, in the language often used in such reports, from specific "risk groups" to the "general population."[8]

Nevertheless, a few recent analyses of the Caribbean epidemic have continued to emphasize the importance of male-to-male HIV transmission in the region. One report on AIDS in the Americas calls men who have sex with men (MSM) one of the region's "forgotten populations," arguing that the continuing high prevalence of HIV among MSM, their generally higher-risk behavior, and the fact that many HIV prevention programs have ignored or underemphasized them, make this population an important priority for future public health programs (PAHO 2001, 22). The report further observes:

Even in those countries where it is believed that the transmission of HIV is generally due to heterosexual relations, and where the proportion of infected men and women is similar, sexual relations between men are a predominant risk factor. . . . Also in the Caribbean it is considered that the prevalence of HIV infection is high among men who have sex with men, even though this population has been partly ignored by prevention measures due to the fact that, at least in number, they generate fewer infections than heterosexual relations (PAHO 2001, 24).[9]

Further, this report represents a relatively rare case in which a major international health agency has emphasized the epidemiological importance of bisexual behavior as a continuing risk factor in the region, citing a growing body of literature demonstrating that most MSM do not engage exclusively in same-sex activities but rather commonly have both male and female sexual partners, often secretively.[10] The discussion concludes by observing that "this overlapping of distinct risk behaviors serves as a bridge to HIV, permitting it to pass from a group of MSM with high risk behaviors to the heterosexual population, whose risk of exposure to HIV is not higher than average" (PAHO 2001, 26).

The question of what label to put on the Caribbean AIDS epidemic—whether it be "heterosexual," "homosexual," or some other term—is more than purely academic, since the language we use to understand HIV transmission, in Susan Sontag's (1990) words, often threatens to "hijack the epidemic," clouding our perceptions and inhibiting our ability to interpret epidemiological patterns. The designation of the region's AIDS epidemic as "heterosexual"—reserving for the moment the historically and culturally specific nature of that term—has influenced funding availability, the design of prevention messages, and the delivery of HIV-related counseling and clinical services. Clearly, the label has been at least partially a response to observable epidemiological trends, particularly the growing proportion of HIV-infected women, but its usage and conceptual limitations have also served to mask or entirely erase certain behavioral risks, particularly those involving certain types of same-sex sexual activity. This chapter uses the specific case of AIDS in the Dominican Republic to highlight some of the ways that the conceptualization of the "heterosexual epidemic" in the Caribbean may draw attention away from a significant domain of sexual activity that may continue to drive HIV transmission. Here, by way of introduction, I draw on a growing body of anthropological and social-scientific literature, focusing my discussion on several factors that have contributed to the conceptual problems in public health approaches to homosexuality and HIV transmission in the Caribbean and, perhaps, in other world areas. These include: (1) the tendency to approach bisexual behavior as a bridge connecting otherwise isolated populations of exclusive homosexuals and heterosexuals; (2) a persistent lack of theoretical and methodological sophistication about the ways that stigma and homophobia influence self-reported data on HIV risk behavior; and (3) the tendency to neglect large-scale structural factors and their influences on patterns of male bisexuality and sex work, particularly in areas highly dependent on the tourism industry.

The potentially problematic usage of the bridge metaphor is suggested in the report cited above, in which male bisexuality is described as the link between an otherwise isolated population of "homosexuals" and a general population of "heterosexuals," ostensibly converting the epidemic from one transmission pattern to another. In fact, the idea of a "bisexual bridge" by which HIV infection passes from "homosexual" to "heterosexual" populations is not new in epidemiological discussions of AIDS. Early in the epidemic, the notion of a bridge between what were often conceived as relatively self-contained high-risk groups and the general population was frequently invoked both as an impending threat to the larger society and as a potential explanation for the more symmetrical male-to-female ratios of HIV infection in certain world areas, especially Africa (see, for example, Padian 1987). Such analyses were also centrally concerned with the global transition from what was then termed "Pattern I"—the epidemiological scenario originally emerging in the United States and Western Europe in which gay men, IV-drug users, and recipients of blood products were the primary victims— to "Pattern II," whose ideal representation is the "generalized," predominantly "heterosexual" epidemic in sub-Saharan Africa. Aggleton (1996a, 1) describes the concept of the bisexual bridge as follows:

Male bisexuals have often been characterized as a "bridging group," enabling HIV to be transmitted from apparently discrete sub-populations of behaviourally homosexual and behaviourally heterosexual individuals. Most usually, it is suggested that bisexual men pose a special threat to their female partners through having had sex with other men, particularly exclusively homosexual men. Such accounts stereotype reality in that they posit the existence of two identifiable and discrete groups of individuals, the "homosexual" and the "heterosexual," that are capable of being "bridged" by a third type.

Early in the epidemic, bisexual behavior and the notion of an epidemiological bridge thus provided a convenient framework for conceptualizing— however crudely—an epidemiological transition that appeared to be occurring particularly rapidly in some world regions.

As some anthropologically oriented analyses have subsequently pointed out, one of the problems with the bridge metaphor is that its usage often suggests a single "crossing-over"—a critical breach of the boundary that presumably cordons off particular high-risk groups from the "general population." A growing literature suggests, however, that a much more likely model, perhaps particularly in certain world areas or among particular ethnic groups, is one in which HIV transmission from bisexually behaving men to their female partners may be a constant and ongoing process, and one which is responsible for a significant proportion of infections. In his discussion of male bisexuality and HIV in Peru, for example, Cáceres (1996, 137) argues that the typical epidemiological construction of AIDS as essentially a "homosexual plague" with bisexuality serving as a "bridge connecting an infected (and infectious) constituency to the 'general population'" serves to falsely essentialize sexual behaviors in a manner that has little relationship to the actual behavioral epidemiology of HIV in Peru. It also tends to ignore the psychosocial perspectives of the majority of behavioral bisexuals in areas such as Latin America and the Caribbean, since prevention programs tend to target only the small proportion of individuals who self-identify as gay or homosexual—the tip of the epidemiological iceberg.[11]

As has been articulated most clearly in the work of anthropologist Richard Parker (1987, 1992, 1990, 1996), the implicit assumption behind such narrow conceptualizations of HIV prevention is that all or most men who engage in homosexual sex will be successfully reached by programs targeting the "gay" or "homosexual" community. This perspective—fostered in part by the overgeneralization and somewhat uncritical exportation of standard approaches to HIV prevention among urban, white, middle-class, gay-identified men in the United States—has therefore tended to conflate a gay sexual identity with homosexual behavior, a conflation that does not reflect the psychosocial reality for some, perhaps most, men who regularly engage in same-sex sexual behavior in areas such as Latin America and the Caribbean.[12] Among the population of *bugarrones* and *sanky pankies* discussed in this book, for example, HIV/AIDS interventions designed to reach men who openly identify themselves as *gay* would be appropriately designed for only 3 percent of the population—the proportion of sex workers who identified themselves as either *gay* or *homosexual* in the survey. This is a point to which we will return later in this chapter in the discussion of HIV risk and intervention approaches among men who have sex with men in the Dominican Republic. For the current discussion, the most important point is that a growing cross-cultural literature on homoeroticism—and perhaps most importantly on Latin American homoeroticism—now exists to conclude that a significant proportion of men who engage in homosexual acts do not identify themselves as *gay,* and their specific needs are rarely addressed by prevention approaches designed for gay-identified men.[13]

This realization is part of the rationale for the shift in public-health language from the use of the terms *gay* or *homosexual* to the use of the acronym *MSM*—men who have sex with men—in an effort to be more inclusive of non-gay-identified men, at least in terminology if not always in practice. Unfortunately, my experience is that the MSM category as used in public health and epidemiology is rarely coupled with a cross-cultural understanding of the highly variable relationships between sexual risk behavior and sexual identity, and the ways these relationships might inform the design of prevention and service programs among specific subgroups of

"MSM."[14] *MSM*, despite the better intentions of some of those who use it, often becomes a euphemism for *gay*, neglecting the potentially large number of men for whom this particular label and social construction of sexuality do not apply.[15] Part of the reason for this may be the persistent tendency in epidemiology to conceptualize sexual "risk behavior" in terms of the bipolar, ideal-type categories typical of Western constructions of sexual orientation: homosexual versus heterosexual. Epidemiological depictions of the "bisexual bridge," therefore, ironically foreclose rather quickly on the importance of transmission through bisexual behavior, relegating it to an explanation for a purported epidemiological shift from "homosexual" to "heterosexual." In the latter type, most HIV transmission is conceptualized as from women to men or from men to women, with male-male transmission accounting for a relatively small proportion of total cases. Thus, male bisexual behavior becomes important only at the critical moment of conversion from one pattern to another—as the link between relatively isolated epidemics among "MSM" (read, "gay"), on the one hand, and "heterosexuals," on the other.

This interpretation not only serves to stigmatize bisexually behaving men by depicting them as infectious to the "general population" but also obfuscates the fact that bisexual behavior may be an integral feature of the epidemiology of HIV/AIDS—as well as sexual life in general—in many populations.[16] Indeed, a few recent studies among African Americans and Latinos in the United States have suggested a different picture of HIV transmission and high-risk scenarios that defies the notion of a marked separation of homosexual and heterosexual epidemics. These studies argue that a high proportion of non-gay-identified black and Latino men regularly have sex with men, and that a growing number of black and Latino women are infected with HIV by bisexually behaving male partners. While such conclusions remain tentative and the data are inconsistent (Millet et al. 2005), several studies offered some suggestive evidence. In Chu et al.'s (1992) study of men with AIDS, for example, the authors find that a disproportionate number of black and Latino men reported engaging in bisexual behavior, and that black women were five times more likely than white women to be infected with HIV by a bisexually behaving man. Similarly, Stokes et al. (1993, 1996) report that among a large sample of bisexually behaving men, African Americans were significantly less likely than whites to have spoken with their female partners about their homosexual activities. The potential epidemiological impact of these trends comes into focus when one considers that most behavioral assessments of HIV risk behavior show that black and Latino MSM—particularly those who do not self-identify as gay—are at significantly higher risk for infection than white MSM and have among the highest HIV prevalence rates of any so-called risk groups tracked by the CDC. One recent epidemiological survey found that among MSM in six U.S. cities, 7 percent of whites, 14 percent of Hispanics, and 32 percent of blacks were HIV-infected (McFarland et al. 2001). Ethnic minority MSM may also be significantly more likely than whites to avoid testing for HIV and to be unaware of their HIV-positive status (Bingham et al. 2002). These trends may be even more pronounced among those men who are, in the terminology of some reports, "non-disclosers" as regards their same-sex experiences (Shehan et al. 2003), although—as described further below—the relationship between disclosure and HIV risk is still quite ambiguous in the literature (Pantalone, Plummer and Simoni 2005).

On the basis of this evidence, some of these scholars have suggested the potential relevance of a different behavioral epidemiology in which a significant proportion of non-gay-identified ethnic minority men are infected through sexual relations with men and later pass this infection—often unknowingly—to their female partners.[17] In this scenario, which has not been definitively proven, women are understood as unable to accurately assess their risk for HIV because of the silences and barriers to communication that characterize their intimate relationships with men, many of whom do not disclose their HIV status or high-risk behavior.[18] Importantly, if such a scenario were operative, there is no necessary reason to believe that this transmission pattern would occur only during a short, circumscribed period of time in the development of a local epidemic, but rather could be a continuous dynamic contributing to an ongoing pattern of transmission, particularly in those populations with a high frequency of male bisexuality and a high background prevalence of HIV. Under these circumstances, any model of HIV transmission positing independent "heterosexual" and "homosexual" epidemics—or treating bisexuality as a "transitional" behavior among a very small group of men ultimately leading to a predominantly "heterosexual" epidemic—would be, at the very least, in danger of glossing over a significant part of the picture.[19]

Figure 8 graphically represents an ideal-type model of the bisexual bridge as often implied in the language used in public health and epidemiological reports, such as those referenced above for the Caribbean. This graphic is not based on a model explicitly described by any particular scholarly report but is, rather, my attempt to extrapolate, for the purpose of drawing a conceptual distinction, an idealized model from the language often used in defense of a hypothesized transition from a "homosexual" to a "heterosexual" AIDS epidemic. The bridge model generally assumes a high HIV prevalence

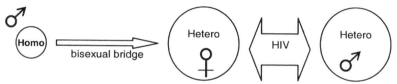

Figure 8. Model of HIV transmission based on the "bisexual bridge"

among a relatively small, isolated group of "homosexuals" (the vast majority of whom have sex exclusively with other men), a correspondingly low frequency of bisexual behavior, and largely independent or parallel epidemics among "homosexuals" and "heterosexuals." Importantly, it also predicts that a relatively high proportion of AIDS cases among men will be due to sex with women, an assumption that runs somewhat counter to studies demonstrating a much higher relative efficiency of male-to-female versus female-to-male HIV transmission.[20] The latter fact necessitates an additional explanation for the high rate of female-to-male transmission presupposed by the bridge model. Thus, the proportion of HIV infections transmitted between exclusively heterosexual men and women in this hypothesized epidemic—visually represented in figure 8 by the thick arrow that links them—is quite large relative to those transmitted between and among MSM, or from "bisexuals" to "heterosexual" women.

The bridge model contrasts with an alternative model of HIV transmission, shown in figure 9, in which male bisexual behavior makes a significant and continuous contribution to HIV infection rates among heterosexual women, many of whom are infected through sex with bisexually behaving men. Drawing on the recent findings in studies of HIV infection among African Americans and Latinos, outlined above, as well as recent culturally informed research on HIV/AIDS among Latin American populations (Carrillo 2002; Díaz 1998), this model entails several different assumptions. First, it assumes that a significant proportion of MSM engage regularly in sex with both male and female partners, a fact that problematizes the presumption of an isolated homosexual epidemic. In addition, it assumes that bisexually behaving men will have high rates of infection (and possibly higher rates than among exclusively homosexual men), will engage in higher-risk behavior (partly because they are not reached by most gay-oriented HIV prevention messages), will have a lower perception of risk for infection, and will be less likely to know that they are HIV-positive. A significant benefit of this model is that it does not attempt to erase behavioral bisexuals in favor of a reified notion of bipolar sexual orientations but rather recognizes a spectrum of rather fluid male sexualities that defy rigid separation.[21] It is therefore more ethnographically consistent for populations, such as those in Latin America and the Caribbean, in which a high proportion of non-gay-identified men engage in discreet—and sometimes elaborately hidden—sexual behavior with other men. Importantly, this model also assumes that men will employ sexual communication styles—*in conjunction with their partners*—that are more typical of "sexual silence" as described in chapter 4. That is, both partners will participate in culturally informed patterns of sexual communication that are indirect and intuitive, rather than direct or rational, and which are informed by larger normative expectations and social stigma.[22] Including sexual silence as an assumption of the model therefore highlights the ways that sexual communication is embedded in larger cultural forms (in this case, Latin American sexual culture), as well as the ways that *both* partners participate in tacit agreements about how to interact with each other both socially and sexually.[23] This avoids presuming (incorrectly, in most cases) that commonly used terms such as *disclosure* and *nondisclosure* reflect the way that most people engage in sexual risk communication, and opens up discussion for a deeper analysis of the social and structural processes that produce and maintain sexual silence.

A limitation of this model is that the proportion of HIV infections among men and women that involve bisexual behavior will inevitably vary depending on a number of factors, and as a result figure 9 would be more or less relevant depending on the behavioral dynamics of specific populations and the base HIV prevalence in each. Here, it serves more as a heuristic for describing the general features of a hypothetical epidemic that is rarely discussed as a *possibility* in epidemiological interpretations of AIDS, particularly in areas such as the Caribbean where the epidemic has been officially designated "heterosexual," with all the implicitly understood, culturally specific assumptions that this label entails. However, as a number of medical anthropologists have shown, the implicit scripts of gender and sexuality that often lead to particular representations of biomedical knowledge—such as the notion that a bipolar system of "homosexual" versus "heterosexual" is the best theoretical model of human sexual behavior or the transmission of HIV—often serve to reinforce oppressive configurations of gender and power, rather than elucidate a "natural" world in the name of "objective" science.[24] The commonsense aspect of the bridge model may therefore have as much to do with the seeming naturalness of a homo-hetero universe as it does with actual patterns of sexual behavior. And, of course, twenty years after the advent of AIDS, it is still sexual behavior that transmits the HIV virus, not the concepts and stereotypes we invoke to explain it.

This tendency to take the lenses of "sexual culture" for granted, rather

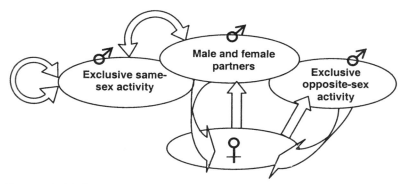

Figure 9. Model of HIV transmission in a hypothetical bisexually driven epidemic

than interrogate the roots of scientific discourses, contributes to another pattern in epidemiological depictions of HIV transmission that has led to a general marginalization of the potentially integral role of bisexual behavior in certain epidemics. This is the persistent lack of methodological and theoretical sophistication about the influence of sociocultural factors on the ways that data about sexual behavior and HIV transmission are collected and interpreted. The fact that "men who have sex with men" are the victims of considerable discrimination in most societies seems remarkably absent in most epidemiological interpretations of transmission patterns, despite the fact that most of these data are gathered in clinical environments in which self-reported sexual histories may be strongly skewed by such factors as an individual's desire to avoid association with marginalized behaviors, the interviewer's conscious or unconscious assumptions about normative and deviant sexualities, and culturally variable definitions of "homosexuality" in which some same-sex behavior may not be regarded as homosexual-typing.[25] Indeed, even among heterosexually identified persons, evidence shows that embarrassment about particular sexual acts may alter self-reported sexual histories to a considerable degree (Wight and West 1999), and that inconsistency in answers to sexual questions is more pronounced when discussing more sensitive topics (Rodgers, Billy, and Udry 1982), when quantitative behavioral data are compared to qualitative data. It is certainly not unreasonable to assume, then, that quantitative (survey) assessments of same-sex behavior would encounter a number of interpretive pitfalls, at least insofar as specific frequencies are taken at face value without serious consideration of the potential influence of the social, cultural, and political-economic environment on statistical results. In the Dominican Republic, for example, counseling staff at one of the primary HIV testing sites in

Santo Domingo have told me that questions about a given patient's sexual history are often asked in the presence of his or her spouse, making any discussion of infidelity and/or secretive homosexual behavior nearly impossible in most cases. To what extent do these realities of data collection—quite understandable in many cases but potentially wreaking havoc on the extrapolation of behavioral trends—contribute to the designation of the country's HIV epidemic as primarily "heterosexual"?

Such questions place us squarely within the realm of epistemological debates about the nature of epidemiological interpretation—debates that have been, somewhat paradoxically, both central to and marginalized within AIDS research. While the complexity of measuring sexual risk based on self-reports is often lamented among AIDS researchers, the methods used to assess the frequency of specific sexual behaviors in a given population have not considerably advanced in response. As Parker (1996) has described, this is due in part to the fact that the purposive methods by which particular groups, such as MSM, must be selected for study do not permit any presumption of generalizability to a larger population, since random sampling is impossible in many cases, particularly among "hard-to-find" or stigmatized groups. Parker explains as follows why this is so:

> Whenever social stigma exists in relation to a given behavioural pattern, not only is there a chance that at least some (if not most) individuals sampled through statistically generalizable methods will hold back information concerning socially disapproved behaviours, but this is in fact very likely. Attempts to gather representative, population-based, data on questions such as the incidence of bisexual behaviour are thus fundamentally problematic, and much of what can be known about sexual risk behaviour among such populations must necessarily rely upon targeted sampling strategies that are inevitably limited by the options open for recruiting participants (Parker 1996, 153).

As a result, the actual frequencies of particular sexual behaviors in a population—perhaps precisely those behaviors that are the most likely to transmit HIV—may be largely impervious to the methods most commonly used in public health to measure them. Combined with the tendency to neglect the influence of social context on the collection and interpretation of data, this fosters a climate in which assumptions and stereotypes about sexuality are more likely to "hijack the epidemic," leading to epidemiological conclusions that are all the more dangerous because they are imbued with the presumption of "scientific rigor."

As demonstrated by a number of medical anthropologists, however, the traditional theoretical and methodological boundaries of epidemiology do not close off the discipline from a critical analysis of the cultural, political, and economic determinants of disease patterns but rather challenge us to question, redefine, and reconfigure those boundaries.[26] In this vein, given the difficulties and potentially misleading consequences of measuring certain HIV risk behaviors using behavioral survey studies or self-reported data from surveillance sites alone, it is important to ask why it is that qualitative and ethnographic evidence does not inform epidemiological interpretations more frequently. Indeed, as discussed in chapter 3, there is now a significant amount of social-science research on MSM in Latin America and the Caribbean that demonstrates that a high proportion of same-sex activity occurs in the absence of a *gay* or *homosexual* identity, and that such activity is unlikely to be accurately reported in formal surveys or clinical contexts. This is particularly true if data collection does not occur in a manner that is sensitive to the stigma and shame that are often associated with same-sex behavior, as well as the influence of such sociological factors as the interviewer's positionality, language choice, and ability to guarantee an environment of trust and confidentiality. Incorporating these elements into epidemiological interpretation requires, first and foremost, an open recognition of the epistemological challenges involved in assessing the epidemiological role of bisexual behavior (or any sexual behavior, for that matter) in the transmission of HIV in specific populations.

Finally, and perhaps most importantly for the current discussion, political-economic trends in the Caribbean suggest that current epidemiological interpretations of the region's AIDS epidemic, as well as the design of most HIV prevention programs, are systematically neglecting a significant subpopulation of bisexually behaving men who are involved in sex work with male tourists. While the appearance of the AIDS epidemic itself may have resulted in decreases in the volume of gay sex tourism to the Dominican Republic in comparison with its "heyday" in the early and mid-1980s (De Moya and García 1998), the present research demonstrates that such tourism has nevertheless not disappeared, and, in fact, forms of gay tourism have diversified considerably in response to the increasing sophistication of tourism marketing, the growth of Internet technologies, and the reemergence of specialized gay tour groups. And although it is quite difficult to assess the behavioral and epidemiological risk for HIV infection among male sex workers and their clients—and perhaps particularly so because no HIV-prevention or service organizations have implemented sustained interventions with this marginalized and underserved population (see below)—the review of the available literature in the following section suggests that tourism continues to function as a potentially important influence on sexual risk behavior among Dominican men employed in the pleasure industry.

Previous chapters have described a number of cultural and political-economic reasons for believing that this is so for the *bugarrones* and *sankies* described here. As discussed in chapter 2, many of these men are responding to decades of structural changes that have dramatically reduced male employment in traditional agricultural sectors, led to their increasing migration to urban and tourist areas, reduced their options for formal-sector employment, and increased demand for their (mostly unskilled) labor. Thus, while structural conditions alone cannot explain all of the same-sex activity in which these men engage, or the specific forms that it takes, it is undeniable that these macrolevel forces increase the likelihood that a given individual will be confronted with the possibility and the necessity to exchange sex for money with tourists.[27] In addition, local constructions of sexuality that are relatively more permissive toward "active" participation in homosexual sex and male philandering in general—combined with gay tourists' projective fantasies about a dominant black male sexuality and their willingness to pay for escapist sexual experiences—facilitate the development of same-sex sexual encounters, some of which evolve into long-term, transnational exchange relationships (chapter 5). At the same time, economic dependence on family, asymmetrical gender norms that reinforce male philandering and "*tigueraje,*" and the stigma and homophobia associated with same-sex behavior—all contribute to a pattern of sexual silence and stigma management that systematically veils male-male sexual behavior from public view and inhibits open, direct sexual communication (chap. 4).

Taken together, these processes raise important questions about the simple designation of the Dominican AIDS epidemic as "heterosexual" and call our attention to significant gaps in HIV prevention and service programs. Just as importantly, examination of the linkages between behavioral bisexuality, sex tourism, and HIV—as well as the ways these linkages have often been obscured by the language and concepts of global health—demonstrates the importance of what Paul Farmer has called a "critical epidemiology," a commitment to the application of an ethnographic sensibility with attention to the discursive power of epidemiological thinking. It is in the spirit of such an analysis that we now turn to a specific discussion of the Dominican AIDS epidemic, focusing in particular on its initial impact and continuing spread among men who have sex with men, as well as the marked—if often underestimated—influence of gay sex tourism on the shape of HIV transmission in this tourist-dependent island-state.

Dominican AIDS: Microcosm of the Caribbean Epidemic

In 1983, just as the first AIDS cases were appearing in the Caribbean, former Dominican President Joaquín Balaguer wrote as follows about the complex "problem" of Haitian immigration to the Dominican Republic:

The commerce with the lowest of Haitian immigration has retarded, in large part, the social evolution of Santo Domingo extending to the inferior classes of its population the most repugnant diseases. A large part of the Negroes that emigrate to Santo Domingo are handicapped beings because of depressing physical defects. Few of them know of hygiene and their infiltration among the native population has brought about a decline in the sanitary indicators in our rural zones. (Balaguer 1983, 49)[28]

Balaguer's words reflect a conceptual model of Haitian contagion that circulates throughout Dominican society, reinforcing an anti-Haitian nationalist mythology of invasion and the looming threat of racial impurity. Given the tumultuous history of ethnic relations and "border anxiety" between Haiti and the Dominican Republic, it is ironic that it was most likely sexual contact with North American tourists—rather than with the "dark," "diseased" Haitian "invaders"—that was responsible for the first cases of AIDS in the country.[29]

Indeed, one of the first studies of HIV prevalence in the Dominican Republic, published in 1987 by Koenig et al. (1987), reported that persons designated "Haitians" and "homosexuals/bisexuals" were the primary victims of the country's first AIDS cases, showing HIV prevalence rates of 10 percent and 19 percent, respectively.[30] Since Haitians were presumed to have little sexual contact with Dominicans, the epidemiological evidence led the authors to conclude that "tourists, and not Haitians, were the most likely source of virus transmission to Dominicans, because contact occurs frequently between tourists (e.g., male homosexuals) and Dominicans" (quoted in Farmer 1999, 119). As Farmer (1996, 301) observes in a footnote, Koenig and colleagues later defended this interpretation, saying that their conclusions were derived in part from "information on the Dominican Republic [that came] from on-site visits to hotels that cater to the gay tourist trade. These places are frequented often by visitors from the United States and Caribbean countries" (see Koenig, Brach, and Levy 1987, cited in ibid.).[31] Yet, following Farmer's argument once again, it should be noted that Koenig and colleagues take their interpretation a step further, concluding that men who consider themselves "heterosexual" and who exchange sex for money with gay tourists were at the highest risk for infection. They describe these men as follows: "Persons who engage in homosexual acts only to earn money usually consider themselves heterosexual. This situation, public health workers have indicated, is particularly prevalent in the tourist areas with young adolescents. It could explain our finding of three positive serum samples in schoolchildren from Santo Domingo" (quoted in Farmer 1999, 119).

While De Moya and García (1998) have shown that gay sex tourism to the Dominican Republic tapered in the late 1980s and 1990s, probably in response to growing fear of AIDS, there is nevertheless a significant number of studies showing that contact with gay tourists continues to be quite common among Dominican MSM. In Ramah et al.'s (1992) KABP survey among Dominican "homosexuals" and "bisexuals," for example, one-third of the study population had engaged in sex with a tourist in the past six months—a very significant finding given that the study population was not sex workers, but a diverse sample of men with same-sex sexual experiences. A more recent KABP study virtually replicated these results, finding that 30 percent of the youngest MSM in the sample had engaged in sex with male tourists (CESDEM 1999). Studies among male sex workers, including this one, have reported even higher frequencies of contact with tourists, with most sex workers indicating that tourists are their preferred clients (De Moya et al. 1992; De Moya and García 1998; Silvestre 1994; see also chapter 5). In Silvestre et al.'s (1994) study in five Dominican cities with a sample of 412 male and female adolescent street children who marginally subsisted through prostitution, most indicated that they catered specifically to foreign tourists. Similarly, Vásquez et al. report that in their study of thirty adolescent male prostitutes in Santo Domingo, eighty-five percent have had sex with a mean of eleven foreign gay clients (1991).

Epidemiological linkages between tourism and the HIV/AIDS epidemic are also suggested by prevalence studies among female and male sex workers whose preferred clients are often tourists. As Fadul et al. (1992) have argued in the case of Dominican female sex workers: "The pervasive sexual interaction of Dominican FSWs [female sex workers] with foreign male tourists during their vacations is a breeding ground for HIV/STD transmission between local women and North American and European males in the Caribbean." This assessment is borne out by the evidence of a national HIV prevalence among female sex workers between 6 and 7 percent, with regional rates as high as 10 percent in some areas (Kerrigan et al. 2001, 222). Similar patterns are suggested among male sex workers, although data are more limited for this population. In 1992, Ramah et al. found that for their diverse sample of MSM, men who had engaged in sex for money were

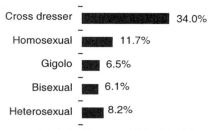

Cross dresser ████████ 34.0%

Homosexual ████ 11.7%

Gigolo ██ 6.5%

Bisexual ██ 6.1%

Heterosexual ██ 8.2%

*Data for Figure published in Tabet et al., *AIDS* 10(2), 1996

Figure 10. HIV prevalence rates among Dominican MSM, by sexual identity (data taken from Tabet et al. 1996)

nearly twice as likely as those who had not to report a history of sexually transmitted infections—a finding that suggested that risk for HIV continued to be elevated in this population as compared to MSM who had not engaged in sex work.[32]

The most important seroprevalence study of HIV among Dominican MSM was conducted by Tabet et al. with 354 men recruited through purposive sampling at "a wide variety of settings where MSM meet" (1996, 202). Participants were categorized into five sexual identities—*cross dressers, homosexuals, gigolos, bisexuals* and *heterosexuals*—with the *gigolo* category roughly corresponding to the category *sanky panky* described in the present study.[33] It is likely that those men categorized by the authors as *bisexuals* and *heterosexuals* included many self-defined *bugarrones*, although neither this term nor any other Spanish identity term is mentioned in their report. Figure 10 shows the rates of HIV seroprevalence found in Tabet et al.'s sample, by sexual identity category.

Notably, while *cross dressers*—most likely corresponding to the identity *travesti* in Dominican Spanish—and *homosexuals* had significantly higher HIV prevalence rates and were more likely to report engaging in receptive anal and oral sex, the authors found a few patterns across all identity categories. First, most of the sample of MSM self-identified as *heterosexual,* and this category accounted for half of participants. Second, sex with women was very commonly reported among all groups, with nearly all *heterosexuals, bisexuals,* and *gigolos* reporting sex with women, as well as more than half of the self-defined *homosexuals* (55.8 percent) and a third of *cross dressers* (31.3 percent). The importance of these results is underlined by the author's finding—paralleling other studies discussed in the following section—that rates of consistent condom use with female partners were significantly lower than with male partners, practiced by only 14 percent of men who reported having sex with women. Third, Tabet et al. make an important statement in their concluding discussion that is worth highlighting here, particularly since it reflects an attention to the accuracy of quantitative behavioral data collected among MSM:

We hypothesize that the strong social stigma against MSM influences bisexual individuals to self-identify as heterosexual. This bias undoubtedly could contribute to an underestimation in the proportion of HIV-positive men reported to be infected by homosexual transmission if risk behaviors are not carefully and appropriately defined. (Tabet et al. 1996, 205)

While the authors do not elaborate on the potentially profound epistemological consequences of this fact, it is important to reiterate that—as already described for the Caribbean region as a whole—the Dominican AIDS epidemic has been defined by government personnel and public health agencies as "heterosexual," with only 10 percent of cases officially attributed to "homo/bisexual" contact (PAHO 1998, 232). Given the historical associations between seropositivity and contact with gay sex tourists, as well as the very high proportion of MSM who report sex with both men and women, the uncritical designation of the Dominican AIDS epidemic as heterosexual seems to obscure more than it reveals. And, as described in the following section, behavioral assessments of risk behavior, condom use, and other potential HIV cofactors—as well as ethnographic evidence from this and other studies—further suggest that a significant domain of HIV transmission continues to be neglected by most epidemiological depictions of the Dominican AIDS epidemic, as well as the programs designed to prevent it. The reasons for this neglect call our attention to large-scale structural dynamics that are rarely considered in epidemiological models, and to the social processes of stigma, homophobia, and shame that systematically veil these linkages.

Reassessing Risk among Male Sex Workers

As discussed further below, the phrase "I always use condoms" is a common response among *bugarrones* and *sanky pankies* to questions about their sexual risk behavior and may be partly a reflection of the increases in condom use rates among male sex workers reported by De Moya and García (1998, 137). As these authors explain, such increases are a logical response to the fear of unprotected sex generated by the expanding AIDS epidemic. To what degree are male sex workers actually incorporating HIV-preventive behaviors into their sexual practices, despite the fact that this population has not been reached by any sustained HIV interventions?

In this section, I engage in an interdisciplinary dialogue between ethnographic and quantitative "measures" of male sex workers' risk for HIV infection, with particular attention to the epistemological problems of assessing sexual behavior based on quantitative surveys alone. As discussed in the introduction, while this project incorporated survey methods, a self-conscious effort was made to compare and contrast survey and ethnographic data, given the sensitivity of questions involved, the stigma and shame that tend to surround them, and the known problems with self-reported data on sexual behavior. The combination of methods thus provided the benefit of "triangulating" or checking the trends suggested by the surveys in a manner that was methodologically complementary. While surveys provided an estimated measure of particular behavioral and socio-demographic trends, qualitative data permitted a much more nuanced understanding of behavior *in process*—as it unfolds in the complex and often contradictory realm of an individual's lived experience. It also provided, I believe, a more accurate picture of actual behavior, particularly regarding the most stigmatized, shameful, or emotionally charged behaviors, such as sex with men, frequency of "passive" sexual acts, and condom use. As much of this ethnography demonstrates, it is the gap between what sex workers say and what they actually do that often defines the boundaries of risk scenarios. At the same time, the extent and commonality of covering and performance creates great challenges for behavioral interpretation, both because some of these "performances" were undoubtedly for the benefit of the researchers themselves and because sex workers may be motivated out of their own fear to underestimate or deny their risk for HIV infection.[34] Yet, in many ways, it is precisely such gaps between what people say and what they do—or between how they wish to project themselves socially and the realities of their private sexual lives—that are often the most revealing of the complexities of sexual experience. The following discussion therefore seeks to emphasize not only convergences and trends, but also the ambiguities and inconsistencies evident in sex workers' behavior, discourse, and self-perception.

It is useful in this regard to begin with the case of Vicente, an experienced *sanky panky* whom I interviewed on the beach in Boca Chica. While early in the interview he had commented that he "always" (*siempre*) used condoms with all sexual partners—effectively sidestepping a deeper discussion of his feelings about HIV and the consistency of his use of "*preservativos*" (a common term for condoms)—later in the conversation, we had the following exchange:

MP: Have you ever been afraid that you're going to get infected with an *enfermedad de la calle* [literally, "street sickness," referring to STDs]?

Vicente: Yes, I've been afraid. That's why I always have my condom.

MP: Okay. And with your girlfriends, you use condoms also?

V: Of course.

MP: Yes?

V: The first time . . .

MP: Always?

V: Always . . . well, no. Because after we get to know each other well, there's no problem, but with the first ones, yes.

MP: And with the girlfriends you have now, do you feel trust [*confianza*] for them?

V: Yes, I trust them.

MP: Okay. So, you're not using condoms with them now?

V: No.

[Later in the interview]

V: So, I'm really afraid of that [getting exposed to HIV from clients].

MP: You're afraid? Okay. And with your girlfriends you're not afraid?

V: Uh . . . the first time I'm afraid . . . but after a month or so, I don't feel afraid.

MP: You don't feel afraid? And do you think that you can tell if somebody has AIDS, for example, is it visible? Can you . . .

V: No, I don't think you can tell [*no se nota*]. Anybody can have it.

MP: Okay. So with your girlfriends, you never know, right?

V: Of course. I don't know.

MP: And that doesn't make you afraid?

V: [silence]

What is fascinating to me about this exchange with Vicente—as well as a number of similar exchanges during the interviews—is the fact that his remarks about risk behavior and condom use transformed so completely in the course of our conversation. Based on his initial statement, one is led to believe that he uses condoms consistently with all partners, an assumption that turns out to be quite inaccurate. Further, it was when we began to discuss his fears about HIV infection that his prior assertion of universal condom use fell apart. This was a common dynamic in the interviews, since open discussion of men's feelings about HIV/AIDS were often more revealing of their "risk behavior" than direct questions about their sexual behavior or condom use, since unstructured conversations tended to evoke spontaneous observations that were less scripted and idealized.

This tendency to report idealized behavior may partly explain why condom use rates reported in the surveys were quite high, with 82 percent of the 168 men who reported having male clients claiming to "always" use condoms during anal penetration with these clients, 5 percent indicating "almost always," and 4 percent "sometimes" (see fig. A.8, appendix). This is significantly higher than some prior quantitative assessments of risk behavior among Dominican male sex workers and MSM and may indicate that condom usage has indeed increased among sex workers since the 1980s. In De Moya's (1989) study of *palomos,* or adolescent male sex workers, in Santo Domingo, for example, sex workers did not believe condom use was necessary as long as the client was "known, clean, and trusted" (cited in De Moya and García 1998, 129). Ruiz and Vásquez's study of seventy-six *palomos* and *bugarrones* in Santo Domingo similarly found that only 35 percent reported using condoms consistently with their last five clients (1993, fig. 2), and Silvestre, Rijo, and Bogaert's (1994) survey of homeless adolescent runaways revealed that only a third of these boys used condoms regularly with their male clients, most of whom were gay tourists.

There are a number of factors that potentially contribute to the relatively higher rates of reported condom use. First, it is possible that condom use has increased among sex workers due to the sheer impact of AIDS and the fear that it has produced among all Dominicans, but perhaps especially among sex workers. This is suggested by the anxiety about AIDS that many sex workers described to me in their interviews, such as that expressed by Juan Carlos, a *sanky panky* in Boca Chica, when we touched upon his fear of getting infected. "AIDS is not a game," he repeated several times under his breath, and then told me about his many friends who have died of AIDS in recent years:

Juan Carlos: Here, many people have died of AIDS.
MP: Have you had friends who have died?
JC: [nodding] Died of AIDS.
MP: How many?
JC: Most of them . . . but just the ones who had sex with—a gay [*maricón*].
MP: More with gays than with women?
JC: Yes. That's why I don't want to do that [have sex with gays] anymore.

Similarly, Ricardo—the *maipiolo* mentioned in chapter 5 who established a sex work "agency" catering to gay male tourists—described in his simple, eloquent way how witnessing the death of many friends was directly related to his personal commitment to use condoms every time with clients, as well as his insistence that his "boys" do the same:

I've lost many coworkers [*compañeros de trabajo*], I mean, lots of sex workers [*trabajadores sexuales*]. I've seen them die. I've seen them in terminal phase. And I've suffered. I've seen them sick in bed. I've lost true friends, dear friends [*amigos de corazón*], because of craziness, in a mome—In an alcoholic amnesia, they've erased [everything] and don't think about the condom. Others say to me that with the condom, they couldn't get it erect [*no se les paraba bien*], and that they don't want to be embarrassed, because if you don't get it erect, they don't pay you. So, I've seen all this that's happened, and all my true friends that I've lost. So because of those guys, because of those guys, thank God, I've gotten a little bit of knowledge. I've never let myself get lost in that, in the issue about work. I'm obsessive about protection.

Ricardo, through his long-term experience as a *maipiolo*, was unusually conscious of the barriers to condom use among sex workers—and particularly young sex workers—such as the economic imperative to perform sexually that was mentioned by a number of sex workers in this study.[35] Comments such as these suggest that *maipiolos* and more experienced sex workers may be effective agents in encouraging safer sex practices among *bugarrones* and *sankies*, as well as among young street children, or *palomos*. For the current discussion, the important point is that direct exposure to those suffering from AIDS seems to have raised consciousness about protection among many sex workers, apparently leading some of them to engage in safer sex practices even in the absence of appropriately designed HIV prevention messages.

This highlights a related reason that the overall estimate of condom use was quite high in this study. Whereas prior studies have focused primarily on the youngest sex workers, including adolescent *palomos* and street children (De Moya 1989; Ruiz and Vásquez 1993; Silvestre, Rijo, and Bogaert 1994), this study selected only adult sex workers. For a number of reasons, child and adolescent sex workers are at the highest risk of HIV infection and are the least likely to use condoms consistently. In the same interview quoted at the beginning of this section, Vicente later explained why he believes that most of the youngest sex workers are unable to use condoms:

Because they're little kids [*chamaquitos*], you understand? They do it out of necessity, like I did . . . without thinking. And they're *palomos*, they don't have anywhere to sleep, you understand? They sleep where the night falls on them [*donde les coja la noche*], they sleep in cheap motels [*pensiones*], you see? It's not the same as a person like me, because now I have my house, and, on top of that, when I didn't have my house, I lived with my grandmother. And I had a roof, somewhere to sleep at least. But most of them who "look for it" [*se la buscan*] here are palo-

mos that sleep where the night falls on them, spending twenty-four hours a day walking on the beach . . . I mean, I think that those people don't take care of themselves, at least not like me. Because *I* take care of myself [*me cuido,* meaning "I use condoms"]!

Vicente's narrative clearly delineates, in his own language and drawing on his lifetime of experience as a sex worker, the structural constraints faced by adolescent sex workers that easily overwhelm their highly limited economic, emotional, and interpersonal resources to successfully negotiate condom use with clients. Thus, condom use rates are likely to be significantly lower among younger sex workers, a pattern that is consistent with the higher-risk behavior among *palomos* and street children reported in other studies.

Despite these facts, an overall rate of consistent condom use of 82 percent seems artificially high—a consequence, I believe, of the context of data collection and the effect of the somewhat idealized attitude toward risk behavior that generally characterized sex workers' responses to questions about AIDS, particularly in the surveys. On the one hand, this may have been related to my and my colleagues' association with local AIDS prevention projects, as well as to the fact that the staff of the NGO Amigos Siempre Amigos were well known among gay-identified men for their HIV prevention work and outreach in the community. This—as well as an extensive informed consent procedure specifying the project's application to HIV prevention programs—probably elicited idealized self-reports of sexual behavior and condom use from some participants. As a result, it often appeared to me that sex workers were expressing a social norm or conviction about consistent condom use that was not necessarily reflected in practice, an interpretation that emerges from inconsistencies in various types of evidence. Vicente's transformation during his interview from a "consistent condom user" to one who rarely, if ever, uses condoms with his many girlfriends provides clues to such gaps.

For example, the survey included a few checks of self-reported behaviors as a means to verify consistency in responses. To a question about how frequently they carry condoms with them, 42 percent of 200 sex workers responded that they "always" have condoms with them, 31 percent said "almost always," 18 percent "sometimes," 4 percent "rarely," and 5 percent "never." This is an important measure of risk behavior, since other data indicate that not having a condom is a factor related to unprotected anal sex in this population.[36] Nevertheless, of the eighty-three sex workers who indicated that they "always" have condoms with them, only 37 percent were able to show a condom to the interviewers upon request. This question frequently produced a barrage of unsolicited excuses and justifications for not having a condom at the time of the interview, despite the fact that the surveys were conducted at times and in places where sex workers could have conceivably negotiated encounters with clients that would have, presumably, required a condom. Again, the fact that sex workers felt compelled to justify their inability to show a condom to the interviewers further suggests that they conceive of condom use as a social norm to which they must conform—at least in discourse, if not always in practice.

The high rate of condom use shown in figure A.8 should also be qualified by a comparison to self-reported condom use with the last *regular* male client, shown in figure A.9 (appendix). As discussed in the previous chapter, these are the clients who are the most likely to become "Western Union daddies," often establishing longer-term visiting relationships involving a certain degree of intimacy as well as regular remittances from abroad. Of the 118 sex workers who indicated that they had had regular male clients, 79 percent said that they always used condoms, a proportion that approximates the overall rate of 82 percent reported above. However, a rather dramatic contrast is evident in the fact that 14 percent of sex workers said that they had *never* used condoms with their last regular client, a fact that most attributed to a feeling of "*confianza*" (trust). This is particularly significant given that the *regular client* category was operationalized as a minimum of just three dates, demonstrating that the dynamics of risk behavior can change considerably after only a few encounters with a client. This association between intimacy with regular clients and the cessation of condom use has also been observed in the case of Dominican female sex workers, many of whom define clients as "*novios*" (boyfriends) after only a few encounters (Kerrigan et al. 2001).

Martín, a *bugarrón* in Santo Domingo, for example, explained to me why he had stopped using condoms with one of his regular clients, who had recently left the country—apparently so abruptly that he neglected to leave a forwarding address. Shortly after his departure, Martín discovered he had symptoms of an STD, which he had self-treated with a brief course of over-the-counter antibiotics.[37] He explained that despite his desire to protect himself from STDs, he had felt pressure to stop using condoms with this regular client. "Lots of times they want you to, like, live with them," he commented, regarding the intimacy these men often seek in their relationships with sex workers, "and they want that without condoms." When I asked him whether he believed it was common among gay clients to avoid condoms in their more sustained relationships with sex workers, he replied: "Many of them don't want to use them because they say they don't feel the pleasure they want to feel."

The pressure to have unprotected sex in his more intimate relationships recalls some of the narratives discussed in chapter 5, in which more romantic encounters are associated with the pressure to engage in behaviors that may cause discomfort or anxiety for some sex workers. On the other hand, not using condoms can also serve to "hook" (*enganchar*) a client, to the degree that it symbolizes intimacy, fidelity, or a true emotional bond. Vicente—who preferred to focus his attention on foreign women, despite his need to resort to gay clients on occasion—explained to me why not using condoms with female tourists could sometimes reap rewards. After explaining that most of the time he uses condoms with these women, even if they request otherwise, he remarked: "Now, if they're in *love* with you, if they're *really* in love with you—like they're ready to take you away [abroad], or to help you out—you might be able to give it to them without a condom." Here, his reference to the potential instrumental gains of unsafe sex makes clear that his decision to use condoms is evaluated against the symbolic effect that this decision may have on his intimacy with female clients. And intimacy, as discussed in chapter 5, can have significant economic benefits.

Andrés, a *bugarrón* in Santo Domingo, had a different rationale for not using condoms with certain male clients, although his logic was no less instrumental. After explaining that he "almost always" uses condoms with his clients, he qualified himself as follows:

Andrés: With a man, it depends on the person. If it gets hard, fine. But if not, if I can't get it hard, sometimes . . .
MP: You mean because of the condom?
A: Yeah. So, I make him suck me, like this [gesturing], with the condom on, and I try to penetrate him, but it depends on if he has a nice ass [*una nalga bonita*] or not. Because if I don't like it, it's difficult.

In fact, a few sex workers described experiences in which a lack of attraction for a client—either because of a general sexual distaste for men or because some clients are considered especially unattractive—created practical obstacles to their consistent use of condoms. This recalls Ricardo's comment above that the exigencies of sex work lead many *bugarrones* to "craziness," that is, discontinuing condom use in order to maintain an erection during intercourse and successfully complete the transaction. In this context, it is worth noting that 70 percent of the sex workers surveyed answered "yes" to a social-norm question about whether most sex workers feel that condoms are "uncomfortable," suggesting that condoms may interfere with sexual pleasure sufficiently to make erection and ejaculation difficult. Those sex workers with the greatest economic need, therefore, are likely to feel the greatest pressure to avoid condoms in order to perform sexually, thereby ensuring the agreed-upon compensation as well as future opportunities for such lucrative exchanges.

The connection between economic need and condom use is most evident in cases in which sex workers are explicitly offered a higher fee for engaging in unprotected sex. Mario, for example, described such offers during an interview with one of my colleagues:

Mario: I mean, I don't have sex without condoms, even though sometimes they've tried to pay me more to do it without a condom.

AM: You mean, they offer you more money?

Mario: I've been offered $5,800 Dominican pesos [approximately U.S.$350 in 2001].

AM: Really?

Mario: Really! Exactly like I'm telling you! And listen, I—when I'm in need [*en necesidad*], I think "You can't take all money!" Because some money stabs you like thorns [*puya como si fuera espinas*]. There's money that has thorns! I go— for example, I go out to have a good time, because I'm going to get my five thousand pesos. I'm going to put it away and do whatever I want! Right? And I'm going to be fine. But what happens when it's over, and I'm burned [*quemado*, implicitly "infected"]? It's stupid to do it, even though at the same time you don't have the same sensation.

While it is impossible to determine how frequent it is for sex workers to be offered additional compensation for unprotected sex, it was mentioned by a few sex workers in the interviews. In addition, 12 percent of survey participants answered "yes" to a hypothetical question about whether they would engage in unprotected sex if a client paid more money for this. Given that some men undoubtedly exaggerated their condom use for the survey, it is likely that an even greater proportion of sex workers would be tempted by such an offer if it were actually made. And, of course, sheer economic necessity is very likely to play a role in such decisions.

In light of these social and structural barriers to condom use, it is not unreasonable to conclude that many sex workers engage regularly in unprotected anal sex with their male clients, and perhaps particularly with their steady clients. This is most likely to occur among younger men and men who are engaging in sex work primarily out of economic desperation. Given this, to what degree do *bugarrones* and *sankies* perceive themselves to be at risk for HIV infection? As with prior studies among male sex workers, this study found that a relatively low proportion of sex workers consider themselves to be at risk. In the KABP study by CESDEM (1999, 2), 78 percent of the sample of MSM believed they had no risk of becoming HIV-infected. While the sex workers surveyed for the present study had a slightly higher perception of risk, 40 percent still believed they had no risk for acquiring HIV/AIDS (see fig. A.10, appendix). In some cases—such as that of Ricardo discussed above—a low perception of risk may be appropriate, to the extent that condoms are used consistently with all clients and regardless of economic circumstance. In other cases, however, it undoubtedly reflects a certain degree of denial, as well as the general tendency to idealize behavior for the sake of the interviewers.

Further, some men may have been unable to accurately assess their risk because they lacked knowledge about how HIV is transmitted. In one interview, for example, Orlando became visibly distraught during our discussion of his risk for acquiring HIV, even though he insisted he had always used condoms with clients. When I asked why he was so fearful, he responded: "My friends have told me that it's not just having sex that you get the virus. You can get AIDS just by kissing." In his study of young male sex workers (*palomos*), De Moya (1989) found that some participants believed HIV was transmitted to the insertive partner in anal sex during ejaculation, since orgasm was thought to produce a temporary vacuum that "sucked" HIV into the body. In this model of transmission, ejaculation outside the body was understood to be a valid way for the insertive partner to avoid infection. During fieldwork, I heard a handful of sex workers describe a similar notion, one of whom—Enrique—expressed it to my colleague in the following interview exchange:

LS: What if, for example, you go with your girlfriend to have sex, and there's no condom. What would you do?

Enrique: Me? I would take it and put it inside like this [gesturing], without a condom, but I would shoot the *leche* [milk] outside.

LS: Why?

Enrique: Because they've told me that if—when you penetrate and you come [*se viene*], uh, it sucks like this [gesturing], when you shoot it [semen], it sucks like—How can I explain it? The penis sucks and that's the way that the disease gets in.

It is clear that, in part, such misconceptions about transmission are due to the fact that most of these men have not been reached by HIV prevention interventions, which have exclusively targeted gay-identified men. The need for such interventions is further demonstrated by the fact that many sex workers used the interview as an opportunity to ask members of our research team about HIV and to clarify the risk associated with various sex acts.[38]

It is possible that some sex workers feel they are at low risk for HIV not because they use condoms consistently, but because they believe that they are able to distinguish clients who may be "sick" from those who are healthy. This emerged in response to a survey question in which participants were asked how often they were able to determine whether a client has AIDS simply by looking at them. While two-thirds (68 percent) of sex workers believed that one could "never" tell if a client has AIDS, the other third believed that there were ways of visually detecting AIDS in a prospective client (see fig. A.11, appendix). Among the latter group, including sixty-four men, a qualitative follow-up question was asked regarding the techniques they used to determine if a client has AIDS, and responses were written textually on the survey. Physical attributes were most commonly mentioned as presumed markers of AIDS, particularly such characteristics as: glassy, bloodshot, yellow, or sunken eyes; excessive thinness or malnutrition; discolored, dry, or pale skin, especially when spots (*manchas*) are present; and a general state of weakness or malaise. Interestingly, particular emotional states were also mentioned as markers of AIDS, including: chronic sadness (*tristeza*); loss of motivation (*animo*); frustration; panic or intense fearfulness; and shyness or aloofness (*timidez*). Finally, some sex workers explained that they simply have a special intuition or "supernatural" ability to detect persons with AIDS and avoid exchanges with them. Again, such notions are undoubtedly related to the fact that most of these men have not received sufficient information about HIV/AIDS, and it is likely that they do not fully understand the distinction between HIV infection and progression to symptomatic AIDS.[39]

Finally, it is not the intention of this analysis of sex workers' HIV risk to extract their same-sex encounters from the entire behavioral context of their lives. Indeed, it is when their sexual relationships with women are brought into focus that the larger epidemiological implications of these behavioral patterns become clear. Sex workers frequently express fear about passing along HIV or other STDs to their unsuspecting wives and girlfriends. Nevertheless, they often reject the idea of using condoms with their female partners, feeling that this would be unnatural or shameful. A decade ago, Ramah et al. (1992) found that only one-fourth (24 percent) of MSM who reported having female partners had used a condom during sex with women in the previous year. Similarly, in the present study, less than a third (31 percent) of survey participants felt that it is necessary to use a condom with one's wife or girlfriend, despite the fact that many of these men engaged in unprotected sex with clients. An even lower proportion (24 percent) believed that their fellow sex workers used condoms consistently with their wives or girlfriends, demonstrating a very low perception of social support for condom use among their peers.

Humberto, a *bugarrón* in Santo Domingo, typifies this somewhat paradoxical juxtaposition of concern about infecting female partners and a categorical refusal to use condoms with them. At the time of our interview, his wife was pregnant, and Humberto explained that this had convinced him to behave more safely with clients, to protect his wife and unborn child:

MP: So, you use condoms with your clients?

Humberto: [nodding] To prevent any disease, because, like I said, my wife is pregnant [*ta preñada*] and I don't want any disease for her or for my son.

MP: Okay. And when was the last time you didn't use a condom with [name of last regular client]?

H: Always. I've always used condoms with him. And there are times that he says no, but I say yes, or otherwise we don't do it.

MP: So, you prefer to use condoms always with him?

H: With him, yes. But with my wife, no, because it would be a shame [*un bochorno*] with my wife.

MP: Have you ever been afraid of infecting your wife with an *enfermedad de la calle* [STD]?

H: Of course! Because of the gays.

MP: "Because of the gays." In what way "because of the gays"?

H: I mean, I use condoms with them [gays] because I'm afraid of making my wife sick.

Here, Humberto articulates a model of selective condom use that was common among sex workers: condoms are seen as a means to shelter the family and the domestic sphere from diseases *de la calle* (from the street), but are not considered appropriate for use with wives or steady girlfriends. The fact that many of these men are exposed to other risks for HIV infection outside of the home, and the fact that some of them do not consistently use condoms with their sex-work clients, does not apparently influence their decision to forgo condoms in their intimate relationships with women. Condoms are construed as something that one does outside of heterosexual marriage and intimacy, partly as a means to protect the sanctity of that institution. The inappropriateness of condoms for the marital context is underlined by Humberto's comment that it would be a "*bochorno*" to use them with his wife, a feeling that he reiterated several times during the interview. Other sex workers expressed similar sentiments, some of them mentioning in addition their desire to have children, which further diminished their receptivity to condoms.

The fact that condom use within heterosexual partnerships was not even considered an option by most sex workers—even when fear about infecting wives was quite high—demonstrates the power of the association between condoms and street behavior. This bifurcation of risk contexts into the discrete domains of the "home" and the "street" is consistent with dominant Dominican gender models that associate (feminine) purity with the domestic sphere and (masculine) impurity with the public sphere (see chapters 2 and 4). In this framework, condoms not only are perceived as unnecessary within the home, but are also symbolic of the moral impurity of the outside world, and may in fact spoil the sanctity of the heterosexual marital bond.[40] Such an interpretation is consistent with sex workers' expressions of shame in response to the prospect of using condoms with their wives.

This moral-spatial bifurcation of the erotic universe is probably more pronounced in the case of male sex workers because homosexuality is seen as highly impure—both by the larger society and by most sex workers themselves—and as a behavior associated with the degeneracy of the street. To the degree that condoms are conceptually associated with impurity and the "outside," then, they are seen as much more appropriate for exchanges with men than with women. This explains why even those men who expressed a very strong conviction to use condoms consistently with their male partners—such as Ricardo, quoted above—did not feel they were appropriate to use with their wives, even when these women were unaware of their involvement in sex work or their high-risk sexual activity. Further, the permissiveness toward male infidelity and philandering within the sex/gender system reinforces men's perceived right to place women at risk without communicating about outside behaviors. Sex workers were not apparently tormented by the question of whether to discuss their risk for HIV with their female partners, or whether to initiate condom use with them in order to protect them from infection. These decisions were made *for* women, rather than *with* them, and their potential implications for women's risk were often regarded—when they were considered at all—with a kind of abstract or diffuse fear, rather than a sense of responsibility to take action to reduce their partners' risk. Thus, it is with an eye toward action that we now turn to a discussion of institutional responses to HIV/AIDS in the Dominican Republic, with particular attention to the ways that the epidemiological and behavioral realities of male sex work have fallen through the cracks of public health programs.

Toward a Critical Epidemiology of the Dominican Aids Epidemic

In light of the historical connections between the Dominican AIDS epidemic and gay sex tourism, the expansion of the sex tourism industry, and the growing number of studies—including this one—that demonstrate a significant amount of sexual contact between Dominican MSM and foreign gay tourists, it is important to ask a few critical questions: Why has the epidemic come to be labeled "heterosexual"? How appropriate is this label for the behavioral dynamics of risk? What is clarified and what is obscured by such a conceptual model of HIV transmission? How much have epidemiological interpretations of modes of HIV transmission taken account of the context of data collection, or the stigma, shame, and secrecy that surround same-sex behavior? And finally, to what degree have local HIV prevention programs responded to the needs of male sex workers and their clients?

Unfortunately, my opinion—both as a consultant for HIV/AIDS projects in Santo Domingo and as an anthropologist—is that the juncture of male sex work, sex tourism, and HIV transmission has not been adequately addressed by either dominant interpretations of the epidemic or public health programs and services. One factor contributing to this neglect is that nearly all interventions that have targeted "MSM" have been oriented toward self-identified gay men, an identity category that excludes a large population of non-gay-identified men, perhaps particularly those who engage in sexual-economic exchanges.[41] ASA, the nongovernmental organization that collaborated with this project, has been funded for over a decade to conduct HIV prevention, counseling, and clinical services in the "gay community," and its staff of peer educators and outreach workers is composed almost entirely of gay men. While the work they have done among gay men is highly innovative—producing a large network of volunteers who assist the organization in its educational and outreach activities—the psychosocial boundaries that separate openly gay men from sex workers such as the *bugarrones* and *sanky pankies* in this project are profound, even though these groups overlap spatially and frequently interact. Indeed, it was precisely ASA's concern about the significant proportion of non-gay-identified MSM and sex workers who were not reached by existing programs that encouraged our initial research collaboration, with the ultimate intention of designing interventions among sex workers. In the year 2001, ASA began its first prevention activities among sex workers, adapting a model of peer education using contacts established through this research to organize "*conversatorios*" (discussion groups) with *bugarrones* and *sanky pankies*. Thus, the critique developed here is somewhat oddly self-referential, since the very production of this text signals an institutional shift in focus in an attempt to be more inclusive of a broader spectrum of "MSM" in ASA's programming (see chap. 1). The fact that the local mission of the United States Agency for International Development (USAID) contributed financially to this project also reflects a growing awareness at various levels that the category MSM is much more diverse than existing interventions imply, and may require very different programmatic approaches.

The question of why Dominican prevention programs among "MSM" remained exclusively gay-focused for so long—particularly in light of the fact that the country's first AIDS cases were among men with a history of sexual contact with gay tourists, rather than a gay identity per se—is a complex one. First, unlike in other countries in Latin America, such as Brazil (see Parker 1999), the Dominican gay community had no institutional base from which to respond to the AIDS epidemic in the early 1980s. As described in chapter 3, even today the country's gay movement is in its formative stages, despite its recent and somewhat dramatic "outing" in certain public events and the media. Thus, the emergence of ASA—the first and only officially gay organization in the country—was a *consequence* of the AIDS epidemic and the availability of funds for HIV prevention projects among gay men. The lack of a preexisting infrastructure organized around homoeroticism undoubtedly inhibited the development of intervention approaches based on local constructions of sexuality and identity, as well as the ability to advocate politically for such approaches.

Further, it is not insignificant that nearly all of the funding that has supported ASA's work in the gay community has come from international—and predominantly North American—donor organizations. This may have facilitated the conceptualization of interventions among Dominican MSM along the lines of those developed by and for gay men in the United States. Yet a "gay" identity politics as conceived in countries such as the United States may not be an appropriate model for conceptualizing homoeroticism or HIV transmission in the Dominican Republic and certainly does not address the very different political-economic circumstances that frame HIV risk behavior and same-sex sexuality in the Caribbean. Moreover, my interactions with officials from various international health agencies in Santo Domingo have convinced me that many are not aware of the large amount of same-sex sexual behavior that occurs between Dominican men in the absence of a *gay* identity, or its relationship to the sex tourism industry, despite a growing amount of anthropologically informed work in this regard (see especially De Moya et al. 1992, De Moya and García 1996, and

De Moya and García 1998). In one case, for example, a North American consultant hired to evaluate local HIV prevention programs received a somewhat hostile reaction from Dominican public health officials when he suggested that male-male HIV transmission may be more common than often implied by predominant epidemiological interpretations of the Dominican AIDS epidemic. It is likely that such biases have encouraged the somewhat uncritical exportation of a North American "gay" prevention model that has unnecessarily constrained the design of intervention approaches and functionally excluded particular groups of MSM, such as the male sex workers described in this study.[42]

Another consequence of an exclusively "gay" intervention model is that the ongoing connections among the tourism industry, male sex work, and the transmission of HIV have been systematically obscured. In the political-economic context of the Dominican Republic, the contemporary dynamics of sexual risk behavior between men cannot be fully understood without considering the structural influences of gay sex tourism on same-sex behavior. Just as economic need was closely linked to the first cases of AIDS among Dominican MSM, the prevailing conditions of poverty within a declining, dependent economy undoubtedly exert an ongoing influence on HIV transmission, particularly among those men who exchange sex for money. Further, the restriction of formal-sector employment options and the simultaneous expansion of male participation in the informal pleasure economy has resulted in a growing number of men who rely on occasional or episodic sexual transactions without defining themselves as "sex workers" or any non-normative sexual identity.

As discussed at the beginning of this chapter, such men are largely invisible to epidemiological models that assume discrete "homosexual" and "heterosexual" populations, or that posit a finite transition, or bridge, from a relatively self-contained homosexually driven epidemic to the "general population." What is obscured by such models may in fact be one of the most neglected dimensions of HIV transmission in the Caribbean: the ongoing process whereby bisexual behavior and male sex work quietly to shape HIV risk among particular populations while rarely being addressed by programs and services. The tendency to marginalize epistemological questions about data collection and the interpretation of self-reported data on sexual behavior, in addition to the stigma and shame that surround homoeroticism, further conspire to marginalize discussion of the role of bisexual behavior in local epidemics. And as evidence mounts of a significant role for male bisexual behavior in the evolving HIV epidemic among black and Latino populations in the United States, debates inevitably revert to what has now become familiar territory for public discourse on AIDS. Bisexually behaving men are increasingly becoming the targets of scapegoating, "silent killers" who engage in "sneaky sex" and then infect their unwitting female "victims." Such discourses do not only distort reality but actually reinforce the stigma and blame that contribute to high-risk behavior among MSM, undercutting a potentially radical social critique of the ongoing influence of structural inequality on the AIDS epidemic.

Conclusion

Sometimes when you want to see things as easy, you accept them. Because that's also our error—the so-called *bugarrones*—because the majority of us don't like to work. I include myself. Because it's not that I don't *like* to work—I've always worked—but the thing is that the kind of work we can do is so hard, and so poorly paid. Working like a "normal" person, I mean. And it's always like that. Nothing. So here we are. And this is our life.

GERMÁN (28), Santo Domingo

In this book, I have examined numerous effects of the pleasure industry on various domains of life among the *bugarrones* and *sanky pankies* whose experiences are described in these pages. Informed by a theoretical approach described as the *political economy of sexuality,* the introduction outlined the parameters for this project, which positions the ethnographic evidence within large-scale structural transformations that are occurring in the Dominican Republic, and their complex intersections with gender and sexuality. Chapter 2 examined recent political-economic changes in detail, including the escalating process of international tourism investment since the Dominican government, encouraged by its international donors, began to cultivate this industry in the late 1960s, and examined the expansion and diversification of the informal sector that resulted from diminishing options for men in the formal wage economy. As a consequence of these and other changes in the country's development approach—changes that have elevated tourism to the most important sector of the economy—a growing number of men have been squeezed out of rural environments and are moving to urban areas and tourism zones in search of work.[1] These transformations have fostered an environment in which men who "look for life" in the expanding pleasure industry—for example, by working as *guías,* vendors, chauffeurs, waiters, or hotel employees—are likely to encounter the necessity and the opportunity to engage in sex-for-money exchanges with tourists.

The fact that these processes have facilitated sexual-economic exchanges between local men and gay tourists has provoked responses in the Dominican Republic that forebode continued suffering and stigmatization for Dominican male sex workers. As described in chapter 3, exposé pieces in the Dominican media and recent proclamations by the Catholic church have framed gay-oriented sex work within a narrative that attributes the purported growth and visibility of such "vices"—often referenced as clear signs of the country's moral "degeneration"—to dependence on foreign tourism and the "perverted" excesses it presumably engenders. Unfortunately, because local Dominicans, and notably *not* tourists, are the ones who suffer most from such demonization, the growth of male sex work has not translated into much-needed social services or HIV/AIDS programs for the men described here, nor has it promoted safer or more humane modalities of tourism work for the growing number of Dominicans who "look for life" in this sector. Continuing to disparage these men only contributes to their stigmatization and further promotes a cultural of silence about the same-sex exchanges with tourists in which many "*hombres normales*" now engage.[2]

In an attempt to remedy this, I have argued in favor of unpacking specifically what is meant by *silence,* and to connect patterns in sexual communication to the ways that stigma is managed and the specific meanings of gender and sexuality in the Dominican context. Chapter 4 presented ethnographic evidence from sex workers' relationships with wives, girlfriends, and families to illustrate sex workers' daily struggles to guard their same-sex encounters from public view or to actively deflect suspicion, using such strategies as the telling of elaborate *cuentos* (stories), inventing *mentiritas* (little lies), creating convincing "scenes," and recruiting accomplices in the construction of protective alibis. I have also sought to place these strategies within local systems of gender and sexuality by examining how such techniques reflect many of the features of contemporary masculine *tigueraje,* such as the ability to use ambiguity and contradiction to one's advantage. While I have borrowed Goffman's (1963) language of "stigma management" to describe certain aspects of these processes, it is not always clear whether it is the *act* of engaging in homoerotic activities or its conversion into *discourse* that is the primary source of social stigma for these men. Indeed, the reactions of family members to moments of intentional or (more often) unintentional disclosure frequently express anxiety about maintaining discretion and preventing gossip, rather than castigating the behavior per se. Thus, the "silence" that envelopes the practices discussed in this book is a *productive* one; it is based on, and informed by, a cultural system of sexual communication that defines the kinds of erotic discourse that are permissible, and assigns meanings to particular types of silences and omissions. In understanding and contextualizing these processes, I have drawn upon recent ethnographically informed work on "sexual silence" in Latin America (Carrillo 2002; Díaz 1998), an exercise which suggests that sexual silence has some relevance for understanding how Dominican male sex workers draw upon notions of gender and sexuality to negotiate their involvement in the pleasure industry. Nevertheless, because of the ways that these men systematically deny homosexual identity or same-sex attraction, and because of their ability to make claims to masculinity vis-à-vis traditional models of sexuality, the masculine meanings of *tigueraje,* and the material benefits of sex work, the operation of sexual silence in these men's relationships takes a particularly Dominican shape.

Because *sanky panky* and *bugarrón* identities are *already* integrated into global circuits of sexual consumption, I have argued that they play a role in the generation and maintenance of a "marketable fantasy." That is, while they have taken their Dominican form in dialogue with "traditional" expressions of homoeroticism, they also function as global erotic commodities that can no longer be interpreted outside of the sexual "investments" of foreigners and the implications of these investments for the local organization of gender and sexuality. I have also argued that, somewhat ironically, the global gay sex market seems to facilitate, rather than attenuate, a contrastive relationship to gay-ness, since the pleasure industry disproportionately commodifies a particular expression of Dominican (hyper)masculinity that is also—and perhaps not coincidentally—defined in opposition to a "modern" gay identity. It should be noted that there are also sexual interactions that occur between gay foreigners and local gay Dominicans, an aspect of global sexual interchange that is not addressed in this book. Nevertheless, while it is certainly the case that some gay Dominican men engage in paid exchanges with foreign gays,[3] it is overwhelmingly clear that the gay commercial sex market within the pleasure industry is primarily oriented toward men whose sense of self-identity and gendered practice conforms to the *bugarrones* and *sanky pankies* described here. As argued in chapter 5, some gay clients draw upon cultural and racial stereotypes to create a fantasy in which *bugarrones* and *sankies* are seen as "real men," true "machos" who are pleased to accept whatever their foreign friends are willing to offer them to "help out." Such fantasies, which are common in heterosexual sex tourism as well (O'Connell Davidson 1998), express an exoticization and commodification of difference that is culturally and historically particular.[4] Here, I would like to suggest that in the case of gay sex tourism in the Dominican Republic, these ideas are related not only to presumed racial and cultural differences (which are nearly always present in sex tourism), but also to the ways that the globalization of the gay market commodifies particular expressions of Dominican homoeroticism.

It is not random, of course, that most of the Dominican men who exchange sex for money with gay tourists do not identify themselves as gay or homosexual. While this might be interpreted as the influence of particular structural constraints on the formation of gay identity and community in Latin America (Murray 1995; Parker and Cáceres 1999), gay tourist narratives such as those expressed by "Jeffrey" in chapter 5—as well as representations of Dominican men in gay publications, Internet sites, and pornography—suggest that most of these tourists are seeking encounters with men whom they regard as decidedly *non-gay*. This particular expression of the "commodification of the other" (hooks 1992) employs real or imagined cultural, racial, and sexual differences, along with the escapism inherent in touristic practice, to realize a fantasy that is not "thinkable" within the sex/gender logic of the "modern" gay world: to have sex with a "straight" man. Thus, Dominican men are not only seen as naturally "macho," sensual, and well endowed—by nature of the racial fantasies of tourists—but also as capable of engaging in same-sex encounters while remaining fundamentally "heterosexual." This logic has entailments on the level of sexual behavior as well, since—to the degree that what sex workers and gay tourists say about their encounters corresponds to their actual sexual practices—*bugarrones* and *sankies* are typically paid to engage in "active" (penetrative) sex. In this sense, sex workers' activity (and, by extension, their symbolic masculinity) in anal sex is both an expression and a reaffirmation of the fact that, in a certain sense, they aren't "really gay."[5] Based on my conversations with gay tourists, I believe that such notions form the foundation for a projective fantasy that motivates, at least in part, the desire for travel to the Dominican Republic among a significant proportion of gay tourists.

Yet, even if one tentatively accepts that the global gay demand for homoerotic services commodifies a particularly *non-gay* expression of Dominican gender and sexuality, it is not simply the absence of a gay identity that accounts for the tourist demand for *bugarrones* and *sanky pankies*. Thus, analytical questions emerge about how to interpret the "performances" described by *bugarrones* and *sanky pankies* in their relations with gay tourists.

What is it precisely that these men are performing, and how can we understand these performances?[6]

The narratives of individual sex workers examined in this book draw attention to these questions, since most of these men are very aware of the impressions that others have of them and are quite skilled at managing these impressions in various spheres of life. As in the case of Orlando, whose interview is quoted at length in chapter 4, many of these men are accustomed to strategically emphasizing or deemphasizing different aspects of gender and sexuality in order to navigate the complex terrain in which they look for life—a terrain in which homoeroticism has different, and often contradictory, implications for one's status as a man. While most sex workers believe that being "burned" as a *bugarrón* in one of Santo Domingo's *barrios* could have severe implications for their social respectability—or, perhaps more importantly, their desirability as husbands and fathers—the global gay market for this particularly Dominican construction of sexuality can be profitable, not only economically but also symbolically (for example, by improving one's masculine status as "household provider"). Indeed, as argued in chapter 4, the very profitability of these identities is linked to discretionary practices in the family, since sex workers often use the financial benefits of their sexual exchanges to evade interrogation about their nonnormative sexual practices. The challenge for *bugarrones* and *sanky pankies*, then, is to perform their various identities strategically, to emerge socially unscathed while continually moving in and out of very different social and sexual spheres. Despite the generally greater sexual license afforded to men by patriarchal gender norms, this is always a precarious game, as demonstrated by sex workers' stories of discovery and their fears that, sooner or later, the elaborate *cuentos* will no longer be enough to evade detection. Longer-term relationships with "Western Union daddies," while potentially profitable, pose additional challenges by threatening a breach of discretion with wives and girlfriends, and—as in the case of Miguel described at the beginning of chapter 4—can create the demand for additional performances, such as convincing shows of "love" and fidelity.

These multifaceted performances by sex workers for the purpose of marketing themselves to tourists demonstrate an intriguing expression of MacCannell's (1973, 1976) now classic analysis of the techniques that people in host countries use to "stage" particular features of "authentic" local culture for consumption on the tourism market. The motivation for touristic experiences, according to MacCannell, is partly the product of the search for authenticity that increasingly characterizes the contemporary world. "Under modern conditions, the place of the individual in society is preserved, in part, by newly institutionalized concerns for the authenticity of his social experiences" (1973, 590). Tourism provides an outlet for these desires through the consumption of "authentic" cultural experiences, but achieving this goal requires access to what MacCannell, following Goffman (1959), describes as "back regions"—the domain of private life that transcends the barriers to "truth" and intimacy that nearly always characterize public social spaces.[7] Nevertheless, this quest for authenticity is a partial one: "Sightseers are motivated by a desire to see life as it is really lived, even to get in with the natives, and, at the same time, they are deprecated for always failing to achieve these goals" (1973, 592). MacCannell summarizes as follows this ambivalent position of the tourist in relation to his or her quest for authenticity:

Touristic consciousness is motivated by its desire for authentic experiences, and the tourist may believe that he is moving in this direction, but often it is very difficult to tell for sure if the experience is authentic in fact. It is always possible that what is taken to be entry into a back region is really entry into a front region that has been totally set up in advance for touristic visitation. In tourist settings, especially in modern society, it may be necessary to discount the importance, and even the existence, of front and back regions except as ideal poles of touristic experience (1973, 597).

This recalls the discussion of Jeffrey in chapter 5, who is tormented by the "what if" question of his financial contributions, never entirely confident about the authenticity of Fernando's shows of affection. As in MacCannell's apt description of the quandary of the tourist, travel to the Dominican Republic allows Jeffrey to purchase exotic experiences that, at least in his view, are not possible in New York, and yet the very instrumentality of these experiences undermines his sense of their authenticity. Importantly, ethnographic evidence described in previous chapters demonstrates that *bugarrones* and *sanky pankies* are indeed highly aware of the suite of meanings associated with a certain notion of Dominican masculinity, and they use this knowledge strategically in marketing themselves to clients. This "strategic" deployment of identity should not be considered, however, a purely rational or conscious phenomenon, since in many cases it is impossible to distinguish between "performances" that are instrumental in nature from those that are more deeply integrated into one's sense of self. Sex workers' performances are therefore fundamentally overdetermined; that is, they are informed by multiple meanings and interests simultaneously.[8]

These observations urge us to return to some of the issues raised in chapter 3 regarding the ways that homoeroticism and gay identity are embedded in the contemporary global economy, as well as the role that tourism plays in these processes. In addressing these questions, it is useful to consider some discussions within gay and lesbian studies that provide a theoretical framework for conceptualizing the relationship between "modern" gay identity and changes in the basic structure of capitalism. Among the most important contributions to the growing literature on the historical emergence of contemporary notions of gay identity in the West is John D'Emilio's analysis of capitalism and gay identity in the United States (1997). Linking the development of a modern notion of gay identity to the historical transformations in the structure of labor in modern industrial society, D'Emilio argues that the gradual reconfiguration of the domestic sphere and the nuclear family that occurred with the expansion of capitalism had the effect of freeing people from many of the traditional moral and economic constraints on sexuality, and particularly homosexuality. As rural agricultural laborers were increasingly incorporated into an urban wage-labor economy, and as the nuclear family became less important as the basic productive unit, "it became possible to release sexuality from the 'imperative' to procreate" (D'Emilio 1997, 171). Whereas heterosexual marriage, fertility, and the gendered division of labor were intimately intertwined and mutually reinforcing within the traditional economic system, industrial capitalism fostered an environment in which an individual's productive capacity was not necessarily dependent upon the (heterosexual) family unit and the private sphere, but rather upon the market for his or her labor within the wage economy and the public sphere:

In divesting the household of its economic independence and fostering the separation of sexuality from procreation, capitalism has created conditions that allow some men and women to organize a personal life around their erotic/emotional attraction to their own sex. It has made possible the formation of urban communities of lesbians and gay men and, more recently, of a politics based on a sexual identity (1997, 172).

Thus, in D'Emilio's analysis, capitalist "free wage labor" fostered a climate in which some individuals could, in fact, find a certain degree of personal freedom to engage in homoerotic behaviors or same-sex partnerships, and their economic independence from nuclear families served to buffer the potential social consequences of these stigmatized practices. Further, the increasingly diverse urban environments in which same-sex practices unfolded enabled the gradual development of a kind of collective consciousness—or a gay "affectional community," in D'Emilio's terms—that both defined and reproduced a particular identity-based construction of same-sex desire.

How well does such an analysis apply to the political economy of same-sex relations and the formation of gay identity in places such as the Dominican Republic? As a growing number of studies of Latin American homoeroticism attest (Carrier 1995; Carrillo 2002; Kulick 1998; Lancaster 1992; Lumsden 1996; Parker 1999), gay identity and same-sex relations in the region are conditioned not only by changes in the structure of labor and capital in specific local settings, but also by the position of these societies within a larger global sphere. In the Caribbean today, new forms of capital accumulation, population movement, communications technology, international gay activism, neoliberal policies, and patterns of HIV/AIDS funding shape contemporary Dominican discourses and practices of homoeroticism. Thus, while the growth of capitalist wage labor may have had important formative effects on the emergence of a particular expression of gay identity and community in the industrialized West, a view of homoeroticism *from the margins* draws our attention to the ways that the globalization of *gay*—and particularly its specific expressions in consumer capitalism— are transforming homoeroticism in places that are differently positioned within the "West Atlantic system."[9] Increasingly, what it means to be gay in places like the United States is intimately related to what it means to be gay—or, perhaps more intriguingly, what it means to be straight—in places like the Caribbean. Yet, as this book endeavors to show, the nature of these connections and the hierarchies they entail place very different constraints on practices of gender and sexuality.

In the Dominican Republic, these global connections cannot be understood without consideration of the role of gay sex tourism in the political economy of same-sex encounters in the new millennium. While the integration of what might be cautiously termed "Western gay culture" into the arena of global capitalism has been remarked before (Altman 1995, 2001), a focus on gay tourism—perhaps particularly in highly tourist-dependent economies—highlights the ways that *the globalization of gay both reflects and reproduces the inequalities through which it operates.* Gay identity in wealthier nations has become not only a means by which to form communities and identities (although it certainly has done that), but also a means to coalesce a powerful economic niche through which a range of consumer products and services are marketed on a global scale. It is not surprising, then, that touristic experiences have become increasingly important to the meanings of *gay* in the contemporary world.[10] Nevertheless, as Puar (2002b) has argued, few of those who would champion queer tourism as a politically justified right to free-market consumerism have considered the political and moral tensions between this presumed "right to global visibility" and the effects of this consumption on local queer populations:

> While it is predictable that the claiming of queer space [abroad] is lauded as the disruption of heterosexual space, rarely is this disruption seen as a disruption of racialized, gendered, and classed spaces, nor is it seen in tandem with a claiming of class, gender, and racial privilege as well . . . And Finally: Whose visibility is enabled here, at the expense of whose invisibility? (Puar 2002b, 137)

In this book, I have traced ethnographically some of the various "disruptions" in local gender and sexuality that result, directly or indirectly, from gay tourism in the Dominican Republic. In this tourism-dependent country, gay tourism dollars function to challenge the gendered moral economy for a group of highly disadvantaged Dominican men. This fact, which is likely to have parallels in many tourism-dependent countries throughout the developing world, requires social scientists to more directly engage the global intersections between queer travel and neocolonial expressions of class and racial privilege, and to develop new theories and methodologies for tracing the structural connections between queer consumption and its local transformations. This, of course, should not be read to justify the attitudes of homosexual contagion with which gay tourists have occasionally been received in the Caribbean but simply makes the point that the very global conditions that permit the practice of gay sex tourism also function to *redistribute the social consequences of homoeroticism from the North to the South.*[11] Such patterns of global "outsourcing" are perhaps not atypical in the realm of traditional commodities, but scholars are only beginning to consider their implications in the arena of gender and sexuality.

In previous chapters I have contrasted the escapism often expressed by gay sex tourists with the complex techniques that sex workers employ to minimize the consequences of their encounters with tourists; I argue that *bugarrones* and *sanky pankies* cope with these social dangers by becoming experts in the management of information about their homoerotic activities. Gender norms—such as the emphasis on discretion about transgressive sexual activities, the notion that masculine "household providers" need not justify their sexual behavior, and the ambiguity and performance embodied in the masculine *tíguere*—assist these men in evading suspicion and discovery. Nevertheless, stories of breaches in discretion and the ruptures they can cause in familial relations suggest that the historical expansion of the gay tourism industry has indeed affected the structure and function of the household for many of the men who provide sexual services to gay tourists. Perhaps even more importantly, these influences are not exclusive to gay-identified Dominican men but rather involve many men who identify themselves as "*hombres normales*," are often married, and commonly have children. This highlights the potential pitfalls of the theoretical separation of "homosexual" and "heterosexual" spheres in anthropological examinations of the globalization of *gay*, and indeed, the fact that gay clients often eroticize and pursue Dominican men whom they regard as "straight" suggests that often it is precisely non-gay-identified men who must manage the potential social consequences of association with gay tourism. The transgressive nature of homoeroticism in many developing contexts, combined with the historical expansion and diversification of the global gay market, implies that these challenges to family structures may be common in gay travel destinations in the Caribbean and elsewhere.

The ways that *bugarrones* and *sanky pankies* participate in household economies provides another contrast with D'Emilio's theory of the emergence of gay communities in the developed West. While D'Emilio regards economic independence from the natal family as a key precondition of the development of non-normative sexual communities, many of the participants in this study depended upon extended family networks for a significant proportion of their routine expenses (see fig. A.2, appendix), and these household ties, in part, *motivated* their decision to engage in non-normative sexual behavior. Rather than enjoying the freedom from familial suspicion and surveillance that D'Emilio describes for urban gay communities in the early- to mid-twentieth century United States, however, these men's sexual "deviance" occurs in the context of close kin relations and obligations, necessitating strategies for balancing their two lives. Stigma management is essential, since any public indiscretion about their same-sex exchanges is potentially damaging to their reciprocal kin relations, as well as their prospects for expanding family networks by establishing relationships with women.[12] Far from facilitating a break with the family, the structures of late capitalism in the Dominican Republic are therefore increasing—or at least maintaining—a reliance on kin networks, at the same time they raise the stakes of potential ruptures with family. This has myriad implications for how sexuality is practiced and socially controlled, and in many cases it is likely to increase the felt need to use culturally available strategies to veil non-normative behaviors.

The "sexual silence" and stigma-management techniques that sex workers use to mitigate the impact of their same-sex encounters on their social and conjugal relations raise questions about epidemiological models that depict the Caribbean HIV/AIDS epidemic as "heterosexual" while obscuring many of the cultural and political-economic factors that facilitate, as well as disguise, same-sex exchanges. This analysis has benefited greatly from a growing literature in anthropology that has addressed the linkages between structural inequalities and the HIV/AIDS pandemic. Anthropologists such as Paul Farmer (1990, 1992, 1996, 2003,), Brooke Schoepf (1990, 1992a, b, c, 1995), and Merrill Singer (1990, 1998) have all pointed to the inadequacies of international health approaches that erase the role of poverty and inequality as the fundamental epidemiological factor influencing both exposure to HIV and progression to AIDS.[13] These scholars have been at the forefront of a considerable movement within medical anthropology—often associated with "critical medical anthropology" (CMA)—that seeks to refocus attention from the microlevel of behavioral "risk factors," typical of international health approaches, to the systemic context of social and structural inequality and both local and global levels.

Nevertheless, much of the literature in the tradition of CMA has not deeply engaged the intersections between political-economic analysis and the functioning of specific sex/gender systems, an area of research that is essential for the next generation of HIV/AIDS research.[14] In an attempt to respond to this need, the theoretical framework advanced here unifies the critical political-economic focus of CMA with a nuanced ethnographic analysis of gender and sexuality. The lack of such a theoretical approach in the Dominican Republic has led to an almost total neglect by existing HIV/AIDS policies and programs of the growing population of men who exchange sex for money with gay tourists. I have discussed a number of interrelated reasons for this neglect: the cultural silence about the commonality of same-sex behaviors among non-gay-identified men; a lack of understanding of the broad range of variation subsumed within public health categories such as "MSM"; a resistance to contextualizing epidemiological data within cultural meanings and political-economic structures; and a strong North American influence on the establishment of intervention strategies and priorities among gay-identified men. Nevertheless, the evidence presented in this book suggests that HIV transmission between men employed in the pleasure industry and their female partners may be a significant factor in the epidemiology of the Dominican AIDS epidemic—and one which most likely has analogous expressions in various developing contexts—but such an interpretation has been obscured by cultural taboos, disciplinary biases, and the persistent marginalization of structural approaches in global health. Overcoming these barriers will be key to confronting the patterns of HIV risk that are associated with the practices described in foregoing chapters. The first step in this process, both in the Dominican Republic and elsewhere, involves the development of an ethnographically informed under-standing of male homoeroticism and the commitment to trace its myriad connections to structural inequalities—a project that requires new theories and methodologies for understanding the complex linkages between health and homoeroticism in the contemporary globalized world.

Appendix: Selected Survey Results

TABLE A.1: Sexual attitudes and preferences, by *bugarrón* vs. *sanky panky* self-professed identity

	n (%)	
	Bugarrón	Sanky panky
Preferred sex partners		
Women	42 (58.3)	17 (51.5)
Men	4 (5.6)	1 (3.0)
Both sexes	26 (36.1)	15 (45.5)
Preferred sexual behaviors with women		
Anal sex	9 (12.5)	5 (15.2)
Vaginal sex	46 (63.9)	18 (54.5)
Oral sex	6 (8.3)	5 (15.2)
Other	5 (6.9)	0 (0)
Doesn't know / no answer	6 (8.3)	5 (15.1)
Preferred sexual behaviors with men		
Anal sex	27 (37.5)	9 (27.3)
Oral sex	40 (55.6)	12 (36.4)
Other	3 (4.2)	6 (18.2)
Doesn't know / no answer	2 (2.8)	6 (18.2)
Could you fall in love with a man?		
No	42 (58.3)	20 (60.6)
Yes	29 (40.3)	6 (18.2)
Don't know	1 (1.4)	7 (21.2)
Could a man be your partner?		
No	39 (54.2)	17 (51.5)
Yes	32 (44.4)	11 (33.3)
Don't know	1 (1.4)	5 (15.2)
Is a man who prefers sex with men a homosexual?		
No	12 (16.7)	4 (12.1)
Yes	58 (80.6)	27 (81.8)
Don't know	2 (2.8)	2 (6.0)
Is any man who has sex with men a homosexual?		
No	34 (47.2)	11 (33.3)
Yes	36 (50.0)	20 (60.6)
Don't know	2 (2.8)	2 (6.1)
Is a man who lets himself be penetrated a homosexual?		
No	5 (6.9)	3 (9.1)
Yes	66 (91.7)	30 (90.9)
Don't know	1 (1.4)	0 (0.0)

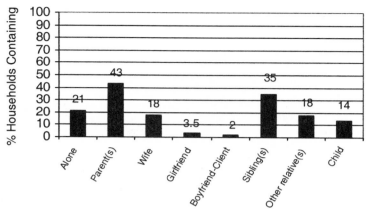

Figure A.1. Sex workers' household composition, by relationship to interviewee (*N* = 199)

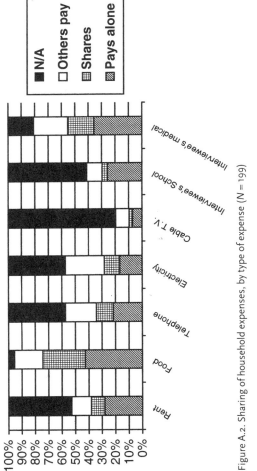

Figure A.2. Sharing of household expenses, by type of expense ($N = 199$)

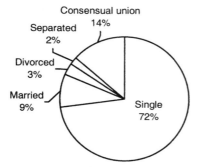

Figure A.3. Sex workers' marital status (*N* = 199)

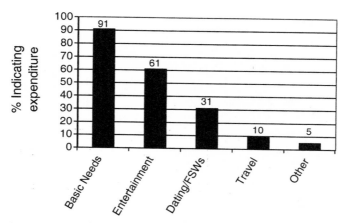

Figure A.4. Expenditure of sex work income (*N* = 199)

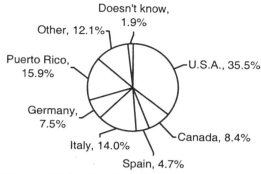

Figure A.5. Nationality of last male tourist-client (*N* = 107)

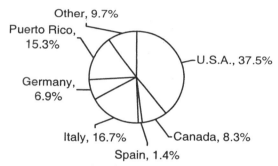

Figure A.6. Nationality of last regular male tourist-client (*N* = 72)

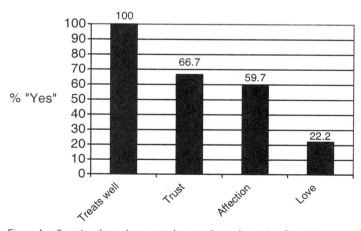

Figure A.7. Emotional attachments to last regular male tourist-client (*N* = 72)

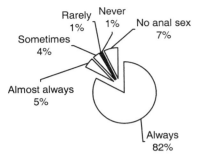

Figure A.8. Frequency of condom use with last male tourist-client (*N* = 168)

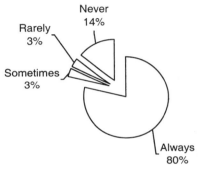

Figure A.9. Frequency of condom use with last regular male tourist-client (*N* = 118)

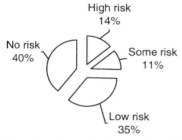

Figure A.10. Sex workers' perception of risk for HIV infection (*N* = 199)

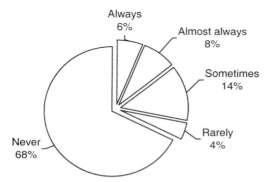

Figure A.11. How often can you detect AIDS just by looking at a client? (*N* = 199)

Notes

Preface

1. Mintz provides a detailed historical analysis of the process by which sugar was converted from a luxury product whose consumption was limited almost exclusively to metropolitan elites to one which, by the mid-nineteenth century, "surrendered its place as luxury and rarity and became the first mass-produced exotic necessity of a proletarian working class" (1985, 46).

2. *Joselito,* as with all sex workers' names throughout the ethnography, is a pseudonym. *Sanky panky* is a local identity term referring to a certain type of Dominican male sex worker. See "Definitions of the research population" in the introduction.

3. Anthropologically informed discussions of Caribbean political economy that have been especially influential to my thinking include the work of Mintz (1971, 1974, 1985, 1987, 1989), Mintz and Price (1981), Hoetink (1985), and Trouillot (1992), as well as historical analyses by Williams (1984) and Knight (1990).

4. Theorists of tourism often trace these experiences, in a neo-Marxian tradition, to the presumed alienation brought about by late capitalist society, in which the socially privileged engage in touristic practices to search for authentic experiences that they lack in their everyday lives (MacCannell 1976; Smith 1978; Urry 2002).

5. CMA overlaps with what has also been termed "the political economy of health" (Morsy 1996); there now exist a number of reviews and theoretical statements on the development of CMA within medical anthropology (Baer, Singer, and Johnsen 1986; Baer, Singer, and Susser 1997; Frankenberg 1988; Morgan 1987; Morsy 1996; Scheper-Hughes 1990; Singer 1986, 1989, 1995a, b).

6. Indeed, as Briggs and Farmer have argued, "the link between infectious diseases and poverty has more commonly prompted responses that stigmatize populations in which epidemics occur, such that developed countries reproach developing nations for their health problems and the latter, in turn, scapegoat their poorest and most marginal sectors" (1999, 2).

7. See Parker, Easton, and Klein (2000) for a useful review of this literature.

8. See, for example, a number of analyses of gender and AIDS among African women by anthropologist Brooke Schoepf (1992a, b, 1993, 1996, 1997, 1998).

9. For a theoretical analysis of the multiple hierarchies and inequalities that structure masculinities, see Connell (1987).

10. I borrow the term *critical epidemiology* from Farmer (1996). For a detailed discussion of its usage and meanings in this book, see chapter 6.

Introduction

1. These issues are taken up more thoroughly in chapter 2. In my reference to "neocolonial," I follow a history of anthropological research in the Caribbean that has framed the region's current political-economic circumstance as one in which the global capitalist system reinstantiates colonial relations of production through a variety of mechanisms, such as development loans, off-shore production, and (coerced) trade favoritism to particular nations. See Basch, Glick Schiller, and Szanton Blanc (1994) for a review of this literature, with examples from the Caribbean.

2. For discussions of the relationship between sexual labor and the colonial project in the Caribbean, see Abraham-van der Mark (1993), Geggus (1996), Henriques (1965), Kempadoo (1999a), Matos-Rodriguez (1995), and Morrissey (1989).

3. See, for example, O'Connell Davidson and Sanchez Taylor's (1999) analysis of the "demand side" of (heterosexual) sex tourism to the Caribbean, as well as chapter 5 of the present work. Joane Nagel has published an excellent global review of the "intimate intersections" of sexuality and race/ethnicity in her recent book *Race, Ethnicity, and Sexuality* (2003).

4. While many of the political-economic changes that have encouraged the growth of the Dominican sex tourism industry have parallels in other Caribbean contexts, it should be mentioned that different islands have been incorporated at different times and at different rates within the global sex tourism industry. For example, while Cuba was the primary Caribbean destination for sex tourists to the region prior to Castro's revolution (Cabezas 1998; del Olmo 1979; Espino 1994; Fernandez 1999; Fusco 1998; Kutzinski 1993; Leiner 1994; O'Connell Davidson 1996; Schwartz 1999), the Dominican Republic became one of the region's primary destinations—as well as the most important "exporter" of female sex workers both within and beyond the Caribbean (Kempadoo 1999b)—following former President Balaguer's incentives to foreign tourism investment in the late 1960s and 1970s (see chapter 2).

5. See Kempadoo (1999a) for a concise historical overview of global representations of Caribbean sexuality as related to patterns of Caribbean sex tourism.

6. "King Tourism" is a somewhat sardonic reference to Williams's (1984) classic historical analysis of "King Sugar," the single cash crop that dominated Caribbean political economy throughout the colonial era, and which generated social and cultural echoes that have been examined by anthropologists since the inception of Caribbean anthropology.

7. This point is elaborated in chapter 5, in the discussion of the market demand for Dominican masculinity and sexuality. As argued in that chapter, the negotiations and accommodations that occur between local sexualities and global tourist demand are often highly racialized, since the qualities that tourists seek in sex workers and the physical or sexual features that are prized on the global tourism market nearly always reflect racial-sexual stereotypes.

8. See, however, Trexler's history of the symbolic role of male-male sexuality in the conquest of the New World, an analysis that focuses on metropolitan interactions with indigenous sexual systems (Trexler 1995). One suggestive, though preliminary, study from the United States

argues that contemporary sexual relationships between black and white men in rural farm settings may be structured by historical relationships of sexualized power in which socioracial hierarchies are reflected in homoerotic expressions of dominance and submission (Lichtenstein 2000).

9. Goffman's (1963) work on stigma and his descriptions of *stigma management* (the strategies and devices used by stigmatized persons to minimize the negative social and psychological impact of their stigma) are central influences on the analysis presented in this book. Interestingly, the term *tapa'o* (literally, "covered") is a common descriptor used by gay-identified Dominican men to refer to the male sex workers described here, who are increasingly considered "closeted" or "repressed"—an opinion, as described in chapter 3, which reflects the growing influence of global gay politics in the Dominican Republic.

10. This team configuration provided another source of ethnographic data, as we were able to consider the ways our individual positionalities as researchers—including a heterosexual Dominican woman, a gay Colombian man, a gay Dominican man, and a gay American man—influenced the kinds of interactions we had and the responses we obtained from *bugarrones* and *sanky pankies*.

11. While De Moya and García's (1998) recent work on Dominican male sex work provides insights into the number and basic features of sex work sites in Santo Domingo over three decades, they do not specify particular geographical locations, a fact that necessitated our team's identification of sex work sites at the beginning of the research.

12. "Pimp" is an inadequate translation in that it suggests a degree of hierarchy and control that is not typical of the relationships between *maipiolos* and sex workers. *Maipiolo* is a term used to describe a man who is a successful social broker between male sex workers and gay clients, who often socializes younger sex workers into the trade, and who can intimidate his peers into giving him commissions for transactions with clients.

13. I first established contact with ASA and learned of their HIV prevention work with gay men in 1996, during a pilot research project funded by the Mellon Foundation and administered through Emory University's anthropology department. This initial association established friendships and professional relationships that greatly facilitated my transition to the field in 1999.

14. As elaborated in chapter 6, ASA's mandate as an HIV/AIDS organization has limited its involvement in purely activist causes. Nevertheless, its intervention approaches explicitly appeal to men who profess a more globalized gay identity, and it has occasionally been involved in gay political organizing, such as the first gay pride march, described in chapter 3.

15. While the ethical and methodological complexities of working as both an anthropologist and an evaluator in the field are too lengthy to address here, it is worth mentioning that my experience in this regard did not convince me that these roles are necessarily contradictory. On the contrary, I see anthropological and ethnographic methods as potentially complementary components of evaluative approaches, both as a means to conceptualize the constraints on programmatic outcomes and as a means to broaden the typical methodological techniques used in program evaluation. It should be mentioned that due to my prior affiliation with ASA, and in order to avoid any potential conflicts of interest, I withdrew myself from any evaluative role in relation to ASA's programs.

16. Both USAID/AcciónSIDA and Fogarty funds for this research were administered by ASA and supervised by me.

17. My own research and living expenses were covered by individual research grants from the National Science Foundation, the Wenner-Gren Foundation for Anthropological Research, and Fulbright IIE.

18. Generous support from AcciónSIDA allowed us to hold extensive training workshops for each formal method used, in order to ensure consistency (when multiple data collectors were involved) and to model appropriate and inappropriate interview techniques.

19. These focus groups are in addition to the focus groups discussed in chapter 3, which were conducted with a broader cross-section of MSM for the purpose of identifying and categorizing sexual identity terms.

20. Because of the clandestine nature of the research population, it was difficult in some cases to identify potential survey participants in order to conduct initial interviews and assess their qualifications for the survey. Recruiters, who were well-known and well-connected sex workers or *maipiolos*, were very useful in this regard and further communicated an environment of trust and confidentiality to potential participants.

21. Surveys, totaling over 700 variables, included measures of: sociodemographic profile (e.g., various measures of socioeconomic status, household composition, marital and extramarital history, patterns of spousal support, education, occupation, and income); sexual self-identifications (e.g., as *bugarrón, sanky panky,* gay, bisexual, etc.); social norms about sex work (e.g., preferred types of clients, perceived behavior of social peers); sexual behaviors and condom use with clients (both male and female) as well as with girlfriends, wives, and intimate male partners; affective and emotional bonds with clients; substance use history; frequency of internal and transnational migration experiences; and numerous relatively standardized measures of potential "co-factors" of HIV and STI risk (e.g., access to condoms, perception of risk, knowledge of HIV/AIDS, and social support). Whenever possible, or when indicated by the validation surveys, questions were structured to permit the broadest range of potential responses, and textual answers were included in many questions to provide additional qualitative data when answers did not correspond to standardized items.

22. As described in chapter 4, however, sex workers' homes are often carefully guarded by the discretionary practices that shield the domestic context from the world of sex work and homoeroticism. My ability to conduct participant observation in informants' homes was therefore limited by the exigencies of privacy and stigma management.

23. See a longer description of this interview conversation in chapter 4.

24. Individuals were included if they reported a history of sex with tourists in exchange for money or benefits in-kind. Because of our particular interest in exchanges with foreign gay men, we purposively targeted men who we knew had engaged in such exchanges. However, a history of sexual-economic exchanges with foreign men was not a strict selection criterion, because it often was not feasible to screen for these rather clandestine and socially delicate behaviors before interviewing and establishing some rapport with participants. For this reason, a small proportion of the survey sample includes men with an exclusive history of sex with foreign women. As described later in this chapter, most of the participants had foreign clients of both sexes.

25. As suggested in the discussion of Jeffrey, a gay sex tourist, in chapter 5, some clients seek to deny the instrumental aspects of their relationships with Dominican men in order to imagine the relationship as based on "authentic" affection.

26. Indeed, De Moya and García (1998), in their study of Dominican male sex work, simi-

larly argue that the typical gender presentation of *bugarrones* expresses an exaggerated masculinity. See chapter 5 for more on the masculine aesthetic typically preferred by gay male sex tourists.

27. The fact that gay sex tourism in the Dominican Republic creates a demand for non-gay-identified men within the pleasure industry is an observation that is further elaborated in both chapter 5 and in the conclusion.

28. Such research is particularly complementary, because within the traditional Dominican sex/gender system, *travestis* are the prototypical sexual partners of *bugarrones,* and vice versa (see chapter 3).

29. Based on my conversations with transgendered persons (including the local identities of *transgéneros, travestis, transformistas,* and *transexuales*) in the Dominican Republic, it is evident that more transgendered persons identify themselves with the term *gay* than do the *bugarrones* and *sanky pankies* discussed here, the vast majority of whom systematically deny this form of self-labeling. Nevertheless, the complexities of sexual identity ascription are likely more complex. For example, it is possible—but not directly studied in this research—that some *travestis* who are in transition to *transexuales* reject (or "disidentify" with) the *gay* label because they consider themselves biological women. Future research will need to elucidate these issues. It should be emphasized that despite their closer affiliation with gay identity, the specific sexual practices and HIV prevention needs of transgendered person in the Dominican Republic are not being addressed by the exclusively gay-focused interventions currently in existence. Amigos Siempre Amigos is now developing new interventions specifically designed for transgendered persons.

30. As described further in chapter 3, the *metálicos,* as a group of men who project a non-normative gender identity in the Dominican context, became strategically aligned with the nascent gay movement in 1999, participating in the organization of what ultimately became the country's first gay pride march.

31. My spelling here of *sanky-panquiar* and *bugarroniar* is based on their most probable spelling in Dominican Spanish.

32. Similar qualities have been associated with beach boys in other Caribbean contexts. See O'Connell Davidson and Sanchez Taylor (1999), Phillips (1999), and Press (1978).

33. The authors do not, however, offer a specific sociohistorical theory for how the French word was introduced and appropriated in the Dominican Republic. *Bugarrón* is also commonly used in Puerto Rico and Cuba, as suggested by conversations with colleagues on those islands. For descriptions of *bugarrones* in Cuba, see also Hodge (2001), La Fountain-Stokes (2002), and Lumsden (1996).

34. Indeed, as discussed further in chapter 3, traditional constructions of Dominican homoeroticism tend to blur the boundaries between *bugarrones* and "normal men," since gender normativity is substantially defined in relation to sexual positionality, as opposed to sexual object choice.

35. To be "maintained" (*mantenido/a*) in the Dominican Republic suggests a relationship in which a person—typically in the context of an intimate relationship—depends entirely on his/her partner to meet basic economic needs. As suggested by Kulick's (1998) ethnography of *travestis* in Brazil, however, there is likely an erotic dimension to this arrangement that contributes to its cultural persistence.

36. See Prieur (1998) and Carrier (1995) on the Mexican *mayate,* and Kulick (1998) and Parker (1999) on the *michê.*

37. Here, and elsewhere in the book, I borrow Rubin's (1975) classic term *sex/gender system* in describing aspects of the cultural organization of homoeroticism and sexual-economic exchange in the Dominican Republic. Rubin used this term to denaturalize sexuality and to interrogate—following a Foucauldian tradition—the deep cultural underpinnings that make sex appear to operate "seamlessly" and "intuitively."

38. Hodge (2001) has argued that the "*pinguero*"—a Cuban male sex work identity—was invented by local men in response to the global tourism market, and thereby functioned as a kind of brand-name marketing. Presumably, the term had no linguistic analogy in older constructions of male sexuality in Cuba. I did not observe such a linguistic transformation or "identity marketing" in the Dominican Republic; however, the emerging term "*parguero*" (designating a local man who takes advantage of relationships with foreigners as a way of gaining a degree of social and financial prestige) may be a related identity term in the Dominican context. Future ethnographic studies in the Caribbean should document and thoroughly describe these social and sexual semantic inventions as they emerge in response to the region's growing tourism industry.

39. This may be related to the fact that relationships with women are more likely than those with men to involve feelings of "romance" or affection, although such relationships also occur with men (see chapter 5).

40. As mentioned above, the methodological approach to participant selection—using purposive or convenience sampling rather than randomization procedures—limits my ability to generalize to a larger population on the basis of survey data alone. Here I report statistical significance measures, but the reader should be cautioned that the sampling frame was not designed to permit reliable measures of statistical differences between groups.

41. This discussion benefits from the important work by Altman (2001) on "sex and political economy."

42. I use the term *queer sexualities* in order to be consistent with its usage in much of the relevant sexuality literature, and as a broad analytical construct that subsumes a wide range of non-normative local genders and sexualities. However, it should be emphasized that this specific term itself carries cultural and academic "baggage," and is problematic to the degree that it draws attention away from local idioms of gender and sexuality.

43. All researchers engaged in critical tourism research among sexual minorities must address this question, since it is inevitably politicized to acknowledge the social inequalities that are expressed and maintained by queer tourism. Ultimately, I believe there is more value in a sensitive and rigorous engagement with these problematics in the effort to minimize the suffering of sexually marginalized populations globally than there is risk in drawing attention to their existence and cultural logic for those who may seek to do us—or more likely, our research subjects—harm.

44. It should be emphasized that contrary to many of the depictions of "trafficking" that are currently circulating in public health, human rights, and feminist circles, I do not interpret male sex workers' involvement in sexual-economic exchanges as necessarily or entirely coerced. Indeed, in the vast majority of cases, these men *make decisions* about their involvement in sex work, even if these decisions are highly constrained by economic considerations and structural inequalities. It is neither ethnographically parsimonious nor respectful of emic perspectives to make the claim that these men have no agency to make decisions regarding their participation in sex work. Indeed, what is more useful analytically is to ask *why* these men

make the decisions that they do—a project which often reveals more about the influence of structural inequalities on individual lives than if we were to assume total coercion, and which allows an entry point into discussions of how to make one's decision-making process safer and more equitable for all concerned.

45. While there is little research on "sexual escapism" among gay male tourists, the theoretical and empirical literature on tourism more generally strongly suggests that tourists' behavior while on vacation is often motivated by the desire to achieve a temporary escape from restrictive socio-moral codes in their home countries, including sexual restrictions (Crick 1989; MacCannell 1976; Urry 1991, 2002). Since the controls on homosexual behavior are presumably highly restrictive in many tourist-sending countries, it is quite possible that a high proportion of queer tourists use travel and tourism as a means of sexual escapism. Indeed, Puar has suggested that tourism may be considered a key component of how queer people construct and maintain their identities, as queer socializing often entails occasional escapes from heterosexism through forays into contained queer spaces (Puar 2002a). Future research will need to document the degree to which queer sexual escapism exists in a distinct form, and investigate its potential impact on local sex/gender systems.

46. As summarized further in chapter 3, the Latin American anthropological literature on homosexuality is extensive, permitting the extrapolation of both regional trends and disjunctures (Adam 1989; Cáceres 1996; Carrier 1995; Carrillo 2002; De Moya and García 1996; Kulick 1998; Kutsche 1995; Lancaster 1992; Lumsden 1996; Murray 1995c; Parker 1999; Prieur 1998).

47. See, for example, Farmer (1990, 1992, 1996) and Singer (1995, 1998).

Chapter One

1. See, however, some important recent works (Bejel 2001; La Fountain-Stokes 2002; Lumsden 1996).

2. The outward-looking posture of Dominican urban gay culture is related to the commonality of migration and travel abroad, particularly to the United States, by the Dominican population more generally, a trend which is described in more detail in chapter 2.

3. The importance of *travestis* as gay cultural translators is consistent with Murray's (Murray 1995; Murray and Arboleda 1995) sociolinguistic suggestion that the term *gay* was initially a simple relexification of the traditional *pasivo* (passive) category in Latin America—a category represented within the Dominican sexual system by the *travesti*. This might result, as I believe may be the case in Santo Domingo, in the conceptualization of *travestis* as quintessential or prototypical gays. In any case, it is clear that in Santo Domingo—the largest urban center in the country—*dragas* and *travestis* perform an important role in the performance of globalized queer identity among a certain segment of Dominican queer youth.

4. As elsewhere in Latin America (Cantú 2002), the phrase *de ambiente* (of the environment) is sometimes used in Dominican queer circles to denote one's participation in homo-erotic social environments or practices. This was also used among some of the sex workers whom I interviewed.

5. Gay tourism agencies, as well as gay movement activists, have tried to document the extent of gay tourism expenditures in an attempt to leverage greater social rights around the world by demonstrating global queer participation in large-scale touristic consumption (Puar

2002b; Ryan and Hall 2001). While such attempts have yielded impressive estimates of the power of the queer dollar, a persistent analytical problem has been to obtain appropriate sample diversity in terms of race, class, nationality, and other relevant axes of diversity in order to accurately assess queer tourism participation.

6. These Internet sites have grown considerably in number and membership since I conducted the fieldwork for this book. There are now annual group trips and parties in the Dominican Republic organized through international gay travel agencies based in New York that attract hundreds of gay tourists, who share information about Dominican men and sex workers via online blogs. Several expatriate gay men have now opened gay hotels, restaurants, and businesses in Santo Domingo to cater to this growing international gay clientele.

7. The countries of origin of these foreign gay tourists are estimated using survey data, and are summarized in chapter 5 and figures A.5 and A.6 in the appendix.

8. My research with Dominican *bugarrones* and *sanky pankies* is consistent with observations by Kempadoo (1999b) and others that Caribbean sex workers almost invariably prefer foreign clients because of the generally higher fees they are willing to pay as well as the potential—real or imagined—for a ticket off the island.

9. For a rich ethnographic description of the Dominican queer diaspora in New York City (Washington Heights), see Decena (2004).

10. It should be emphasized, however, that I encountered very few Dominican gay men who were "out" about their sexuality in a way that parallels the urban gay ghettos of North America and Europe. Indeed, most Dominican gay-identified men with whom I interacted who could "pass" as straight openly expressed their gayness only at circumscribed times and places. This is at least partially related to the restrictive structure of family life and economic interdependence with kin. See chapter 4 and Murray (1995). Nevertheless, recent activism in the Dominican Republic suggests this pattern is beginning to change, particularly among a younger generation of gays who are professing a more public gay identity and politics.

11. In this system, gender performance organizes the selection of *gender*-appropriate sexual partners, and also presupposes particular sexual roles (active vs. passive) for each partner, such that all homoeroticism is structured along cross-gender ("exogamous") lines. The logic implicit in this system is evident in the somewhat cryptic comment by a gay-identified male informant to my inquiries about his coresidence with his gay-identified partner: "Everyone says we're lesbians." The fact that their relationship was not defined along the lines of *activo-pasivo* (or *bugarrón-gay*) necessitated its interpretation as same-*gender*, that is, pseudo-lesbian (since *gay* is constructed as pseudofemale), within the traditional sex/gender system. Nevertheless, this remark was nearly always made in jest, demonstrating an element of flexibility and play in these cultural logics. See in particular Murray (1995b).

12. See chapter 3 for a detailed description of traditional models of sexuality.

13. *Tomando trago* in the Dominican Republic, as in much of Latin America and the Caribbean, is a highly homosocial activity among men that is associated with street behavior, mostly at night, and through which many men establish some of their key peer relationships.

14. The dangers of tourist areas to locals deemed "delinquents" are on the rise due to the recent commitment by Dominican President Hipólito Mejía of 80 million pesos (approximately U.S.$2.5 million) earmarked to increase "surveillance" and the presence of the tourist police in the country's tourist zones (Medina 2003). In response to this commitment, one of the country's largest multinational resort chains commented, "We believe that the economic

stability of the Dominican Republic and the social peace is in the hands of President Mejía" (quoted in ibid., translation by author).

15. Clearly, race and color play significant roles in the ascription of a tourist identity. I once spoke with a black American woman in the Dominican Republic who told me about her experience of being publicly scorned by local Dominicans when she walked through a tourist town on the north coast while holding hands with her white American boyfriend. Local Dominicans had assumed—on the basis of color alone—that she was a Dominican prostitute.

16. A small minority of participants in this study had spent significant amounts of time in jail for other crimes, such as drug dealing, theft, and crimes of violence. This even influenced my research process. After his mysterious disappearance, I heard that one of my key informants had been arrested and was serving a long sentence in the infamous detention center "La Victoria," featured in Dominican director José Enrique Pintor's dark film *Cárcel de La Victoria: El cuarto hombre* (2004).

17. The reticence of most hotel and business owners to allow interviews on the premises made it necessary in Boca Chica to conduct interviews in public and semipublic spaces, such as beaches and adjacent abandoned lots.

18. As described in chapter 3, police abuses and raids on gay establishments have been common in the Dominican Republic, and—as with the gay movement in the United States—such abuses spurred the first public protest by Dominican gays in 1999.

19. A clear exception to this is demonstrated by cases in which foreigners are suspected of involvement in child prostitution or pornography, and incidents in which such foreigners have been incarcerated are commonly discussed among sex workers.

20. The importance of the Zona Colonial (colonial zone) as a nodal point of both sex work and tourism is described in chapter 3.

21. The highly ambivalent fact of being ascribed a tourist status while conducting research is something that has been extensively discussed in the social science literature on tourism and is perhaps particularly problematic in the context of ethnographic research on sex tourism (Burns 1999; Chambers 1999; Clifford 1997; Crick 1989; Graburn 1983; Nuñez 1989).

22. My childhood exposure to Ecuadorian Spanish through my father's side of the family—while not fully preparing me for the rapid-fire *cortao* (cut off, or abbreviated) speech pattern typical of the Hispanic Caribbean—undoubtedly improved the depth of my communication with Dominican sex workers.

23. Sex workers' tendency to associate me with tourists was further amplified by my self-identification as a gay man, since most of the foreign clients of sex workers were also gay-identified men. My sexual identity therefore tended to position me as a potential sex work client, and in fact *bugarrones* and *sankies* commonly tried to negotiate paid exchanges with me, especially toward the beginning of fieldwork when my social status in sex work environments had not been clearly established. After several months of fieldwork, however, I began to make a transition in my friendships with *bugarrones* that enabled some of them to refer to me as "*medio bugarrón*" (half *bugarrón*)—a humorous nickname that reflected, I believe, both their desire to distinguish me from the gay clients with whom they regularly interacted and the belief that I, in some sense, was not entirely gay, and therefore not an appropriate target for their sexual advances.

24. Interestingly, research on sex tourists suggests that empathy for sex workers' economic deprivation is, in fact, motivational for some clients, who feel fulfilled by the opportunity

to "help out" local people through their redistribution of wealth (O'Connell Davidson and Sanchez Taylor 1999). See chapter 5 for an example of this rationale in the case study of a gay sex tourist whom I call Jeffrey.

25. See chapter 4 for a discussion of the gender logic behind the image of the Dominican *tíguere*.

26. My interactions with gay male sex tourists suggest that many clients are, in fact, quite concerned about their vulnerability to robbery or aggression, and are often victims of theft by sex workers. Therefore, many clients highly value sex workers whom they perceive as both attractive sex partners and capable bodyguards. This configuration of the relationship is also highly gendered, placing the gay tourist in the stereotypically feminine position of requiring protection by the sex worker—an arrangement that was highly eroticized by the sex tourists with whom I spoke.

27. I do not intend to imply that the "stories" that have always been told to ethnographers can be easily divided into the reified categories of "truth" and "fiction," since often it is the blurring of these boundaries—either consciously or unconsciously—that is most revealing of ethnographic "reality." Nevertheless, the rules of social engagement between sex workers and tourists, and sex workers' concern for projecting an attractive image, raise important epistemological questions about the interpretation of ethnographic data.

28. The latter was certainly a genuine concern, since sex workers were often arrested and jailed on charges of theft, whether justifiable or fabricated by the police. Therefore, sex workers' reticence to discuss their involvement in illegal activities is also an understandable adaptation to the real threat of incarceration.

29. Caribbean ethnography demonstrates that masculinity in the region—and particularly its lower-class manifestations—tends to valorize men's artful verbal ability, a trait that is particularly well developed in the men discussed in this book (Chevannes 2001; Dann 1987; Wilson 1973). See chapter 4 for more on Dominican *tigueraje*.

30. See Staff (2003) for a description of the Dominican Republic's five *polos turísticos*, and the Dominican government's attempts to revive them in the post-September eleventh environment.

31. Nevertheless, there are two caveats to this generalization. First, a few older *sanky pankies* mentioned in interviews that during the eighties and early nineties, there was a gay hotel in operation in Boca Chica in which exchanges between gay tourists and local men were common. This hotel is now closed, possibly because of the increased surveillance of these businesses resulting from recent scandals about child prostitution in the area (see, for example, Pantaleón 2001 and Silvestre, Rijo, and Bogaert 1994). Second, one business located on the beach in Boca Chica, while not specifically gay, was owned by a gay foreigner and served as an important networking site for both gay tourists and local *sanky pankies*/sex workers.

32. See chapter 5 for survey results on the specific nationalities of gay sex tourists.

33. Such trips are an important source of symbolic capital for local men, precisely because of the elitism and exclusivity that access to tourist areas connotes.

Chapter Two

1. Throughout the book, *pleasure industry* is used instead of the more common *sex industry*, in order to draw attention to the fact that sex-for-money exchanges are one niche in the

informal-sector economy that caters to the generalized pleasure-seeking and hedonism that is especially characteristic of tourist enclaves.

2. Nevertheless, one study of Dominican gender and informal entrepreneurship shows that men generally make more than comparable women in this sector, and contribute a lower proportion of their income to the household economy (Espinal and Grasmuck 1997).

3. It is, of course, inherently reflecting a gender bias to declare a "crisis" when men begin to experience dramatic increases in informal-sector employment and job insecurity—situations that have long confronted Caribbean women.

4. The expansion of free trade zones (FTZs) continues to form, along with tourism, the foundation of the Dominican development approach. In 2001, more than 85 percent of the country's exports came from FTZs, increasing from 52 percent in 1990 (World Trade Organization 2001, xi). This dramatic change also reflects the simultaneous decline of traditional agricultural exports.

5. Following its involvement in the assassination of the Dominican dictator Rafael Trujillo in 1961 (Diederich 1978), the U.S. government—at its peak of anticommunism and military buildup prior to Vietnam—became increasingly concerned about the popularity of the liberal, reformist politician Juan Bosch, who was democratically elected to the Dominican presidency in 1962 (Wiarda and Kryzanek 1992, 41). In 1965, when a U.S.-supported Dominican military coup aimed at removing Bosch from power failed, President Lyndon Johnson ordered 23,000 American troops to invade the country to remove the president-elect and "prevent another Cuba" (ibid.) (also see Lowenthal 1995).

6. There are historical echoes in such policies, recalling the hoarding of enormous tracts of prime agricultural land by foreign companies for the purpose of mass sugar exportation, a process which began in the late nineteenth century (Hoetink 1982).

7. For other discussions of the impact of structural adjustments and Balaguer's economic reforms on the Dominican economy, see Bray (1984, 1987), Deere et al. (1990), Freitag (1996), Silié and Colón (1994), and Wiarda (1995). Tracing the relationships between these structural changes and their numerous social and economic consequences, several authors have drawn attention to the connections between structural adjustments programs and the practices of offshore banking, money laundering, drug trafficking, informal commercial trading, information processing, and export manufacturing in the Caribbean (Block and Klausner 1987; Kempadoo 1999a; Maingot 1993; Watson 1994).

8. In 2001, some 2,294,121 nonresident foreigners (not of Dominican descent) entered the Dominican Republic. The vast majority of these arrivals were from North America (963,521) or Europe (1,108,471), and nearly all of them indicated that they were visiting the country for "pleasure" (Banco Central de la República Dominicana 2001). By the early 1990s, intensive investment in tourism infrastructure made the Dominican Republic one of the regional leaders in tourism development, boasting the largest number of hotel rooms of any Caribbean country (Wiarda and Kryzanek 1992, 90).

9. As Safa (1995, 20) argues in her discussion of Dominican free trade zones, "the sharp increase in export manufacturing is directly attributable to currency devaluation mandated by the International Monetary Fund, which lowered the cost of labor and other expenses in the Dominican Republic to one of the lowest levels in the Caribbean."

10. Georges (1992, 31), citing Bray (1984), notes that "the number of university graduates increased nearly 800% between 1970 and 1977."

11. Bray (1984, 1987), in his analyses of Dominican development and emigration, reaches similar conclusions.

12. Indeed, the saturation of the informal labor market—which is the direct result of diminishing economic prospects in the formal sector—is one reason that tourists may feel overwhelmed by vendors in Dominican tourist enclaves. Tourists' annoyance at the "bothersome" vendors, in turn, motivates the occasionally abusive practices of law enforcement personnel seeking to stop locals from "harassing" the tourists. See Mullings's (1999) excellent analysis of these dynamics in Jamaica.

13. Freitag describes the philosophy of the Caribbean tourism-as-development approach as follows: "A central thesis of early proponents of tourism was that the industry promoted secondary growth in other sectors of the economy, was a 'smokeless' industry which safeguarded resources, both human and natural, and, being a service-intensive industry, employed large numbers of people. The United Nations deemed tourism to be such a panacea for the economic problems of many Third World nations that the organization chose 1967 to be the International Tourism Year. International mass tourism since has grown into one of the largest global industries, even surpassing the combined earnings of petroleum companies for a brief period during the early 1980s" (1996, 226).

14. "Making do" is a Jamaican phrase described by Mullings (1999) and is similar in its general semantic characteristics to the Dominican analog *buscársela,* discussed later in this chapter.

15. Following the September 11 , 2001, attack on the World Trade Center in New York City, which was tragically punctuated only a few days later by the crash of an American Airlines flight leaving New York and bound for Santo Domingo, created deep concerns among local Dominicans about the future of the tourism industry—and their livelihood. Indeed, the number of North Americans entering the Dominican Republic dropped from 74,321 in August to 28,614 in September 2001—a decrease of 65 percent in a single month (Banco Central de la República Dominicana 2001). In early 2002, tourism experts in the Dominican Republic complained of dramatic drops in hotel occupancy rates in the country's tourism enclaves, most of them in the double digits (Collins 2002).

16. Of the notorious unpredictability of the tourism industry, Crick (1985, 315) observes that the inherent seasonality of tourist arrivals is compounded by the vagaries of foreign economies: "Not only are there the obvious seasonal fluctuations in arrivals, but the developed economies themselves also go through economic cycles; and during recessions, demand for overseas travel declines."

17. These terms are used here to set up a contrast between traditional explanations of Caribbean family forms and the contemporary pressures that more often typify Dominican families, not to legitimate the problematic usage of such terminology. Indeed, as Barrow (1996, 5–7) has argued, the centrality of kinship and household studies to Caribbean anthropology is related to the persistent assumption that Caribbean families are in some way "deviant," "fractured," or "disorganized," and therefore in need of analysis and explanation. While more recent anthropological research has sought to overturn or qualify this core assumption, much of the influential early scholarship on lower-class Caribbean kinship took for granted that these family forms were either suboptimal or seriously pathological, and then framed their analyses as attempts to explain the existence of these forms.

18. While leading a household-level reproductive health survey in seven Dominican sugar

cane plantations in the course of my work for USAID's Prime II project, I had the opportunity to witness these dynamics directly over the course of six months of fieldwork in 2000.

19. Nevertheless, as discussed throughout the ethnography, the fact that Dominican law does not specifically prohibit commercial sex work most emphatically does *not* mean that law enforcement officials are respectful of sex workers' rights.

20. International donor agencies—particularly in the area of HIV/AIDS prevention—have done much to spur the development and institutionalization of the self-advocacy movement among female sex workers.

21. The nongovernmental organization Centro de Orientación e Investigación Integral (COIN)—with financial support from USAID—has recently expanded its innovative, grassroots HIV/AIDS prevention intervention among Dominican female sex workers into what they call the "*nuevas modalidades*" (new modalities) of sex work, which now compose approximately 90 percent of sex establishments in Santo Domingo (Kerrigan et al. 2001). Among these new modalities are the "*liquor store*" and the "*car wash*," both of which are English designations that are linguistically "creolized" in Dominican Spanish.

22. On the dramatic effects of sex tourism on Dominicans' lives, see also Brennan (2004), O'Connell Davidson (1996), Manier (1996), and Cabezas (1998).

23. *Cabañas,* usually located on the periphery of tourist zones or urban centers, are short-term motels known for their discreet drive-in garages that guarantee a measure of anonymity for people engaging in sex-for-money exchanges or casual encounters. Aside from their discretion and generally lower cost, *cabañas* fill an additional market niche for sex-work clients who are staying in hotels that prohibit entrance to sex workers—an obstacle that is particularly salient for clients seeking homosexual encounters.

24. The complex term *marido* is roughly glossed here as "husband" to signify its general reference to a steady partner, but *marido* carries a number of cultural connotations that are missed by this crude translation, including the fact that it tends to imply a less formalized relationship or consensual union. Through their community work in the area of female sex work, staff members of one of the HIV prevention NGOs have commented to me that clients are often considered *maridos* after just a few dates.

25. An educational comic book for Dominican female sex workers (*Maritza*) tells the story of a fictional Dominican sex worker who is duped by a foreign client to travel abroad, where she discovers she was brought to dance in a strip club and suffers a series of abuses.

26. As Kempadoo (1999a, 20) notes, work conducted on the Jamaican informal sector, such as Harrison's (1991) study of a Jamaican urban slum, has consistently found that women are often involved in multiple interrelated occupations such as "barkeeping, ganja trading, and housekeeping," and that a significant proportion are also employed as "sportin' gals" or prostitutes. Kempadoo remarks that "there is little to suggest that these strategies have changed in the 1990s but rather . . . point to an intensification of this process" (Kempadoo 1999a, 20). Note that the concepts of "making do" and "buscársela" are both similar to descriptions of "hustling" in African American urban communities in the United States (Whitehead 1997, 427–28).

27. Note that when more than one additional economic activity was mentioned, only the first job mentioned was used in constructing figure 4.

28. In figure 4, "informal sales" includes street and beach vendors selling products or services such as food/drink (commonly tropical fruit, seafood, and soft drinks) or local artwork.

"Bar/rest./hotel" includes waiters, bartenders, and street/beach promoters (*"fizgones"*) working for businesses near tourist or beach areas, either formally or by commission. "Mech./elec." includes jobs oriented toward auto mechanics, electrical services (e.g., the popular *"electricista del barrio"*), carpentry, and other forms of semi-skilled manual labor. "Beach rentals" refers to the rental of beach equipment and services (scuba diving, banana boats, jet skis, etc.) to tourists. "Chauffeurs" includes taxi drivers and *"motoconchistas"* (motorcycle taxi drivers), as well as individuals who occasionally offer tours in their own private vehicles. "Studies," while not an income-generating activity per se, was a common response to this question, apparently because sex workers regard it as an "occupation" or "profession."

29. Other research on Dominican male sex workers has also noted the commonality of informal-sector work as *guías*. De Moya et al.'s (1992) study of sanky pankies in Sosúa on the north coast of the country demonstrates that many *sanky pankies* work in the informal sector as "independent tour guides." Cabezas (1999) also notes that a "study conducted in 1996 by COVICOSIDA disclosed that 38.5 percent of the male sex workers in the area [of Puerto Plata] had jobs in hotels as waiters, porters, and security guards, and 36.8 percent work as motoconchos (motorcycle taxis operators)."

30. A common scenario among Dominican female sex workers is the maintenance of a job as a *camarera/mesera* at a business such as a *discoteca,* bar, *car wash,* or *colmado* (small corner store). In many cases, the businesses in which these women work are implicitly or explicitly oriented toward sex work, but when asked about their profession, most of these women will answer *"soy camarera"* (I'm a waitress). In this case, formal-sector work as a *camarera* serves a dual purpose: it provides a consistent (if inadequate) income, and it provides a cover for stigmatized activities in the sex industry.

31. The recent diversification of female sex-work establishments in Santo Domingo seems to represent a trend toward a more informal, less "traditional" (i.e., brothel-based) modality of female sex work that would more closely resemble the informality of male sex work. In the historically recent modalities of the *car wash* and the *liquor store,* waitresses are not accountable to the owners for any sex-work activities they conduct after hours and are not required to pay a fee. Nevertheless, formal ties are still discernible in the fact that these sex workers are generally employed as waitresses (*meseras/camareras*) (Deanna Kerrigan, personal communication).

32. Dominican male sex workers would likely use *cliente* (client), *amigo* (friend), *pareja* (stable partner), *maricón* (roughly, "fag"), or *loca* (literally, "crazy," but meaning an exaggeratedly effeminate gay man) to describe their clients, depending on the gender expression of both the sex worker and the client, the degree of affection between them, and the context of the conversation. When clients are foreigners, I have also heard many sex workers refer to them simply by their nationality, such as *"el italiano,"* *"el español,"* or *"la americana."* Descriptive nicknames are also commonly used. See chapter 3 for a more detailed discussion of sexual identity terms.

33. Another prejudice is evident in some of the growing "gay" establishments in Santo Domingo, where gay management is occasionally openly annoyed by the "self-deception" of sex workers' purported heterosexuality, or by their hypermasculine *"machista"* performance of gender. Recall, for example, the description of the attempted *bugarrón* ban in the gay bar that I call Tropicalia, described in the previous chapter.

34. Some cross-cultural literature may suggest that male sex workers are generally more mobile and independent of sex work businesses than female sex workers. McCamish et al.

(2000), for example, make precisely this argument in their discussion of Thai male sex workers serving a homosexual clientele.

35. The ethnographic research upon which this book is based was conducted in conjunction with the nongovernmental organization Amigos Siempre Amigos (ASA), which has fifteen years of experience in HIV prevention among gay-identified men. Partly as a result of this research, the administration of ASA, as well as the local USAID mission and other donor agencies, have become aware of the need to expand HIV prevention services to the population of male sex workers that composes a distinct subgroup of men who have sex with men. Beginning in January 2002, ASA began a series of exploratory interventions with male sex workers, with support from the USAID-funded project AcciónSIDA. See chapter 6 for details.

36. See, however, the various short-term projects undertaken in the area of HIV prevention among male sex workers, described in chapter 6.

37. Some male sex workers, in fact, work in the bars and discos where they also meet clients. In Santo Domingo, one of the most common ways that sex workers are incorporated into commercial businesses is as strippers, usually involving an informal fee-for-performance payment system. Often the *porteros* (doormen), security personnel, and bartenders dabble in sex work to a greater or lesser degree.

38. Cabezas (1999, 110) observes of the Dominican Republic: "Working-class women, and sex workers in particular, routinely fuse the traditional dichotomy of public and private spaces. Consequently, they are suspect and are stigmatized as *cueros* (skins) and *putas* (prostitutes). The connotations surrounding 'puta' are the worst that a woman can be, the lowest person in the society. Sex workers are also known as the *mujeres libres* (free women) or *mujeres de la calle* (women of the streets). Women who work in the sex trade are the opposite of the *Dominicanas de su casa* (Dominican women of their homes)."

39. In a recent book of person-centered interviews with Dominican female sex workers, women frequently discussed the hardship and isolation that can result from the social ascription of the identity "*puta*" (Murray 2001). At a recent launching of the book held in Santo Domingo by the members of a grass-roots advocacy organization for female sex workers, sex workers argued that their stigma was unjust, because they were victims of necessity and systematic abuses by a *machista* culture.

40. The numerous travel diaries and conversational sites on the Internet documenting clients' experiences with sex work in the Dominican Republic (and elsewhere) offer a wealth of potential research projects on the sexual and racial stereotypes that circulate in the global sex industry (see chapter 5). The fieldwork on which this book is based took advantage of this medium to correspond with and interview—formally or informally—a number of male sex-work clients, some of whose observations will be discussed at various points in the following pages.

41. This trend toward anonymity is particularly evident in sex-work interactions between Dominicans and foreign tourists. This is because sex-work interactions between locals reflect in some ways a more traditional structure of sexual-economic exchange in which relationships are characterized by patronage or ongoing material support, and "clients" are sometimes neighbors residing nearby. The group of male sex workers with whom this study was conducted was highly diverse, ranging from men whose pattern of sexual exchange could be considered more "traditional" or local to those whose exclusive focus was foreign tourists.

42. Nevertheless, young Dominicans (whether male or female) who are seen with foreign

tourists are often *assumed* to be sex workers, particularly in tourist enclaves or other "hot" sex-work areas. Thus, while focusing on foreign clients may be more effective as a boundary maintenance strategy, it can still lead to suspicion if one is seen consorting too often or too closely with tourists. See chapter 4 on sex workers' strategies to avoid being burned by their relationships with tourists.

43. The overall Dominican trend toward increasing rural-urban migration cannot be understood without consideration of the "ethnic division of labor" that has characterized the development of the sugar industry in the twentieth century. During the U.S. military occupations of the Dominican Republic (1916–24) and Haiti (1915–34), North American plantation owners—concerned about the global competitiveness of the Dominican sugar crop—encouraged the country's dependence on the cheaper migrant laborers from neighboring Haiti (Betances 1995; Calder 1984; Cambeira 1997; Logan 1968; Martinez 1995; Wiarda and Kryzanek 1992). To meet this labor demand, the United States encouraged the emigration of over 300,000 Haitians to Dominican plantations during the U.S. occupation of Haiti (Wilhelms 1994, 29–30). Consequently, sugar plantations in the Dominican Republic showed "a progressively greater reliance on the cheaper laborers from Haiti" (Grasmuck and Pessar 1991, 27), a pattern that has provoked massive Haitian emigration to Dominican plantations and the "replacement" of a significant proportion of rural Dominican laborers with ethnic Haitians.

44. In a household study in five poor neighborhoods of Santo Domingo, 91 percent of household heads were migrants, largely from rural areas (Duarte 1980, cited in Georges 1990, 35).

45. Georges argues that the increasing mobility of Dominican women and the associated work vacuum it has created in the household context "contributed to the commodification of previously nonwage work performed within the domestic economy. When a woman migrated and children were left behind, her labor in the household had to be replaced. Many women, often close kin, were employed as caretakers for the children of migrants; they were sent remittances for their services and also for household expenses" (1990, 133).

46. New York City is the destination for 90 percent of Dominican immigrants to the United States, and there are now approximately 20,000 Dominican-owned businesses in this city (Howard 2001, 98).

47. Note that these figures do not include the children of Dominican immigrants born in the United States, since they are U.S. citizens.

48. Howard (2001, 99) notes that a "survey of 8,000 households in the Dominican Republic showed that 16.7 percent had members living overseas (Profamilia 1993)."

49. On Dominican migration to Puerto Rico, see Angueira (1998) and Duany (1985).

50. Eighteen of the sixty sex workers who indicated they had traveled abroad, or 30 percent, reported they had engaged in sex work abroad. Of these, nine individuals (50 percent) had done so in the continental United States or Puerto Rico.

51. "Technical training" mentioned by sex workers ranges from service-sector skills (bartending, scuba diving, restaurant service [*camarería*]) to more intensive education in such things as accounting, computer programming, and languages. "Professions" mentioned by participants include such positions as electrician, refrigeration technician, plumber, marketing professional, and salesman.

52. As discussed in subsequent chapters, the fact that these behaviors are stigmatized and therefore hidden from public view may serve as a partial explanation for the tendency to

neglect same-sex exchanges with tourists in most prior scholarly analyses of male sex work in the Caribbean.

Chapter Three

Richard Parker, *Beneath the Equator: Cultures of Desire, Male Homosexuality, and Emerging Gay Communities in Brazil* (New York: Routledge, 1999).

1. As I have argued more thoroughly elsewhere (Padilla, Vásquez del Aguila and Parker 2006), terms such as "LGBTQ," "queer," and so on, are useful analytically in permitting a language for scholarly discourse, but are quite problematic when viewed cross-culturally. I use such terms occasionally in this chapter because, in part, many of the Dominican activists with whom I have interacted themselves often use such terms and categories in conceptualizing local sexual politics. Nevertheless, the reader should keep in mind that cross-cultural variability in the meanings and practices of sexuality makes even the language and terminologies we use complicated and occasionally problematic.

2. Sex workers are not the only informal-sector laborers who benefit from the gay tourism market, as is evident when one observes any scene outside a gay bar or disco late at night, particularly during high tourism season; a combination of "*motoconchistas*" (motorcycle taxi drivers), *taxistas,* artisans, promoters for other businesses, and vendors of various sorts seek to take advantage of the buying power of gay tourists with dollars in hand.

3. *El Drake* was the name of a gay bar previously located on the Plaza España, and after the bar's closure, the surrounding area became a generalized gay cruising and socializing area referred to by the same name.

4. Most of the information on police abuses against gays in the Plaza España was gathered through informal conversations with gay men who had either been arrested or knew of others who had been arrested. One of the most important sources was a firsthand account provided by a staff member at an HIV/AIDS organization, who had narrowly escaped arrest while conducting HIV prevention outreach among gay men in the area of El Drake.

5. Gay male informants alluded to the alleged rape of gay men by arresting police officers, often described as an incipient motive behind police arrests. While, as far as I am aware, none of these reports was officially documented in formal complaints against the authorities, they are commonly mentioned by Dominican gay men as characteristic of police treatment of gays. It is also likely that such abuses are more commonly perpetrated against *travestis* (transgendered persons), particularly those involved in sex work, than against gay-identified men whose gender performance is less readily marked in public space. Analogous reports of sexual abuse of Dominican female prostitutes have been described by Cabezas (1998, 1999).

6. Incidentally, gay tourists may not even be aware that they are paying these *multas.* I have witnessed many interactions in which a police officer requests a bribe from a sex worker who is accompanied by a tourist, and—due to language barriers and a lack of understanding about the nature of these social transactions—the tourist may pay a police officer without thoroughly understanding the larger context of these exchanges in the gay sex tourism economy.

7. See the analysis of Dominican gay language later in this chapter for more detail on the impressive variety of terms used to describe the "*locas.*"

8. Perhaps the most significant body of regional academic work in this regard focuses on

the temporal fluctuations in social restrictions on homoeroticism and cross-gender behavior surrounding Carnival celebrations (Kulick 1998; Miller 1994; Parker 1991, 1999).

9. While the question of the origin of the Dominican identification with all things Hispanic is a complex one, it is undoubtedly related to the particular brand of racist anti-Haitianism and nationalist "border anxiety" (Derby 1994) promulgated by the infamous dictatorship of Rafael Trujillo. Since his assassination in 1961, Trujillo's racist philosophy and policies have continued their legacy through the political influence of his right-hand man, Joaquín Balaguer, who until his death in 2002 dominated Dominican politics for thirty years. Balaguer shows his continuity with Trujillo in his diatribe and scapegoating of Haitians in *La isla al revés* (The island reversed)(1983).

10. With an estimated cost of U.S.$250 million (Ferguson 1992, 2), the Columbus lighthouse raised serious questions regarding the equity of such conspicuous expenditures in light of the extreme economic deprivation of much of the country's population. Cambeira, for example, observes: "Amid a ruinous shortage of electrical energy, a lighthouse stands, believed to be the world's largest and expected to overtax the limits of energy consumption under any normal circumstances" (Cambeira 1997, 200; see also Anderson 1995). Nevertheless, as Krohn-Hansen (2001, 167) has aptly noted, public debates focusing on the cost of the monument have tended to sidestep a more critical perspective on the Dominican state's troubling appropriation of Spanish colonialism and the history of external domination in order to further its political-economic interests and symbolically reinstantiate the country's oppressive "racial regime."

11. "For the international tourism conglomerates, the availability of sexual services as an exotic commodity functions as a source of tourist attraction and helps to fill airplane seats and hotel rooms. National accounts benefit from taxes on accommodation, food, drinks and services" (Truong 1990, 128).

12. For another notable example from the same period, see Sosa (1982).

13. Some of the volunteers at an HIV prevention NGO were among the principal organizers of the event.

14. I was later told that these flags were donated by a gay Puerto Rican tourist who had access to surplus flags from a previous gay pride event abroad, but this was not confirmed, and their origin remains somewhat mysterious.

15. It is also quite possible that police harassment of gays is more likely to occur during the late-night hours, when common citizens are less likely to directly witness law enforcement abuses.

16. Nevertheless, as described in the previous chapter, the *bugarrón*'s gender expression—precisely because of his exaggerated performance of hypermasculinity—entails an ambiguous relationship to normative male gender constructs.

17. However, it is difficult to determine how coherent this statement was for either the protesters or the observing public, since the ad hoc nature of the march seriously undermined the representational clarity of the group's message.

18. There is a final historical irony in the fact that this march—narrated by the participants as the country's "first gay pride" event—has not been subsequently memorialized as such in the subcultural memory of the nascent Dominican gay and lesbian movement. Indeed, a second gay pride event—now widely recognized by both the Dominican media and the gay community as the "first"—occurred on July 1, 2001, in the port area adjacent to the Plaza España (Ramírez 2001). In contrast to the ad hoc and spontaneous nature of its predecessor, this sec-

ond "outing" of the Dominican gay community was part of a self-conscious political strategy led by a nucleus of academically trained activists and professionals, composed of both Dominicans and foreign ex-pats residing in Santo Domingo.

19. It is important to mention that the Latin American homosexual's stereotyped passivity in anal sex is an ideological construction that may or may not be borne out in actual sexual practice. For example, my conversations with Dominican transvestite prostitutes, as well as the rich ethnographic work of anthropologist Don Kulick (1997), demonstrates that *travestis* commonly perform the penetrative role with their male clients. This calls analytical attention to the issue that has been at the heart of much AIDS-related research on sexuality: the potential pitfalls of interpreting the relationship between idealized sexual norms and the private realities of sexual behavior.

20. The Dominican term *plomero* (plumber), referring to the active participant in anal sex, provides the converse example.

21. It should be mentioned, however, that anthropologist Stephen Murray emphatically disagrees with the claims by Lancaster and others that Latin American men can actually *enhance* social esteem by being the active participant in homosexual intercourse (Murray 1995c, 54): "I would infer (especially since Latinos have told me so) that boasting about fucking men is risky to all but the most solidly established macho reputations. Too-frequent forays into this kind of Banco de Inversiones undercut a macho reputation, as does emotional investment in those he uses sexually."

22. Interestingly, the latter fact leads Carrillo to the interesting observation that this emerging construction of gender and sexuality may actually alleviate some of the burden of masculine performance for all Mexican men, since the fact that one's masculinity is no longer necessarily accepted as "proof" that one is heterosexual allows straight men to stop obsessing about demonstrating their *machismo*.

23. From a feminist consciousness-raising perspective, however, this may be interpreted as a consequence of their oppression within a sex/gender system that does not acknowledge the existence or value of *bugarrones* in the public sphere. This, however, was not a political perspective expressed by the vast majority of the men in this study.

24. Recall, however, that this idea of *bugarrones*' sexual repression is pervasive among many Dominican gays, who consider them to be "*unos tapa'os*" (covered, meaning "repressed") who will eventually "*soltar las plumas*" (let their feathers loose).

25. An interesting expression of this "testing" of sexual desires came up in conversations about how men perform sexually with men. Some men expressed that they were sure that they were "*hombres normales*" because they were always forced to imagine a woman during sexual behaviors with male clients, in order to maintain their erection and complete the sexual act.

26. There are also cases of *bugarrones* developing long-term relationships with one another. One heterosexually identified interviewee in this study, Edgar, lived with and confessed to "loving" another sex worker with whom he frequently shared clients.

27. See chapter 4 for additional examples of participants' contrasts between the sexual talents of *maricones* and wives/girlfriends.

28. It bears mentioning that most of the gay tourists with whom I have spoken have never attempted or requested to penetrate a Dominican sex worker, although this certainly occurs on occasion. See chapter 5 for a discussion of how these sexual roles—when they occur across transnational space—encode racialized fantasies of the Dominican phallus.

29. See Octavio Paz for a classic discussion of this phallic symbolism—embodied in the figure of the "*chignón*"—which Paz claims is a fundamental feature of masculinity and sexuality in Mexico (1985). For a parallel discussion on Dominican men, see De Moya (2003).

30. Interestingly, De Moya (2003) also makes the argument that this intense negative socialization not only represses homosexual practices, but also gives an erotic charge and excitement that, in some cases, may motivate a man to engage in same-sex practices.

31. Parker (1999, 40) provides ethnographic data from interviews in which informants note the recent attenuation of the *activo-pasivo* model, as imported notions of "homosexuality" and "bisexuality" have become more salient in Brazil. Similarly, Carrier (1995) describes the invention of the category "*internacional*" in Mexico, making explicit reference to foreign (specifically U.S.) concepts of homosexuality that are less bound by sexual roles. In Carrier's words, "it has become 'politically correct' for Mexican gay men to move away from being a '*puro pasivo*' or '*puro activo*' (that is, only anal receptive or anal insertive) and to be more like their gay male counterparts in the United States who, according to common knowledge in the Mexican gay world, are not into role playing" (1995, 193).

32. Nagel writes: "Ethnicity and sexuality join together to form a barrier to hold some people in and keep others out, to define who is pure and who is impure, to shape our view of ourselves and others, to fashion feeling of sexual desire and notions of sexual desirability, to provide us with seemingly 'natural' sexual preferences for some partners and 'intuitive' aversions to others, to leave us with a taste for some ethnic sexual encounters and a distaste for others. Ethnicity and sexuality blend together to form sexualized perimeters around ethnic, racial, and national spaces. Ethnic and sexual boundaries converge to mark the edges of ethnosexual frontiers" (Nagel 2003, 1).

Chapter Four

Peter J. Wilson, "Reputation and Respectability: A Suggestion for Caribbean Ethnology," *Man* 4 (1969):81.

Paul Kutsche, "Two Truths about Costa Rica," in *Latin American Male Homosexualities*, edited by Stephen O. Murray, 111–37 (Albuquerque: University of New Mexico Press, 1995), 116–17.

1. Hirschman (1984, 13) estimates there are 5,000 "*tricicleros*" (tricycle riders) in Santo Domingo, who make a meager living by distributing fruits, vegetables, coal, and a variety of other items. Driving *triciclos* is a common source of employment among poor urban males.

2. Interestingly, Campbell et al. (1999, 135), in their life-history study of sixteen male and female sex workers in Jamaica, mention that "four of the sex workers reported having to run away from home because of hostile relationships with stepparents." Similarly, among adolescent female sex workers in Cartagena, Mayorga and Velásquez (1999, 165) find that "in virtually all . . . cases, family difficulties were related to the separation of the young woman's biological parents and the subsequent union of the custodial parent with a new partner."

3. While both of the above examples involve instances of coresidence with a father and stepmother, most of the cases of single-parenting involved a mother who had been either divorced or abandoned. In fact, comments about absent or neglectful fathers were common when sex workers were asked open-ended questions about their childhood.

4. Ramah et al. (1992), in their survey study of a diverse group of 188 Dominican men who

have sex with men, similarly report that two-thirds of their sample still lived with parents. They comment that "given the large proportion of the sample living with their families, it is not surprising that over half of all sexual encounters take place in hotels or motels (59%)."

5. In their study of seventy-six "*palomos*" (street children who engage in sexual exchanges with men) and *bugarrones* in Santo Domingo, Ruiz and Vásquez (1993) find that 43 percent of them were helped economically by their families.

6. The reference to Goffman's (1963) definition of "covering" as an information management technique is a self-conscious one and will be discussed further toward the end of this chapter.

7. Campbell et al. (1999, 143) describe how Jamaican female sex workers employed in sex-work establishments will cooperate with a fellow sex worker if the latter's family should suddenly appear, "pretending that their main occupation is nonsex work" (for example, waitressing). The authors do not, however, mention cases in which these alibis were compensated with cash in the ways I observed among Dominican male sex workers.

8. Campbell et al. (1999), in their discussion of female sex workers in Jamaica, report that sex workers' greatest fear is that their children will discover the true nature of their work, as illustrated by one informant who "consistently fabricates stories of what she does for a living in order to protect the child and hopes that she will never find out before she gets a chance to leave the sex trade, which she intends to do in the very near future" (143).

9. In their work with female sex workers in the mining camps of Guyana, the Red Thread Women's Development Programme has recently noted that "for some of the women, family members, including current partners, knew how they were earning an income and there appeared to be no negative consequences, especially where financial support was forthcoming" (Red Thread Women's Development Programme 1999, 274).

10. This quotation is paraphrased.

11. This parallels Mayorga and Velásquez's (1999, 163) argument for female sex workers in Cartagena, Colombia, who rely to a greater degree on local clients during the low tourist season.

12. While heterosexual exchanges across class lines have been described in many classic Caribbean ethnographic accounts (Alexander 1984; Barrow 1996; Smith 1974, 1988)—consistently noting that these relationships are ways that some lower-class (and often darker-skinned) women establish crucial ties to higher-class (lighter-skinned) men—there has been almost complete silence in the ethnographic literature on similar exchange relationships between local men. This is undoubtedly more about disciplinary biases regarding what are considered "appropriate" research questions in Caribbean ethnology than it is a reflection of the real existence or extent of these relationships.

13. Such an interpretation parallels observations by some tourism researchers (Harrison 1992; Kinnaird, Kothari, and Hall 1994) who suggest that interaction with tourists creates a "demonstration effect" that promotes certain forms of commodification and consumer practices.

14. Paralleling these findings, Ruíz and Vásquez (1993) report that most of the *bugarrones* above the age of twenty-four in their study of "homotropic" male sex workers functioned as informal pimps or role models for younger initiates, teaching them how to make contacts with clients and negotiate prices.

15. A subgroup of *bugarrones* and *sankies* are involved with women who work in brothels

or bars as sex workers. These relationships typically have the benefit of greater openness about sexual exchanges but can also lead to abuses if the male controls his partner's income or brokers her sex work contacts.

16. This is similar to arguments by ethnographers in other Latin American contexts, such as Parker's (1991) suggestion that public norms of Brazilian sexuality do not necessarily reflect the realities of men's sexual behavior "between four walls" (i.e., in private). It is also related to more recent ethnographic discussion of "sexual silence" in Latin America, a point to which I will return later (Carrillo 2002; Díaz 1998).

17. Indeed, in his Ph.D. dissertation on Dominican homosexuality and transnational identities in New York City, Carlos Decena argues that the use of the "*sujeto tacito*" (tacit subject) in Dominican language problematizes the very notion of the open "disclosure" of sexual identity, since "these men assume that most people in their lives either know they are homosexual or can infer it from the way these men live" (Decena 2004, viii).

18. This figure may be slightly skewed by the participants' overestimation of their actual contributions, since ethnographic observations suggest that sex workers' wives and girlfriends are frequently unsatisfied with their economic support. It is likely that the desire to portray themselves as good providers for their children within the context of the interview moved some participants to answer positively to the question regarding their economic support for children, when actually there was no such support or support was negligible.

19. These preestablished categories were chosen for the survey based on comments made by sex workers in prior focus group discussions regarding their use of sex-work income. When sex workers mentioned an expense that was not appropriate for any of these categories, responses were included in "other." Multiple answers were allowed for each participant.

20. De Moya (1989, 9) similarly reports that many adolescent male sex workers spend the money they earn through their sex-for-money exchanges on girlfriends or on female sex workers in order "to avoid being discredited as homosexuals and lose their position in the group." Ruíz and Vásquez (1993) also observe that 43 percent of their sample of *bugarrones* reported having sexual relations with female sex workers, suggesting an important epidemiological link between male and female sex work.

21. Victor Turner's analysis of the ritual state of "liminality" in human societies is relevant here (Turner 1970, 1975). While Turner's classic theory used the notion of liminality to describe a transient state of "antistructure" during rites of passage in small-scale societies, he also acknowledged in his book *Dramas, Fields, and Metaphors* that modern societies may create permanent "marginals" who are not reincorporated into the social structure and "have no cultural assurance of a final stable resolution of their ambiguity" (Turner 1975, 233).

22. As Carrillo points out, however, Mexican culture does encourage frank expressions of sexuality in the form of *albures*, an elaborate form of mostly lower-class joking or jabbing that also derives its cultural salience from humorous ambiguities in sexual communication.

23. Gerardo's use of *maricón* here implies more than sexual preference, since it suggests that the man was highly effeminate and "obviously" *maricón*.

24. Merengue and bachata are quintessentially Dominican musical forms, heard constantly in streets, businesses, and public areas. Although their evolution and social history are distinct (see Austerlitz [1997] on the social history of Dominican merengue, and Hernandez [1995] on bachata), many of the musical features of merengue and bachata are becoming increasingly *blended* in contemporary Dominican music, as each genre borrows from the other.

25. It is also important to remember that these musical styles tend to reproduce markedly *male* representations of gender, since the vast majority of writers, performers, and producers of popular music are men. As Austerlitz (1997) has also pointed out, even the recent emergence of women as *merengueras* or back-up singers has been coopted by the machismo of the Dominican music industry, as female performers have been incorporated principally for their sensual presence and the provocative visuals of gyrating young women in bikinis.

26. As support for his argument, Wilson repeatedly cites the contributors to the influential volume *The People of Puerto Rico* (Steward et al. 1956), which discusses a similar dichotomized gender ideal embodied in the *casa/calle* distinction. See in particular the contributions by Manners, Mintz, and Scheele.

27. As with most models, Wilson's reputation/respectability distinction is perhaps most useful in highlighting that which it does *not* explain. While several recent analyses of Caribbean gender norms have found Wilson's framework at least partially useful for conceptualizing lower-class Caribbean gender relations in widely varying contexts (Brana-Shute 1989; Dann 1987; Freeman 1993; Lieber 1981; Manning 1973; Olwig 1990; Yelvington 1995), others have pointed out problems with its basic assumptions. Besson (1993), for example, questions Wilson's assumption that Caribbean women subscribe exclusively to European-derived, colonial values of respectability. She draws upon more recent anthropological research to show that: (1) Caribbean women often participate in resistant, anticolonial social structures and institutions, and (2) they also participate actively in many of the activities subsumed under the value system that Wilson describes as reputation.

28. For published examples, see the life-history interviews of Dominican female sex workers collected in Murray (2002), as well as Brennan's discussion of female sex workers' in her excellent ethnography *What's Love Got to Do with It?* (2004).

29. Nevertheless, *sanky pankies* have a higher female-to-male client ratio than do *bugarrones*, whose sex work clients are overwhelmingly male (see chap. 1).

30. Interestingly, in his discussion of men and masculinity in Jamaica, Chevannes (2001, 114) has made a similar argument about men's information management as regards their extramarital affairs: "The sexual problem facing men is not whether to have sex before or outside marriage, or to get a woman pregnant, or whether to have more than one woman. What they face instead is the question of how open they ought to be about multiple partnerships."

31. The commonality of expressions of shame by sex workers regarding their exchanges with men calls into question the interpretation that Latin American men gain social esteem by participating in active (*activo*) homosexual relations, a point that has been debated among some scholars (Lancaster 1997; Murray 1995c, 54).

32. As suggested by Castaneda et al.'s (1996) description of stigma management techniques among Mexican female sex workers, women involved in sex work may have fewer strategies for covering their stigmatized activity than do their male counterparts. In Goffman's framework, then, it may be useful to conceive of female sex workers as already "discredited"—due to the greater surveillance of their sexual activities—whereas male sex workers (at least those who do not display cross-gender behavior) may be more accurately described as "discreditable." "Passing," therefore, may be a more realistic possibility for male sex workers, because of the nature of patriarchal gender norms.

33. The idea that Caribbean men are "marginal" to the household has been one of the primary theses of gender studies in the Caribbean since some of the earliest ethnographic treat-

ments of the region (Barrow 1996). See, for example, Clarke (1970), M. G. Smith (1962), and R.T. Smith (1974). This has also been argued by anthropologists in the Dominican Republic (Brown 1973; Brown 1975b; Cross Beras 1980).

Chapter Five

Epigraph: Hall, Stuart (1991, 19–39). "The Local and the Global: Globalization and the World System." Binghamton, NY: State University of New York. Excerpt from p. 31.

1. Amazingly, Leonardo chased the perpetrator for several blocks and managed to retrieve my belongings, confirming his status as a skilled *portero* as well as solidifying my relationship with him. This was one of three occasions in which he came to my rescue in the course of my fieldwork.

2. In the early 1990s, Charlie's was the target of a widely publicized police raid—largely instigated by a television exposé piece by a popular Dominican talk show host—in which all tourists and sex workers were jailed under charges of alleged prostitution by minors and drug use. While the tourists were eventually released after weeks in jail and hefty payoffs to the police, Charlie's was destroyed by looters. It later reopened under a different name and Simon's management.

3. Some sex workers lack the identification occasionally required to make Western Union pickups, which was the motive for my assistance on two occasions.

4. Ruiz and Vásquez (1993, 58) report as follows: "Around 9 of every ten [sex workers] preferred foreign tourist-clients, mainly because they say that they pay better (74 percent), even though one of every ten thinks that these clients can transmit diseases. Virtually all of them (92 percent) had had sexual relations with foreign tourist-clients. The average number of lifetime foreign clients was 21, mainly from the United States, Italy, Spain, and Canada" (translation by author).

5. In their description of the overt racism of some male sex tourists to the Caribbean, O'Connell Davidson and Sanchez Taylor (1999, 44–45) have argued that black female prostitutes are viewed as the most appropriate objects for degrading sex but are not sought for romantic encounters.

6. Mullings (1999, 66) summarizes Pruitt and LaFont's argument as follows: "Pruitt and LaFont (1995) have argued that male sex workers are involved in romance rather than sex tourism, because there is often a level of emotional involvement that is not often present in sex tourism. These holiday relationships tend to be longer term, involving a much higher level of social and economic commitment on the part of both parties in the exchange."

7. Cabezas's translation of *tíguere* as "pimp" is somewhat problematic, given the much broader usage of the term in actual discourse, as discussed in the previous chapter.

8. Only those respondents with experience with male clients are included (n = 166). For this question, survey participants were read a list of client types from which they were requested to choose the one that represented the "best" client according to their own preferences/criteria. The client types included in this question were established in prior focus-group discussions with sex workers, who identified the categories shown here as the primary client types that were relevant for this question. It bears mentioning that "married man" was a somewhat odd category, both because it raises questions about why married men would be preferred by sex workers and because it is not a category that is exclusive of other categories (i.e., a client could be a foreigner *and* a married man). Nevertheless, a small number of focus group participants

expressed a preference for married men (regardless of nationality), because they felt these men were highly likely to be discreet about their sexual-economic exchanges and therefore were perceived to represent a lower risk of public disclosure.

9. At this point in the survey, an internal check was included to verify prior answers regarding experience with male clients. Two participants who had previously denied having male clients confessed to having them, increasing the number of respondents to this question from 166 (shown in figure 6) to 168.

10. Puerto Rico is considered here as a separate country, despite its official status as a U.S. territory, because sex workers tended to conceive of it as distinct from the United States. Those countries of origin falling within the "other" category in figure A.5 (appendix) include: Cuba, Curaçao, Denmark, France, Greece, England, Mexico, Norway, Switzerland, Surinam, and Yugoslavia.

11. Some sex workers prefer to avoid regular clients, because of the greater danger of discovery by family and friends. Indeed, many cases of traumatic family discoveries, as described in the previous chapter, are due to the greater degree of intimacy resulting from relationships with regular clients, leading to familial suspicion.

12. Those countries of origin falling within the "other" category in figure A.6 (appendix) include: Colombia, Cuba, Denmark, France, Greece, Holland, Norway, and Switzerland.

13. Nevertheless, as mentioned in chapter 4, support for children as a primary motive for involvement in sex work is much less common among male sex workers than female sex workers. This is consistent with Espinal and Grasmuck's (1997) finding that male informal entrepreneurs contributed 60 percent of their income on average to their households, whereas their female counterparts contributed 80 percent.

14. Georges (1990, 151, 236) reports that by the mid-1980s, remittances received by Dominicans from migrant family members, primarily from the United States, were already nearly equal to the annual profits from the country's sugar exports and equivalent to the total budget of the Dominican government. In addition, "the contribution of remittances to the Dominican balance of payments was considerably greater than in some other major Caribbean [migrant] sending nations, such as Jamaica and Barbados" (ibid., 236).

15. As described in chapter 3, stories abound among sex workers of *bugarrones* who are "converted" into *maricones,* and are canonized linguistically in such creative identity terms as "*bugaloca,*" which refers to a *bugarrón* who has slipped into the role (implicitly the sexual role) of a *loca* (effeminate gay man).

16. Original Spanish: *¿Dirías que tu último cliente fijo te trata bien?; ¿Sientes confianza con tu último cliente fijo?; ¿Sientes cariño por tu último cliente fijo?; ¿Sientes amor por tu último cliente fijo?*

17. These findings are consistent with a study of Dominican male sex work among minors by De Moya (1989), who finds that lower-class boys between the ages of fourteen and fifteen are often pressured by their peers to engaged in sex-for-money exchanges with older men in order to "prove" to their peers that only the money interests them and that "they are not afraid of men" (*no tienen miedo a los hombres*). According to De Moya, through sex work the adolescent satisfies basic needs at the same time he demonstrates that he is not emotionally or physically involved in relations with other men. Thus, and somewhat ironically, the adolescent sex worker's emotional detachment during his sex-for-money exchanges with other men reinforces a homophobic norm and functions to preserve his social status among his peers.

18. In his study of male sex workers in a Costa Rican brothel, Jacobo Schifter (1998, 60) sim-

ilarly argues that *cacheros* (an identity of male sex workers roughly analogous to Dominican *bugarrones*) "cannot conceive of how two men can love each other." He quotes one informant who commented that clients often "want you to tell them they're attractive and interesting and I just don't give a shit" (ibid.).

19. The only apparent pattern is that Puerto Rican clients are generally disparaged as being among the worst, which is perhaps an expression of the regional tension between Dominicans and Puerto Ricans.

20. Nelson H. H. Graburn, 1983, "The Anthropology of Tourism," *Annals of Tourism Research* 10, p. 11.

21. The feminine pronouns frequently used in Jeffrey's correspondence are a gay discourse style and invariably refer to gay men.

22. *Pinga* is colloquial Spanish for "dick" and is frequently used by gay sex tourists and the pornography industry as a racialized reference to the Latin phallus.

23. The notion that Dominican *bugarrones* are relatively more drug-free than urban hustlers in the United States may have some basis in fact; however, as noted in chapter 6, drug use among Dominican *bugarrones* and *sankies* is fairly common, especially in the context of their sexual exchanges with tourists.

24. The erotic charge of this fantasy seems to be reflected in the fact that many gay sex tourists do not object to their "boys" being sexually involved with women or married, and may even prefer this arrangement.

25. Jeffrey's reference to the idealized lack of "blatant materialism" among poor Dominicans is also ironic, given the fact that his remittances would seem to encourage, rather than inhibit, such materialism.

26. Gay sex tourists often enjoy these conflicts, since they provide them the opportunity to be perceived as a desirable object worthy of being aggressively defended. In their discussion of heterosexual male sex tourists to the Dominican Republic, O'Connell Davidson and Sanchez Taylor similarly quote one sex tourist as follows: "The problem is getting rid of [the girls]. Once you've bought them, they stick to you. They even fight with each other over you. It's wicked" (O'Connell Davidson and Sanchez Taylor 1999, 39).

27. Given increasingly strict U.S. immigration policies, as well as the inability of same-sex couples to legally validate their relationships for immigration purposes, it is unlikely that Fernando would be able to migrate to the United States legally. Nevertheless, as demonstrated by a few success stories (see De Moya and García 1998), gay tourist-clients have occasionally been able to take their Dominican partners abroad by sponsoring them, adopting them, or providing financial backing for the many expenses related to legal or illegal migration. Little is known about the development of these relationships once migration has occurred; however, see De Moya and García (1998, 134–35) for a brief note on this matter.

28. De las Casas's condemnatory tone in relation to indigenous homoeroticism is ironic, given his historic role as a staunch advocate for the rights of the island's indigenous people and the use of imported African labor rather than exploiting the island's natives (Benitez 1992). Prior to this, Gonzalo Fernández de Oviedo, the colonial governor of Hispaniola, wrote: "What I have said of these people is very public on this and neighboring islands, and even in the continent, many of these male and female Indians were sodomites. . . . Indeed, this is a very usual, ordinary and common thing among them. . . . And you should know that the man who plays patient or takes the position of being the woman in that beastly and anathematized act is

given the role of a woman, and wears naguas (skirts) as women do. . . . This abominable *contra natura* sin was very usual among the male Indians of this island; but to women it was abhorrent, because of their own interest rather than because of any scruples of consciousness" (Oviedo/Las Casas 1988, translated and quoted by De Moya and García 1996, 123).

29. In Kempadoo's (1999b) important recent volume on Caribbean sex tourism, for example, homosexual exchanges were observed by several of the contributors (for example, by Joan Phillips in Barbados [p. 200] and Jacqueline Martis in St. Maarten and Curaçao [p. 205]) but in all cases were explicitly marginalized from analysis. Perhaps the rationale for this marginalization is provided by a footnote to chapter 12 by the Red Thread Women's Development Programme: "Given the taboo nature of homosexuality, discussing such matters would also have been difficult in light of the short timescale of our research" (287).

30. Mullings notes that "unlike the East Asian sex tourism sector, where women appear to be the dominant sex workers, both women and men in Jamaica appear to be equally active in the supply of sex services to tourists" (1999, 66).

31. Thomas and Sillen (1972, cited in Whitehead 1997, 425) argue that the symbolic hypersexualization of black men and women in Western society is related to the historical construction of blackness as "sinful" and the religious view of sex as sinful—ideologies that functioned in plantation society to reinforce white male fears about black male sexuality and the "safety" of white women.

32. Despite this, some male heterosexual clients of female sex workers, as described by O'Connell Davidson and Sanchez Taylor (1999, 45), express a contradictory set of fantasies, including both the desire for traditional expressions of feminine submissiveness and the sexual aggressiveness and insatiability of so-called LBFMs (little brown fucking machines).

33. However, De Moya and García (1998) argue that this aesthetic was not the dominant one when gay sex tourism first began in the 1970s. At that time, younger adolescent boys, rather than "muscular working-class dark mulattos with large cocks," were the erotic ideal for sex tourists seeking homoerotic encounters in Santo Domingo. By the 1980s, this preference had shifted toward adult "macho" men (1998, 135).

34. Indeed, as described in chapter 3, sexual positionality is the key behavioral marker that defines the symbolic boundary between *maricones* and *hombres normales,* resulting in anxiety and denial on the part of many sex workers regarding their engagement in "passive" anal sex. Nevertheless, when asked a general opinion question about whether a *bugarrón*—that is, *any bugarrón*—occasionally allows himself to be anally penetrated, 68 percent (135/199) of sex workers answered affirmatively. In contrast, only 7 percent (12/168) of those survey respondents with experience with male clients admitted to having engaged in receptive anal sex. This difference is more than coincidental; it represents a considerable denial of so-called passive sexual acts among sex workers, as these imply a stigmatized homosexuality.

35. bell hooks (1992) has similarly described the racial objectification of black women's bodies in contemporary Western imagery: "Most often attention [is] not focused on the complete black female on display at a fancy ball in the "civilized" heart of European culture, Paris. She is there to entertain guests with the naked image of Otherness. They are not to look at her as a whole human being. They are to notice only certain parts" (62).

36. De Moya and García argue that Dominican adolescent boys often compete with one another over genital endowment, "conferring special privileges upon the winner, which might include, in some instances, orally or anally penetrating peers in secret encounters" (1996, 127).

37. The ease with which sex workers lower their pants is demonstrated by the fact that during the surveys, when participants were asked about sexually transmitted infections, several sex workers attempted to lower their pants to show the researchers a rash, irritation, or lesion. They did this despite the fact that most surveys were conducted in semipublic areas such as streets, parks, and bars.

38. For an analysis of the ways that tourism marketing—and the exoticizing it entails—can present challenges to local movements for gender equity in the Caribbean, see Alexander (1997).

39. Nevertheless, representations of masculinity in advertising permit alternative readings by gay men, and these readings may be either intended or unintended by marketing executives.

40. These Internet sites have become noticeable enough to attract the attention of the Dominican media. See one recent discussion of the intersection between gay sex tourism and the Internet in Canó (2000).

41. Nevertheless, just as Mullings (1999, 73) argues that much of the tourism advertising and imagery of Caribbean people is actually produced by foreigners and therefore beyond local control, in most cases it was foreign clients who had published sex workers' "personal" Web pages on the Internet. This attests to the fact that, even among the more professionalized sex workers, access to Internet technology is constrained by class and nationality, resulting in representations that are more often loaded with the erotic projections of foreigners.

42. Simon, the owner of Charlie's bar, had a collection of these videos, since traveling porn directors often provided him complimentary copies of their latest productions.

43. Similarly, it is likely that the language barrier that characterizes most relationships between sex workers and tourist-clients, while creating certain problems for communication, may also be functional for the client in that it enables the maintenance of a certain distance that permits the construction of an essentialized, eroticized Other.

Chapter Six

Paul Farmer, *Infections and Inequalities: The Modern Plagues* (Berkeley: University of California Press, 1999), 101.

1. Actually, as Agar has pointed out, it is problematic to claim that "traditional" epidemiology does not account for political-economic perspectives, since the discipline's nineteenth-century ancestors were actually quite influenced by the analysis of disease patterns in light of social inequalities. It was, rather, epidemiology in its twentieth-century manifestations that reflected a more myopic clinical focus and moved away from a structural analysis of health and disease.

2. However, the earmarking of this funding exclusively for programs in Haiti and Guyana—two of the circum-Caribbean countries most devastated by AIDS—has led some to question the wisdom of leaving neighboring countries dangerously underfunded as the regional epidemic escalates (Gonzales 2003).

3. Farmer's work highlights the tragic irony of the ways that exoticizing, racist theories about the presumed linkages between Haiti and Africa entirely ignored the fact that none of the initial AIDS cases in Haiti was associated with travel to Africa, but "10–15 percent of these patients had traveled to North America or Europe in the five years preceding the onset of their illness, and several more admitted sexual contact with tourists" (Farmer 1996, 104).

4. Guyana, where the AIDS epidemic is accelerating at an alarming rate, is the clear excep-

tion to the positive association between tourism dependence and HIV prevalence, since Guyana's epidemic has been driven much more by the rapid growth of its interior mining industry and the local prostitution this has engendered than it has by its nascent tourism industry (Red Thread Women's Development Programme 1999). In this sense, Guyana's epidemic parallels more closely that described by Jochelson and colleagues (1991) for South Africa, where similar interrelationships between labor migration, large-scale mining, and concentrated prostitution are typical.

5. However, two attempts have been made in the Dominican Republic to incorporate the tourism sector into HIV prevention programs. The NGO COVICOSIDA (currently CEPROSH) in Puerto Plata implemented a pilot project between 1993 and 1997 in an effort to educate hotel employees about HIV prevention (CEPROSH 1997; Family Health International 2003), and the Punta Cana Group, which has developed several popular resorts in the country's easternmost tourist enclave, has recently agreed to sponsor, along with the Dominican government, HIV awareness programs in the area (Gonzales 2003).

6. See the various contributions to Kempadoo's (1999b) volume for specific examples of less-than-enlightened responses to AIDS (and sex workers) by Caribbean governments. Cuba's response to the AIDS epidemic, particularly in the 1980s, differed significantly from its neighbors', not only because of its highly controversial quarantine policy toward persons living with HIV, but also because the motives behind its denial of an "AIDS problem" were more politically oriented (and specifically anticapitalist) than in other Caribbean societies more dependent on tourism. This, however, may be changing as tourism continues to gain ground in the Cuban economy. On Cuba's AIDS policies and political rhetoric, see Granich et al. (1995), Bayer and Healton (1989), Santana et al. (1991), Leiner (1994), and Santana (1997).

7. Camara (2001) argues that the notion that HIV was first introduced to the Caribbean through North American gay tourism is reinforced by the fact that the genetic clade of the virus first detected in the region, known as Clade B, was the same as that which was then circulating in the primarily homosexually driven epidemic in the United States.

8. Some social scientists have rightly observed that the use of the "risk group" concept in AIDS discourse, as well as the implicit or explicit associations often made between marginalized groups and their presumed contamination of the "general population," have led to the stigmatization of particular "deviant" groups and to a false sense of security among those who are considered—or who consider themselves to be—"normal" (Patton 1990, 1996; Treichler 1988a, b).

9. Translation from Spanish by author.

10. For another recent example, see UNAIDS/WHO/PAHO (2003).

11. For various critical commentaries on the notion of the bisexual bridge, see the contributors to Aggleton's (1996b) edited volume, *Bisexualities and AIDS*.

12. As Murray (1995a, 45) mentions, the globalization of AIDS services can lead to a dissemination of Euro-American notions of "modern" gay identity. Nevertheless, AIDS funding—often from international sources—also places particular constraints on the degree to which an organization can respond to local concerns or engage in counter-hegemonic practices.

13. In addition to the work by Parker cited above, other examples of scholarly analyses of the relationships between homoerotic "sexual cultures" and HIV/AIDS in Latin America (and among Latinos in the United States) include: Alonso and Koreck (1993), Cáceres (1996), Carrier (1995), Carrillo (2002, 2003b), De Moya and García (1996), Díaz (1997, 1998, 2001), and Schifter (1996).

14. As Parker (1990, 501) has observed, "qualitative research must focus on examining in precisely what ways sexual behaviors and sexual identities are in fact linked, and researchers must be prepared to examine a relatively high degree of diversity in at least some research settings. . . . In [some] contexts, for example, sexual activity, in same-sex as well as opposite sex interactions, may actually be relatively unproblematic, and may translate into a high degree of bisexual behavior without ever being transformed into a distinct bisexual identity."

15. Conversely, gay-identified men may feel delegitimized by the generalized designation *MSM*, which they may see as a denial of a politicized and socially meaningful collective identity (Díaz 1998).

16. Indeed, the commonality of bisexual behavior—even within the sexual system of the United States that supposedly entails a more rigid separation of homosexual and heterosexual "orientations"—is suggested by numerous behavioral surveys, most notably the Kinsey studies (Kinsey 1948, 1953).

17. Research among African-American MSM demonstrates that most of them have a very low perception of their risk for infection, and that those who are HIV-seropositive are very unlikely to be aware of their HIV infection (Bingham et al. 2002).

18. Indeed, Lichtenstein (2000, 385) finds that many HIV-positive black women in Alabama whom he interviewed believed their husbands were infected because of their philandering with other women, but his male informants scoffed at such suggestions, arguing that homosexual encounters were primarily responsible for these infections.

19. It should be emphasized, however, that many of the growing number of studies and popular reports on bisexuality and HIV among ethnic minority populations—most sensationally represented in the recent media frenzy regarding the "down low" phenomenon among African American men—have made problematic claims about the responsibility of non-gay-identified men for women's growing HIV prevalence rates based on evidence that is still largely ambiguous (Millet et al. 2005). This has been exacerbated by the fact that few of these reports highlight the stigma and systematic discrimination that many bisexually behaving ethnic minority men experience, leading to decontextualized, exoticized conclusions that contribute to a demonization of minority MSM.

20. For evidence supporting the notion that male-to-female HIV transmission is significantly more efficient than female-to-male, see the report by the European Study Group on Heterosexual Transmission of HIV (1992). This disparity in transmission efficacy is one of the reasons that some scholars have hypothesized that other cofactors, such as lack of male circumcision (Baeten et al. 2005; Bongaarts et al. 1989; Cameron et al. 1989; Fink 1987; Halperin and Bailey 1999; Jessamine et al. 1990; Reining 1991) or concurrent STDs (Wasserheit 1992), may account for the apparently more efficient transmission of HIV from women to men in certain regions, particularly parts of Africa.

21. For the sake of simplicity, and because it is intended to represent the most probable routes of HIV transmission, figure 9 depicts an artificially low degree of diversity in women's sexual behavior.

22. Carrillo explains that while most public-health prevention programs in Guadalajara, Mexico, advocated a rational risk assessment procedure during risk-reduction counseling sessions, this approach "contrasted sharply with the more intuitive, silent assessments that often informed decisions about what to do with any given sexual partner" (Carrillo 2002, 147).

23. For important research on the ways that women may participate in or even promote de-

cisions to engage in high-risk unprotected sex with their male partners, see Hirsch et al. (2002), Hirsch (2003), and Sobo (1993, 1995).

24. See, for example, Martin (1987, 1988, 1991), Inhorn (1994), Treichler (1988a, b), and Patton (1990, 1996).

25. As a consequence of the latter, some men—perhaps particularly those who behave bisexually and do not consider themselves to be "gay"—may not understand questions about homosexual behavior to be relevant to them. Parker (1996), for example, has described this phenomenon among Brazilian *activos*—the supposedly exclusive penetrative partners in homosexual intercourse and those usually considered "normal men" (see chap. 3)—who may underreport their same-sex activities and HIV risk behavior because they consider such questions to be relevant only to "true" homosexuals.

26. See, for example, Farmer (1992, 1996), Singer (1995a, b, 1998), and Inhorn (1995).

27. This is particularly evident in cases of child prostitution, some of which are discussed at the beginning of chapter 4. See Silvestre, Rijo, and Bogaert (1994) for more on the dire situation of child prostitution in the Dominican Republic.

28. Balaguer's words are echoed by Dominican writer Victor Manuel Soñé Uribe, who, concerning Haitian migration to the Dominican Republic, writes: "In truth, it is a very complex problem: . . . the situation is framed by the peaceful 'invasion' by Haitian workers and other nationals of the country that come to the Dominican Republic and establish themselves with a loaded bundle of superstitions, promiscuity and diseases . . ." (quoted in Murphy 1991:134–35).

29. See Derby's (1994) discussion of border anxiety and Dominican cultural myths about Haitians.

30. As I have argued elsewhere, in some early AIDS rhetoric in the Dominican Republic, the tendency to represent Haitians as an independent risk factor for HIV and as a reservoir of disease, as well as the assumption that those ascribed "Haitian" acquired the infection on the other side of the border rather than within Dominican space, reflect long-standing racist assumptions and a denial of the ways that those ascribed a Haitian identity face numerous structural risks for HIV and other illnesses in Dominican society (Padilla 1996). Persons who are categorized as "Haitian" and who live on sugar cane plantations continue to show the highest rates of HIV infection in the Dominican Republic (Brewer et al. 1996; Capellan et al. 1990; Koenig et al. 1987).

31. The authors' apparent suggestion here that people from neighboring Caribbean countries were purchasers of the sexual services of Dominican sex workers—while certainly possible among a small segment of sex-work clients—is not consistent with the general pattern in which European and (especially) North American tourists are the primary clients. See Kempadoo (1999b).

32. Ramah et al.'s finding that a self-reported history of sexually transmitted infections was more common among MSM residing outside of the capital city may be related to the fact that proximity to tourist enclaves increased risk for such infections. Kerrigan et al. (2001) similarly note the higher rates of HIV among female sex workers outside of Santo Domingo but suggest that this may be due to successful prevention activities focused in this area of the capital. A similar argument cannot be made for male sex workers, given the lack of sustained interventions with this population.

33. The authors do not clearly articulate their method for identifying these five identity terms, or to what degree they are exhaustive or mutually exclusive, except to refer to them as terms of self-definition. They note that "gigolos are a previously described distinct group of

CSW [commercial sex workers] from the beach areas of Santo Domingo (Boca Chica) and Puerto Plata who accept money and gifts from female tourists, yet will also engage in sex trade with male tourists" (Tabet et al. 1996, 204).

34. In their study of gay men's assessment of their risk for HIV infection, Bauman and Siegel (1987) find that these men often expressed "unrealistic optimism" and "denial" about the potential risk associated with their sexual behavior, a response that may represent a coping mechanism for dealing with their fear of infection. See also Odets's (1995) excellent book on the "psychological epidemic" among HIV-negative gay men, which discusses various emotional coping strategies.

35. As described further below, *bugarrones* and *sanky pankies* are sometimes denied payment by gay clients if they are either unable to achieve full erection or to ejaculate. In some instances, this can lead to physical conflicts between sex workers and clients, as sex workers may insist on payment regardless of the outcome of the encounter.

36. In the survey, not having a condom at the time of the encounter was one of the most common explanations given by sex workers for not using condoms consistently with clients. One sex worker explained this as follows in an interview: "If I have three condoms and I use them in a week, and I have a client and there aren't any condoms, and I have to do the job, I do it. . . . So, I use them [condoms], but if I don't have them, I still do it [have sex]."

37. Despite my attempts to convince him otherwise, Martín declined to discuss his ongoing symptoms—primarily genital itch and some urethral discharge—with a physician at ASA or another medical facility, apparently afraid that this would subject him to rumors. Eighteen percent of the sex workers surveyed in this study indicated that they had been diagnosed with an STD at some point in the past.

38. As mentioned above, this may also reflect the fact that the members of the research team were associated with HIV prevention programs, which tended to elicit such discussions during the interviews and surveys.

39. This distinction may be particularly problematic in developing contexts in which HIV testing is not widespread and antiretroviral therapies are unavailable, since in such situations persons are frequently diagnosed with AIDS shortly before their death, contributing to the perception that HIV infection is concurrent with the onset of symptoms.

40. In her study of AIDS risk denial among Mexican women and their male partners, Hirsch (Hirsch et al. 2002; Hirsch 2003) has argued that while young couples often profess a "modern" understanding of companionate marriage based on love and mutual sexual satisfaction, this cultural model can also result in the emphatic denial of outside infidelities and inhibit the perceived need for condom use in marriage.

41. Nevertheless, one HIV prevention project among male sex workers bears mentioning here. Between 1990 and 1992, the nongovernmental organization CASCO (Coordinadora de Animación Socio-Cultural) conducted a needs assessment of adolescent street sex workers based on thirty interviews, designed some educational materials for distribution, and began conducting a pilot intervention incorporating volunteer peer educators (CASCO 1992; Vásquez, Ruiz, and De Moya 1991). The intervention component of this project was discontinued after less than a year.

42. It is interesting in this regard that while studies were conducted by public health organizations themselves that demonstrated a highly diverse population of MSM (e.g., Ramah et al. 1992), HIV/AIDS programs among MSM continued to be exclusively gay-focused, per-

haps suggesting the belief that interventions oriented toward gays would inevitably reach all types of MSM.

Conclusion

1. This pattern is reflected in the relatively large proportion of survey participants (51%) who had moved to the study sites from other parts of the country in order to engage in informal income generation in the tourism market (see fig. 5). Evidence from other studies reviewed in chapter 2 suggests that these migratory patterns may be even more pronounced among women, who generally have fewer options in the rural, predominantly agricultural economy. Nevertheless, recent closures of state-held (CEA) sugar plantations are likely to accelerate rural-urban migration among young men, many of whom have fewer options for formal-sector employment than do comparable women.

2. Antonio de Moya and Rafael García (1996), social scientists who have studied Dominican homoeroticism and HIV/AIDS, have alluded to this silence, attributing it to the contradictions inherent in a model of sexuality that derives, according to the authors, from the historical tensions and mutual appropriations that occurred between indigenous and colonial sexual systems. In this "syncretic" model, homoerotic encounters commonly occur and may even be valorized, but are rarely discussed in the "respectable" context of public or familial space—an interpretation that resonates with analyses of homoeroticism in other Latin American contexts (see especially Parker 1991).

3. Indeed, 3 percent of the survey sample for this study included gay- or homosexual-identified men. See Cantú (2002) for a useful discussion of interactions between local and foreign gays.

4. Indeed, the cultural particularity of these constructions is suggested by the regional differentiation of sex tourist fantasies and motivations for travel that appears to be evidenced in the growing cross-cultural literature on sex tourism (Jackson and Cook 2000; O'Connell Davidson 1998; Seabrook 1996; Truong 1990).

5. While I do not seek here to analyze the psychosocial roots of the quest for encounters with the elusive "straight" man that seems to be prevalent among gay men in the United States, the existence and erotic charge of such encounters seem to be demonstrated by the preponderance of fantasies involving straight men in gay publications, classified ads, and pornography.

6. Here, I use the metaphor of performance in the analytical sense of "gender performance," not to delegitimate these expressions of gender or to imply that they are in some way contrived. See Morris (1995) on the use of performance theory in anthropological studies of gender.

7. The use of "front" and "back" in MacCannell's terminology derives from Goffman's use of the dichotomy of "front stage"/"back stage" in his theoretical model, which employs theatrical performance as a metaphor for the contextual nature of public and private social relations.

8. It is this blurring between "performance" and "authenticity"—between "front" and "back" regions—that leads MacCannell to describe touristic performance as a continuum, since these self-representations are frequently informed by multiple, and even contradictory, meanings.

9. Orlando Patterson describes the West Atlantic System as follows: "Originally a region of diverse cultures and economies operating within the framework of several imperial systems, the West Atlantic region has emerged over the centuries as a single environment in which the

dualistic United States center is asymmetrically linked to dualistic peripheral units. Unlike other peripheral systems of states—those of the Pacific, for example—the West Atlantic periphery has become more and more uniform, under the direct and immediate influence of its powerful northern neighbors, in cultural, political and economic terms. Further, unlike other peripheral zones in their relation to their centers, the West Atlantic system has a physical nexus in the metropolis at the tip of Florida" (quoted in Farmer 1999, 258).

10. Ryan and Hall (2001, 104) report on studies of the U.S. gay travel industry that indicate that the gay and lesbian travel sector is worth approximately U.S.$47.3 billion, reflecting a higher propensity for travel among gay populations than among heterosexuals, and a higher expenditure of personal funds for this purpose. Nevertheless, as Puar has aptly observed, these statistics represent a particularly affluent vision of the "cosmopolitan gay consumer" that effaces other kinds of stratification within the "West" (Puar 2002b).

11. In 1999, the Cayman Islands received international media attention after refusing docking privileges to gay and lesbian cruise ships (Human Rights Campaign [HRC] 1998). A government minister observed that the Cayman Islands had a "mandate from God" to maintain its legal ban on gay sex, despite British demands that it eliminate it. A gay activist later made implicit reference to the country's dependence on tourism when she remarked, "denying berthing rights to a ship because it is carrying gay passengers is morally wrong, as well as economically foolish" (ibid.).

12. As mentioned in previous chapters, the fact that *bugarrones* and *sanky pankies* are concerned with the potential consequences of their involvement in homoerotic activities complicates suggestions in prior ethnographic accounts in Latin America (e.g., Lancaster 1988, 1992) that the "*activo*" participant in such exchanges is not stigmatized and may even improve his masculine status. The present study suggests that this question is better conceived as a situational one; that is, the degree of stigma varies depending on the social context. Nevertheless, my experience in the Dominican Republic is that open discussion of homosexual practices in the context of the family—regardless of sexual role—is rarely if ever condoned, and sex workers' anxieties about such interactions provide further evidence that acknowledgment of same-sex activities is actively avoided in familial relations.

13. Drawing on various theoretical traditions—such as world systems theory, the political economy of health, and various neo-Marxist approaches—this body of anthropological literature has also offered important contributions to the analysis of HIV/AIDS by emphasizing the importance of placing the epidemic within the history of neocolonial dependency, global capitalism, migration, and work (see Singer 1998).

14. Conversely, Padilla, Vásquez del Aguila, and Parker (2006) have recently argued that relatively little attention has been placed within cross-cultural studies of LGBTQ communities on what has been described as "dependent development and gay identity" (Parker and Cáceres 1999), in which the shape of queer cultural forms and identities is analyzed within local and global systems of power and inequality. Such a framework is essential in considering the influence of structural violence on LGBTQ health, and therefore has many consequences for conceptualizing the health of queer populations in the developing world.

Bibliography

Abraham-van der Mark, Eva. 1993. "Marriage and Concubinage among the Sephardic Merchant Elite of Curacao." In *Women and Change in the Caribbean,* edited by Janet Momsen, 38–50. Bloomington: Indiana University Press.

Adam, Barry. 1989. "Pasivos y activos en Nicaragua: Homosexuality without a Gay World." *Out/Look* Winter: 74–82.

Aggleton, Peter. 1996a. "Introduction." In *Bisexualities and AIDS,* edited by Peter Aggleton, 1–6.

———, ed. 1996b. *Bisexualities and AIDS: International Perspectives.* London: Taylor & Francis.

AIDSCAP/FHI. 1993. "Technical Assessment of AIDS in the Dominican Republic. A Report to the U.S. Agency for International Development." Santo Domingo: AIDSCAP.

Alexander, Jack. 1984. "Love, Race, Slavery, and Sexuality in Jamaican Images of the Family." In *Kinship and Ideology in Latin America,* edited by Raymond T. Smith, 147–80. Chapel Hill: University of North Carolina Press.

Alexander, M. Jacqui. 1997. "Erotic Autonomy as a Politics of Decolonization: An Anatomy of Feminist and State Practice in the Bahamas Tourist Economy." In *Feminist Genealogies, Colonial Legacies, Democratic Futures,* edited by M. Jacqui Alexander and Chandra Talpade Mohanty, 63–100. New York: Routledge.

Alonso, Ana Maria, and Maria Teresa Koreck. 1993. "Silences: 'Hispanics,' AIDS, and Sexual Practices." In *The Lesbian and Gay Studies Reader,* edited by Henry Abelove, Michele Aina Barale, and David M. Halperin, 110–26. New York: Routledge.

Altman, Dennis. 1995. "Globalisation, the State and Identity Politics." *Pacifica Review* 7, no. 1:69–76.

———. 2001. *Global Sex.* Chicago: University of Chicago Press.

Anderson, George M. 1995. "Darkness in the Dominican Republic." *America* 173, no. 16:10–11.

Anderson, Patricia, and Michael Witter. 1994. "Crisis, Adjustment and Social Change: A Case Study of Jamaica." In *The Consequences of Structural Adjustment: A Review of the Jamaican Experience,* edited by Elsie LeFranc, 1–55. Kingston: Canoe Press.

Angueira, Luisa Hernández. 1998. "Across the Mona Strait: Dominican Boat Women in Puerto

Rico." In *Daughters of Caliban: Caribbean Women in the Twentieth Century*, edited by Consuelo López Springfield, 96–111. Bloomington: Indiana University Press.

Appadurai, Arjun. 1996. *Modernity at Large*. Minneapolis: University of Minnesota Press.

ASONAHORES. 1995. "Estadísticas seleccionadas del sector turístico." Santo Domingo: Asociación Nacional de Hoteles y Restaurantes.

Austerlitz, Paul. 1997. *Merengue: Dominican Music and Dominican Identity*. Philadelphia: Temple University Press.

Baer, Hans A., Merrill Singer, and John H. Johnsen. 1986. "Toward a Critical Medical Anthropology." *Social Science and Medicine* 23:95–98.

Baer, Hans A., Merrill Singer, and Ida Susser. 1997. *Medical Anthropology and the World System: A Critical Perspective*. Westport, CT: Bergin & Garvey.

Baeten, Jared M., Barbara A. Richardson, Ludo Lavreys, Joel P. Rakwar, Kishorchandra Mandaliya, Job J. Bwayo, and Joan K. Kreiss. 2005. "Female-to-Male Infectivity of HIV-1 among Circumcised and Uncircumcised Kenyan Men." *Journal of Infectious Diseases* 191, no. 4:546–53.

Balaguer, Joaquín. 1978. *Guía emocional de la cuidad romántica*. Barcelona: Los Telleres Sirven.

———. 1983. *La isla al revés: Haité y el destino dominicano*. Buenos Aires: Ferrari Hermanos.

Banco Central de la República Dominicana. 2001. Report: "Llegada mensual de pasajeros, via aérea, por nacionalidad, 2000–2001." Santo Domingo: Departamento de Cuentas Nacionales y Estadísticas Económicas.

Barrow, Christine. 1996. *Family in the Caribbean: Themes and Perspectives*. Kingston: Ian Randle Publishers.

Barry, Tom, Beth Wood, and Deb Preusch. 1984. *The Other Side of Paradise*. New York: Grove Press.

Basch, Linda, Nina Glick Schiller, and Cristina Szanton Blanc. 1994. *Nations Unbound: Transnational Projects, Postcolonial Predicaments, and Deterritorialized Nation-States*. Amsterdam: Gordon & Breach.

Bastide, Roger. 1968. "Color, Racism, and Christianity." In *Color and Race*, edited by John Hope Franklin, 34–49. Boston: Beacon Press.

Bauman, Laurie J., and Karolynn Siegel. 1987. "Misperceptions among Gay Men of the Risk for AIDS Associated with Their Sexual Behavior." *Journal of Applied Social Psychology* 17, no. 3:329–50.

Bayer, Ronald, and Cheryl Healton. 1989. "Controlling AIDS in Cuba: The Logic of Quarantine." *New England Journal of Medicine* 320, no. 15:1022–24.

Beckles, Hilary. 1989. *Natural Rebels: A Social History of Enslaved Black Women in Barbados*. London: Zed Books.

Bejel, Emilio. 2001. *Gay Cuban Nation*. Chicago: University of Chicago Press.

Benitez, Antonio. 1992. *The Repeating Island: The Caribbean and the Postmodern Perspective*. Durham, NC: Duke University Press.

Besson, Jean. 1993. "Reputation and Respectability Reconsidered: A New Perspective on Afro-Caribbean Peasant Women." In *Women and Change in the Caribbean*, edited by Janet Momsen, 15–37. Bloomington: Indiana University Press.

Betances, Emelio. 1995. *State and Society in the Dominican Republic*. Latin American Perspectives, no. 15. Boulder, CO: Westview Press.

Bingham, Trista A., William McFarland, Douglas A. Shehan, Marlene LaLota, David D.

Celentano, Beryl A. Koblin, Lucia V. Torian, Duncan A. MacKellar, Linda A. Valleroy, Gina M. Secura, Robert S. Janssen, and G. W. Roberts. 2002. "Unrecognized HIV Infection, Risk Behaviors, and Perceptions of Risk among Young Black Men Who Have Sex with Men—Six U.S. Cities, 1994–1998." *MMWR* 51, no. 33:733–36.

Bishop, Ryan, and Lillian Robinson. 1998. *Night Market: Sexual Cultures and the Thai Economic Miracle.* New York: Routledge.

Black, Jan Knippers. 1986. *The Dominican Republic: Politics and Development in an Unsovereign State.* Boston: Allen & Unwin.

Block, Alan A., and Patricia Klausner. 1987. "Masters of Paradise Island: Organized Crime, Neo-colonialism and the Bahamas." *Dialectical Anthropology* 12:85–102.

Bolles, A. Lynn. 1992. "Sand, Sea, and the Forbidden." *Transforming Anthropology* 3, no. 1:30–34.

———. 1996. *Sister Jamaica.* Lanham, MD: University Presses of America.

Bongaarts, John, Priscilla Reining, Peter Way, and Francis Conant. 1989. "The Relationship between Male Circumcision and HIV Infection in African Populations." *AIDS* 3, no. 6:373–77.

Bourdieu, Pierre. 1977. *Outline of a Theory of Practice.* Cambridge: Cambridge University Press.

Bourgois, Philippe. 1995. *In Search of Respect: Selling Crack in El Barrio.* Cambridge: Cambridge University Press.

Brana-Shute, Gary. 1989. *On the Corner: Male Social Life in a Paramaibo Creole Neighborhood.* Prospect Heights, IL: Waveland.

Bray, David. 1984. "Economic Development: The Middle Class and International Migration in the Dominican Republic." *International Migration Review* 18, no. 2:217–36.

———. 1987. "Industrialization, Labor Migration, and Employment Crises: A Comparison of Jamaica and the Dominican Republic." In *Crises in the Caribbean Basin,* edited by Richard Tardanico, 79–93. Newbury Park, CA: Sage.

Brennan, Denise E. 1998. "Everything Is for Sale Here: Sex Tourism in Sosúa, the Dominican Republic." PhD dissertation, Yale University, New Haven.

———. 2004. *What's Love Got to Do with It? Transnational Desires and Sex Tourism in the Dominican Republic.* Durham and London: Duke University Press.

Brewer, Toye, Julia Hasbún, Jorge Sanchez, Caroline Ryan, Martha Butler de Lister, Stephen Hawes, Jose Constanzo, Jose Lopez, and King Holmes. 1996. "Prevalence of STD among Women on the Sugar Cane Plantations (Bateyes) of the Dominican Republic (D.R.)." *International Conference on AIDS* 11, no. 1:131 (abstract no. Mo.C.1436).

Brown, Susan E. 1973. "Coping with Poverty in the Dominican Republic: Women and Their Mates." *Current Anthropology* 14, no. 5:555.

———. 1975a. "Low Economic Sector Female Mating Patterns in the Dominican Republic." In *Women Cross-Culturally: Change and Challenge,* edited by Ruby Rohrlich-Leavitt, 221–39. The Hague: Mouton.

———. 1975b. "Love Unites Them and Hunger Separates Them: Poor Women in the Dominican Republic." In *Toward an Anthropology of Women,* edited by Rayna Rapp Reiter, 322–32. New York: Monthly Review Press.

Brussa, Licia. 1989. "Migrant Prostitutes in the Netherlands." In *Vindication of the Rights of Whores,* edited by Gail Pheterson, 227–40. Seattle: Seal Press.

Burns, Peter M. 1999. *An Introduction to Tourism and Anthropology.* New York: Routledge.

Butcher, Kate. 2003. "Confusion between Prostitution and Sex Trafficking." *Lancet* 361, no. 9373:1983.

Cabezas, Amalia L. 1998a. "Discourses of Prostitution: The Case of Cuba." In *Global Sex Workers: Rights, Resistance and Redefinition,* edited by Kamala Kempadoo, 79–86. New York: Routledge.

———. 1998b. "Pleasure and Its Pain: Sex Tourism in Sosúa, the Dominican Republic." PhD dissertation, University of California, Berkeley.

———. 1999. "Women's Work Is Never Done: Sex Tourism in Sosúa, the Dominican Republic." In *Sun, Sex, and Gold,* edited by Kamala Kempadoo, 93–123.

Cabrera, Federico. 2001. "Anuncio policial saca a flote derechos de los homosexuales." *Listín Diario,* February 18:3.

Cáceres, Carlos F. 1996. "Male Bisexuality in Peru and the Prevention of Aids." In *Bisexualities and AIDS,* edited by Peter Aggleton, 126–47.

Calder, Bruce. 1984. *The Impact of Intervention: The Dominican Republic during the U.S. Occupation of 1916–1924.* Austin: University of Texas Press.

Caldwell, John C., Pat Caldwell, and Pat Quiggin. 1989. "The Social Context of AIDS in Sub-Saharan Africa." *Population and Development Review* 15, no. 2:185–233.

Camara, Bilali. 2001. *20 Years of the HIV/AIDS Epidemic in the Caribbean.* Port of Spain, Trinidad: CAREC-SPSTI.

Cambeira, Alan. 1997. *Quisqueya la Bella: The Dominican Republic in Historical and Cultural Perspective.* Armonk, NY: M. E. Sharpe.

Cameron, D. William, J. Neil Simonsen, Lourdes J. D'Costa, Allan R. Ronald, Gregory M. Maitha, Michael N. Gakinya, Mary Cheang, J. O. Ndinya-Achola, Peter Piot, Robert C. Brunham, and Francis A. Plummer. 1989. "Female to Male Transmission of Human Immunodeficiency Virus Type 1: Risk Factors for Seroconversion in Men." *Lancet* 2, no. 8660:403–7.

Campbell, Shirley, Althea Perkins, and Patricia Mohammed. 1999. "'Come to Jamaica and Feel All Right': Tourism and the Sex Trade." In *Sun, Sex, and Gold:,* edited by Kamala Kempadoo, 125–56.

Canan, Penelope, and Michael Hennessey. 1989. "The Growth Machine, Tourism and the Selling of Culture." *Sociological Perspectives* 32, no. 2:227–43.

Canó, Pedro. 2000. "El turismo sexual: la cara oscura de la industria sin chimeneas." *[A]hora,* Sept. 25.

Cantú, Lionel. 2002. "De Ambiente: Queer Tourism and the Shifting Boundaries of Mexican Male Sexualities." *GLQ* 8, no. 1–2:139–66.

Capellan, M. R., L. Reyes, E. Antonio De Moya, and E. L. Koenig. 1990. "A Comparative Study between Sugar Cane Workers in the Dominican Republic: A Search for HIV and Its Co-Factors." *International Conference on AIDS* 6, no. 2:227 (abstract no. F.C.586).

Carrier, Joseph. 1995. *De los tros: Intimacy and Homosexuality among Mexican Men.* New York: Columbia University Press.

Carrillo, Héctor. 1999. "Cultural change, hybridity and male homosexuality in Mexico." *Culture, Health & Sexuality* 1, no. 3:223–38.

———. 2002. *The Night Is Young: Sexuality in Mexico in the Time of AIDS.* Chicago: University of Chicago Press.

———. 2003a. "Neither Machos nor Maricones: Masculinity and Emerging Male Homosexual Identities in Mexico." In *Changing Men and Masculinities in Latin America,* edited by Matthew C. Gutmann, 351–69. Durham: Duke University Press.

———. 2003b. "Another Crack in the Mirror: The Politics of Aids Prevention in Mexico." In *Sexual and Reproductive Health Promotion in Latino Populations: Parteras, Promotoras y*

Poetas: Case Studies across the Americas, edited by M. Idali Torres and George P. Cernada, 307–29. Amityville, NY: Baywood.

CASCO. 1992. "Informe del proyecto Bugui-Bugui." Santo Domingo: CASCO.

Castañeda, Digna. 1995. "The Female Slave in Cuba during the First Half of the Nineteenth Century." In *Engendering History: Caribbean Women in Historical Perspective,* edited by Verene Shepherd, Bridget Brereton, and Barbara Bailey, 141–54. New York: St. Martin's Press.

Castaneda, Xochitl, Victor Ortiz, Betania Allen, Cecilia Garcia, and Mauricio Hernandez-Avila. 1996. "Sex Masks: The Double Life of Female Commercial Sex Workers in Mexico City." *Culture, Medicine and Psychiatry* 20:229–247.

Cepeda, Carlos. 1984. "Falta de legislación impide detener auge de la prostitución homosexual." *La noticia,* Apr. 2, 12–13.

CEPROSH. 1997. "Proyecto Hotelero." Puerto Plata: Centro de Promoción y Solidaridad Humana.

CESDEM. 1997. "República Dominicana: encuesta demográfica y de salud." Calverton, MD: PROFAMILIA, ONUPLAN, and Macro International, Inc.

———. 1999. "Informe de resultados: encuesta sobre conocimientos, creencias, actitudes y prácticas acerca del VIH/SIDA en hombres que tienen sexo con hombres." Santo Domingo: AcciónSIDA.

Chambers, Erve. 1999. *Native Tours: The Anthropology of Travel and Tourism.* Long Grove, IL: Waveland.

Chen, Martha Alter, Joann Vanek, and Marilyn Carr. 2004. *Mainstreaming Informal Employment and Gender in Poverty Reduction: A Handbook for Policy-makers and other Stakeholders.* Ottawa: International Development Research Centre.

Chevannes, Barry. 2001. *Learning to be a Man: Culture, Socialization, and Gender Identity in Five Caribbean Communities.* Kingston: University of the West Indies Press.

Chu, Susan Y., Thomas A. Peterman, Lynda S. Doll, James W. Buehler, and James W. Curran. 1992. "AIDS in Bisexual Men in the United States: Epidemiology and Transmission to Women." *American Journal of Public Health* 82, no. 2:220–24.

Clarke, Edith. 1970. *My Mother Who Fathered Me: A Study of Three Selected Communities in Jamaica.* London: George Allen & Unwin.

Clifford, James. 1997. *Routes: Travel and Translation in the Late Twentieth Century.* Cambridge: Harvard University Press.

Cohen, E. 1972. "Towards a Sociology of International Tourism." *Sociological Research* 39:164–82.

Collins, John. 2002. "Direction of Tourism Being Debated in D. R." *Pymesdominicanas.com* Accessed July 28, 2003: http://www.pymesdominicanas.com/english/articles/hotel_dr.htm.

Connell, R. W. 1987. *Gender and Power: Society, the Person, and Sexual Politics.* Cambridge, MA: Polity Press.

Contreras, Alonso de. 1999. "Estados Unidos deportará a 3,000 Dominicanos." *El nuevo herald.* Feb. 18, 1B.

Crassweller, Robert D. 1966. *Trujillo: The Life and Times of a Caribbean Dictator.* New York: Macmillan.

Crick, Malcolm. 1985. "'Tracing' the Anthropological Self: Quizzical Reflections on Fieldwork, Tourism and the Ludic." *Social Analysis* 17:71–92.

———. 1989. "Representations of International Tourism in the Social Sciences: Sun, Sex, Sights, Savings, and Servility." *Annual Review of Anthropology* 18:307–44.

Cross Beras, Julio A. 1980. "The Dominican Family." In *The Family in Latin America*, edited by Man Singh Das and Clinton J. Jesser, 270–94. New Delhi: Vikas.

Dann, Graham. 1987. *The Barbadian Male: Sexual Attitudes and Practice*. Kingston: Macmillan Caribbean.

D'Emilio, John. 1997. "Capitalism and Gay Identity." In *The Gender/Sexuality Reader: Culture, History, Political Economy*, edited by Roger N. Lancaster and Micaela di Leonardo, 169–79. New York: Routledge.

De Moya, E. Antonio. 1989. "La Alfombra de Guazábara o el Reino de los Desterrados." Paper read at El Primer Congreso Dominicano sobre Menores en Circunstancias Especialmente Difíciles, Santo Domingo.

———. 2003. "Power Games and Totalitarian Masculinity in the Dominican Republic." In *Interrogating Caribbean Masculinities: Theoretical and Empirical Analyses*, edited by Rhoda E. Reddock, 68–102. Kingston: University of the West Indies Press.

De Moya, E. Antonio, and Rafael García. 1998. "Three Decades of Male Sex Work in Santo Domingo." In *Men Who Sell Sex: International Perspectives on Male Prostitution and AIDS*, edited by Peter Aggleton, 127–40. London: Taylor & Francis.

———. 1996. "AIDS and the Enigma of Bisexuality in the Dominican Republic." In *Bisexualities and AIDS*, edited by Peter Aggleton, 121–35.

De Moya, E. Antonio, Rafael García, Rosario Fadul, and Edward Herold. 1992. "Sosua Sanky-Pankies and Female Sex Workers: An Exploratory Study." Unpublished report. La Universidad Autonoma, Santo Domingo.

Decena, Carlos Ulises. 2004. "Queering the Heights: Dominican Transnational Identities and Male Homosexuality in New York City." PhD diss., Program in American Studies, New York University, New York.

Deere, Carmen Diana, Peggy Antrobus, Lynn Bolles, Edwin Melendez, Peter Phillips, Marcia Rivera, and Helen Safa. 1990. *In the Shadow of the Sun: Caribbean Development Alternatives and U.S. Policy*. Boulder, CO: Westview Press.

del Olmo, Rosa. 1979. "The Cuban Revolution and the Struggle against Prostitution." *Crime and Social Justice* 12:34–40.

Derby, Lauren. 1994. "Haitians, Magic, and Money: Raza and Society in the Haitian-Dominican Borderlands, 1900–1937." *Comparative Studies in Society and History* 36, no. 3:488–526.

Díaz, M. 1987. "La tención crece entre ilegales criollos en Puerto Rico." *Ultima hora*. May 5, 17.

Díaz, Rafael M. 1997. "Latino Gay Men and Psycho-Cultural Barriers to Aids Prevention." In *In Changing Times: Gay Men and Lesbians Encounter HIV/AIDS*, edited by Martin P. Levine, Peter M. Nardi, and John H. Gagnon, 221–44. Chicago: University of Chicago Press.

———. 1998. *Latino Gay Men and HIV*. New York: Routledge.

Díaz, Rafael M., George Ayala, Edward Bein, Jeff Henne, and Barbara V. Marin. 2001. "The impact of Homophobia, Poverty, and Racism on the Mental Health of Gay and Bisexual Latino Men: Findings from 3 US Cities." *American Journal of Public Health* 91, no. 6:927–32.

Diederich, Bernard. 1978. *The Death of the Goat*. Boston: Little, Brown.

Duany, Jorge. 1985. "Ethnicity in the Spanish Caribbean: Notes on the Consolidation of Creole Identity in Cuba and Puerto Rico." *Ethnic Groups* 6, no. 2–3:99–123.

Duarte, Isis. 1980. *Capitalismo y superpoblación en Santo Domingo*. Santo Domingo: CODIA.

Enloe, Cynthia. 2000. *Bananas, Beaches & Bases: Making Feminist Sense of International Politics*. Berkeley: University of California Press.

Espinal, Rosario, and Sherri Grasmuck. 1997. "Gender, Households and Informal Entrepreneurship in the Dominican Republic." *Journal of Comparative Family Studies* 28, no. 1:103–28.

Espino, Maria Dolores. 1994. "Tourism in Cuba: A Development Strategy for the 1990s?" In *Cuba at the Crossroads: Politics and Economics after the Fourth Party Congress,* edited by Jorge F. Peres-Lopez, 147–65. Gainesville: University of Florida Press.

European Study Group on Heterosexual Transmission of HIV. 1992. "Comparison of Female to Male and Male to Female Transmission of HIV in 563 Stable Couples." *British Medical Journal* 304:809–13.

Fadul, Rosario, E. Antonio De Moya, Rafael García, and Edward Herold. 1992. "Sexual Interaction and HIV/STD Risk between Females Sex Workers and Foreign Tourists." *International Conference on AIDS* 8, no. 2: D492 (abstract no. PoD 5618).

Fanon, Franz. 1963. *The Wretched of the Earth.* New York: Grove Press.

Farmer, Paul. 1992. *AIDS and Accusation: Haiti and the Geography of Blame.* Berkeley: University of California Press.

———. 1996. "Social Inequalities and Emerging Infectious Diseases." *Emerging Infectious Diseases* 2, no. 4:259–69.

———. 1999. *Infections and Inequalities: The Modern Plagues.* Berkeley: University of California Press.

———. 2003. *Pathologies of Power: Health, Human Rights, and the New War on the Poor.* Berkeley: University of California Press.

Farmer, Paul, Margaret Connors, and Janie Simmons, eds. 1996. *Women, Poverty, and AIDS: Sex, Drugs, and Structural Violence.* Monroe, ME: Common Courage Press.

Ferguson, James. 1992. *The Dominican Republic: Beyond the Lighthouse.* London: Latin America Bureau.

Fernandez, Nadine. 1999. "Back to the Future? Women, Race, and Tourism in Cuba." In *Sun, Sex, and Gold:,* edited by Kamala Kempadoo, 81–89.

Fernández-Kelly, Patricia. 2004. "Neoliberal Hopes Stir Up Growing Inequalities: Evidence from Latin America." *Points of Development, Bulletin for the Center for Migration and Development* Jan: 1–2.

Family Health International. 2003. "Final Report for the AIDSCAP Program in the Dominican Republic, October, 1993 to April, 1997." Family Health International.

Findlay, Eileen J. 1997. "Decency and Democracy: The Politics of Prostitution in Ponce, Puerto Rico, 1890–1900." *Feminist Studies* 23, no. 3:471–99.

Fink, A. J. 1987. "Circumcision and Heterosexual Transmission of HIV Infection to Men." Letter *New England Journal of Medicine* 316, no. 24:1546–47.

Frankenberg, Ronald. 1988. "Gramsci, Culture, and Medical Anthropology: Kundry and Parsifal? Or Rat's Tail to Sea Serpent?" *Medical Anthropology Quarterly* 2, no. 4:324–37.

Freeman, Carla. 1993. "Designing Women: Corporate Discipline and Barbados's Off-Shore Pink-Collar Sector." *Cultural Anthropology* 8, no. 2:169–86.

———. 1997. "Reinventing Higglering across Transnational Zones: Barbadian Women Juggle the Triple Shift." In *Daughters of Caliban: Caribbean Women in the Twentieth Century,* edited by Consuelo López Springfield, 68–95. Bloomington: Indiana University Press.

———. 2000. *High Tech and High Heels in the Global Economy: Women, Work, and Pink-Collar Identities in the Caribbean.* Durham, NC: Duke University Press.

Freitag, Tilman G. 1996. "Tourism and the Transformation of a Dominican Coastal Community." *Urban Anthropology and Studies of Cultural Systems* 25, Fall:225–58.

Fuller, Anne. 1999. *Tourism Development in the Dominican Republic: Growth, Costs, Benefits and Choices.* http://kiskeya-alternative.org/publica/afuller/rd-tourism.html (accessed 9/21/2005).

Fusco, Coco. 1998. "Hustling for Dollars: Jineterismo in Cuba." In *Global Sex Workers: Rights, Resistance, and Redefinition,* edited by Kamala Kempadoo and Jo Doezema, 151–66. New York: Routledge.

Gallardo Rivas, Gina. 1995. "Buscando la vida: dominicanas en el servicio doméstico en Madrid." Santo Domingo: Centro de Investigación para la Acción Femenina.

García Canclini, Néstor. 1995. *Hybrid Cultures: Strategies for Entering and Leaving Modernity.* Minneapolis: University of Minnesota Press.

Geggus, David P. 1996. "Slave and Free Colored Women in Saint Domingue." In *More Than Chattel: Black Women and Slavery in the Americas,* edited by David Barry Gaspar and Darlene Clark Hine, 259–78. Bloomington: Indiana University Press.

Georges, Eugenia. 1990. *The Making of a Transnational Community: Migration, Development, and Cultural Change in the Dominican Republic.* New York: Columbia University Press.

———. 1992. "Gender, Class, and Migration in the Dominican Republic: Women's Experiences in a Transnational Community." *Annals of the New York Academy of Sciences* 645:81–99.

Goffman, Erving. 1959. *The Presentation of Self in Everyday Life.* Garden City, NY: Doubleday.

———. 1963. *Stigma: Notes on the Management of Spoiled Identity.* New York: Simon & Schuster.

Gonzales, David. 2003. "Governments in Denial as AIDS Ravages Caribbean." *New York Times,* May 18.

González, Mercedes. 2001. "Pineda: es inconstitucional expulsar homosexuales de PN." *El siglo,* Aug. 10.

González, Peterson, and Carlos O. Pérez. 2001. "Candelier sostiene ley orgánica prohíbe homosexuales en la PN." *El siglo,* Feb. 14, 9A.

Graburn, Nelson H. H. 1983. "The Anthropology of Tourism." *Annals of Tourism Research* 10:9–33.

Granich, Reuben, Bradley Jacobs, Jonathan Mermin, and Allan Pont. 1995. "Cuba's National AIDS Program. The First Decade." *Western Journal of Medicine* 163, no. 2:139–44.

Grasmuck, Sherri, and Patricia Pessar. 1991. *Between Two Islands: Dominican International Migration.* Berkeley: University of California Press.

Hall, Stuart. 1991. "The Local and the Global: Globalization and Ethnicity." In *Culture, Globalization, and the World-System,* edited by Anthony D. King, 19–39. Binghamton: Department of Art and Art History, State University of New York.

Halperin, Daniel T., and Robert C. Bailey. 1999. "Male Circumcision and HIV Infection: 10 Years and Counting." *Lancet* 354, no. 9192:1813–15.

Harrison, David, ed. 1992. *Tourism and the Less Developed Countries.* London: Belhaven.

Harrison, Faye V. 1991. "Women in Jamaica's Urban Informal Economy: Insights from a Jamaican Slum." In *Third World Women and the Politics of Feminism,* edited by Chandra Talpade Mohanty, Ann Russo, and Lourdes Torres, 173–96. Bloomington: Indiana University Press.

Harvey, David. 1990. *The Condition of Postmodernity.* Cambridge: Blackwell.

Henriques, Fernando. 1965. *Prostitution in Europe and the Americas.* New York: Citadel Press.

Hernandez, Deborah Pacini. 1995. *Bachata: A Social History of a Dominican Popular Music.* Philadelphia: Temple University Press.

Hirsch, Jennifer. 2003. *A Courtship after Marriage: Sexuality and Love in Mexican Transnational Families.* Berkeley: University of California Press.

Hirsch, Jennifer S., Jennifer Higgins, Margaret E. Bentley, and Constance A. Nathanson. 2002. "The Social Constructions of Sexuality: Marital Infidelity and Sexually Transmitted Disease—HIV Risk in a Mexican Migrant Community." *American Journal of Public Health* 92, no. 8:1227–37.

Hirschman, Albert O. 1984. *Getting Ahead Collectively.* New York: Pergamon Press.

Ho, Christine. 1999. "Caribbean Transnationalism as a Gendered Process." *Latin American Perspectives* 26, no. 5:34–54.

Hobson, J. S. Perry, and Uta C. Dietrich. 1994. "Tourism, Health and Quality of Life: Challenging the Responsibility of Using the Traditional Tenets of Sun, Sea, Sand, and Sex in Tourism Marketing." *Journal of Travel and Tourism Marketing* 3, no. 4:21–38.

Hodge, G. Derrick. 2001. "Colonization of the Cuban Body: The Growth of Male Sex Work in Havana." *NACLA Report on the Americas* 34, no. 5:20–45.

Hoetink, Harry. 1982. *The Dominican People, 1850–1900: Notes for a Historical Sociology.* Translated by Stephen K. Ault. Baltimore: Johns Hopkins University Press.

———. 1985. "'Race' and Color in the Caribbean." In *Caribbean Contours,* edited by Sidney W. Mintz and Sally Price, 55–84. Baltimore: Johns Hopkins University Press.

hooks, bell. 1992. *Black Looks: Race and Representation.* Boston: South End Press.

Howard, David. 2001. *Coloring the Nation: Race and Ethnicity in the Dominican Republic.* Boulder: Lynne Rienner.

Human Rights Campaign (HRC). "British Embassy Pledges That Cayman Islands Will Review Cruise Ship Policy after Turning Away Gay Tourists." http://www.hrc.org/newsreleases/1998/980116cayman.asp (accessed 11/3/03).

Imbert Brugal, Carmen. 1991. *Tráfico de mujeres: visión de una nación exportadora.* Santo Domingo: CE-Mujer.

Inhorn, Marcia C. 1994. *Quest for Conception: Gender, Infertility, and Egyptian Medical Traditions.* Philadelphia: University of Pennsylvania Press.

———. 1995. "Medical Anthropology and Epidemiology: Divergences or Convergences?" *Social Science and Medicine* 40, 3:285–20.

International Organization for Migration (IOM). 1996. *Trafficking in Women from the Dominican Republic for Sexual Exploitation.* Budapest: Migration Information Programme.

Jackson, Peter A., and Nerida M. Cook, eds. 2000. *Genders and Sexualities in Modern Thailand.* Chiang Mai: Silkworm Books.

Jessamine, P. G., Frank A. Plummer, J. O. Ndinya-Achola, Mark A. Wainberg, I. A. Wamola, Lourdes J. D'Costa, D. William Cameron, J. Neil Simonsen, P. Plouroe, and Allan R. Ronald. 1990. "Human Immunodeficiency Virus, Genital Ulcers and the Male Foreskin: Synergism in HIV-1 Transmission." *Scandinavian Journal of Infectious Diseases* 69:181–86.

Jochelson, Karen, Monyaola Mothibeli, and Jean-Patrick Leger. 1991. "Human Immunodeficiency Virus and Migrant Labor in South Africa." *International Journal of Health Services* 21, no. 1:157–73.

Kane, Stephanie C. 1993. "Prostitution and the Military: Planning AIDS Intervention in Belize." *Social Science and Medicine* 36, 7:965–79.

Karch, Cecilia A., and G. H. S. Dann. 1981. "Close Encounters of the Third World." *Human Relations* 34:249–68.

Kempadoo, Kamala. 1999a. "Continuities and Change: Five Centuries of Prostitution in the Caribbean." In *Sun, Sex, and Gold,* edited by K. Kempadoo, 3–33.

———, ed. 1999b. *Sun, Sex, and Gold: Tourism and Sex Work in the Caribbean.* New York: Rowman & Littlefield.

Kempadoo, Kamala, and Ranya Ghuma. 1999. "For the Children: Trends in International Policies and Law on Sex Tourism." In *Sun, Sex, and Gold,* edited by Kamala Kempadoo, 291–308.

Kerr, Paulett A. 1995. "Victims or Strategists: Female Lodging Housekeepers in Jamaica." In *Engendering History: Caribbean Women in Historical Perspective,* edited by Verene Shepherd, Bridget Brereton, and Barbara Bailey, 197–212. New York: St. Martin's Press.

Kerrigan, Deanna, Jonathan M. Ellen, Luis Moreno, Santo Rosario, Joanne Katz, David D. Celentano, and Michael Sweat. 2003. "Environmental-Structural Factors Significantly Associated with Condom Use among Female Sex Workers in the Dominican Republic." *AIDS* 17:415–23.

Kerrigan, Deanna, Luis Moreno, Santo Rosario, and Michael Sweat. 2001. "Adapting the Thai 100% Condom Programme: Developing a Culturally Appropriate Model for the Dominican Republic." *Culture, Health & Sexuality* 3, no. 2:221–40.

Kincaid, Jamaica. 1988. *A Small Place.* London: Virago.

Kinnaird, Vivian, Uma Kothari, and Derek Hall. 1994. "Tourism: Gender Perspectives." In *Tourism: A Gender Analysis,* edited by Vivian Kinnaird and Derek Hall, 1–34. New York: John Wiley & Sons.

Kinsey, Alfred. 1948. *Sexual Behavior in the Human Male.* Philadelphia: W. B. Saunders.

———. 1953. *Sexual Behavior in the Human Female.* Philadelphia: W. B. Saunders.

Knight, Franklin W. 1990. *The Caribbean: The Genesis of a Fragmented Nationalism.* New York: Oxford University Press.

Koenig, E. L., G. Brach, and E. R. Smith. 1987. "Response to K. W. Payne." *Journal of the American Medical Association* 258, no. 1:46–47.

Koenig, E. R. 1989. "International prostitutes and transmission of HIV [letter]." *Lancet* 1, no. 8641:782–83.

Koenig, Ellen, Juan Pittaluga, Marie Bogart, Manolo Castro, Francisco Nuñez, Israel Vilorio, Luis Delvillar, Manuel Calzada, and Jay Levy. 1987. "Prevalence of Antibodies to the Human Immunodeficiency Virus in Dominicans and Haitians in the Dominican Republic." *Journal of the American Medical Association* 257, no. 5:631–34.

Kreniske, John. 1997. "AIDS in the Dominican Republic: Anthropological Reflections on the Social Nature of Disease." In *AIDS in Africa and the Caribbean,* edited by George C. Bond, John Kreniske, Ida Susser, and Joan Vincent, 33–50. Boulder, CO: Westview Press.

Krohn-Hansen, Christian. 1996. "Masculinity and the Political among Dominicans: 'The Dominican Tiger.'" In *Machos, Mistresses, Madonnas: Contesting the Power of Latin American Gender Imagery,* edited by Marit Melhuus and Kristi Anne Stølen, 108–33. New York: Verso.

———. 2001. "A Tomb for Columbus in Santo Domingo: Political Cosmology, Population and Racial Frontiers." *Social Anthropology* 9, no. 2:165–92.

Kulick, Don. 1997. "The Gender of Brazilian Transgendered Prostitutes." *American Anthropologist* 99, 3: 74–85.

———. 1998. *Travesti: Sex, Gender and Culture among Brazilian Transgendered Prostitutes.* Chicago: University of Chicago Press.

Kutsche, Paul. 1995. "Two Truths about Costa Rica." In *Latin American Male Homosexualities,* edited by Stephen O. Murray, 111–37.

Kutzinski, Vera M. 1993. *Sugar's Secrets: Race and the Erotics of Cuban Nationalism.* Charlottesville: University Press of Virginia.

La Fountain-Stokes, Lawrence. 2002. "De un pájaro las dos alas: Travel Notes of a Queer Puerto Rican in Havana." *GLQ* 8, no. 1–2:7–33.

Lancaster, Roger N. 1988. "Subject Honor and Object Shame: The Construction of Male Homosexuality and Stigma in Nicaragua." *Ethnology* 28, no. 2:111–25.

———. 1992. *Life Is Hard: Machismo, Danger, and the Intimacy of Power in Latin America.* Berkeley: University of California Press.

———. 1997. "On Homosexualities in Latin America (and Other Places)." *American Ethnologist* 24, no. 1:193–202.

Larson, Ann. 1989. "Social Context of Human Immunodeficiency Virus Transmission in Africa: Historical and Cultural Bases of East and Central African Sexual Relations." *Reviews of Infectious Diseases* 2, no. 5:716–31.

Leiner, Marvin. 1994. *Sexual Politics in Cuba: Machismo, Homosexuality, and AIDS.* Boulder, CO: Westview Press.

Levine, Martin P., ed. 1979. *Gay Men: The Sociology of Male Homosexuality.* New York: Harper & Row.

Lewis, Linden. 2004. "Caribbean Masculinity at the Fin de Siècle." In *Interrogating Caribbean Masculinities: Theoretical and Empirical Analyses,* edited by Rhoda E. Reddock, 244–66. Kingston: University of the West Indies Press.

Lichtenstein, Bronwen. 2000. "Secret Encounters: Black Men, Bisexuality, and AIDS in Alabama." *Medical Anthropology Quarterly* 14, no. 3:374–93.

Lieber, M. 1981. *Street Scenes: Afro-American Culture in Urban Trinidad.* Cambridge: Schenkman.

Lim, Lin Lean, ed. 1998. *The Sex Sector: The Economic and Social Bases of Prostitution in Southeast Asia.* Geneva: International Labour Office.

Link, Bruce G., Mary E. Northridge, Jo C. Phelan, and Michael L. Ganz. 1998. "Social Epidemiology and the Fundamental Cause Concept: On the Structuring of Effective Cancer Screens by Socioeconomic Status." *Milbank Quarterly* 76, no. 3:375–402.

Link, Bruce G., and Jo C. Phelan. 1995. "Social Conditions as Fundamental Causes of Disease." *Journal of Health and Social Behavior* 36 (spec. no.): 80–94.

Logan, Rayford Whittingham. 1968. *Haiti and the Dominican Republic.* New York: Oxford University Press.

López, Kleiner. 2001. "Una débil zapata sostiene el turismo de Boca Chica." *Listín diario,* Oct. 26, 8.

Lowenthal, Abraham F. 1995. *The Dominican Intervention.* Baltimore: Johns Hopkins University Press.

Lumsden, Ian. 1996. *Machos, Maricones, and Gays: Cuba and Homosexuality.* Philadelphia: Temple University Press.

MacCannell, Dean. 1973. "Staged Authenticity: Arrangements of Social Space in Tourist Settings." *American Journal of Sociology* 79:589–603.

———. 1976. *The Tourist: A New Theory of the Leisure Class.* New York: Shocken Books.

Magaña, J. Raul, and Jospeph M. Carrier. 1991. "Mexican and Mexican American Male Sexual Behavior & Spread of AIDS in California." *Journal of Sex Research* 28, no. 3:425–41.

Maingot, Anthony P. 1993. "The Offshore Caribbean." In *Modern Caribbean Politics,* edited by Anthony Payne and Paul Sutton, 259–76. Kingston: Ian Randle Publishers.

Manalansan, Martin. 2003. *Global Divas: Filipino Gay Men in the Diaspora.* Durham, NC: Duke University Press.

Manier, Benedicta. 1996. "RD está entre países de turismo sexual." *El Nacional.* Feb. 6, 3.

Mann, Jonathan M. 1991. "AIDS: Challenges to Epidemiology in the 1990s." In *AIDS and Women's Reproductive Health,* edited by Lincoln C. Chen, Jaime Sepulveda Amor, and Sheldon J. Segal, 11–15. New York: Plenum Press.

Manners, Robert. 1956. "Tabara: Subcultures of a Tobacco and Mixed Crop Municipality." In *The People of Puerto Rico,* edited by Julian Steward, 93–171. Urbana: University of Illinois Press.

Manning, Frank E. 1973. *Black Clubs in Bermuda: Ethnography of a Play World.* Ithaca, NY: Cornell University Press.

Martin, Emily. 1987. *The Woman in the Body: A Cultural Analysis of Reproduction.* Boston: Beacon Press.

———. 1988. "Medical Metaphors of Women's Bodies: Menstruation and Menopause." *International Journal of Health Services* 18, no. 2:237–254.

———. 1991. "The Egg and the Sperm: How Science Has Constructed a Romance Based on Stereotypical Male-Female Roles." *Signs* 16:485–501.

Martinez, Samuel. 1995. *Peripheral Migrants: Haitians and Dominican Republic Sugar Plantations.* Knoxville, TN: University of Tennessee Press.

Martis, Jacqueline. 1999. "Tourism and the Sex Trade in St. Maarten and Curacao." In *Sun, Sex, and Gold,* edited by K. Kempadoo, 201–15.

Matos-Rodriguez, Felix V. 1995. "Street Vendors, Pedlars, Shop-Owners and Domestics: Some Aspects of Women's Economic Roles in Nineteenth-Century San Juan, Puerto Rico, 1820–1870." In *Engendering History: Caribbean Women in Historical Perspective,* edited by Verene Shepherd, Bridget Brereton, and Barbara Bailey, 176–93. New York: St. Martin's Press.

Mayorga, Laura, and Pilar Velásquez. 1999. "Bleak Pasts, Bleak Futures: Life Paths of Thirteen Young Prostitutes in Cartagena, Colombia." In *Sun, Sex, and Gold* edited by Kamala Kempadoo, 157–82. McCamish, Malcom, Graeme Storer, and Greg Carl. 2000. "Refocusing HIV/AIDS Interventions in Thailand: The Case for Male Sex Workers and Other Homosexually Active Men." *Culture, Health & Sexuality* 2, no. 2:167–82.

McFarland, William, Mitchell Katz, Susan Stoyanoff, Douglas Shehan, Marlene LaLota, David Celentano, Beryl Koblin, Lucia Torian, Hanne Thiede, Clinical Biochemistry Br., Div. of Environmental Health Laboratory Sciences, National Center for Environmental Health; Prevention Svcs. Research Br., Statistics and Data Management Br., Office of the Director, Div. of HIV/AIDS Prevention—Surveillance and Epidemiology, National Center for HIV, STD, and TB Prevention, CDC. 2001. "HIV Incidence among Young Men Who Have Sex with Men—Seven U.S. Cities, 1994–2000." *MMWR* 50, no. 21:440–44.

McNeill, William H. 1976. *Plagues and Peoples.* New York: Anchor.

Medina, Lidia. 2003. "Gobierno invertirá en zonas turísticas." *Hoy.* April 12.

Medrano, Néstor. 2006. "El cardenal pide sacar lacras de la Zona Colonial." *Listín diario,* April 7.

Mercer, Kobena. 1993. "Looking for Trouble." In *The Lesbian and Gay Studies Reader,* edited by Henry Abelove, Michèle Aina Barale, and David M. Halperin, 350–59. New York: Routledge.

Miller, Daniel. 1994. *Modernity: An Ethnographic Approach.* Oxford: Berg.

Millet, Gregory, David Malebranche, Byron Mason, and Pilgrim Spikes. 2005. "Focusing

'Down Low': Bisexual Black Men, HIV Risk and Heterosexual Transmission." *Journal of the National Medical Association* 97, no. 7: 52S–59S.

Mintz, Sidney W. 1956. "Canamelar: The Subculture of a Rural Sugar Plantation Proletariat." In *The People of Puerto Rico*, edited by Julian Steward, 314–417. Urbana: University of Illinois Press.

———. 1971. "The Caribbean as a Socio-cultural Area." In *Peoples and Cultures of the Caribbean*, edited by Michael M. Horowitz, 17–46. Garden City, NY: Natural History Press.

———. 1974. *Worker in the Cane*. New York: Yale University Press.

———. 1985. *Sweetness and Power: The Place of Sugar in Modern History*. New York: Penguin.

———. 1987. "Labor and Ethnicity: The Caribbean Conjuncture." In *Crises in the Caribbean*, edited by Richard Tardanico, 47–57. Newbury Park, CA: Sage.

———. 1989. *Caribbean Transformations*. New York: Columbia University Press.

———. 1996. "Enduring Substances, Trying Theories: The Caribbean Region as Oikoumen." *Journal of the Royal Anthropological Institute* 2, no. 2:289–311.

Mintz, Sidney W., and Richard Price. 1981. *An Anthropological Approach to the Afro-American Past: A Caribbean Perspective*. Philadelphia: Institute for the Study of Human Issues.

MODEMU. 1997. "Movimiento de Mujeres Unidas: ¿Quiénes somos?" Santo Domingo: MODEMU.

Moitt, Bernard. 1996. "Slave Women and Resistance in the French Caribbean." In *More Than Chattel: Black Women and Slavery in the Americas*, edited by David Barry Gaspar and Darlene Clark Hine, 239–58. Bloomington: Indiana University Press.

Momsen, Janet Henshall. 1994. "Tourism, Gender, and Development in the Caribbean." In *Tourism: A Gender Analysis*, edited by Vivian Kinnaird and Derek Hall, 106–20. London: John Wiley & Sons.

Moodie, T. Dunbar. 1988. "Migrancy and Male Sexuality on the South African Gold Mines." *Journal of Southern African Studies* 14, no. 2:228–56.

Morgan, Lynn M. 1987. "Dependency Theory in the Political Economy of Health: An Anthropological Critique." *Medical Anthropology Quarterly* 1:131–54.

Morris, Rosalind C. 1995. "All Made Up: Performance Theory and the New Anthropology of Sex and Gender." *Annual Review of Anthropology* 24:567–92.

Morrissey, Marietta. 1989. *Slave Women in the New World: Gender Stratification in the Caribbean*. Lawrence: University Press of Kansas.

Morsy, Soheir A. 1996. "Political Economy in Medical Anthropology." In *Medical Anthropology: Contemporary Theory and Method*, edited by Carolyn F. Sargent and Thomas F. Johnson, 21–40. Westport, CT: Praeger.

Mullings, Beverley. 1999. "Globalization, Tourism, and the International Sex Trade." In *Sun, Sex, and Gold*, edited by K. Kempadoo, 55–80.

Multilateral Investment Fund. 2001. Conference Document: "Remittances to Latin America and the Caribbean: Comparative Statistics." Washington, DC: Multilateral Investment Fund.

Muñoz-Laboy, Miguel. 2004. "Beyond 'MSM': Sexual Desire among Bisexually-Active Latino Men in New York City." *Sexualities* 7, no. 1:55–80.

Murphy, Martin F. 1991. *Dominican Sugar Plantations: Production and Foreign Labor Integration*. New York: Praeger.

Murray, Laura, ed. 2001. *Rien mis labios y llora mi alma*. Santo Domingo: AccionSIDA/AED.

———, ed. 2002. *Laughing on the Outside, Crying on the Inside*. Santo Domingo: AcciónSIDA/AED.

Murray, Stephen O. 1995a. "Family, Social Insecurity, and the Underdevelopment of Gay Institutions in Latin America." In *Latin American Male Homosexualities*, edited by Stephen O. Murray, 33–48.

———. 1995b. "Homosexual Categorization in Cross-Cultural Perspective." In *Latin American Male Homosexualities*, edited by Stephen O. Murray, 3–33.

———, ed. 1995c. *Latin American Male Homosexualities*. Albuquerque: University of New Mexico Press.

Murray, Stephen O., and Manuel Arboleda. 1995. "Stigma Transformation and Relexification: Gay in Latin America." In *Latin American Male Homosexualities*, edited by Stephen O. Murray, 111–37.

Nagel, Joane. 2003. *Race, Ethnicity, and Sexuality: Intimate Intersections, Forbidden Frontiers.* Oxford: Oxford University Press.

Nuñez, Theron. 1989. "Touristic Studies in Anthropological Perspective." In *Hosts and Guests: The Anthropology of Tourism*, edited by Valene L. Smith, 265–74. Philadelphia: University of Pennsylvania Press.

O'Connell Davidson, Julia. 1996. "Sex Tourism in Cuba." *Race and Class* 38 (July/Sept.): 39–48.

———. 1998. *Prostitution, Power, and Freedom*. Ann Arbor: University of Michigan Press.

O'Connell Davidson, Julia, and Jacqueline Sanchez Taylor. 1996. "Child Prostitution and Sex Tourism: The Dominican Republic." Bangkok: ECPAT.

———. 1999. "Fantasy Islands: Exploring the Demand for Sex Tourism." In *Sun, Sex, and Gold*, edited by Kamala Kempadoo, 37–54.

Obbo, Christine. 1993. "HIV Transmission through Social and Geographical Networks in Uganda." *Social Science and Medicine* 36, no. 7:949–55.

Odets, Walt. 1995. *In the Shadow of the Epidemic: Being HIV-Negative in the Age of AIDS.* Durham, NC: Duke University Press.

Olwig, Karen F. 1990. "The Struggle for Respectability: Methodism and Afro-Caribbean Culture on 19th-Century Nevis." *New West Indian Guide* 64, no. 3/4:93–114.

Oviedo/Las Casas. 1988. *Crónicas escogidas*. Santo Domingo: Ediciones de la Fundación Corripio.

Padian, Nancy. 1987. "Heterosexual Transmission of Acquired Immunodeficiency Syndrome: International Perspectives and National Projections." *Reviews of Infectious Diseases* 9, no. 5:947–60.

Padilla, Mark B. 1996. "AIDS, 'Haitians,' and Border Anxiety: Lessons for an Epidemiology of Ethnicity in the Dominican Republic." Unpublished seminar paper, Department of Anthropology, Emory University, Atlanta.

Padilla, Mark, Ernesto Vásquez del Aguila, and Richard Parker. 2006. "Globalization, Structural Violence, and LGBT Health: A Cross-Cultural Perspective." In *The Health of Sexual Minorities: Public Health Perspectives on Lesbian, Gay, Bisexual and Transgender Populations*, edited by Ilan H. Meyer and Mary E. Northridge, 209–41. New York: Springer.

PAHO. 1998. "Health in the Americas, Vol. 2." Pan American Health Organization.

———. 2001. "VIH y SIDA en las Américas: una epidemia multifacética." Pan American Health Organization.

PAHO/WHO. 2002. "AIDS Surveillance in the Americas: Biannual Report." Pan American Health Organization.

Pantaleón, Doris. 2001. "El SIDA mata 270 personas en once años en Boca Chica." *Listín diario*, Oct. 24, 12A.

Pantalone, David W., Mary D. Plummer, and Jane M. Simoni. 2005. "HIV Disclosure and Risk Reduction Research: Practical Implications." *Focus* 20, no. 5:1–5.

Pape, Jean William, and Warren D. Johnson. 1988. "Epidemiology of AIDS in the Caribbean." *Baillière's Clinical Tropical Medicine and Communicable Diseases* 3, no. 1:31–42.

Parker, Richard. 1987. "Acquired Immunodeficiency Syndrome in Urban Brazil." *Medical Anthropology Quarterly* 1, no. 2:155–75.

———. 1991. *Bodies, Pleasures, and Passions: Sexual Culture in Contemporary Brazil.* Boston: Beacon Press.

———. 1992. "Male Prostitution, Bisexual Behaviour and HIV Transmission in Urban Brazil." In *Sexual Behaviour and Networking: Anthropological and Socio-cultural Studies on the Transmission of HIV,* edited by Tim Dyson, 109–22. Liege, Belgium: International Union for the Scientific Study of Population.

———. 1996. "Bisexuality and HIV/AIDS in Brazil." In *Bisexualities and AIDS,* edited by Peter Aggleton, 148–60.

———. 1999. *Beneath the Equator: Cultures of Desire, Male Homosexuality, and Emerging Gay Communities in Brazil.* New York: Routledge.

———. 2001. "Sexuality, Culture, and Power in HIV/AIDS Research." *Annual Review of Anthropology* 30: 163–79.

Parker, Richard, and Carlos Cáceres. 1999. "Alternative Sexualities and Changing Sexual Cultures among Latin American Men." *Culture, Health & Sexuality* 1, no. 3:2016.

Parker, Richard, and Manuel Carballo. 1990. "Qualitative Research on Homosexual and Bisexual Behavior Relevant to HIV/AIDS." *Journal of Sex Research* 27, no. 4:497–525.

Parker, Richard, Delia Easton, and Charles Klein. 2000. "Structural Barriers and Facilitators in HIV Prevention: A Review of International Research." *AIDS* 14, no. S1: S22–S32.

Patton, Cindy. 1990. *Inventing AIDS.* New York: Routledge.

———. 1996. *Fatal Advice.* Durham, NC: Duke University Press.

Pattullo, Polly. 1996. *Last Resorts: The Cost of Tourism in the Caribbean.* London: Cassell.

Paz, Octavio. 1985. *The Labyrinth of Solitude.* New York: Grove Press.

Phillips, Joan L. 1999. "Tourist-Oriented Prostitution in Barbados: The Case of the Beach Boy and the White Female Tourist." In *Sun, Sex, and Gold,* edited by Kamala Kempadoo, 183–200. Poon, Auliana. 1989. "Competitive Strategies for a 'New Tourism.'" In *Progress in Tourism, Recreation and Hospitality Management,* edited by C. Cooper. London: Belhaven Press.

Press, C. M. 1978. "Reputation and Respectability Reconsidered: Hustling in a Tourist Setting." *Caribbean Issues* 4, no. 1:109–19.

Prieur, Annick. 1998. *Mema's House, Mexico City: On Transvestites, Queens, and Machos.* Chicago: University of Chicago Press.

Pruitt, Deborah, and Suzanne LaFont. 1995. "For Love and Money: Romance Tourism in Jamaica." *Annals of Tourism Research* 22, no. 2:422–44.

Puar, Jasbir. 2002a. "Introduction" (Special Issue: "Queer Tourism: Geographies of Globalization"). *GLQ* 8, no. 1–2:1–6.

———. 2002b. "Circuits of Queer Mobility: Tourism, Travel, and Globalization." *GLQ* 8, no. 1–2:101–37.

Ramah, Michael, Reynaldo Pareja, and Julia Hasbún. 1992. "Lifestyles and Sexual Practices. Results of KABP Conducted among Homosexual and Bisexual Men." Santo Domingo: USAID.

Ramírez, Leonora. 2001. "Homosexuales consideran marcha un hito." *Hoy.* July 2, 19.

Ramírez, N. 1984. "Planificación familiar, crecimiento demográfico y condiciones de vida en la República Dominicana." In *Población y pobreza en la República Dominicana,* edited by Frank Moya Pons, 175–98. Santo Domingo: Forum.

Red Thread Women's Development Programme. 1999. "'Givin' Lil' Bit fuh Lil' Bit': Women and Sex Work in Guyana." In *Sun, Sex, and Gold,* edited by Kamaa Kempadoo, 263–90.

Reddy, Gayatri. 2004. *With Respect to Sex: Negotiating Hijra Identity in South India.* Chicago: University of Chicago Press.

Reining, Priscilla. 1991. "Male Circumcision's Status in Relation to Seroprevalence Data in Africa: A Review of Method." Unpublished manuscript.

Richard, Lucie, Louise Potvin, Natalie Anne Kishchuk, Helen Prlic, and Lawrence W. Green. 1996. "Assessment of the Integration of the Ecological Approach in Health Promotion Programs." *American Journal of Health Promotion* 10, no. 4:318–28.

Rodgers, Joseph L., John O.G. Billy, and J. Richard Udry. 1982. "The Rescission of Behaviors: Inconsistent Responses in Adolescent Sexuality Data." *Social Science Research* 11:280–96.

Rogers, Beatrice Lorge. 1995. "Alternative Definitions of Female Headship in the Dominican Republic." *World Development* 23 (December): 2033–39.

Rubin, Gayle. 1975. "The Traffic in Women: Notes on the 'Political Economy' of Sex." In *Toward an Anthropology of Women,* edited by Rayna Reiter, 157–210. New York: Monthly Review Press.

Ruiz, C., and R. E. Vásquez. 1993. "Características psicosociales y motivación para la prevención del SIDA en trabajadores sexuales homotrópicos," master's thesis, Psychology Department, Universidad Autónoma, Santo Domingo.

Ryan, Chris, and C. Michael Hall. 2001. *Sex Tourism: Marginal People and Liminalities.* New York: Routledge.

Safa, Helen I. 1986. "Economic Autonomy and Sexual Equality in Caribbean Society." *Society of Economic Studies* 35, no. 3:1–21.

———. 1995. *The Myth of the Male Breadwinner: Women and Industrialization in the Caribbean.* Boulder, CO: Westview Press.

Santana, Sarah. 1997. "AIDS Prevention, Treatment, and Care in Cuba." In *Aids in Africa and the Caribbean,* edited by George C. Bond, John Kreniske, Ida Susser, and Joan Vincent, 65–84. Boulder, CO: Westview Press.

Santana, Sarah, Lily Faas, and Karen Wald. 1991. "Human Immunodeficiency Virus in Cuba: The Public Health Response of a Third World Country." *International Journal of Health Services* 21, no. 3:511–37.

Scheele, Raymond. 1956. The Prominent Families of Puerto Rico. In *The People of Puerto Rico,* edited by Julian Steward. Urbana: University of Illinois Press.

Scheper-Hughes, Nancy. 1990. "Three Propositions for a Critical Applied Medical Anthropology." *Social Science and Medicine* 30, 2:189–97.

Schifter, Jacobo. 1998. *Lila's House: Male Prostitution in Latin America.* Binghamton, NY: Harrington Park Press.

Schifter, Jacobo, Johnny Madrigal, and Peter Aggleton. 1996. "Bisexual Communities and Cultures in Costa Rica." In *Bisexualities and AIDS,* edited by Peter Aggleton, 99–120.

Schoepf, Brooke Grundfest. 1992a. "AIDS, Sex and Condoms: African Healers and the Reinvention of Tradition in Zaire." *Medical Anthropology* 14:225–42.

———. 1992b. "Gender Relations and Development: Political Economy and Culture." In *Twenty-First- Century Africa: Towards a New Vision of Self-Sustainable Development,* edited by Ann Seidman and Frederick Anang, 203–41. Trenton, NJ: Africa World Press.

———. 1992c. "Sex, Gender, and Society in Zaire." In *Sexual and Behavioral Networking: Anthropological and Sociocultural Studies on the Transmission of HIV,* edited by T. Dyson, 353–76. Liège, Belgium: International Union for the Scientific Study of Population.

———. 1992d. "AIDS, Sex and Condoms: African Healers and the Reinvention of Tradition in Zaire." *Medical Anthropology* 14: 225–42.

———. 1993. "Gender, Development and AIDS: A Political Economy and Culture Framework." In *The Women and International Development Annual,* edited by Rita S. Gallin, Anne Ferguson and Janice Harper, 55–85. Boulder, CO: Westview Press.

———. 1995. "Culture, Sex Research, and Aids Prevention in Africa." In *Culture and Sexual Risk: Anthropological Perspectives on Aids,* edited by Han ten Brummelhuis and Gilbert Herdt, 29–51. Amsterdam: Gordon & Breach.

———. 1996. "Health, Gender Relations, and Poverty in the AIDS Era." In *Courtyards, Markets, and City Streets: Urban Women in Africa,* edited by Kathleen Sheldon, 153–68. Boulder, CO: Westview Press.

———. 1997. "AIDS, Gender and Sexuality during Africa's Economic Crisis." In *African Feminism: The Politics of Survival in Sub-Saharan Africa,* edited by Gwendolyn Mikell, 310–32. Philadelphia: University of Pennsylvania Press.

———. 1998. "Inscribing the Body Politic: Women and AIDS in Africa." In *Women and Biopower: What Constitutes Resistance?* edited by Margaret Lock and Patricia Kaufert, 98–126. New York and London: Cambridge University Press.

———. 2001. "International AIDS Research in Anthropology." *Annual Review of Anthropology* 30:335–61.

Schoepf, Brooke G., Engundu Walu, Wa Nkara Rukarangira, and Ntsomo Payanzo. 1990. "Gender, Power and Risk of AIDS in Central Africa." In *Women and Health in Africa,* edited by Meredith Turshen, 187–203. Trenton, NJ: World Africa Press.

Schwartz, Rosalie. 1999. *Pleasure Island: Tourism and Temptation in Cuba.* London: University of Nebraska Press.

Scott, James. 1985. *Weapons of the Weak: Everyday Forms of Peasant Resistance.* New Haven: Yale University Press.

Seabrook, Jeremy. 1996. *Travels in the Skin Trade: Tourism and the Sex Industry.* London: Pluto Press.

Secretaria de Estado de Trabajo. 1998. "Cuadros estadísticos." Santo Domingo: Secretaria de Estado de Trabajo.

———. 2000. "Cuadros estadísticos." Santo Domingo.

Selwyn, Tom. 1993. "Peter Pan in South-East Asia: A View from the Brochures." In *Tourism in South-East Asia,* edited by Michael Hitchcock, Victor King, and Michael Parnwell, 117–37. London: Routledge.

Senior, Olive. 1991. *Working Miracles: Women's Lives in the English-Speaking Caribbean.* Bloomington: Indiana University Press.

Shehan, Douglas A., Marlene LaLota, Denise F. Johnson, David D. Celantano, Beryl A. Koblin, Lucia V. Torian, Hanne Thiede, Duncan A. MacKellar, Gina S. Secura, Stephanie Behel, Linda A. Valleroy, and G. W. Roberts 2003. "HIV/STD Risks in Young Men Who Have Sex with Men Who Do Not Disclose Their Sexual Orientation—Six U.S. Cities, 1994–2000." *MMWR* 42, no. 5:83–85.

Silié, Ruben, and Manuel Colón. 1994. "Ajuste estructural y modelo neoliberal en República Dominicana." In *Los pequeños países de América Latina en la hora neoliberal,* edited by Gerónimo de Sierra, 89–120. Mexico: Editorial Nueva Sociedad.

Silvestre, Emmanuel, Jaome Rijo, and Huberto Bogaert. 1994. "La neo-prostitucion infantil en República Dominicana." Santo Domingo: UNICEF.

Singer, Merrill. 1986. "Developing a Critical Perspective in Medical Anthropology." *Medical Anthropology Quarterly* 17, no. 9:128–129.

———. 1989. "The Coming of Age of Critical Medical Anthropology." *Social Science and Medicine* 28, no. 11:1193–1203.

———. 1995a. "Beyond the Ivory Tower: Critical Praxis in Medical Anthropology." *Medical Anthropology Quarterly* 9, no. 1:80–106.

———. 1995b. *Critical Medical Anthropology.* New York: Baywood.

———. 1997. "Forging a Political Economy of AIDS." In *The Political Economy of AIDS,* edited by Merrill Singer, 3–32. Amityville, NY: Baywood .

———, ed. 1998. *The Political Economy of AIDS.* Amityville, NY: Baywood.

Singer, Merrill, Candida Flores, Lani Davison, Georgine Burke, Zaida Castillo, Kelley Scanlon, and Migdalia Rivera. 1990. "SIDA: The Economic, Social, and Cultural Context of AIDS among Latinos." *Medical Anthropology Quarterly* 4, no. 1:72–114.

Smith, M. G. 1962. *West Indian Family Structure.* Seattle: University of Washington Press.

Smith, Raymond T. 1971 [1956]. *The Negro Family in British Guiana: Family Structure and Social Status in the Villages.* London: Routledge & Kegan Paul.

———. 1974. "The Matrifocal Family." In *The Character of Kinship,* edited by Jack Goody, 121–44. London: Cambridge University Press.

———. 1988. *Kinship and Class in the West Indies.* Cambridge/New York: Cambridge University Press.

Smith, Valene, ed. 1978. *Hosts and Guests: The Anthropology of Tourism.* Oxford: Blackwell.

Sobo, Elisa J. 1993. "Inner-City Women and AIDS: The Psycho-social Benefits of Unsafe Sex." *Culture, Medicine, and Psychiatry* 17, no. 4:455–85.

——— 1995. *Choosing Unsafe Sex: AIDS Risk Denial among Disadvantaged Women.* Philadelphia, PA: University of Pennsylvania Press.

Sontag, Susan. 1990. *AIDS and Its Metaphors.* New York: Anchor.

Sosa, José Rafael. 1982. "Relatan vida en bares homosexuales." *¡Ahora!* June 24, 13–14.

Staff. 2001. "La policía expulsará hoy agentes homosexuales." *El siglo.* Feb. 13, 11A.

———. 2003. "Presentan plan para mejorar entornos polos turísticos." *Hoy.* Apr. 3.

Standing, Hilary. 1992. "AIDS: Conceptual and Methodological Issues in Researching Sexual Behaviour in Sub-Saharan Africa." *Social Science and Medicine* 34, no. 5:475–83.

Steward, Julian, Robert Manners, Eric Wolf, Elena Padilla, Sidney Mintz, and Raymond Scheele, eds. 1956. *The People of Puerto Rico.* Urbana: University of Illinois Press.

Stokes, Joseph, David McKirnan, Rebecca G. Burzette, Peter Vanable, and Lynda Doll. 1993. "Female Sexual Partners of Bisexual Men: What They Don't Know Might Hurt Them." *International Conference on AIDS* 9, no. 1:111 (abstract no. WS-D08–5).

Stokes, Joseph P., David J. McKirnan, Lynda Doll, and Rebecca G. Burzette. 1996. "Female Partners of Bisexual Men: What They Don't Know Might Hurt Them." *Psychology of Women Quarterly* 20:267–84.

Tabet, Stephen R., E. Antonio de Moya, King K. Holmes, Melissa R. Krone, M. R. de Quinones, Martha Butler de Lister, Ivelissa Garris, Mónica Thorman, César Castellanos, P. D. Swenson, Gina A. Dallabeta, and Caroline A. Ryan. 1996. "Sexual Behaviors and Risk Factors for HIV Infection among Men Who Have Sex with Men in the Dominican Republic." *AIDS* 10, no. 2:201–6.

Tejada, Argelia. 2001. "Resumen ejecutivo: bateyes del estado: encuesta socioeconomica y de salud de la población materno-infantil de los bateyes agricolas del CEA (Consejo Estatal de Azúcar)." Santo Domingo: USAID.

Thomas, Alexander, and Samuel Sillen. 1972. *Racism and Psychiatry.* New York: Brunner/Mazel.

Treichler, Paula A. 1988a. "AIDS, Gender, and Biomedical Discourse: Current Contests for Meaning." In *AIDS: The Burdens of History,* edited by Elizabeth Fee and Daniel M. Fox, 190–266. Berkeley: University of California Press.

———. 1988b. "AIDS, Homophobia, and Biomedical Discourse: An Epidemic of Signification." In *Aids: Cultural Analysis, Cultural Activism,* edited by Douglas Crimp, 31–70. Cambridge: MIT Press.

Trexler, Richard. 1995. *Sex and Conquest: Gendered Violence, Political Order, and European Conquest of the Americas.* London: Polity Press.

Trouillot, Michel-Rolph. 1992. The Caribbean Region: An Open Frontier in Anthropological Theory. *Annual Review of Anthropology* 21:19–42.

Truong, Than Dam. 1990. *Sex, Money and Morality: The Political Economy of Prostitution and Tourism in South East Asia.* London: Zed Books.

Turner, Victor. 1970. *The Forest of Symbols: Aspects of Ndembu Ritual.* Ithaca, NY: Cornell University Press.

———. 1975. *Dramas, Fields, and Metaphors: Symbolic Action in Human Society.* Ithaca, NY: Cornell University Press.

UNAIDS. 2002a. Epidemiological Fact Sheet on HIV/AIDS and STIs, Dominican Republic: UNAIDS/UNICEF/PAHO/WHO.

———. 2002b. *Report on the Global HIV/AIDS Epidemic 2002.* Barcelona: UNAIDS and Joint Agencies.

UNAIDS/WHO/PAHO. 2003. *Provisional Report: HIV infection and AIDS in the Americas: Lessons and Challenges for the Future.* Havana: Joint agency document from 2nd Forum on HIV/AIDS/STD in Latin America and the Caribbean.

Urry, John. 1991. The Sociology of Tourism. In *Progress in Tourism, Recreation and Hospitality Management,* edited by C. Cooper, vol. 3, 48–57. London: Belhaven.

———. 1995. *Consuming Places.* New York: Routledge.

———. 2002. *The Tourist Gaze.* London: Sage.

Vásquez, R. Eduardo, C. Ruíz, and E. Antonio De Moya. 1990. "Motivación y uso de condones en la prevención del SIDA entre muchachos de la calle trabajadores sexuales." Santo Domingo: UASD/PROCETS.

———. 1991. "AIDS Prevention Motivation and Condom Use among Dominican Male Street Kid Sex Workers." *International Conference on AIDS* 7, 2:71 (abstract no. TH.D.61).

Wasserheit, Judith N. 1992. "Epidemiological Synergy Interrelationships between Human

Immunodeficiency Virus Infection and Other Sexually Transmitted Diseases." *Sexually Transmitted Diseases* 19, no. 2:61–77.

Watson, Hilbourne A., ed. 1994. *The Caribbean in the Global Political Economy.* Boulder, CO: Lynne Rienner.

Whitehead, Tony L. 1997. "Urban Low-Income African American Men, HIV/AIDS, and Gender Identity." *Medical Anthropology Quarterly* 11, no. 4:411–47.

Wiarda, Howard J. 1995. *Democracy and Its Discontents: Development, Interdependence, and U.S. Policy in Latin America.* New York: Rowman & Littlefield.

Wiarda, Howard J., and Michael J. Kryzanek. 1992. *The Dominican Republic: A Caribbean Crucible,* 2nd. ed. Boulder, CO: Westview Press.

Wight, Daniel, and Patrick West. 1999. "Poor Recall, Misunderstandings and Embarrassment: Interpreting Discrepancies in Young Men's Reported Heterosexual Behavior." *Culture, Health & Sexuality* 1, no. 1: 55–78.

Wilhelms, Saskia Katenka Susanne. 1994. *Haitian and Dominican Sugarcane Workers in Dominican Bateyes: Patterns and Effects of Prejudice, Stereotypes, and Discrimination.* Interethnische Beziehungen und Kulturwandel, vol. 19. Münster: Lit.

Williams, Eric. 1984. *From Columbus to Castro: The History of the Caribbean.* New York: Vintage Books.

Wilson, Peter J. 1969. "Reputation and Respectability: A Suggestion for Caribbean Ethnology." *Man* 4:70–84.

———. 1973. *Crab Antics: The Social Anthropology of English-Speaking Negro Societies of the Caribbean.* New Haven: Yale University Press.

Winn, Peter. 1992. *Americas: The Changing Face of Latin America and the Caribbean.* Berkeley: University of California Press.

World Trade Organization. 2001. "Trade Policy Review: Dominican Republic." Report from the Secretariat: #WT/TPR/S/105.

Yanagisako, Sylvia, and Carol Delaney. 1995. "Naturalizing Power." In *Naturalizing Power,* edited by Sylvia Yanagisako and Carol Delaney, 1–22. New York: Routledge.

Yelvington, Kevin. 1995. *Producing Power: Ethnicity, Gender, and Class in a Caribbean Workplace.* Philadelphia: Temple University Press.

Index

homoeroticism (*continued*)
structed and socially perceived in different locales, 6. *See also* Latin American
homoeroticism
"homoerotic mediascapes," 165–66
homosexual concentration camps of early
1950s, 83
homosexuality (*homosexualidade*): Latin
American model of male, 89–90; and
medical/scientific model of sexual classification, 100; notion of based primarily on sexual object choice, 101–2. *See
also* homoeroticism; Latin American
homoeroticism
hooks, bell, 162, 208, 253n35
Hurricane Georges, 54

illegal migrants, 70
immigration restrictions, 52
indentureship, 57
in-depth interviews, 13
informal interviewing, 13, 14
informal labor market, 50; employs more
men than any other sector of the Dominican economy, 47–48; female sex workers
largest sector in tourist economy, 57; fluid
boundary between formal and informal
sectors in pleasure industry, 54; male sex
workers in, 31, 59, 61–62; saturation of,
238n12; sex work one of the fastest growing sectors of, 56; tourist economy, 53–55
international AIDS funding, 255n12
international donor agencies, 239n20
International Monetary Fund, 52, 237n9
international travel: effect on sex work in
Caribbean, 3, 70; and increased imported
diseases, 171; by male sex workers, 72–74.
See also gay sex tourism; tourism
Internet: influence on the organization of
sex tourism to the Caribbean, 164, 254n40;
sites documenting clients' experiences
with sex workers in Dominican Republic,
234n6, 241n40; technology constrained by
class and nationality, 254n41

Jamaica: "beach boy" phenomenon, 138;
concept of masculinity, 140; female sex

workers, 80, 246n2, 247nn7–8; informal
sector, 239n26; "making do" in, 59; middle-
class men, 134; "rent-a-dread" or "rent-a-
Rasta," 137; tourism development in, 53
John Paul II, Pope, 81
Johnson, Lyndon, 237n5
Johnson, Warren D., 172
Juan Dolio, 50

Kempadoo, Kamala, 5, 49, 54, 57, 59, 137, 163,
166, 234n8, 239n26, 253n29, 255n6
Kerrigan, Deanna, 62, 257n32
"King Tourism," 6, 228n6
Knight, Franklin W., 227n3
Koenig, E. R., 185–86
Krohn-Hansen, Christian, 82, 135, 244n10
Kulick, Don, 231n35, 245n19
Kutsche, Paul, 106, 139, 140

LaFont, Suzanne, 137, 144, 250n6
Lancaster, Roger N., 89, 90, 245n21
La Romana, Dominican Republic, 50
Las Terrenas, Dominican Republic, 50
Latin American homoeroticism: active participant in anal sex not stigmatized by engagement in homoerotic relations, 90; and
changes in the structure of labor and capital in local settings, 212; high proportion of
non-gay-identified men engage in sexual
behavior with other men, 176, 180; "homosexual exogamy," 32; homosexual's stereotyped passivity in anal sex, 245n19; "sexual
silence," 130–32; traditional model of, 89
Latin American sex/gender systems, weakened by the introduction of a globalizing
model of sexual orientation, 101
Latino MSM, highest HIV prevalence rates
of any group tracked by the CDC, 178
Law, 153, 49
Lewis, Linden, 48
Lichtenstein, Bronwen, 256n18
"liminality," 248n21
limpiabotas (shoe shiners), 111
"liquor store," new sex-work modality,
239n21, 240n31
loca (effeminate), 64, 81, 96
"looking for life," 92, 206

MacCannell, Dean, 209, 259nn7–8

macho homosexual, 91

"maintained" (*mantenido/a*), 231n35

maipiolos (roughly, "pimps"), 10, 15, 62, 107, 117, 191, 192, 229n12, 230n20

"making do," 59, 238n14, 239n26

male sexual communication styles, 180

male sex workers: and anxiety over what will become of them, 95; appeal to role as household provider to justify participation in stigmatizing behaviors, 129–30; art of the *cuento,* 37–40; belief that sex work does not define identity, 92; commodity fetishism among, 72; concerns about neighbors' suspicion and gossip, 116–17; "covering" techniques, 66, 114–17, 138–40, 206–7, 213, 247n6; "decoding" of social cues in interactions with gay tourists, 43–45; "delocalization" of sex-for-money exchange that fosters anonymity and discretion, 65; demonization in Dominican media and by the Catholic church, 206; few formal ties to the businesses in which they meet *clientes,* 62–63; highly mobile, 63; internal migratory pathways of, 69; international travel, 72–74; on Internet sites dedicated to sex tourism or pornography, 65; minors among, 251n17 (*see also* adolescent male sex workers); natal family may provide a reinforcement of safer sex practices, 120; negotiation of prices for particular sexual acts, 97–99; no institutional representation, 63; participation in pornographic video productions, 165; "performing poverty" for regular clients, 157; police abuses of, 25, 36–37; reliance on cell phones, 65; reporting of grossly inflated prices for passive sexual acts, 98–99; residence of by self-identified sexual identity, 19; sexual self-identifications among, 17; sex work abroad, 72–73; similar to non-sex-working peers in the formal-sector tourism economy, 47; sometimes barred from upscale bars and *discotecas,* 63; subject to heightened scrutiny in hotels, 36; use financial benefits of their sexual exchanges to evade interrogation about

their nonnormative sexual practices, 209; use of sexual identity terms, 240n32; vulnerability to social prejudice and censure for sexual behaviors, 64; wives, girlfriends, and evasion, 121–32

male sex workers, backgrounds and families: absent or neglectful fathers, 246n3; childhood and the natal family, 110; concerns about raising a family and having children, 127–28; dependence upon extended family networks for routine expenses, 114, 214; divorce, separation, or remarriage in natal family, 112; economic contributions to the family, 117–18; fears about the end of relationships with women, 126–27; "fleeing" the natal home at very early age, 68, 107, 111, 112–13; household composition, by relationship to interviewee, 220; marital status, 124–25, 222; parental neglect and abuse, 68, 111–12; percent living with family, 113; relationships with siblings, 120–21; rural origins, 68; sharing of household expenses, by type of expense, 221; traumatic family discoveries resulting from relationships with regular clients, 251n11; wives/girlfriends and evasion, 121–32; wives/girlfriends frequently unsatisfied with economic support, 248n18

male sex workers, clients: age range of their last regular tourist-client, 146–47; ambivalence toward regular clients, 149–53; "best" client according to their own preferences/criteria, 250n8; contacts with clients made in public places, 63; emotional attachments to last regular male tourist-client, 223; importance of regular clients to general economic situation, 147–49; last-client nationality, 146, 223; locations of initial contacts with clients, by research site, 43; preference for foreign clients, 145–46; preference for older clients, 147; preference for tourists as clients, 186; reliance on wealthier local clients, 119–20; sex of clients over previous month, by self-defined sexual identity, 21; types of economic support from last regular tourist-client, 148